A Life with Wildlife

Celebrating
30 Years of Publishing
in India

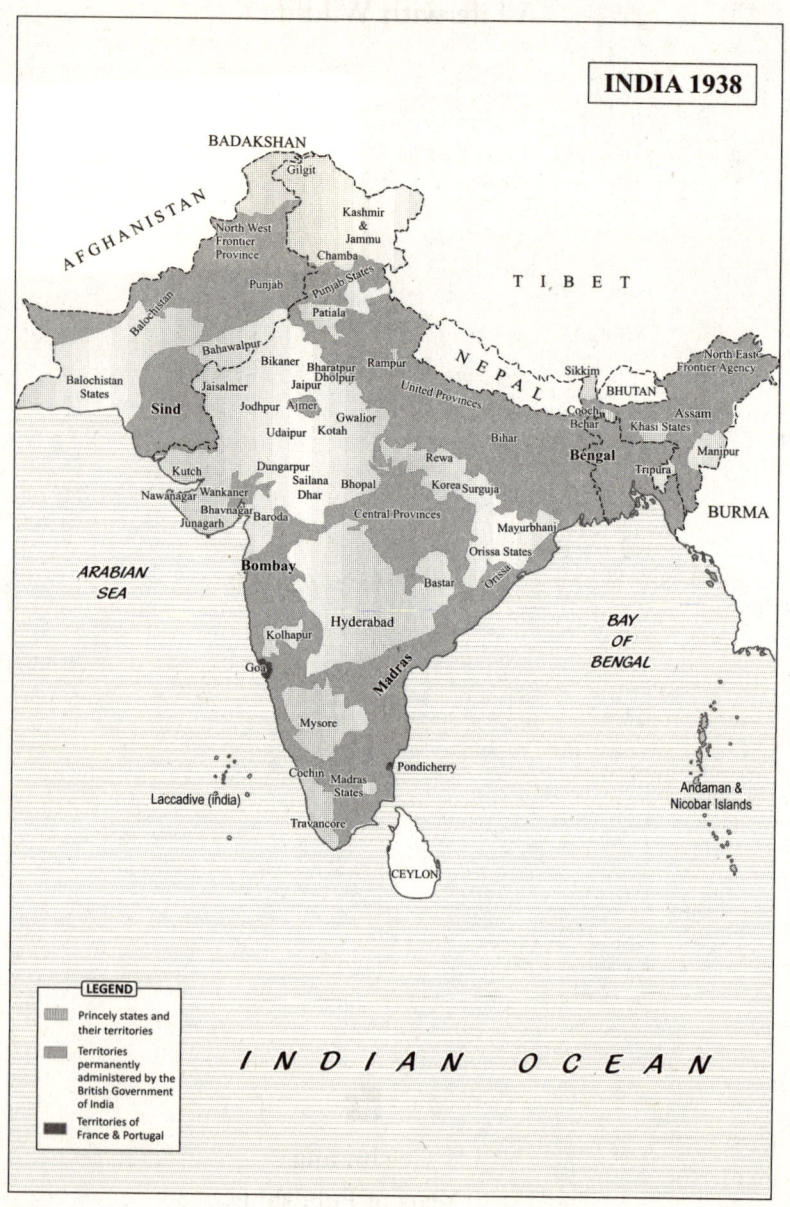

A Life with Wildlife

From Princely India to the Present

M.K. RANJITSINH

HarperCollins *Publishers* India

First published in hardback in India by
HarperCollins *Publishers* India 2017
4th Floor, Tower A, Building No. 10, DLF Cyber City,
DLF Phase II, Gurugram, Haryana – 122002
www.harpercollins.co.in

This edition published in paperback by HarperCollins *Publishers* 2023

2 4 6 8 10 9 7 5 3 1

Copyright © M.K. Ranjitsinh 2017, 2023

P-ISBN: 978-93-5699-114-9
E-ISBN: 978-93-5264-423-0

The views and opinions expressed in this book
are the author's own and the facts are as reported by him,
and the publishers are not in any way liable for the same.

M.K. Ranjitsinh asserts the moral right
to be identified as the author of this work.

The colour photographs are by the author. Unless otherwise specified,
copyrights of all photographs are vested in the author.

The map on page ii is for representational purposes only and the international
boundaries as shown do not purport to be authentic as per directives of
the Survey of India.

All rights reserved. No part of this publication may be reproduced,
stored in a retrieval system, or transmitted, in any form or by any means,
electronic, mechanical, photocopying, recording or otherwise,
without the prior permission of the publishers.

Typeset in 11/14.2 Brioso Pro
by Jojy Philip, New Delhi

Printed and bound at
Replika Press Pvt. Ltd.

This book is produced from independently certified FSC® paper to ensure
responsible forest management.

Dedicated with affection,
To
Kalpana Kumari, Meenal and Radhika.

Contents

	Preface	ix
1	Wankaner	1
2	Dungarpur	13
3	Wildlife in Princely India	23
4	Kashmir	53
5	Bhutan	77
6	Madhya Pradesh	87
7	Indira's India	111
8	The Wilds of Asia	158
9	The Forests of Central India	184
10	Bhopal, Gas and Union Carbide	214
11	Environment and Forests, Ganga and Narmada	234
12	Conservation Outside of Government	275
13	Cheetah	327
14	Conservation in the Twenty-first Century	339
	Bibliography	351
	List of Species Mentioned in Text	357
	Index	369
	Acknowledgements	379

Preface

Being a student of history and fascinated by nature and wildlife since childhood, I have been attracted to legends and facts associating history, especially my family history, with wildlife. In circa 1077 CE, when Harpaldev Makwana – the founder of our lineage – lost his father and the kingdom of Kerantigarh, in modern-day southern Sindh, Pakistan, as a result of internecine warfare so common amongst Rajput princes, he sought refuge at the court of his cousin Karan Solanki, the ruler of Patan in north Gujarat. Patan today is famous for Rani-ni-vav, the most exquisitely carved step well in the world. In Mughal times it was famous as one of the principal sites for the capture of cheetah for royal sport (Habib 1982). *Mirat-i-Ahmadi*, a contemporary account of the Mughal period, goes on to say that the cheetah of this region (north Gujarat) '... is better and superior in relation to those available in other places' (cited in Divyabhanusinh 1999). Why was it so? Was it because the cheetah here had to tackle the robust wild ass and the numerous nilgai, amongst the largest to be found in India? Wild asses ranged wide and have never been an object of the hunters' pursuit, except for an interlude. Mughal emperor Babur (r. 1526–30 CE), an inveterate hunter who mentions all animals he killed and ate, from a rhinoceros to the quail, does not mention the wild ass (*Babur Nama* 1921). Yet his great-grandson Jahangir killed wild asses as far north as Lahore (*Tuzuk-i-Jahangiri* 1978). Slaying of the 'ghorkhar' (wild ass) with swords from horseback was the privilege of the Persian nobility, in which Humayun partook whilst he sought refuge with the Shah of Persia after being ousted from India by Sher Shah Suri. When he returned to India and reclaimed his lost empire, he and his successors continued with this 'sport'. India owes the origin of the Mughal style of painting and the adoption of Persian as the court language, which persisted till its substitution with English and contributed to the evolution of the Urdu language, to Humayun's exile in Persia. Can the beginning of the decline of the wild ass also be attributed to this Persian sojourn?

Legend has it that in Patan, Harpaldev married Goddess Shakti, after being subjected to a stern test, and that while she would appear before Harpaldev as a woman, to others she would appear to be lioness (Shukla, undated). Harpaldev acquired his own kingdom and established Patdi as his capital, at the edge of the Little Rann of Kutch. There, in the palace jharokha, or balcony, as Shakti sat combing her tresses, she saw an elephant that had escaped from the royal stables, bearing down upon her three children playing below. Shakti stretched her arms supernaturally, caught her children and lifted them to safety. Thereby the Makwanas came to be called Jhalas – 'jhallya' being the Gujarati word for caught. So my family name owes its origins to an elephant – mad or in musth.

The tryst with animals continues. When Mohammad Begda, the ablest and the most ruthless of the sultans of Gujarat invaded northern Saurashtra, still referred to as Jhalawad, the Jhalas had to move westwards. In 1488 CE, whilst out hunting, Jhala ruler Rajodharji's horse flushed a desert hare (*Lepus nigiricollis dayanus*). Instead of fleeing, the hare stood its ground. Attributing the hare's plucky behaviour to the quality of the soil and water of the place, Rajodharji built his capital there. Halvad remained the political capital of the Jhalas for three centuries and remains their spiritual capital till this day.

From Halvad two significant exoduses occurred, when the rightful heirs were denied the throne by palace coups. In the first instance, the ousted Ajoji, with his brother Sajoji, sought service with the Maharana of Mewar at Chittor, fought under his leadership against the Mughal emperor Babur at Khanwa, in 1527 CE, and when the redoubtable Maharana Sanga fell in battle, Ajoji led the Rajput confederacy till he himself was killed. Ajoji's descendant, Jhala Rana Mansingh, saved the life of Maharana Pratap at the battle of Haldighati against Akbar.

The other instance of exile was that of the brothers Surtanji and Rajoji a century later. Surtanji founded the state of Wankaner, Rajoji that of Wadhwan, now Surendranagar.

C.E. Walker, the vice principal of St Stephen's College, Delhi, once gave us a very sane piece of advice. 'One retires from one job or task to another,' he said, 'but one retires from life only when one is dead or a dummy.'

Many of my colleagues in the Indian Administrative Service (IAS) got busy writing their memoirs after retirement, and when I completed my service, well-wishers advised me to do the same. My father suggested that I write not just my life story, but about my times, of the transition of wildlife from princely and British India to the present, since he said, I had been a part of this change. However, I chose to continue with my interest in conservation and for viewing wildlife in as many parts of the world as possible. Recently, my daughters Meenal and Radhika and friends once again urged that I write, and after crossing the age of seventy-five, I realized that I do not have much time left. Hence, this text, before memory fades.

1
Wankaner

The nine decades from 1857 to 1947 were, politically, the period of Pax Britannica and India's growing aspirations to freedom. From the standpoint of natural history, it was the era of the breech-loading gun and the evolution of the hunting ethos; of Darwinism and the discovery of new species; and, finally, a nascent consciousness of the need to conserve nature, in India and the world over.

Some 60 km south of Halvad and 40 km north of the city of Rajkot, lies Wankaner, in the north-central part of the Saurashtra peninsula of Gujarat. Though recognized as a first-class princely state with a gun salute, Wankaner was small in comparison to the territories of other princely states. The premier states of Saurashtra (or Kathiawad as it was then called) were Junagadh, Jamnagar, Bhavnagar, Porbandar, Gondal and Dhrangadhra, in the last of which Halvad was situated.

In 1881, Banesinhji, the ruler of Wankaner, died and was succeeded by his two-year-old son Amarsinhji, my grandfather. Amarsinhji was the thirteenth descendant of Surtanji, the founder of Wankaner, and the forty-first after Harpaldev, the first Makwana-Jhala ruler. Banesinhji brought over from Porbandar state its deputy diwan, Karamchand Gandhi, and appointed him the diwan or prime minister of Wankaner. The child Mohandas, the future Mahatma, spent seven years in Wankaner before his father moved to Rajkot, where again he served as diwan.

In 1899, at the age of twenty, Amarsinhji was vested with full powers as the ruler of Wankaner. He inherited an almost empty treasury along with the worst famine in a century. Famine management, by way of irrigation tanks, was started with borrowed money and to supervise them he had to ride up to about 50 km a day, changing horses en route. In the next forty-nine years of his rule, Raj Amarsinhji left his mark on every square kilometre of Wankaner. He ruled personally, and not through a diwan.

※

Active conservation of wildlife in India has invariably descended from its rulers: from the British administrators and the Indian princes and, later, from prime ministers like Jawaharlal Nehru, Indira Gandhi and Rajiv Gandhi. The exceptions to this rule have been the indigenous communities which, inspired by religious sentiment, superstition or tradition, have conserved fauna and flora in their neighbourhood. Another very significant factor has been the practice of vegetarianism and the religious tenet of ahimsa or non-violence amongst large segments of the populace, which has contributed to what can be called passive conservation by the people. This is not the case in Africa, where almost all members of the population are consumers of meat.

At the time of Independence in 1947, all the three factors above were in operation – the firm, autocratic control over hunting and woodcutting in British and princely India; the zealous protection of trees and animals by some communities in a few localities; and the passive conservation by the vegetarian sections of the population. All combined, India had a unique advantage in saving its natural heritage over every other newly liberated developing nation in the twentieth century. The traditions and even the infrastructures were there. Unfortunately, we squandered this advantage.

Jawaharlal Nehru was a genuine lover of nature and wildlife and it was at his instance that the Indian Board for Wildlife was created. But he was too occupied with the humungous social and economic problems that new India faced to pay personal attention to issues of conservation. A cardinal mistake was to designate forests and wildlife as a state subject under the Indian Constitution, instead of including them in the Central or Concurrent List. This was rectified by Nehru's daughter Indira Gandhi three decades later. However, the damage was already done by then.

Vast tracts of grasslands were parcelled out to agriculture under the 'Grow More Food' campaign. Forests were cleared to make way for new projects and settlements. Weapons were issued by the thousand, to shoot 'vermin' such as blackbuck, wild pig, and even carnivores in order to protect crops and livestock. In the Saurashtra peninsula alone, the blackbuck population, in my estimation, was reduced from over 80,000 in 1947 to about 3,000 in 1960 (Ranjitsinh 1989a). States like Odisha offered bounties for a killed tiger as late as the 1950s. Conservation, especially of wild animals, was regarded in some segments as elitist, reactionary and even a hangover of a bygone era. One chief minister of Saurashtra actively encouraged people to destroy wild animals that raided crops (Dharmakumarsinh 1978). The attitude of the state governments would have been worse, but for Nehru.

Pre-Independence accounts of Indian wildlife are replete with mentions of the huge 'bags' of the British and of the princes, with photographs to prove the slaughter. The ethos of the day, indeed, was that tigers were meant to be hunted and partridges were meant to be eaten. There was more wildlife in the princely states than in the British territories, because hunting was personally controlled by the rulers. By 1947, the difference was even more marked, because of the preoccupation of the British with World War II and the presence of British troops, who were given a relatively free hand to hunt in the British-administered territories.

As a corollary, another interesting phenomenon became apparent. There was more wildlife in the princely states whose rulers were keen on hunting than in those that were not. The reason for this is not hard to see. The act of killing a wild animal or bird for 'sport', different from killing for food, is the ultimate act of selfishness. By killing a creature, the hunter believes he has succeeded in possessing it, making it his own. There is also an element of machismo in the idea of vanquishing the biggest, most powerful game, of obtaining a trophy that would find mention in Rowland Ward's 'Records of Big Game' or of claiming the biggest 'bag'. This selfishness and braggadocio resulted in the most stringent protection of wildlife: only the privileged few could hunt, and everything possible was done to prevent others from hunting and to ensure the propagation of the quarry. Besides, the greatest form of entertainment or honour one could bestow upon state guests was to offer them the opportunity to shoot a tiger, or a lion in Junagadh, or duck in Bharatpur, or the imperial sandgrouse in Bikaner.

My grandfather Amarsinhji was not a very keen shikari. He did shoot the customary lion in Gir with his school friend Ranjitsinhji and a marauding elephant and a tiger in the Simlipal Forest in Mayurbhanj, Odisha, where his daughter was the maharani. The Simlipal hunting reserve was to become one of the nine earliest tiger reserves of the country.

The south-west monsoon pours its waters more generously on the southern coast and south-western parts of the Saurashtra peninsula. Here, in the Gir and Girnar, occur the sturdy teak and an unparalleled profusion of the stately banyan trees. Northwards, the climate becomes drier and the flora less lush. Wankaner is semi-arid, while trees are non-existent in the salt pans of the Little Rann of Kutch, the abode of the wild ass, beyond which lies the Great Rann of Kutch. In the precincts of the state of Wankaner were some of the only surviving 'videes' – xerophytic forests interspersed with grasslands – in northern Saurashtra. It also marked the northernmost extent of leopard habitat in the peninsula.

Wankaner had lost its lions in the early part of the nineteenth century and leopards were the apex predator here. Even these were scarce at the outset of Amarsinhji's reign and for his first leopard shoot he had to go to the borders of Wankaner, in the Thanga

Hills, near Chotila. These hills also held some of the last remnant populations of the Indian cheetah in Saurashtra. In 1894, three sub-adults were shot by British officers mistaking them for leopards, just outside of Rajkot town. Next day, two more of the same family of cheetah were speared from horseback by C.W. Waddington, principal of Rajkumar College, and Lt Col. Fenton (Fenton 1924).

In 1907, the year my father Pratapsinhji was born, Amarsinhji shot a cheetah over a natural sheep kill, just off the Wankaner–Rajkot road, mistaking it for a leopard in the dark. A few years later, a leopard was reported to be causing havoc amongst small livestock in the Vadsar Hills, west of Wankaner. Not wanting to shoot the marauder but instead planning to introduce it in the Gadhia forest just behind the palace in Wankaner, Amarsinhji sent his head shikari, Vasram Pugee (tracker), to trap the animal. The trap was set and a female cheetah, not a leopard, walked in. A search in the vicinity revealed two small cubs, which were put in the same cage as the mother and hauled back to Wankaner, on a cart drawn by bullocks. The pacing of the overstressed mother resulted in one of the cubs being trampled to death by the time the caravan reached Wankaner. The mother and the surviving cub were promptly sent back to the Vadsar Hills and released. They were the last cheetah to be reported in Wankaner.

Leopards were specially nurtured, and soon repopulated their former habitats in the thorn forests of Rampara, Bhenslo and Mesariya. No member of the royal family was permitted to shoot a leopard without the permission of the ruler. The ladies of the family, my two aunts and my three sisters, were allowed to shoot one leopard each, but the male members of the family were permitted to shoot only on the borders of the state, mostly stragglers from outside. Guests such as Maharao Khengarji of Kutch and Jam Ranjitsinhji were also taken to the Mandav Hills on the border of Wankaner.

In 1907, the year Ranjitsinhji became the jamsaheb of Jamnagar, he laid the foundation stone of the palace at Wankaner, named Ranjit Vilas, one of the finest and most imposing palaces in Gujarat. Despite the damage of the earthquake of 2001, it is still our home.

It was Ranjitsinhji who persuaded grandfather to send my father Pratapsinhji to Cheltenham College and then to Clare College, Cambridge, to join his schoolmate, Duleepsinhji or 'Duleep', the other renowned cricketer from Jamnagar and a nephew of Ranjitsinhji. Father would spend summer vacations with Ranji at the latter's mansions at Staines in England and in Ballynahinch, Ireland. Ranjitsinhji was my father's idol, though he never admitted it. When I was born in 1938, the stars at birth indicated that my name should start with an 'R'. My mother, a devotee of Lord Ram, wanted me to be named after him, but Father had only one name in mind – Ranjitsinh. I am told that I was not named for over a year over this tussle. Then a lottery was arranged. Mother wrote out five slips of paper, each with a different name of Ram starting with an 'R', while father had just one slip and one name. I am told that I picked his ticket three times running, till poor mother, a believer in providence, gave up.

The proximity of the Gadhia Hills to the town of Wankaner had resulted in their denudation, due to extraction of fuelwood. With the stoppage of this practice, the tree cover improved, as also happened in recent years when the townsfolk changed to cooking with gas rather than wood. The next step was to entice the leopards from Rampara, their nearest population, over to Gadhia, a distance of 9 km straight. According to Bechar Pugee, the son of grandfather's legendary pugee, Vasram, a male was baited from Rampara and brought across over an open patch of grassland and scrub forest called Foshido. The technique was to lay a bait every third day some 300 metres further along the direction they wanted the leopard to move. In Foshido, they allowed the animal to settle for a week and then started shifting the bait towards Gadhia. As that involved traversing open fields, a frequented road and a railway line, the distance between the sequential baits was reduced to about 200 metres. The entire process of bringing that male leopard from Rampara to Gadhia took a little over two months. Once there, he was fed intermittently. Then he disappeared for about ten days and returned with a female. After that, there was a permanent leopard population in the Gadhia Hills of not less than three adults and going up to seven, including cubs, for the next forty years, until 1952. Till 1975, wolves too lived in Gadhia, which my father kept as his private property after 1947.

Ranjit Vilas Palace itself is surrounded by the Gadhia Hills. The hilltops held nilgai and the valley a substantial population of wild pig that used to enter the palace premises in summer, to crop the green lawns in front of the palace. Leopards sometimes stalked them there and I have seen the footprints of a male on the driveway leading to the main porch of the palace. When I was a child, Father would wake me, over the protestations of my mother, as a leopard started its sawing call in the hill above the palace. He would test me by asking whether it was the call of a male or a female leopard, as there is a perceptible difference between the calls of the two.

There were some four to six adult leopards in the Rampara Forest, and another four or five in Bhenslo. At the time of the merger of the state of Wankaner with the Union of India in 1948, there was a resident population of eighteen to twenty-three adult leopards. Each was known by its size, gender and locality, and its movements were regularly reported. The leopards fed on a fairly substantial population of wild pig, nilgai and peafowl. There were no wild primates in Wankaner. As grazing was not permitted within these protected forests, grass was cut and baled after the rains and supplied to the villages in summer, with always a stock kept in case of a famine year. There was surprisingly little livestock killing by leopards prior to 1948, though they ventured out of the forest at night and picked up the itinerant pi-dogs around villages. Matters changed with the drastic decimation of natural prey after 1948. Leopards became dependent on livestock, and the last leopards in Wankaner were either poisoned or suffocated to death in their caves by avenging shepherds. After 1956, there were no leopards reported in Wankaner, except for a transient animal in the Mandav Hills, despite Rampara becoming an official sanctuary in 1988.

On 31 December 2015, my wife Kalpana and I spent an idyllic New Year's Eve amongst the solitude of Rampara Forest, now greatly recovered and at par with what it was in 1948. Next morning, I saw the footprints of a young male leopard, the first I had seen in sixty years in Rampara. I could not hold back tears. It was the best new year's gift I ever got, proving the efficacy of a protected area and the propensity of nature and wildlife to recover, if given the chance.

On top of the hill, above Ranjit Vilas, my grandfather had built a tower to celebrate the Allied victory in World War I, in which he had participated. Below this tower was a tunnel that led to a hexagonal pillbox hide, with sliding shutters for viewing, and a removable wooden roof. About 8 m from it was a platform, 1.5 m high and above the reach of hyenas. One could park a car at the entrance of the tunnel and walk in without disturbing the leopard on the kill on the platform, enter the pillbox hide and switch on the light – 2,500 candle power – focused on the platform and its surrounds. I can still recall most vividly that brilliant tableau when the powerful light came on.

Usually, a leopardess would make the kill and vanish if she had cubs. The next sight would be of her marching into that bright circle of light, her cubs in tow. She would gently pick up each cub and effortlessly jump to the top of the platform, deposit the cub near the kill and repeat the process. After the meal, the cubs would either jump down if they were large enough, or be brought down by the mother, and proceed to the water trough sunk into the ground, just 5 m from the hide and at almost eye level with it. The sound of multiple tongues lapping up the water was unforgettable, all the animals crouched low and facing us, as they sensed humans were inside that hide.

The next day, the kill would be moved by the pugees to the top of the hide at the end of the tunnel, with the detachable wooden roof removed. Below the roof were two large, transparent slabs of reinforced glass, held in place by a steel girder, just above the heads of the occupants of the hide below. The leopards and their cubs, if any, would feed just above one's head in brilliant light, while we would remain in total darkness in the hide below.

Perhaps the most wonderful moments of my boyhood were

spent in that hide, watching those leopards. And the greatest thrill was to have Father raise me up to the glass roof so that I could put my hands under the leopard's belly and feel its warmth through the glass, or draw circles tracing those rosettes visible through the glass. Whenever I got up to mischief, not an uncommon occurrence, Father only had to threaten that he would not take me to see the leopards for me to be on good behaviour once more.

After the disappearance of the leopards from Wankaner and vandalization of the hide by intruders, Father gave me those glass roofs, with the suggestion that I should convert them into a dining table. I still have them.

My uncle Chandrabhanusinhji had even trained a male leopard to come to the site, on the playing of a gramophone record associated with the providing of food, so that guests could be shown a leopard without any bait or preparation. One night, the leopard didn't show up. So uncle went back up the tunnel to go back home, only to find the leopard walking into it from the other end, curious to investigate the source of that strange sound associated with its food. I cannot say which of the two was more surprised, but that was the end of gramophone calling the leopard, on the orders of Grandfather.

Sometimes the male leopard would make a kill and if the female came over, they would feed in succession. Twice, I remember, the male killed, jumped off the platform and sat aside in the full glare of the light, making way for the female and the cubs to feed first. Twice again I saw a striped hyena circle the platform helplessly as the leopard fed, with much snarling from the cat. From the same hide, Father had seen a leopard forced to take a refuge in a tree by a large hyena. Only twice have I seen a hyena worsted by a leopard in India, each time the hyena making off with an almost beelike buzzing drone that I have never heard otherwise. Hyena fat was in great demand in Saurashtra, as an ostensible cure for rheumatism and led to the drastic decline in the numbers of this most useful scavenger.

I must record here the debt I owe to the pugees of Wankaner: Nathu and Bechar, Jivraj, Savshi, Kunvro and Kano. Their knowledge of the geography and of the habits of wild animals was astounding. But what was perhaps most valuable for me was learning from them the art of tracking and the recognition of pugmarks. I remember Nathu stopping our jeep, getting down and examining the leopard tracks on the road and wondering aloud as to what that particular male leopard of Rampara was doing in Bhenslo, 6 km away from his home range and across a river and open fields, risking entry into the territory of another male of about equal size. Kunvro could even tell the difference between the tracks of a heavily pregnant leopardess and one with a full belly, but I never learnt to do that. The Bushmen of the Kalahari in southern Africa can also tell the difference between the two. Such skills are a legacy of primitive man, in both Asia and Africa, and we have all but lost them.

The counting of carnivores by the pugmark method has led to much abuse and controversy. Enumeration by camera traps is far superior, but these cannot be supplied everywhere. In any case foresters must be encouraged to recognize the tracks and the sex of the animal that makes them. That is one way to make foresters walk the forest and to get 'down to earth'. There is already far too much reliance on vehicles and computers and too little knowledge of 'ground realities'. It is likely that one day the art and skill of tracking may be forgotten forever. If and when that happens, mankind will have lost a skill of immeasurable conservation value and will stand even more divorced from Mother Earth.

In 1948, a small group of sambar appeared in Wakaner for the first time in at least a century. Their nearest known population then and now is in the Girnar Hills near Junagadh, 150 km away, across human habitation. They took up residence in Rampara and once demographic pressure increased there after Independence, they moved to the Gadhia Hills and lived in a valley behind Ranjit Vilas Palace. In 1954, they disappeared. We never found out who killed them.

In 1988, as director of wildlife preservation of India, I was able to persuade the Government of Gujarat to declare Rampara a wildlife sanctuary. In 2013, a sambar hind appeared there, as mysteriously as earlier. It was an emotional experience to see the animal again in Rampara, after a lapse of almost sixty years.

The most common wild ungulate in Wankaner was the blackbuck, followed by the nilgai and chinkara. They did cause significant damage to crops, aided by the wild pig, and from time to time my grandfather would direct my father and uncle to go reduce the numbers in chosen areas. Uncle would argue that the complaints were exaggerated, whereupon Grandfather, who used to visit three different villages of the state in a day, thrice a week, would retort that he had verified the damage himself and if his sons would not reduce the number even marginally, he would issue hunting permits to the locals.

It was common to spot up to 400 blackbuck on a morning's drive in Wankaner. A blackbuck herd was in permanent residence on the airstrip just outside Wankaner town, and the pastime I loved most as a boy, after leopard watching, was to chase those poor creatures on the airstrip in a Chevrolet station wagon and see them go into those incomparable bounds. That stopped when I succeeded in setting fire to the station wagon.

No wild animal in India has suffered such a drastic decline after Independence as the blackbuck. In Wankaner, they had disappeared from the open plains by 1960, the last population having taken refuge in the Jambudiya Videe, a large, open thorn forest of gorad, *Acacia senegal*, interspersed with grasslands, in the northern part of Wankaner. By 1965, even this herd was wiped out. As a boy I used to scan the countryside from the moving car, eager to be the first in the family to spot the inevitable herds of blackbuck. Today, the countryside anywhere in India is empty, except for the ubiquitous livestock. The showpiece of the plains has gone and, with it, some of India's soul. Jamubudiya Videe is a very significant wildlife habitat. Until about 1970, there were never less than a couple of hundred nilgai there, some of the largest in size and horn to be found anywhere in India. Twice I have seen female nilgai with small horns there. Hermaphrodites?

There was a resident population of wolves and hyenas, and the houbara or MacQueen's bustard would visit it in the winter. Jambudiya Videe was the extreme north-western patch of xerophytic forest in Saurashtra and it was a great pity that the Gujarat government did not heed my advice to declare it a sanctuary, when they established Rampara as one. Though I have seen the great Indian bustard just 3 km out of Wankaner, the best place to see this magnificent bird was beyond Jambudiya. In 1952, I saw a monsoonal congregation of twenty-eight birds in an area of less than 2 sq. km, the males strutting about with extended gular sacs in breeding display, emitting their booming calls. Today, the bird is extinct in Saurashtra and I fear I may live to see the day when it is extinct from the world. I estimate the current global population of the bird to be less than a hundred.

The third bustard, the lesser florican in its exquisite black- and-white breeding plumage, would first come to the open grasslands in scrub forests like Rampara, Vadsar and Mesariya, and start its nuptial display. Once the crops in the agricultural fields were several centimetres high to afford some cover, the birds would shift to the croplands, where the insect population and other food were more plentiful. They arrived at known spots and their arrival and distribution were carefully noted. The migration depended upon the timing and the quantum of the monsoonal rains. Occasionally, stragglers stayed behind after the monsoon. I have seen them in Wankaner in the winter and summer thrice. The moulting males assume the pelage of the female and though they are smaller in size than the female, only the lyre-shaped feathers on the upper neck reveal their sex when in moult. Today, they are rarely recorded here, even in good monsoon years; the fields, shorn of insect life because of insecticide spraying, are hardly a habitat for them.

When I visit Wankaner now, I do not go to these old haunts. I would like to remember them with the wildlife they once had, rather than view the desiccation, desolation and emptiness that has set in. Nostalgia has a resuscitative value.

2

Dungarpur

At the end of the twelfth century, Samant Singh, heir to the throne of Chittor, Rajasthan, lost the succession to his younger brother. He established a kingdom of his own further south, over a hilly forested terrain occupied by the Bhil tribe and later to be called Dungarpur, in south Rajasthan, between Udaipur and Gujarat. Centuries later, at the battle of Khanwa, the then Rawal of Dungarpur, Udai Singh, with his younger son Jagmal, joined the Rajput confederacy led by Maharana Sanga, against the Mughal invader Babur. Udai Singh was killed in the battle; Jagmal was wounded, but recovered, and returned to set up his own kingdom eastwards of Dungarpur—Banswara. From this lineage came my late friend Hanumant Singh, who scored a century on his first appearance in a cricket Test match, like some other Indian princes – Ranjitsinhji, Duleepsinhji and Iftikar Ali, the Nawab of Pataudi.

As the name suggests, the topography of Dungarpur is undulating (dungar means hill), being at the southern extremity of the Aravalli Range. The hillsides were covered with dry, deciduous forests in which teak was the most valuable timber.

The story of the wildlife of Dungarpur may begin from the early twentieth century, during the reign of my maternal grandfather, Rai Rayan Maharawal Bijay Singhji. The prevalent situation in Dungarpur at that time is graphically portrayed in a contemporary account: 'The country being full of woods, these beasts of prey find both food and shelter in plenty. Indeed, they are still in such large numbers that it is quite unsafe to travel alone at night when these gentleman of the carnivore fraternity prowl about in search of prey' (Misra 1911).

Bijay Singhji died in 1918, a victim of the influenza epidemic that was brought by Indian soldiers returning from World War I. He left behind four sons and a daughter. The eldest who succeeded him as Maharawal, Lakshman Singhji, was just ten years old. His widowed mother, Devendra Kunwar, a princess of Sailana, arguably one of the most capable women of her time and circumstance, was to leave some of the most lasting impressions on my life. She ruled Dungarpur during the minority of her son, keeping at bay the British political agent at Udaipur. In that almost medieval milieu, the young boys were sent to Mayo College, Ajmer and Rajkumar College, Rajkot; the girl was tutored at home by an Englishwoman. The second son, Virbhadra Singhji went to Oxford, became the prime minister of Dungarpur and, after Independence, a senior officer in the Indian Administrative Service (IAS) in Madhya Pradesh (MP). The third son, Nagendra Singhji, stood first in his class in Agra University, went to Cambridge and topped his batch in the Indian Civil Service. He was a member of the Constituent Assembly that drafted the Indian Constitution under B.R. Ambedkar, became secretary to the Government of India and died as the president of the International Court of Justice at The Hague. The fourth, Pradyuman Singhji, became the director of agriculture in MP. The daughter, Rama Kunwer, was my mother.

The story of the forests and wildlife of Dungarpur is best described in the words of Lakshman Singhji himself, extracted from notes he sent me in 1982 and '83.

> The preservation of forests in Dungarpur district could not have been possible without the active cooperation of the people living in and around the forests. These forests were one of the finest in the whole of Rajputana [Rajasthan]. The Dungarpur state forest department was established in 1907 and the Reserve Forests were

demarcated after consulting and taking into confidence the locals. The demarcation was announced in the villages concerned by beat of drum. The Great Famine of Chhappania in 1899–1901 had reduced the population of Dungarpur to one lakh. This indirectly helped the establishment of the forest department, as the pressure of illicit cutting of timber had become light. It was during the rule of Maharawal Bijay Singhji (1909–18) that the foundation of the forest department was laid. Enthusiastic forest guards were screened and selected. They served under the direct eye of the ruler who each year toured his state for three and a half months or more. The forests were mixed forests, with teak and bamboo in abundance. There was no dearth of grass and forest lands were heavily laden with jungle fruit such as mahua, ber, timru, karamda, rayan and there were thousands of mango and jamun trees growing wild. All these trees annually bore a heavy crop of fruit. It was amazing to see the forest floor covered with abundance of fruit, no matter how many men, women, children, monkeys, wild animals and birds ate them ... these forests could maintain one million cattle free of cost. Tonnes of dry leaves provided excellent fertilizer and enriched thousands of acres of soil free of cost. Bamboo provided cottage industry to adivasis for weaving supra (baskets/winnowing pans), chatai (mats) and dhabka (screens). All this has become a dream as millions of bamboos have been wiped out.

Grass in 'beeds' was grown. Each area was divided into four parts and grass was cut on partnership basis. Fifty per cent of the grass cut was surrendered to the forest department and the remaining 50 per cent retained by the cutter. Cattle grazing, in grass 'beeds' and reserve forests, was permitted on scientific basis, i.e., one fourth of the area was allotted for the purpose. Each bloc, thus, remained closed for three years out of four. Villages situated on the border of reserve forest paid land revenue at concessional rates, to partly compensate for the depredation of wild herbivores. The villagers of these areas were given privileges of 'Aam Nistar', i.e., they could take out forest produce for their personal use on head loads. They could not use carts and there were no trucks then.

Forty years of careful preservation (1907–48) ended in complete destruction within ten years (1950–60) ... The people were just allowed to do what they liked and the process of destruction took place under the very nose of authorities, with their tacit but silent approval. The adivasis have, thus, lost their greatest benefactor, the forests, and this has left them in a state of perpetual poverty and famines to cope with ... The hunger of fuel has risen to such proportions that basketfuls of tree roots dug up in forests are available in abundance daily in the city of Dungarpur as fuel. It is a pity to see 100-year-old trees being cut illicitly under the nose of the Administration ... The position of forests in this district has been reduced to such a low ebb that the situation has now become irreversible ... The way to preserve forests is not through driving in jeeps. There must be some footwork, to enter the forest interior and if there is no footwork, the idea of preservation of forests is an eyewash.

How very true. But matters have become even worse. Forest officials and district collectors have given up jeeps and have moved to sedans and SUVs.

As for the wildlife of Dungarpur, Lakshman Singhji had the following to say:

The situation of game in Dungarpur after the Great Famine of Chhappania had become precarious. Thousands of chinkara, nilgai and pigs perished. But with effective preservation in the reserve forests, the game steadily increased.

The area of Dungarpur state was 1,460 sq. miles [about 3781 sq. km] and the population of leopard in the Dungarpur reserve and village forests was quite 200. The area of the reserve forest was about 500 sq. miles [about 1295 sq. km] and that of the village forests roughly 300 sq. miles [about 777 sq. km]. I imagine that in these village forests quite 50 to 60 leopard had their permanent abode. Dungarpur was, perhaps, the most prolific part of Rajasthan for panthers and four-horned antelope. From 1900 to 1948, more than 600 panthers were shot and yet, their number remained stationary. After the great famine of 1900, tigers had vanished but they reappeared in 1915 ... although their number was confined to three or four, they started multiplying in 1930 and their number increased to 20 to 25 between 1935 and 1949.

The area of Rajdhani Jungle, including Tadi Obri, Ambanal, Gangeli and Do-Dungra was approximately 160 sq. miles [414 sq. km]. In the Rajdhani forest, after the advent of tigers, I do not think there were more than 20 leopards, as there were constantly four to six tigers living in this area from 1928 to 1948. Before 1928 (and the reintroduction of the tiger), the number of leopards in the Rajdhani forest and the adjoining village forests would be twice the number, viz., 40 or even more but now, in what was once Tadi Obri, there may be an occasional wandering leopardess. This forest is totally destroyed and there is hardly any place where a leopard can live.

The only fauna that the state protected were tigers, panthers, bears, sambar, chital, blackbuck and lynx [caracal]. None of these species was found in large numbers ... Whatever the advasis killed in the course of the year was replaced within that year, be they chinkara, pigs or nilgai ... Care was taken in compensating people generously for the cattle killed by tigers. Each head, be it calf, bullock, cow or buffalo killed by tiger, was compensated for at a price fixed by Panchas [village headmen] in consultation with the owner and immediate payment made, which invariably exceeded the price fixed by the Panchas.

A list of Dungarpur's fauna is appended below to show the position of wildlife in 1948 and 1982, as assessed by Maharawal Lakshman Singhji:

	1948	*1982*
Tiger	25	Nil
Panther [leopard]	200	2 or 3
Bear	20	Nil
Hyena	300	5
Lynx [caracal]	30	Nil
Sambar	2,000	Nil
Chital	500	Nil
Four-horned antelope [chowsingha]	200	10 or 15

	1948	1982
Nilgai	5,000	Nil
Chinkara	25,000	50
Pig	25,000	Nil
Peacock	500,000	200

I have written at length about Dungarpur not just because of my relationship with the place and the fact that I spent some of the most exciting days of my childhood and youth there, but because of the availability of detailed notes and statistics – a very rare occurrence in princely India. There were also two very significant endeavours at conservation there. In 1928, Lakshman Singhji introduced tigers in Dungarpur, which had become almost extinct in the state during his minority as a ruler. Three wild-caught tigers, a male and two tigresses, were introduced in the Rajdhani Jungles. In what was the first recorded successful tiger reintroduction, the male named Bokha or 'the toothless' – as he had lost three canines during his captivity – sired cubs from both the tigresses and established a lineage which lasted till 1951.

By 1935, the tiger population in the erstwhile Dungarpur state had been built up to over twenty, which was about the optimum for the habitat. The surplus population started moving to neighbouring states. While maintaining a stable population, which stood at around twenty-five in 1948 as mentioned by Lakshman Singhji in the above table, a total of forty-eight tigers were shot between 1930 and 1950 (Ranjitsinh 1997).

The other innovation of the Maharawal was the initiation of the cattle compensation scheme. 'I had brought in the tigers,' he told me. 'The tigers and the people were, therefore, both mine. I had to devise a method of keeping those tigers of mine without harming my people.' The boundaries of the reserves were demarcated; local people were made aware of these and told not to graze their livestock within them. If they did and the tiger made a kill, they would receive no compensation. If, on the other hand, the tiger ventured outside the reserves and killed livestock in the open forest areas where grazing was permitted, they would receive generous and immediate compensation.

In 1973, in my first stint as director, wildlife preservation of India, I introduced the cattle compensation scheme in the country on the same lines, and few know today that the plan originated in Dungarpur. The success of the scheme depends upon three factors: receiving early information of a kill and immediate arrival on the spot; prompt payment of a liberal compensation in full and, thus, the transference of the ownership of the kill to the compensator; and the prevention, thereof, of vindictive killing of the carnivore. Today, state governments in India take months to reimburse the affected livestock owners and that too involves kickbacks. No wonder the aggrieved owner would rather deal with the predator his own way.

India frames some excellent laws and schemes. The problem is with their implementation. In Dungarpur, the implementation of the cattle compensation scheme was ensured by the tiger itself. Bokha, the paterfamilias of the Dungarpur tigers, had teamed up with the larger of his two tigresses, Gwaliorwali, so named because she had been captured in the forests of the Gwalior state. With three canines broken, Bokha could strangulate but could not puncture the jugular nor sever the vertebrae necessary to break the neck of a sambar, nilgai or of livestock. Later, he found it difficult to even tear out chunks of flesh and his health deteriorated. But he had teamed up with Gwaliorwali and the two would kill in tandem, the tigress often driving the prey towards her mate, whereupon Bokha would latch on to the neck and Gwaliorwali would deliver the coup de grâce.

The cattle compensation scheme had been announced but the Bhil tribes were accustomed to transgressing the rules during the minority of Lakshman Singhji and would sneak their cattle into forbidden forests. One hot summer afternoon, when the locals thought no one would be about, they took their cattle into the Ambanal Reserve, and to the waterhole in the gorge with its precipitous banks. But unknown to them, the tigers were already there. Bokha blocked one end of the gorge and Gwaliorwali the other. She attacked and killed, whereupon the hapless cattle rushed to the other end of the gorge, where Bokha bowled over another bullock. The herd turned back, and the tigress faced with the stampede of the panic-stricken herd left her kill and caught another one from the advancing stampede. The herd turned back again to where Bokha was, and he did what the tigress had done. At the end of this macabre tennis match, eighteen cattle were left dead.

Lakshman Singhji came, saw the slaughter, went to the villages and explained why they could not be compensated. The lesson was learnt. No livestock invaded the reserve forests till Independence. Outside the reserve forests, the compensation scheme proceeded successfully.

I do not think I have learnt so much about wildlife from any single human being as from my uncle Lakshman Singhji. The morning walk with him in the Udai Bilas Palace premises was a vivid experience. The customary look-in to see his beloved pigeons would be followed by a brisk walk in the garden, accompanied by a retinue of servants and shikaris in saffron Mewari pagdis (turbans) and flowing achkans (upper garments). Then came a drone-like recitation of the movements of beings with human names – where the pugmarks had been found and where the trail had led to. Each tiger had a human name, according to the sex. Each one's life history from birth was known. If there was a kill, news would have come over the heliostat, transmitted across hilltops with reflected flashes in code. If the pugmarks of a male leopard with a pad width not less than four fingers of a male human hand were encountered, that would also be reported.

Bokha's son from the first litter, named Babo, left the Rajdhani Jungle and occupied the Ratapani forest, some 35 km away. He started a lineage of his own and in six years had attained a weight of 507 lb (230 kg). Babo's son, the largest tiger recorded in Dungarpur, was offered by Lakshman Singhji as a trophy to his only brother-in-law, my father Yuvraj Pratapsinhji of Wankaner, in 1942.

There was much to be learnt from the shikaris and trackers of Dungarpur – Bheru Singh and Naniya Bhil particularly. Along with the incomparable Haidu Jamadar of Sasan–Gir and the Gonds and Baigas of Madhya Pradesh, they taught me how to approach a kill on foot with the tiger or lion in occupation; how to interpret the warning growls of the protesting predator; what to do if the kill was a special one such as a porcupine or a pig and, of course, the precautions to take if there were cubs about.

With the recitations of the nightly movement of familiar tiger names ringing in my ears, I would eagerly await the evening drive into the neighbouring forests. But before that there would be pleasant hours of watching crocodiles and waterfowl in the Gebsagar Lake which abuts the Udai Bilas Palace, and a session of that other passion – cricket – with my cousins Mahipal Singhji, Jai Singhji and, most of all, Raj Singhji of Dungarpur, whose knowledge and love for the game has never been surpassed. Raj Singhji was to become a national cricket selector and the president of the Board of Control for Cricket in India.

A lifetime with wildlife has given me the opportunity to experience some marvellous outings, but few could match that of seeing the vast multitudes of mammals one was certain to come across while driving through the Rajdhani jungle of Dungarpur. Just behind the palace, one would meet about a hundred chital and the resident blackbuck in Naramagra. Then at the waterhole at Gangeli, another seething mass of chital; more chital and sambar in Ambanal; four-horned antelope and sambar, including a white doe, in Adadari; and finally, Tadi Obri, stocked with the nutritious fodder-bearing kardhai trees (*Anogeissus pendula*). Nowhere have I seen such a concentration of sambar as in Tadi Obri. In a 9-km drive up the valley to Khuman Sagar Lake, my cousin Samar Singh and I counted 436 sambar in 1948. In 1949–50, after Independence and the merger of Dungarpur state with Rajasthan, grazing restrictions were flouted and livestock entered the reserves. This led to the sambar population being struck by rinderpest and some 1,400 rotting sambar carcasses were found in Tadi Obri (Ranjitsinh 1997).

The four-horned antelope, or chowsingha, indigenous to India and the only animal in the world with four horns, has a wide distribution across peninsular India, inhabiting open deciduous forest and grassland mosaics. In southern and northern India, the anterior horns are usually poorly developed. Nowhere have I found the anterior horns (and even the posterior ones) of the chowsingha so well-developed as in the stretch of land from southern Rajasthan to the Satpura Range in Madhya Pradesh, and Dungarpur had some of the finest specimens.

It was in Tadi Obri in 1947 that I saw my first tiger ever, the tigress named Lunti. She was to be the last in the line of Bokha. When the sambar population crashed in Tadi Obri in 1950, she shifted to Naramagra, behind Udai Bilas Palace, for safety and prey. She was poisoned in 1951. In three years after the merger of Dungarpur state with the Union of India, the tiger went extinct in the state. But Lunti will always live in my memory. When I went to Mandla as district collector in 1967, the most commonly seen tiger in the Kanha meadows, around the Schaller Hide, was a tigress with two cubs. She was exceptionally graceful and gracious, and I named her Lunti.

On a bright winter morning in 2007, I went up to the Fort of Bijaygarh, towering above Dungarpur town. Behind the fort, I could see the entire tract from Gangeli to Tadi Obri. There were practically no trees to be seen, not even in the valley floors, and hardly any grass either. The only visible signs of life were some distant brown and white specks – cattle. I silently wept and vowed never to go there again.

3

Wildlife in Princely India

Until the first half of the twentieth century, writings on the wildlife of India were mainly hunting accounts, reflecting the ethos of that time. Some notable exceptions were the books of F.W. Champion and A.A. Dunbar Brander. Almost all the hunting accounts were confined to the British territories, barring hunting forays of British officers into the princely states, especially Kashmir, where they were encouraged to travel to prepare them for a possible military showdown emanating from the 'Great Game' – a perceived threat from imperial Russian expansion and the British strategy to counter it. Other than records of numbers of game bagged and photographic evidence of the same, there is hardly any contemporary writing to portray the status of wild fauna in princely India. This was the main reason why Salim Ali encouraged me, three decades ago, to write about the wildlife in the erstwhile princely states, based upon old hunting records.

The status of wildlife and its conservation varied from state to state, according to the personal interest and, often, the idiosyncrasies of the ruler. After Independence, in the deadly decade of the 1950s, the wildlife of India was almost annihilated and the forests hugely damaged. The maximum destruction was caused in the former British territories outside the jurisdiction of the forest departments, and in those parts of the princely states which were not kept as private properties by the erstwhile rulers themselves.

Only those areas which had the status of a wildlife sanctuary and the infrastructure for protection were able to save something. In the erstwhile princely states, where the aura of the ruler had been the most important deterrent to hunting or cutting of trees, the existing staff, such that remained, were demoralized and lacked the support of the state forest departments in whose charge they were now placed. The state forest departments, on the other hand, were facing problems in their own forest areas in the former British territories. The best preserved 'islands' of all were the hunting reserves of the former princes, which they had been able to retain as their private properties when their states acceded to India. Wildlife continued to exist in these properties for about a quarter-century, till they were acquired by the government and the princes' titles, privy purses and the privileges, including hunting rights, were extinguished by the constitutional amendment of 1971. In Wankaner, my father Pratapsinhji's private reserves – Rampara and Gadhia – had more wildlife and vegetative cover even in 1972 than the other forests of Wankaner, which were now under the control of the Gujarat government. The same applied to the properties of most other former princes such as Gajner in Bikaner, Sunderpura in Baroda, Naramagra in Dungarpur, Chadva in Kutch, Shikarbadi in Sailana, and Hingolgadh in Jasdan.

I have mentioned before how India lost the conservation opportunity in the decade after Independence, despite the favourable milieu and the existence of infrastructure. It would be pertinent to point out that of the 617 national parks and sanctuaries that currently stand notified, more than half were hunting reserves – eighty-seven of the British and 277 of the Indian princes. Unfortunately, almost all of them were established as protected areas after the Wild Life (Protection) Act of 1972 came into force, a quarter of a century after Independence. If they had been designated sanctuaries under the various existing laws and decrees from 1947 onwards, the history of Indian wildlife would have been different. However, as the preserves and reserves in 1947 were for the purposes of hunting, a privilege of the few and not for the enjoyment of the people, it is small wonder that they were regarded as elitist in the new democracy.

Some of the more famous parks and sanctuaries that were once the hunting reserves of the princes include: the Gir, Girnar, Barda, Mitiyala and Velavadar in Gujarat; Bhadra, Nagarhole and Bandipur in Karnataka; Periyar in Kerala; Nagarjunasagar–Srisailam, Eturnagaram and Pakhal in Telangana; Radhanagari in Maharashtra; Indravati, Kanger Valley, Gomarda, Ghasidas, Semarsot and Tamor Pingla in Chhattisgarh; Simlipal, Bhitarkanika and Satkosia in Odisha; Panna, Bandhavgarh, Sanjay–Dubri, Madhav–Shivpuri, Palpur–Kuno, Sailana and Ratapani in Madhya Pradesh; Ranthambore, Sariska, Tal Chhapar, Sita Mata, Jaisamand and Kumbhalgarh in Rajasthan; Chandra Prabha and Suhelva in Uttar Pradesh; Gangotri and Askot in Uttarakhand; Simbalbara, Chail, Kugti and Kalatop Khajjiar in Himachal Pradesh; and Dachigam, Hokesar, Shikargah–Tral and Overa–Aru in Kashmir. Corbett (Uttarakhand), Tadoba (Maharashtra) and Kanha (MP) were once hunting reserves of the British.

It is interesting to note that as the Vaishnavite Hindu rajas of Manipur were not interested in hunting, they did not take steps to preserve the wildlife in their territories, and whatever nature preservation was done in that state was by the British administrators who were implanted there from time to time. As a result, the very rare sangai, a subspecies of the brow-antlered deer, endemic to this region, was wiped out in the Vale of Manipur, surviving only in the small, remote, floating morass of vegetation at Keibul Lamjao, where it was saved from extinction in the 1970s.

This brings to mind a similar tale told to me by Boonsong Lekagul of Thailand, undoubtedly one of the greatest conservationists of the twentieth century. The highly endemic and swamp-specialized cervid, the Schomburgk's deer, whose stags carried antlers with as many as twenty-eight points, was on the verge of extinction in Thailand. In 1905, an expedition had been sent from Germany to Bangkok to obtain live specimens for breeding in captivity. But since there was no tradition of hunting in the Buddhist country, the only information the Germans received was of the common sambar deer (Lekagul and McNeely 1977). England's Duke of Bedford – whose family had saved the Chinese Père David's deer, another very rare and localized deer, from extinction and preserved them at their estate in Woburn Abbey – was also keen to get Schomburgk's deer for captive breeding. He sent emissaries twice in the 1920s to the king of Thailand, but they found no information at the royal court. Instead, they were referred to a prominent nobleman, Prince Rangsit Prayurasakdi, who was said to be knowledgeable about animals, but he was interested only in racehorses and had never heard of this deer. Rangsit sent the Bedford mission to the forests of Chiang Mai in the north. Predictably, they only found sambar in the hilly forests. The second Bedford mission was sent to the forests of Korat in eastern Thailand. More sambar and, of course, no Schomburgk's deer. Yet, ironically, Schomburgk's deer survived barely 4 km from the royal palace, in the marshes of the Chao Phraya river, until they became extinct in 1938.

The purpose of the above narrative is not to justify the unjustifiable – the hunting extravaganzas of the British and the princes – but, rather, to chart the course of wildlife conservation in the country in the twentieth century and to identify the motivating factors for wildlife preservation, the most important of which, in the first half of the century, was almost invariably shikar.

One may at this juncture take a bird's-eye view of the wildlife scenario in the various princely states, beginning with Junagadh and its lions.

In the year 1880, the lion population in Junagadh state was estimated to be a mere dozen; in 1891 the official estimate was thirty-one. During the Great Famine of 1899–1901, when lions took to eating man, their numbers in Junagadh reportedly dropped lower. It was around this time that Lord Curzon, the viceroy of India, made his celebrated decision of declining the invitation of the Nawab of Junagadh to shoot a lion, and urged the Nawab instead to save the animal from extinction (Ranjitsinh 1997).

The low numbers reported pertained only to the Junagadh state and not to the Gir in the territories of Baroda state and other principalities, and the low figures were, perhaps, exaggerated. But it is certain that the lion population suffered a serious depression and the total world population of the Asiatic lion in India was, in all probability, much below a hundred.

The nawabs of Junagadh regarded themselves as the custodians of the Indian lion. Though they did hunt, especially leopards, they very rarely killed a lion. But British viceroys, governors and political agents visiting the state could not be denied the permission to shoot a lion. An annual quota of four to six animals was allowed for shooting, and British officials and prominent princes were to be accommodated within that. However, in the then prevalent shikar milieu, every prince and influential Englishman wanted a trophy lion. Most were refused or given evasive answers, even at the cost of offending the persons concerned. The nawabs never went to the Chamber of Princes and almost never socialized with brother princes, one reason for which could well have been to avoid the embarrassment of having to personally refuse requests for a lion shoot.

Junagadh was honeycombed with the principalities of other states, particularly of Baroda, Bilkha and Jetpur. Barring Baroda, whose sagacious ruler Sayaji Rao III was more interested in the administration of his state than in shikar, the chiefs and rulers not only shot lions in their own territories but used baits to entice them from Junagadh territories. The Junagadh shikar department reacted by beating drums, burning fires all night and firing blank shots on the borders of their own territory, to discourage lions from crossing the boundary in quest of the baits.

Ranjitsinhji, now the Jamsaheb of Jamnagar and an inveterate lion hunter, had loaned money to the chief of Jetpur and had, thereby, acquired from him the right to shoot in Endhaniya, an enclave of Jetpur in the middle of Junagadh Gir. From the hilltop hunting lodge of Endhaniya, which still stands, he and that other very prominent prince, Maharaja Ganga Singhji of Bikaner, began their operations against the local black-maned lions. They then sought permission from the young nawab Mahabat Khanji of Junagadh to shoot in Junagadh Gir. Not only was the request refused but, when approached, the nawab refused even to meet them. The letter that the nawab wrote, thereafter, to the British political agent at Rajkot is worth quoting from:

> It is an unquestionable fact that the house of the lion is the Gir forest and equally unquestioned that the forest is my ancestral property. The preservation of the forest which covers about 500 sq. miles [1,295 sq. km] of my territory is supposed to be of value to the province as a whole, not only as a constant source of grass and firewood but also because of its effect on rainfall. But what has weighed with the Nawabs of Junagadh in the past and carries weight also with me is that the forest is the last sanctuary of Indian lions. If the lions were eliminated, I would certainly adopt a policy of disafforestation which would add to my revenues and simplify the difficulties of administration. The sacrifice that the neighbouring jurisdictional holders are called upon to bear by reason of the existence of the lions is small. The brunt of it is borne by Junagadh and ownership, with all that it implies, rightly appertains to Junagadh.
>
> I would, therefore, ask that the [imperial] Government may fully consider the matter and use their influence to see that my rights are respected and especially the scandal of tying up buffaloes within sight of my borders is stopped ... If I were to take the law into my own hands, the result would be a constant series of border affrays which would endanger the peace of this part of Kathiawad (Divyabhanusinh 2006).

It is interesting to note the nawab's clear statement that the Gir Forest was surviving because of the lions. Just as many forests survive today because of tigers and other animals.

One of Mahabat Khanji's last surviving shikaris, Haidu Jamadar, told me that if there was a very large male lion, they were required to report it to the nawab, set a bait for it, and await the nawab's arrival. Mahabat Khanji would come with his retinue, rifles and all. The lion would be dutifully driven up close to the machan of the nawab, who would let it go, telling the shikaris to keep looking for even a better male lion. After Independence in 1947, when Mahabat Khanji was persuaded by his diwan Shah Nawaz Bhutto (the father of Zulfiqar Ali Bhutto who would become prime minister of Pakistan) to flee from Junagadh to Karachi, the plane took off from Keshod airport and circled over the adjacent Gir. My father often recounted the tale of the nawab looking longingly at the Gir and the Girnar, with tears in his eyes, and lamenting, 'Who will protect my lions now?' When I visited Karachi in 1977, Mahabat Khan was dead, but the first question that his eldest son Dilawar Khan asked me, after the customary pleasantries, was about the status of the Gir lions.

Having a substantial Muslim population to whom pork is taboo, the Gir had a large wild pig population. I first visited the forest in 1950, during the first comprehensive lion enumeration for Saurashtra that was conducted by M.A. Wynter-Blyth, principal of my school, the Rajkumar College, Rajkot. He was assisted by the noted ornithologist R.S. Dharmakumarsinhji of Bhavnagar – nicknamed Bapa – and my father. The lion population was worked out to be a minimum of 217 to 227 and a maximum of 243 to 251 (Wynter-Blyth and Dharmakumarsinh 1950). I distinctly remember the excitement of seeing each of my five first lions on that visit, their behaviour being very different from that of the animals observed in Gir today. Thanks to Uncle Bapa, I also saw in the Gir my first grey hornbills, now rendered locally extinct by people's belief in the medicinal properties of its bones and beak. It was also my first meeting with another set of outstanding pugees (trackers) – Kanthad, Viram and Haidu Jamadar.

Next to Junagadh, the most important state in Kathiawad (Saurashtra) was Jamnagar or Nawanagar. Its ageing ruler Jam Vibhaji had failed to produce a male heir from any of his fourteen wives. In 1878, he had, therefore, adopted Ranjitsinhji, the second son of his nearest kin, the Jagirdar of Sarodar, and had sent him to Rajkumar College. Then one of Vibhaji's concubines 'produced' a son, widely believed to have been smuggled into the *janana* – not an uncommon occurrence in those days. Vibhaji requested the recognition of the newborn son, Jassoji, as the heir apparent of Jamnagar, and the consequent derecognition of Ranjitsinhji. The British government granted Vibhaji's wish, mainly in recognition of his loyalty to them during the uprising of 1857.

Ranjitsinhji became persona non grata in Jamnagar, and at the behest of Vibhaji, was taken to England. There on the playing fields of Cambridge, 'he turned a cricket bat into a wizard's wand,' in the words of Neville Cardus (Cardus 1948). Always a spendthrift and almost always in debt, matters became much worse for young Ranji when gratuities from Jamnagar stopped, following Vibhaji's death. His friends, including my grandfather, helped him, but he continued to live beyond his means. Then in 1907, Jam Jassoji died, leaving no heir despite having had five wives. The Indian princes, especially Sir Pratap Singhji of Jodhpur, clamoured for the reinstatement of Ranjitsinhji. The British government that had earlier agreed to his being disowned complied, as Ranjitsinhji had become the beloved legendary Ranji of England. As an Englishman put it, he became the prince of a small state, when he was already the king of a great game! Had Jassoji lived a couple of summers longer, Ranji would probably have become the second batsman in the history of cricket, after W.G. Grace, to score a hundred centuries in first-class cricket.

With Ganga Singhji of Bikaner, Ranjitsinhji was perhaps the most lavish 'hunting host' amongst all princes. Since his state had lost its lions in the second half of the nineteenth century and there were never any tigers in Saurashtra, the 'noblest game' that Ranji could offer his guests were leopards.

Jamnagar state was mostly flat, the only hilly forested tracts being the Dalasa and Alech Hills and the larger Barda Hills, where today plans are afoot to reintroduce the lion. Till the 1970s, Barda Hills were the westernmost distribution in the world of the sambar and of the four-horned antelope, now locally extinct. Today, sambar and chital are being reintroduced here. Encompassing hills like the Abhaparo and Venu, which are over 600 metres in height and where I saw sambar in 1959, and endowed with a dense cover of babool, gorad, dhav and bamboo, the Barda was the second-largest forest in Saurashtra after the Gir, but floristically quite distinct from the Gir. One-third of it was in the state of Jamnagar and the rest in Porbandar. Ranji introduced chital near the exquisite ruins of Ghumli, where I saw them in 1959, but they were subsequently wiped out. However, it was the leopard that was the main quarry of Ranjitsinhji.

Ensconced in his hunting lodge at Kileshwar, Ranji would await the killing of his baits that were tied along the Porbandar border. Male leopards were offered to his guests, not only because they were more desirable as trophies but also because their vacant home ranges were more readily occupied by other male leopards from across the border, especially if the females were left unscathed on the Jamnagar side. Some of the most noteworthy names in the land and in the cricketing world, such as Ranji's Sussex teammate and lifelong friend C.B. Fry, shot leopards at Kileshwar (Fry 1939). Being the master predators here, unlike in the Gir, leopards continued to thrive in the Barda Hills. Dharmakumarsinhji reports seeing six on one evening drive (Dharmakumarsinh 1978) and I saw them there as late as in 1959.

But Barda alone would not suffice for Ranji's guests. Close to his birthplace, Sarodar, he built a campsite at Samana, fitted with permanent plumbing for bathrooms. Large, luxurious tents would be put up here when guests were expected.

Blackbuck, chinkara and feathered 'game' were the routine quarry, but leopards were always the main item on the 'menu'. The printed daily programme for the camp would mention a panther shoot in the morning: 'If khabbar (news) comes'. At breakfast, Ranji would announce which of his guests was to have the privilege of shooting the leopard, if of course, khabbar came. Sure enough, an equerry would make an appearance with a note. Ranji would read it, exclaim that the welcome khabbar had indeed come. A leopard had been located, and complimenting the chosen hunter on his luck, Ranji would send him and some others off for the leopard shoot.

Ranji maintained a special unit for trapping leopard, mostly in the Vijaynagar forests on the border of Gujarat and Rajasthan. Leopards would be caught, secretly brought in their cages, hidden near Samana and on the appointed day released in an isolated valley with no contiguous forests, mostly around the Dalasa Hill. From there, they would be driven up to face the guns of the novice hunters. No wonder khabbar never failed to come.

My father, one of the recipients of this hospitality, shot a leopard with a broken canine and a forehead lacking hair, obviously the result of the trauma suffered by the creature during its internment.

Father requested Ranji to allow him a sambar, which he had never shot. Ranji warned that being midsummer, sambar stags would have long shed their antlers, but 'we will see,' he comforted. A beat was arranged on Venu Hill at Kileshwer and a stag without antlers appeared. The Jamnagar shikari sitting with Father forced him to shoot. When the beaters came up, one of them produced a pair of antlers, which the beater claimed he had seen the stag 'shed' when it was disturbed by the beaters! Later, Father gave me one of the antlers he had kept. From one Ranjitsinh to another, he said. It will always be a treasured possession.

On the island of Rozi near Jamnagar port, Ranji introduced chital. He also stocked it regularly with grey partridge and hare. Father would relate how every evening a truck carrying grain would feed the thousands of partridges and other fowl. When on a hunt, Ranji – sitting on an elephant – would direct the line of 'guns' (hunters) walking with the beaters, who would flush out the birds and other small game. At the end of the island, the guns would stop and form a line, and the beaters would drive the birds and the hare back to them. Each bush yielded something and the 'bags' would often exceed a thousand birds. The greatest danger was from being 'peppered' with gunshot from other shooters. Ranji himself had lost an eye in a similar manner, on a shoot in England.

No part of Kathiawad had so many blackbuck and chinkara as Jamnagar. In the early 1930s the farmers complained to Ranji that it was not worth their while to plant crops, with the damage caused by the antelope. Ranjitsinhji's successor Digvijaysinhji estimated that there were some 30,000 to 40,000 blackbuck in an area of 8,500 sq. km of Jamnagar state (Ranjitsinh 1989a).

The third princely state in Saurashtra was Bhavnagar, the ruling family of which practised the most diverse forms of hunting. Maharaja Bhavsinhji, the ruler at the beginning of the twentieth century, went out early every morning, with his shikaris, mainly to shoot birds. The blackbuck was strictly protected and Bhavnagar had the largest blackbuck population in Kathiawad, after Jamnagar. The maximum population was on the flat, alluvial, semi-saline grassland tract called the Bhal. R.S. Dharmakumarsinhji, a doyen amongst India's early ornithologists and naturalists and the third son of Bhavsinhji, told me that he estimated that there were some 8,000 blackbuck in an area of some 25 sq. km, a part of which now constitutes the Velavadar Blackbuck National Park. It was a treeless flatland, the exotic *Prosopis juliflora* (vilayati babul) not having invaded it then. It was also a prime breeding area for the rare lesser florican in the monsoon, and the best area for coursing the blackbuck with cheetah in the winter. Uncle Bapa showed me a 16-mm black-and-white movie where a phalanx of blackbuck trots across the field of a stationary camera, filling the entire screen in an unending stream for a duration of seven minutes. In 1957, when I visited Velavadar, the blackbuck population was estimated at around 2,400. By 1969, there were less than 500 (Ranjitsinh 1989a).

The Bhal was earmarked for cheetah hunts only. However, when Bhavsinhji's only daughter was to marry Maharaja Yadvendra Singhji of Panna (Madhya Pradesh), a huge marriage party was to arrive. Bhavsinhji asked his younger brother to get enough venison for the large gathering. The brother proceeded to the Bhal, drove into a large all-male blackbuck group, and from one 'stand', in the manner of the buffalo hunters of the prairies of the United States, shot twenty-one antelope, all black males. Bapa told me that he had seen all-male groups of over 500 animals in the Bhal. The largest group of this type that I have seen was 162 in 1981.

Wild boar was the next most numerous wild animal. Dharmakumarsinhji records populations of 2,000 to 4,000 wild pigs in the mango and coconut plantations in Mahuva alone, and the ordering of the Bhavnagar armed forces to reduce their numbers, as the pig-sticking forays from horseback were not enough to reduce them sufficiently (Dharmakumarsinh 1978).

Through the rapid reduction of its territory in the nineteenth century, the lion had become extinct by 1856 in the thorn forest of Sihor, the old capital of Bhavnagar (Dharmakumarsinh 1986). From 1917 onwards, nomadic lions started visiting the isolated hilly scrub forest, Mitiyala, an enclave of Bhavnagar at the edge of the eastern Gir. In 1931, during the reign of Krishnakumarsinhji, the eldest son of Bhavsinhji and the elder brother of Bapa, the preservation of lions began in Mitiyala and the nomadic lions started occupying Mitiyala regularly for varying periods, during winter and the monsoon. The maharaja, his family and guests would hunt the itinerant male lions periodically.

Two ardent American falconers, John and Frank Craighead, later to become renowned bear experts, spent a year with Bapa in Bhavnagar. They reported that some maharajas who had never shot a lion offered Krishnakumarsinhji 'six to ten tigers in return for one lion, but H.H. [His Highness] says he wouldn't do it for forty tigers!' (Craighead and Craighead 2001). Mitiyala is now a wildlife sanctuary.

After Independence, Krishnakumarsinhji became the governor of Madras and in that capacity introduced the white blackbuck from Bhavnagar into Guindy National Park in Chennai, thereby mixing the two subspecies of the antelope – *Antilope cervicapra cervicapra* of south India and *A. cervicapra rajputanae* of Saurashtra.

Bhavsinhji of Bhavnagar is known for introducing falconry in Saurashtra and hunting with cheetah and caracal. He employed Makke Khan, a hereditary trainer of falcons (bazdar). Makke Khan and his sons also trained cheetah and caracal, but he specialized in falcon (baz) training, especially goshawks and saker falcons (Craighead and Craighead 2001).

Each autumn, Makke Khan Bazdar would go to Amritsar market to buy shahins, peregrines, laggar falcons, and other hawks. After careful inspection and weighing of the birds, purchases would be made. The birds would then undergo intensive training, which would involve giving them dope, the ingredients of which was the most closely guarded secret of the hereditary falconers. The hawks would be ready to hunt in a month or so. After the winter hunting season was over, the hawks would be released so that they could fly back north on their annual migrations. In autumn, a fresh lot would be purchased, trained and deployed. The bazdars were also expert trappers, and falcons were captured in Bhavnagar as well.

Makke Khan could train a pair of female sakers (cherrugs), which are (as in most falcons) larger than the male, to attack a chinkara. The pair would hit the gazelle on the head in tandem, blind it and down it. My grandfather Amarsinhji found this to be very gruesome and requested his host Bhavsinhji to stop this method of hunting in future, which was agreed to.

Saker pairs would hunt hare in the same way, in tandem, with the hunters following on horseback. These falcons were also trained to strike at the necks of the migratory eastern common crane from above and send them plummeting down.

When indigenous cheetah became unavailable in the plains of India where they could be spotted and trapped, their import from Africa began, in the early decades of the twentieth century. They were trained to pursue only the darkest alpha male blackbuck. If they killed a doe or an immature blackbuck, not only did they have to forgo the customary reward of blood or venison from their kill but were punished by being kept hungry for a couple of days. Cheetah with hoods covering their eyes would be taken in bullock carts or vans and released in the proximity of a blackbuck herd, entailing the rush of the fastest terrestrial animal on earth after the fastest animal in South Asia, over a distance of some 200 m. Uncle Bapa showed me a slow-motion movie of his favourite cheetah named Badshah Pasand (Beloved of the Emperor), slicing through a galloping herd of blackbuck, ignoring the does and immature bucks darting across, just pursuing the master buck, catching up with him, tripping his hind legs with his foreleg and, finally, gripping the fallen buck by the throat to kill him.

The falconers would also net the migratory grey quail. The best males would be segregated and kept in cages, and these would be put out in the fields on the evening before the shoot. The calls of these birds, called bularas or 'callers', would attract other wild grey quail to the vicinity, which would be flushed out and shot on the wing by the hunters next morning.

When I went to Bhavnagar in 1960, Makke Khan was dead and his son Gulam Hussain (GH) was the bazdar. A basha or female Eurasian sparrowhawk was released after a grey partridge, but it failed to catch its prey and sat panting on a tree stump. GH walked up, talking endearments to the hawk and showed it a piece of meat. Thus distracting it, he dexterously blindfolded the hawk with the topi (leather hood) with a quick sleight of hand. Back in the jeep, Krishnakumarsinhji laconically commented to GH that his basha was not a good performer. GH protested. The maharaja told me in English to watch carefully. While caressing the hawk and talking to it incessantly and when GH thought I was not looking, a dark brown pill was put in its mouth. The next partridge stood no chance. That basha went like a bullet and hit its prey in a flurry of free-flying feathers. No wonder athletes do drugs.

Kutch was another princely state. Its geographic isolation had its own impact, and it has been described as 'a place apart'. Not only the place but also the people and wildlife are quite apart. Isolated from Saurashtra by the Little Rann and from Sindh in the north by the Great Rann of Kutch, the area has its own special ecology. The extremely arid Great Rann, apparently, was a lesser ecological barrier than the smaller but totally barren salt pan which is the Little Rann. The fauna of Kutch has greater affinity to that of Sindh and Rajasthan than to Saurashtra. Kutch has the black partridge, Saurashtra the painted; the two francolins not being sympatric. Saurashtra has the rusty-spotted cat, and Kutch the caracal, the desert cat and the desert fox. Once, flying low over the Banni Grasslands that separate the Kutch 'mainland' from the Great Rann, I saw what appeared like a pair of Blanford's fox (Ranjitsinh 1985a). However, I could not be certain. The greylag goose, imperial or black-bellied sandgrouse, and spotted sandgrouse or waku-waku migrate to Banni in winter, not to Saurashtra. The only record of an albino great Indian bustard and black partridge, that I am aware of, are from Kutch. The last surviving great Indian bustard population in Gujarat is now in western Kutch. Banni also had the only relict population of the blackbuck in Kutch; separated from the nearest other population of this antelope by some hundred kilometres across the Little Rann. It is now locally extinct.

The only habitat of the Indian wild ass is the Little Rann of Kutch. There is also an isolated small population of about thirty animals in the Great Rann, west of the Kutch Desert Wildlife Sanctuary. Just north of this and between the islands of Khadir and Paccham, close to the imposing rock outcrop of Bhanjdo that is jutting up from the salt pan, is the only breeding site in South Asia of both greater and lesser flamingoes.

I went to Kutch first in 1954. My eldest sister was married to the noted ornithologist M.K. Himmatsinhji, the youngest brother of Maharao Madansinhji. I have never before or since seen such numbers of chinkara as I did in Kutch then. Driving along the coast from Lakhpat Fort, on the Kori Creek border with Pakistan, to the shrine at Narayan Sarovar further south, one was almost never out of sight of chinkara. Groups of this gazelle rarely exceed half a dozen animals. Near Lakhpat I saw herds of over thirty. Narayan

Sarovar is an offshore island. Yet, in the lake near the temple, I saw a freshwater crocodile. Pigs and wolves were numerous in Kutch and large numbers of the migratory houbara bustard arrived in winter, especially in the coastal dunes around Vijay Vilas, the palace of the royal family at Mandvi.

Mirza Maharao Khengarji III ruled Kutch from 1876 to 1942. An archetypal benign ruler and a very keen big-game hunter, his forte was the shooting of large 'heads', not large bags. Each autumn, shikaris would be sent out to scour the landscape for large-horned chinkara. Any male with horns well over 13 inches would be marked down and reported, the world record being of $15^{5}/_{8}$ inches. Khengarji 'Bawa' (an honorific for male members of the Kutch royal family) would camp close to the sites of the largest heads reported, proceed in a bullock cart to the chosen animal and watch it for hours through binoculars, trying to determine the exact length of the horns to the last decimal point. Undecided, he would return to camp and go again the next day. As he grew older, he became more and more choosy. In 1921, he camped out for four days, going each morning and evening to look at the same animal and returning undecided whether the gazelle was worth shooting or not. Finally, his shikari got fed up. With the brazen frankness permitted only to the favourite shikaris of old, he remarked that the animal was only a chinkara, not a camel. If the Bawa wanted the head, he should shoot. Otherwise, they should pack up and go home. The Bawa laughed and did shoot. It turned out to be the seventh-largest pair of chinkara horns ever reported, just an inch shorter than the world record (Ward 1928).

The same Maharao Khengarji, however, had no qualms about shooting leopards and he succeeded in wiping out the leopard population of Kutch. Later, leopards were brought from Sirohi state near Mount Abu and reintroduced successfully in Kutch. I saw their progeny in 1960, and a few still manage to survive.

The largest and most important princely state in western India was Baroda, which was then the only political entity in the world to have both the tiger and the Asiatic lion, as the eastern part of the Gir was in Baroda state. Its sagacious ruler Sayaji Rao III was not interested in hunting, but did maintain a 'stable' of cheetah for coursing the blackbuck. Being meticulous about any state activity and expenditure, he ordered the preparation of a unique almanac on the training and maintenance of captive cheetah for the purpose of hunting.

Rajputana, now Rajasthan, consisted almost entirely of princely states. The centre stage here for shikar was taken by Maharaja Ganga Singh of Bikaner and his family. There were no leopards in Bikaner. The single sighting of one in Bikaner resulted in Ganga Singhji going to shoot it in a special train. The main animal pursued was the blackbuck, which reached its maximum horn proportions in Bikaner and in neighbouring Punjab. Before Ganga Sinhji brought the Ganga Canal from the Sutlej river to irrigate the northern parts of Bikaner, Hanumangarh and Suratgarh held some of the largest concentrations of this antelope in India: over 30,000 animals according to one estimate, with large populations of chinkara in the undulating terrain southwards and westwards. Today, the blackbuck is almost extinct in that region.

From Hanumangarh–Suratgarh, Ganga Singhji captured blackbuck and introduced them into Tal Chhapar and the Gajner oasis. Today, they are wildlife sanctuaries where the antelope are still the main attraction.

Ganga Singhji gave finesse to shikar and converted it into almost a science. As chancellor of the Chamber of Princes and spokesperson of the Indian princes, he deployed shikar as an instrument of diplomacy and statecraft. All viceroys of India, especially those interested in hunting like Lord Hardinge and Lord Linlithgow, were frequent visitors to Bikaner for buck, duck and grouse shoots. Brother princes were invited in rotation.

Unlike Ranji, Ganga Singhji did not 'stock' his game reserves. He did not have to, and even the blackbuck he introduced in Gajner were only offered to very important guests who could not spare the time to go to his special blackbuck areas.

Every autumn when the principal blackbuck rut was on, experienced shikaris would be sent out to Hanumangarh, Suratgarh and Dulmani to 'headhunt'. Any male with horns not less than 25 inches, from the base to the tip, would be marked and reported to Ganga Singhji. If the distance between the tips of the two horns was the same as the length, forming an equilateral triangle, it was considered a 'royal' buck. If a 'head' of over 27 inches was reported, Ganga Singhji would go in a special train to shoot it himself. Anything over 25 inches would be offered to his very special guests. The modus operandi was to take the guest to the selected specimen in a bullock cart to which that blackbuck had already been made accustomed prior to the arrival of the guest, thus allowing close approach. The record blackbuck had horns of $32^{1}/_{4}$ inches in length and 28½ inches from tip to tip, and was shot in Jind by the Maharaja of Jind in the Punjab. Ganga Singhji himself had a trophy measuring $28^{3}/_{16}$ inches and would accept nothing less than 27 inches for himself. Every fraction of an inch mattered.

In two consecutive years, a shikari reported heads of over 27 inches. Both times Ganga Singhji went by special train from Bikaner to Hanumangarh, and both times the measurements were not even 26 inches. The maharaja threatened the shikari with dismissal if he was let down a third time. The next year, a telegram arrived from the same shikari – $27^{3}/_{8}$ inches. Intrigued by the precise measurement but keen as ever for a great head, Ganga Singhji went again by special train. The blackbuck was shot and measured – $27^{3}/_{8}$ inches. Ganga Singhji caught the shikari by the ear and asked him to confess how he knew the exact length. The shikari replied that after marking the large buck, he had gone every morning and evening in a bullock cart and circled round the animal, feeding it with green fodder for over a fortnight until it got so accustomed to the cart as to allow it within touching distance. He then leapt out of the cart on to the back of the buck, pinioned it down with the help of a companion, measured it and set it free. It was a matter of his bread and butter, he said, and pleaded the maharaja's forgiveness. That buck is in Rowland Ward's *Records of Big Game*.

Once the best 'heads' of the season had been accounted for, shikar camps would be held at Suratgarh and Hanumangarh, where hunters would go hurtling after fleeing blackbuck, shooting them with rifles from open convertible cars.

※

Indian sandgrouse were very common and it was considered infra dig to shoot them. The large pintail sandgrouse were infrequent visitors and the only ones I ever saw were at Gajner. But it was the imperial or black-bellied sandgrouse shoots that Bikaner was most famous for. This species of sandgrouse, the second-largest in Asia after the Tibetan sandgrouse, is, like other members of its family, a complete creature of habit. Flocks fly in and congregate near water a little after dawn, and then, in a matter of an hour and a half, descend en masse at chosen points to drink. If they do not get a chance to drink during that limited period, they depart and the routine is repeated the next morning. Before the irrigation canals brought water to the parched Thar Desert, the sandgrouse drank only at selected lakes during the winter months, when it migrated there.

One of the most favoured watering spots was the oasis of Gajner in Bikaner, where an exquisite palace stands abutting the lake. Bikaner shikar records mention over 125,000 birds visiting the lake each morning for their beak-fuls of water. There are photographs in which there is less sky than birds to be seen. In 1956, I must have seen over 30,000 in one morning. On the high ground surrounding the twin Gajner and Sugan Sagar Lakes, where the grouse first congregate, circular masonry 'butts' were built over selected spots, which still stand. On the edge of the lakes were moveable butts of grass. The flyways of the birds, to both the high ground and the lake edge, were known. A few days before a big shoot the butts on both high ground and on the lakeside would be occupied by shikaris, who recorded how many separate coveys of sandgrouse flew over each of the most prized butts and the estimated total number of birds. The butts were then allotted to privileged hunters, according to their order of precedence and priority.

Two days prior to important shoots, Gajner and all the surrounding lakes over a radius of 80 km would be manned, and the birds prevented from drinking. The accumulated thirst made them desperate. On the appointed day, they would be shot as they came on to the high ground for their pre-drink congregation, and then on a signal, the 'guns' would be whisked away to the lakeside butts, where the desperately thirsty birds would come in coveys, wings folded and hurling themselves to land, despite the barrage of blazing guns. Over 5,000 sandgrouse have been shot in one morning; one 'gun' has shot over 900. There have not been any grouse shoots for some sixty years but only a few sandgrouse now migrate to India each winter, and they now have water to drink almost everywhere. Only a handful of birds come to Gajner.

Where heavy shooting was practised in Europe and India, a pair of shotguns was required. But for the imperial sandgrouse in Bikaner, three double-barrel shotguns were employed, with two loaders constantly loading and handing over guns to the shooter. Holland & Holland and Purdey made these triplet sets of guns especially for such shoots. It was called sport in those days; it would certainly be deemed slaughter today. Holland & Holland, makers of the famous English guns, told my father that their guns were heirlooms, to be handed down from one generation to another. Only in two cases, they said, had individual sportsmen worn down their weapons – the Bikaner royal family their shotguns, and the Surguja family their rifles.

Gajner and its neighbouring lakes were also a haven for migratory duck, and over 1,000 have been shot in one day. The houbara bustard was a common visitor, and I have seen the great Indian bustard around Gajner till 1961. Demoiselle cranes came to water at Gajner and Kodamdesar, and were shot with the help of wooden decoys.

Sambar was introduced by Maharaja Ganga Singhji into the Gajner Reserve, and would wade into the lake to supplement their meagre xerophytic diet. Both chital and hog deer had been introduced. In the confined unnatural habitat, the two *Axis* species interbred, as would be expected, and curious mixed specimens emerged. These and all hog deer were shot and thus eliminated, and chital were again introduced in Gajner. Today, both sambar and chital are extinct in Gajner, but a few blackbuck, nilgai, chinkara and pig survive in the sanctuary. Caracal have also been recorded in the area.

Next to Bikaner was the larger state of Jodhpur. Large herds of blackbuck were preserved near Pali town, at Kharda and around the Bishnoi hamlets of Doli, Guda Bishnoia and others. Jodhpur state had the highest population of chinkara in India, partly due to the protection afforded by the Bishnois. Their religious sentiments were respected and the royal families did not shoot blackbuck and gazelle in Bishnoi areas. Around the Sardar Samand hunting lodge, leopards were carefully preserved and the lake had a large population of crocodiles. On the Pokhran Lake en route to Jaisalmer, over 5,000 imperial sandgrouse have been shot in a morning, by a fewer number of guns than were responsible for the record bag at Gajner. Now, hardly any imperial sandgrouse come to Pokhran.

Bharatpur was the other state where large-scale organized shoots occurred annually, accounting for over 4,000 ducks and geese in a day. There was a prevalent assumption then that migratory birds required no bag limits – that it was in fact not India's responsibility to protect them. After the passage of the Wild Life (Protection) Act in 1972, I, as the then director of wildlife preservation of India, was repeatedly badgered with requests that hunting of migratory birds should be permitted. Kashmir, indeed, continued with the practice under their law till the 1980s.

Next to Bharatpur was the state of Dholpur, ruled by the Jat prince Maharaj Rana Udai Bhan Singhji. He was a superb exponent of the shotgun, but had become an ardent conservationist.

C.W. Waddington, the former principal of the Rajkumar College, recounts how in one day's drive in a car in Dholpur, he saw a tiger, a leopard, a sloth bear, a caracal, several hyenas, wild boar, jackals and foxes, mongooses, hare and chinkara.

> None but dangerous beasts are ever molested in Dholpur, for His Highness the Maharaj Rana is a true lover of wild animals. One day, he kindly offered to show me a sight which he promised would be unique in my experience, and it certainly proved to be so. Leaving the road which runs due west from Dholpur some ten miles [16 km] from the city, His Highness steered his car into the thick jungle, winding skilfully among the trees and rocks, until we reached a small clearing surrounded by thickets. Here he sounded his motor-horn and we waited in silence. Presently, a sambhur hind showed herself, peering at us from the cover, then another and another, followed by the stags, and they all finally clustered round the car to take carrots from the Maharaj Rana's hands, allowing him to stroke their nozzles and showing no signs of fear, although naturally they are among the shyest of the denizens of the forest. It was a miracle worthy of Saint Francis, and for once I regretted the absence of a movie camera!' (Waddington 1933).

Just across the River Chambal with its gharial and Gangetic dolphins, lay Gwalior, the largest Maratha state in the country. Its very able ruler Madho Rao Scindia was not as keen a shikari as many of the other princes of his era. He was, however, an avid hunter of the innumerable tigers that his state held. His summer capital was shifted to Shivpuri, adjacent to which lay his favourite hunting reserve, now the Madhav National Park, with its spectacular lakes. On one of them, Sakhya Sagar, was the boat club of the Gwalior court, just across from the dam that filled the lake. On the dam was a hide; below it was a bait site for tigers. When the tiger arrived to feed below the dam, a light would be flashed from the hide to the boat club across the water. Anyone interested could travel by boat to the dam, climb into the hide and watch the tiger feeding below, under electric lights.

Being a very important ruler with a keenness to please the British implied organizing tiger shoots for the viceroys of India and visiting British nobility. A 10-foot tiger was the 'blue riband' of shikar, an object of envy and something to boast about. Large tigers were marked down, fed and provided as game to special guests, both white- and brown-skinned. But Madhav Maharaj wanted to go a step further. A 10-foot tiger was not good enough for a viceroy – it had to be a world record. A clever way was found: a special tape measure was made, in which 12 inches were really no more than 11 inches. This was to become famous as the 'Gwalior tape'. Viceroy Lord Reading shot a 'monster' tiger measuring 11 ft 5 inches from tip of nose to tip of tail. However, the problem with viceroys – as with all bureaucrats – was that they got transferred after a while, and the next viceroy must better the record of the previous one. So when Viceroy Lord Hardinge shot a tiger, it was found to be 11 ft 5½ inches long (Ward 1928)!

Some five years after Independence, the Maharaja of Kolhapur and his party were allowed to shoot thirty-two tigers in twenty-nine days in the Kuno forest. Today, practically no tiger survives in this area of the former Gwalior state. Madho Rao attempted to introduce the African lion in this forest, which was one of his favourite hunting areas. The forest type was right, the prey was ample. But there were a very large number of tigers, and the lions had been kept in captivity too long. To avoid the tigers, the lions had to move to other forests. One was shot by the Maharao of Kota in the neighbouring forest of Shahbad. Another was killed in the state of Panna, over 300 km away.

Historically, Udaipur was the predominant princely state in western India. Their rulers had never accepted the suzerainty of Delhi sultans, and the maharanas – the descendants of Sanga and Pratap – had vowed never to go to the court at Delhi. Maharana Fateh Singh spurned the invitation of Lord Curzon to the Delhi Durbar of 1903, and risked being dethroned. Maintaining a constant population of about 200 adult tigers in his state, Fateh Singhji shot more than 500 tigers in his reign of forty-five years. In later years, he would only shoot male tigers. As his eyesight was failing, a shikari would sit with him to warn him if a tigress approached. Only sixteen noblemen of the state were permitted to shoot in Udaipur, and this rarely happened as they all knew that it would be frowned upon by Fateh Singhji. Between 1949 and 1954, Udaipur lost 70 per cent of its 200 tigers when almost no legal hunting was allowed (Lakshman Singhji of Dungarpur, personal communication). By the 1960s, Udaipur had lost all its tigers, as it had most of its forest and almost all its wild ungulates.

In eastern Rajasthan, large concentrations of blackbuck were preserved near Patan in Jhalawar state. Towards the north, the royal family of Kota had long traditions of hunting. Paintings of the Kota school show lions and tigers emerging from the same drive. Darrah Wildlife Sanctuary, now ruined by grazing and human ingress, was a wonderful valley for wildlife. It is now part of the Mukundra Hills (Darrah) National Park, made a tiger reserve after it had lost all its tigers. The Chambal river, on which the city of Kota stands, is bound by steep, rocky banks upstream. At the bottom of the gorge along the riverside, baits would be tied, sometimes resulting in tussles between tigers and crocodiles. With human 'stops' blocking the upward retreat of the tiger, the only option for the tiger was to run below the precipitous gorge, where it could be shot at from a speedboat racing alongside.

Both the chinkara and the blackbuck reached their maximum proportions in both body and horn, in what is today Punjab and Haryana. The largest heads on record come from these areas, despite their relatively smaller populations here (Ward 1928). As the land is flat and fertile and has been cultivated for millennia, the only areas which could be set aside for these animals were in special beeds or grasslands, the 'rakhs' or reserves of the princes. On agricultural land outside these reserves, they could survive only in those princely states where the rulers were keen on shikar and hunting of the antelope and gazelle was prohibited, despite the damage they caused the crops. As we have seen, the small state of Jind produced the largest-known blackbuck horns. Some of the others on record also came from Jind and from Patiala, Nabha and Faridkot. Today, outside of the Bishnoi areas like Abohar in Punjab, both the chinkara and blackbuck are almost extinct in this region.

In the Himalaya south of Kashmir, the largest state was Chamba. It held in its reserves some of largest populations of brown bear, goral and Himalayan tahr. In the valleys of Bharmour and Pangi, there were Himalayan ibex and snow leopards. The pursuit of mountain fauna was almost a preserve of the British in India. Hardly any Indian hunters, who were almost entirely of the princely order in those days, pursued the high-altitude animals because of the hardships it entailed. Englishmen almost exclusively went to Kashmir for mountain game and, thus, hill states such as Chamba, Jubbal and Bushahr were not exploited. On the border of Chamba and Bhadarwah lies Gamgul–Siyabehi, the only area outside of the state of Kashmir where the rare and endemic hangul, or Kashmir stag occurred in the last century. They moved down here during the rutting period and winter, and were zealously protected but periodically hunted by the rajas of Chamba. In the summer, the hangul moved up into the high alpine forests of Bhadarwah in Kashmir. Gamgul is a marvellous terrain of dale and forest, so beloved of the hangul. When I visited it in 1988, the hangul had been extinct for some years, but I did see the gorgeous and very rare western tragopan pheasant.

Now to tiger land in central India. No one in the history of the world has shot more tigers than Maharaja Ramanuj Saran Singh Deo of Surguja, in what is now north Chhattisgarh. Though he stopped recording his tiger trophies after their number reached about 1,150, it is assumed that the total figure was over 1,400. His grandson and my senior colleague in the IAS, Maharaja M.S. Singh Deo, told me that when Ramanuj Saran Singh Deo began his reign in 1918, there were so many tigers and such a high incidence of man-eating that it led to a human exodus and at one point it was questionable as to who would survive in Surguja, man or tiger.

The shooting of tigers became a consuming passion with the Surguja royal family, almost its raison d'être. The police stations in that vast, forested state were equipped with heliostat signalling facilities. Tiger kills were signalled to the state capital at Ambikapur. Within twenty minutes of receipt of the message, the maharaja would be in his hunting van, which was equipped with food, weapons, shikaris and two bales of white cloth, each 65 m long and some 1.8 m wide. He was familiar with the technique used by the Ranas of Nepal of surrounding tigers in the Nepal terai with a phalanx of elephants and the placement of white cloth in a ring to enclose them (Smythies 1942). The maharaja adopted and evolved this technique for tiger beats in his sal forests. The machan or shooting platform, usually an inverted string cot, would be in place and beaters ready for the arrival of the hunting party. The bales of white cloth would be strung out in a huge V-shaped funnel, with the narrower end opening in front of the machan. Tigers do not barge through white cloth, nor do they jump over it. Even half a dozen beaters were enough to drive a tiger into the funnel and out of its open end to the waiting gun.

Ramanuj Saran Singh Deo's three sons were also keen to kill tigers. So a rotational scheme was evolved. After the maharaja had shot five tigers, his elder son would be allowed to shoot one, followed by another five by the father, followed by one for the second son, then five more for the father, then one for the third son, and then back to the father (M.S. Singh Deo of Surguja, personal communication). In the palace compound, a stuffed tiger mounted in a galloping posture was strung over a rail. Operated by electricity, the dummy would be made to suddenly dart forward, providing vivid target practice from various angles, usually done the first thing in the morning.

The maharaja's shikar diary in his later years reads like a laundry list – the number of tigers and leopards shot in each shikar camp are noted without any further details (Unpublished, seen by the author courtesy of M.S. Singh Deo of Surguja). As his sons grew older and there being jealousies over opportunities to shoot tigers, the forests of the state were divided for hunting rights, with the best areas, of course, being apportioned to the father. In my estimation, the family and their guests were responsible for the death of over 1,900 tigers. At the end of it, there were very few tigers left in Surguja, though the prey species and the forests were still intact. Nevertheless, there were still more tigers surviving then than there are today.

Next to Surguja was the state of Korea, where the last Indian cheetah – three young male siblings – were shot by Maharaja Ramanuj Pratap Singh Deo of Korea in 1947. The royal family of Korea accounted for another 150 to 200 tigers (Ram Chandra Singh Deo of Korea, personal communication). Bordering both Korea and Surguja lay the large state of Rewa, famous for its white tigers. Here, Maharaja Gulab Singhji and his family shot about 900 tigers, 100 being accounted for in just fourteen months. On the whole, some 3,000 tigers were shot in these three neighbouring princely states, from around the end of World War I to the end of World War II. In 1950, there were still some 200 tigers left in the area. At the time of the 1972 enumeration, when there had hardly been any legal hunting in this area for almost a quarter-century, less than thirty had survived (Ranjitsinh 1997).

Bhopal was another state with shikar traditions and, consequently, strict protection. Muhammad Nasrullah Khan, son of the Nawab Begum of Bhopal, wished to shoot ten tigers in a single day. He did get nine. The world record for both sambar (over 50 inches) and chital (over 42 inches) was from Bhopal. The only record ever of a totally black blackbuck, a male, is also from Bhopal (Ranjitsinh 1989a).

The huge sprawling state of Bastar, however, had no hunting tradition and the administration frequently lay with appointees of the political department of the British government. It was the latter that first paid attention to the relict population of the wild buffalo, for which restricted permissions to hunt were given by the state. In the maharaja's reserve at Makri lived some of the last central Indian barasingha surviving outside of the Kanha National Park. Now, the barasingha is extinct in Bastar and there are less than thirty wild buffalo left in the Indravati National Park in Bijapur district.

Eastwards in Odisha, the largest princely state of Mayurbhanj encompassed the Simlipal massif, the highest in the Eastern Ghats. It forms a part of the most extensive and contiguous sal forests in the country and once held large concentrations of elephants and deer. Elephants were captured by the kheda method of driving the herd into a wooden stockade. My father, who participated in one kheda, had a fascinating film that captured the process. In this, the leader of the herd was a tusker, not the usual matriarch. The magnificent trapped animal repeatedly charged the camera and then entwined his trunk around a sal stump, slumped to the ground and, despite all efforts of the kunkis (tame elephants), refused to eat or drink and, ultimately, died. As a boy, I used to weep over this most poignant scene. The Maharaja of Mayurbhanj also had a remarkable movie of a fight between two wild tigers and a wild cow elephant. I don't know what the cause of the fight was, but at the end, all three combatants perished.

Further eastwards, Maharaja Nripendra Narayana of Cooch Behar killed a very substantial number of animals between 1871 and 1907 in the Duars of West Bengal, around what is today the Buxa Tiger Reserve. According to his own account, he shot 365 tigers, 311 leopards, 207 rhinos, 438 buffalo, 133 bears, 259 sambar, 318 barasingha, and forty-eight bison (Nripendra Narayana Bhupa 1908). After his demise, neither active shikhar nor conservation seems to have continued in the region, and this prime high-grassland–forest-mosaic habitat was largely decimated and occupied for agriculture.

In the Deccan, the royal family of Kolhapur, the descendants of Chhatrapati Shivaji Maharaj, pursued the multitude of blackbuck in the state with cheetah. Chhatrapati Sahu, venerated by the backward classes of India for being a pioneer in giving them equal rights, maintained a stable of cheetah (Divyabhanusinh 1999).

Nearby lay the dominions of the Nizam of Hyderabad, the largest and the wealthiest of the Indian states. Till the beginning of the twentieth century, cheetah could be caught in the wild in Hyderabad state, and the flamboyant nizam, Mehboob Ali Pasha, maintained captive cheetah for hunting and was a keen shikari himself. His son Osman Ali was not at all keen on hunting, and though his grandson, the prince of Berar, shot thirty-five tigers in thirty-three days in one district of Hyderabad, the preservation of wildlife in the state was not as stringent as in other princely domains.

In the state of Mysore, G.P. Sanderson, a British naturalist who worked in the Public Works Department, had in the later part of the nineteenth century refined the kheda technique of group capture of elephants, which became the standard method in peninsular India (Sanderson 1912). A permanent site for elephant capture was identified at Kakanakote on the Kabini river, and elephants were periodically captured there, right until 1972. That year, the Wild Life (Protection) Act had been promulgated and, moreover, the dam on the Kabini River was filling up. This was to be the last kheda and tickets for the show had already been sold at high prices to foreign tourists. In my capacity as director of wildlife preservation of India, I protested that since the Act had come into force, elephants could not be captured. But the then Union minister for tourism hailed from Mysore, and the state chief wildlife warden gave permission to capture elephants in the better interest of wildlife management, under the provisions of the Act! The last kheda was thus held, in which the elephant herd broke back and one animal was killed. This led to the amendment of the Act, whereby the state chief wildlife wardens would have to take prior permission of the Union government's director of wildlife preservation of India to allow hunting or capture of an animal specified in Schedule I of the Act.

The last maharaja of Mysore, Jayachamaraja Wodeyar, was a keen but very selective hunter and the first chairman of the Indian Board for Wildlife. It was during his reign and that of his predecessor, the sagacious Krishna Raja Wodeyar, that the foundations of conservation were laid in the state, the results of which we see in

Bandipur, Nagarhole, Bhadra and Biligiriranga Swamy parks and sanctuaries.

In the present state of Kerala, the rajas of Cochin were uninterested in shikar and the most notable conservation occurred at the hands of the tea planters of the Kanan Devan tea estates. Their interest in shikar saved the largest population of Nilgiri tahr that survive on their estate, which today constitutes the Eravikulam National Park. The enlightened rulers of Travancore, who were also not greatly interested in hunting, did protect what is now the Periyar Tiger Reserve.

This long litany of blood sport is not to justify the huge bags and the swagger that went with them, but rather to record the course of wildlife conservation history and to highlight three basic factors. First, the resilience of the Indian subtropical ecosystems and species and their ability to recover despite heavy hunting, provided that the habitats were saved from demographic impact and the prey species remained adequate. Second, just as no carnivore drives its prey to extinction, no single hunter or family can, but a multitude driven by need or greed can. Lastly, in a country with a teeming population riven by poverty and illiteracy, conservation efforts must come from the 'top' and be motivated by individual interest – in the past, the interest was shikar but today, thankfully and hopefully, it is a nascent love for and appreciation of nature. I was privileged to witness the transition.

4

Kashmir

There is no political entity in the world to rival the former princely state of Jammu and Kashmir in its diversity of montane flora and fauna. Covering 222,441 sq. km, it was once the largest princely state in India. Stretching from the Hindu Kush mountain range in the west to the Kunlun Mountains and Rupshu in the east, and from the mighty Karakoram in the north to the Kandi–Shivalik Range of Jammu in the south, it encompasses vast stretches of the Kailash, Ladakh, Zanskar, Pir Panjal, Kajinag and the Great Himalayan mountain ranges besides vast tracts of the Trans-Himalaya and over 800 km of the upper Indus river. With eight different forest types; cold, arid and temperate grasslands; altitudes ranging from Mount K2, the second highest peak in the world at 8,611 m, to the plains of Jammu barely 200 m above sea level; Jammu and Kashmir's ecology and faunal wealth are unparalleled (Champion and Seth 1968).

Situated at the junction of the Indo-Malayan and Palaearctic realms, the mega diversity of the flora of Kashmir also has no equal in the world (ibid.). As for its fauna, 367 species of birds belonging to 180 genera, seventy species of reptiles belonging to forty-three genera and 154 species and subspecies of mammals representing seventy-five genera, occur in the state (Bacha 2013). Few know that even tigers roamed the forests of Poonch until the latter half of the nineteenth century (Adams 1867). As for large, truly montane mammals, more species occur in Kashmir than the whole of central and northern Asia put together. In the words of C.H. Stockley, the foremost hunter-naturalist of the Himalaya, 'Kashmir is the Ultima Thule of mountain sport and the finest big game field in the world' (Stockley 1928).

The state of Jammu and Kashmir was created in 1846 by the Dogra chieftain Maharaja Gulab Singh, in the aftermath of the disintegration of the Sikh Empire of Maharaja Ranjit Singh of Punjab. To Kashmir, Gulab Singh added Ladakh. Being at the junction of three empires and a fulcrum for the Great Game, the state was accorded special attention by the British government in India. In the early years, Englishmen were advisors and functionaries in the administration and even chiefs of the state's game department. Prior to the accession of Maharaja Hari Singhji in 1925, the Kashmir royal family was not interested in shikar and even Hari Singhji did not pursue mountain fauna other than the hangul.

The hangul, being a large-bodied *elaphus* deer, is primarily a grazer. In autumn and winter, it has to descend to the valley floors and to the lower-altitude margs (grassy dales) to forage. The fertile vale of Kashmir has been occupied by man for millennia. As the human population grew in the nineteenth and twentieth centuries, habitation crept upwards along the valleys and streams. The riparian forests were destroyed by human settlements, the margs taken over by shepherds. Only in those valleys where the deer could find some succour in the winter did they survive. Of these – the upper Sindh and Lidder, Gurez, Bringhi and Dachigam – only Dachigam was a royal rakh or game reserve. Now a national park, it is the last home of, and hope for, the hangul.

In the early years of the twentieth century, the Duke of Bedford, with his penchant for collecting deer of all kinds, persuaded Maharaja Pratap Singh to capture and send hangul to the Woburn Abbey in England, where they survived till World War II. The grateful Duke sent brown trout to Kashmir on two occasions, to be introduced there (Ward 1921). While the English trout still thrives in the streams of Kashmir, the hangul is on the verge of extinction and there are none breeding in captivity.

The waters of Dachigam have been witness to another wildlife drama. Kashmir once had a good population of wild pig. In cold climes, these animals assume greater proportions than in hotter regions, and one of the heaviest Indian wild boars on record was shot by Raja Amar Singh, the father of Maharaja Hari Singh. In lower Dachigam, cut grass was stacked. This provided fodder to the hangul and a shelter for wild pigs on severe winter nights. In the winter of 1960, I used to run into them frequently while in search of the hangul. A decade later, a powerful chief minister (CM) of Kashmir saw a sounder of pigs cross the stream above the trout hatchery at Harwan in Dachigam, just above the point from where water is siphoned off for Srinagar. Pigs being taboo to Muslims, the CM was incensed on seeing the drinking water of Srinagar being polluted by these creatures, and ordered the destruction of all wild pigs in the catchment area of the Dachigam stream. This is the only instance that I am aware of in which a species was made extinct by a government in a national park for religious reasons.

I regard a true montane mammal as one that has evolved in the mountains and whose main populations, past and present, live in the mountains. The longest mountain range in the world is the Andes; the main Himalayan range is the shortest of the great mountain chains of the world. However, while the Andes has but three species of large montane mammals, the whole of Africa another three and Europe four, the Himalaya and its adjoining ramparts hold more than half the large montane mammal species of the world and most of these occur in the state of Jammu and Kashmir. Riding on horseback for some twelve hours along one nala (valley) of the Chang Chen Mo Valley in Ladakh in 2008, I saw six species – wild yak, chiru (Tibetan antelope), Tibetan argali or nyan, bharal, kiang (wild ass) and the Tibetan grey wolf.

As mentioned above, the early rulers of Kashmir were not keen on hunting and the early chief game wardens of the state were

Englishmen. The management of wildlife and its shikar, therefore, barring the royal rakhs in the Kashmir Valley and Jammu, was not for the benefit of the ruler and his guests only, but for the British hunter. Kashmir was unique in this regard, with a system of game rules, licences, bag limits and hunting blocks set in place. We also have extensive records of the travels and exploits of the European shikaris. These are of interest, partly because they show the abundance of 'game' and also because they are a part of the wildlife legacy of the past, whose ramifications prevail even today.

Following is a list of the licences that were available for hunters, circa 1928, and the number of animals each licence holder was allowed to shoot.

Summer Licence – ₹125		Winter Licence – ₹75	
Hangul	2	Hangul	1
Markhor	2	Markhor	2
Ibex	3	Ibex	2
Tahr	4	Tahr	3
Goral	4	Goral	3
Tibetan argali	2	Tibetan argali	1
Tibetan antelope	4	Tibetan antelope	3
Tibetan gazelle	1	Tibetan gazelle	1
Bharal	4	Bharal	2
Shapu	2	Shapu	2
Serow	1	Serow	1
Brown bear	2	Brown bear	1
Total	31		22

Both licences covered the shooting of 'small game' and there was no limit to the number of leopard, snow leopard, black bear, wolf and pig that could be shot by the licensees. For an additional ₹50, a hunter could shoot any additional specimen of the above, barring markhor and argali. For a special licence of ₹30, a musk deer could be shot. A licence of ₹40 covered the shooting of only black bear, leopard and pig, without limit. The minimum size of horn length that could be shot for the species on the licence were: markhor, 44"; ibex, 35"; Tibetan argali, 38"; shapu, 24"; bharal, 23"; hangul, 30" with ten antler points. The summer hunting season, from mid-April to October, was divided into two periods of three months each. In the Kajinag and Shamshabari mountains, six guns were allowed in each period, and in Ladakh twelve guns in the first half and twenty in the second, including three in Chang Chen Mo in each period. The walk from Srinagar to the precipices of Haramosh and Skardu entailed a month one way, and to Leh three weeks. This was no 'cakes and ale' shikar of the plains.

The prevalent predilection for large daily 'bags', however, persisted. With the onset of winter, black bears from the southern side of the Pir Panjal Range moved down to the Poonch region, causing considerable damage to the ripening crops and orchards. The periodic Poonch bear 'battues' were famous. There is a record of fifty-four bears being shot in three days of drives with beaters (Ward 1923a).

Large bags of chakor, snipe and duck were other status symbols. Barring Keoladeo Ghana of Bharatpur, I have not seen so many waterfowl and geese anywhere as were to be encountered in Hokersar, Haigam, Mirgund and Wular in 1955 and 1960, and they were but a fraction of the number found in the pre-Independence era. One T.M. Kennard is reported to have shot 129 greylag geese in one day and a Major Radcliffe shot 6,998 duck and geese, including 2,000 mallards, in one season (Ward 1923b).

In the 1950s and even later, open waterbodies of Hokersar and Haigam could hardly be seen for the rafts of duck floating on it, even in mid-winter when a portion of the migrants would have flown further south to warmer climes. Every evening, hunters would line up on the Srinagar–Baramulla road to shoot greylag geese and mallard flying out of Hokersar, with spectators cheering every hit and plummeting bird. I last went to Hokersar in the autumn of 2015, when the concentration of migratory birds should have been at its peak. However, there were more coots than ducks or geese on the water body and the total waterfowl count would not have exceeded a thousand.

In the early years of the twentieth century, an event occurred that changed the faunal history of Kashmir and of India. The city of Srinagar was growing and needed a sufficient supply of potable water, not the polluted plenty from the River Jhelum and the Dal Lake. The nearest perennial stream of adequate size was the Dagwan, debouching from a valley above Harwan, adjacent to the famed Mughal gardens of Shalimar. But the valley had ten villages situated on the stream and hence the name – Dachigam. If the source of drinking water for the capital of Kashmir was to be pollution-free, these villages had to be relocated, and that is what Maharaja Pratap Singh did from 1910 onwards. The last resettlement occurred during the reign of his successor Maharaja Hari Singh in 1934, when Dachigam had already become a royal reserve (Kurt 1978). These were the first cluster of villages ever to be moved out of a protected area in recent history, and served as a constant inspiration to me when I was attempting to move out the first village from a national park or sanctuary in independent India – the village of Sonph, from Kanha National Park, in 1969.

The shifting of those ten villages not only provided safe water for Srinagar, it also helped secure the survival of the Kashmir stag, the only member of the *elaphus* family of red deer to now exist in the Indian subcontinent and is today endemic to Kashmir. The barasingh or hangul, like a true montane cervid, requires undisturbed upland pastures to feed, and forests for cover and safety and to bear their young. Unlike other montane mammals that move vertically up and down the slopes of a valley with the changing seasons, the hangul moves diagonally up or down the length of a valley, sometimes from one valley into another. They follow known paths and during the autumn rut, known in Kashmir as the 'awaz ki wakht' (calling time), they make their presence known by their eerie, shrill calls. In winter, they need to go to the lowest valley bottoms, where the snow is the least and temperature the highest, to procure forage, as they neither have the underwool of the wild sheep and goats nor the tubular hollow hair of the musk deer.

Thus, to save the hangul, one must save the ecosystem. How does one achieve that in an insurgency-ridden, heavily populated, democratic set-up where all the available grasslands are grazed by a vote bank of Gujar shepherds, where a deer is the most sought-after wild meat of an almost 100 per cent meat-eating populace who have been provided – the cruellest joke of all – weapons to ostensibly safeguard themselves, and the state, from insurgents? Today, only one valley, one ecosystem provides the needs of the hangul, and that too only partially – Dachigam. Around 1940, when the hangul population in Kashmir was between 5,000 and 6,000, Dachigam held about 3,000 (Holloway 1970). Twenty years later, they were down to less than 200 in the rakh (Gee 1964). Today, between 140 and 170 survive in Dachigam, with the total population in the Kashmir Valley – indeed in the world – not exceeding 200. This is despite the fact that the hangul is the state animal of Kashmir. The Dachigam ecosystem is this deer's only hope now. Outside of it, the scattered few would, perhaps, number less than ten. Upper Dachigam, which was their traditional summer breeding ground, is now occupied by the Gujar shepherds and their dogs in the summer.

I have had some memorable wildlife experiences in Kashmir over the past six decades. From the end of November 1960, after writing my IAS entrance examination, I spent five weeks in the Kashmir Valley. The rut of the hangul was nearing its end. In Dachigam, the ochre and gold hues of the broadleaf forests were turning sombre and some trees were already stark and leafless. The exceptions were the groves of English oak planted by Maharaja Hari Singh, which not only provided fodder for the hangul and acorns for the pig and black bear, but also a welcome cover during inclement weather. These two oak groves still flourish, though the pigs have gone and close to one oak patch stands an anachronistic sheep farm. Yet, at the height of the acorn season in September and October, black bears sneak into the oak grove near the sheep farm to gorge themselves the whole night and lay on fat in preparation for the onset of winter. In the autumn of 2013, I saw sixteen black bears in a day in these two oak groves.

In 1960, artificial salt was still being offered to animals at chosen sites in open fire lines that were then being maintained. These salt licks were areas of deer congregation and for rutting activity. The hinds would first approach the licks with all caution, hesitating and peering around. The stag would then strut up in measured steps; antlers laid back, orbital glands everted. Nuzzling and sniffing the posteriors of the hinds to ascertain their receptivity, it would raise its snout to vent the haunting, long-drawn rutting call, a wail ending in a roar, which would be answered by a rival across the valley. Occasionally, the hinds would raise themselves on their hind legs and flail at each other with their forelegs, even crinkling their noses in a classic grimace of 'flehmen'. Though an adult stag usually has ten to twelve tines and hence the name barasingh, as many as sixteen tines on an antler pair have been recorded.

Around midday, when the deer would be in cover and resting, I would go to the Draphahama hunting lodge of the former maharaja, a wooden hut built on a height, commanding an idyllic view of the valley slopes and grasslands favoured by the hangul. Indira Gandhi loved this hut; and on her visits to Srinagar, she always took the opportunity to stay a day or more in this retreat. On one trip, her efforts to see the hangul having been foiled by the security vehicles piloting her entourage, she resorted to a stratagem. Excusing herself from the front portico of the hut where she sat with her companions, she went to the toilet at the back, slipped out of it through its back door, marched up to one of the jeeps parked at the back, and ordered the driver to take her down the road. When her chief of security, the legendary R.N. Kao, discovered that she had sneaked off alone with a driver, he jumped into a vehicle and drove frantically down to find Mrs Gandhi happily watching a herd of hangul at the salt lick below the oak grove. Of course, his approach put the deer to instant flight and Indira Gandhi was livid. 'What are you doing here, Mr Kao,' she yelled. 'I am doing my duty, madam,' replied Kao. She drove off straight to Srinagar in a huff, never to return, and refused to go to any national parks thereafter. During my first tenure as director of wildlife preservation of India, I requested her to visit Corbett National Park in April 1973, for the inauguration of Project Tiger. 'I will never go to a park,' she replied wistfully and then almost under her breath added, 'It causes too much disturbance to the animals.'

That exquisite little wooden hut at Draphahama was destroyed in a fire, and was replaced by another anachronistic intrusion – a plush, modernistic concrete structure out of sync with the surroundings, with vast, manicured lawns and flower beds. Still, one night during the Snow Leopard Conference in the autumn of 1989, when I was staying with my family in the outhouse on this property, my wife Kalpana came face-to-face with a leopard on the lawn.

Up the valley, the motor road ends at what used to be another hut, at Pahlipora, which was later burnt down by insurgents. The long walk downhill from Pahlipora to Draphahama, on the northern flank of the valley through the favoured grasslands of the hangul, is one of the most exhilarating treks in the Lower Himalaya and the surest way to see the deer. In the winter of 1979, whilst looking for hangul on this walk, I stumbled upon a large male serow in the meadows, a most uncharacteristic habitat, and took the best pictures I have of this remarkable, elusive and reclusive rupicaprid (goat-antelope).

Dachigam, however, is one of the best places to see the serow, if one has the patience and perseverance. Being solitary and a creature of habit with restricted movements, it is persecuted by poachers with relative ease and comes to bay if chased by dogs. It needs total protection and freedom from disturbance, which it gets in lower Dachigam. Having failed to see serow in the Aijas Rakh in the Wangat in the north-western corner of the Kashmir Valley, despite bivouacking under rock shelters in heavy snowfall, I returned to Dachigam at the end of December 1960. Amongst the sheer rock cliffs interspersed with scrub and pine so beloved of the serow, between Gratnad and Chandranad below Sangri Top, I came within 100 m of a large male. But as I rested to regain my breath, he took that one extra step and disappeared from view, forever. Two days later on Christmas Eve, as I was struggling up a steep gully in knee-deep drifts of snow, I heard crunching thuds of onrushing hooves on snow. Suddenly, a serow with a kid came hurtling down the gully, head lowered for the upward thrust of those short, sharp backward curving horns. Grabbing a protruding rhododendron branch, I was able to yank myself sideways out of their path. Serow are known to be aggressive when cornered and this female perhaps felt that her kid was being threatened.

Lower Dachigam has the highest concentration of Himalayan black bear in the world today. They take their share of the hangul young as do leopards, and used to be culled in earlier times. In that December of 1960, I saw a bear on the premises of the Palace Hotel, above the Dal Lake. This was the former palace of Maharaja Hari Singh, and from the windows of which Maharaja Umaid Singh of Jodhpur had shot a hangul in the past.

One late evening in December 1960, close to the Dagwan stream below Rajnari, we heard the typical, measured cawing of ravens. They were perched atop a tree, looking down in one particular direction, giving repeated plaintive calls and inviting attention to an obvious kill. The fact that they were not descending to the ground meant that the 'owner' of the kill was in attendance. Accompanied by the forest guard Mir, I went to look for the predator, presuming it to be a leopard, armed with a small stick to part the thorns and brambles. We approached the spot very carefully, and sure enough, there lay a disembowelled hangul yearling, obviously the work of a leopard. Slowly we stepped out into a small opening to secure a better look, when Mir suddenly grabbed my arm and shouted, 'Haput' (bear). Barely 15 m to our right was a huge hulk of a bear, crouched over the viscera of the hangul that had been expertly extricated by the leopard. His broad, white chest sash vividly visible, the bear peered at us with its beady eyes, head thrust belligerently forward. We started inching backwards, which was the best course under the circumstances. Then Mir lost his nerve and yelled at the bear, whereupon it lunged towards us with loud, guttural snarls. Mir bolted in one direction and I in another. Turning back to see whether I was being pursued or Mir, I fell headlong to the ground and cut my lower lip. Trying to raise myself, I found that my leg had been entwined in a creeper. The best course, I then thought, was to lie on my chest and cover my head with my hands to prevent, if possible, the mauling of my face. I could hear the bear snorting and mulling about, but obviously he had lost sight of both of us. After about three or four minutes, which of course seemed like eternity, I got up, peered about and not seeing the bear, decamped forthwith with a bleeding lip. The doctor at Srinagar wanted to put in a couple of stitches, but I refused. The scar is a memento of a lifetime.

From the wildlife perspective, the most diverse, rich and fascinating area of Kashmir is Ladakh. Indeed, it has hardly any peer in the world in many respects. Its vast uninhabited vistas, its sentinel-like monasteries towering above in splendid isolation, its awesome highlands, lakes and peaks, make Ladakh a place without parallel. Perhaps I am biased; it was here that I undertook my first montane trek in 1958 while still in college and came under the undying spell of the mountains and their fauna. And it is to Ladakh that I keep returning ever so often, for inspiration and solace. It is one of the very few places left in the world where the wildlife in its remoter parts is almost as abundant as when I first saw it.

British hunters stopped visiting Ladakh during World War II, since no leave was being granted to them for hunting; and after the intrusions of Pakistan and China, Ladakh became an area closed to visitors. My lifelong friend and the father of my future sister-in-law Sudha, Maharaj Kamal Singhji of Dumraon was a member of parliament and an ardent mountain wildlife enthusiast. He asked permission of the then defence minister, Krishna Menon, to travel in the wilds of Ladakh in 1958 with my elder brother Digvijaysinhji and myself. Permission was refused. Kamal Singhji then appealed to Prime Minister Nehru whose love for mountain trekking was well known. Jawaharlal gave permission, with the caveat that we should not go near the international borders in Chang Chen Mo and Changthang.

In May 1958, we flew from Srinagar in a propeller-driven Dakota DC-2 aircraft, with only a part-pressurized cabin. It would only take off if the weather was clear over both the Zoji La and Fotu La passes, and it followed the traditional trek route: Sonamarg, Zoji La, Dras, Kargil, and up the Indus to Leh, flying as low as possible and just clearing the two high passes. The scenery was simply superb and daunting. Leh was a town with less than 3,000 inhabitants and no electricity then. In the main street running up to the derelict but very imposing palace of the Raja of Ladakh, shops were shut in the evening, and polo was played. Shops sold goods brought overland from Yarkand and Kashgar, over the fearsome Karakoram Pass over 6,000 m high. A school had recently opened, but signage in English was hardly to be seen, though one house displayed a placard 'No life without a wife'! Men wore their traditional gunchas and women sported their perak headdress bedecked with turquoise stones – the richer the person, the greater the number of stones.

We were housed with the army in the old Moravian Mission House. With us was the Raja of Ladakh, with the rank of a major. The only vehicle in Ladakh was a jeep brought overland and reassembled, and the only jeepable track was to the airstrip and to the Hemis Gompa (Monastery) 22 km away. We hired ten ponies and mules as pack animals and three Zanskari ponies for riding, at ₹5 per day. If an animal died a natural death or by a fall, we were to pay a compensation of ₹500; if it was killed by a 'shan' (snow leopard), the compensation would be ₹700.

We marched out of Leh, seen off by a good part of its population lining the streets and camped the first day at Ranbirsinghpura, named after the Dogra general of Maharaja Gulab Singhji who conquered Ladakh. The next day while walking through Shisher Lungpa (valley), we saw our first wild animal – a shapu ram. Upstream and on the same right bank of the Indus in the Kulum Lungpa, we saw our first bharal and after a heavy snowfall, our first ibex.

As the causeway over the Indus at Upshi had been washed away by floods, we crossed by a rope bridge and walked up the spectacular gorge to Gya, seeing confiding bharal, chakor partridge and the Himalayan snowcock along the way. The gorge is the most scenic in Ladakh, with rocks of vivid hues and sharp spires and ridges rising perpendicularly. Above Gya village where the valley opens out into the vast, rolling uplands of the Changthang, we turned left into Kyamer Lungpa and paradise. I have been into this nala half a dozen times and have never failed to see the nyan or the Tibetan argali, the tallest and heaviest wild sheep in the world, the rams standing up to 1.2 m at shoulder and reaching over 180 kg in weight.

It was early June and the adult rams of the great sheep – nyan, shapu and bharal – as well as males of the ibex, had long segregated from the flocks of their ewes and nannies and had sequestered themselves on the highest pastures and crags. All along we had encountered wild animals and birds that were strikingly confiding. Bharal would meander about within 100 m of our caravan; the chakor would come up to our camp. No sportsman had hunted in these parts since the onset of World War II, and in 1958 the army presence was negligible. Yet, the shapu were very wary and the nyan would not allow us to approach closer than 1,000 m.

In the uppermost reaches of the Kyamer Lungpa, we saw a band of nine rams, creamish yellow underparts merging with their darkish brown bodies, contrasting with the white neck ruffs in the alpha males, carrying horns of over 40 inches in length and 18 inches in diameter at base. At the top of each 'la' or mountain pass that we crossed, there would be a 'lato', a pile of stones on which were deposited the skulls and horns of animals that were found dead by the local Changpa shepherds, and were an indication of the fauna to be found in the vicinity. I weighed the dry skull and horns of a nyan ram picked up from a lato: they weighed 18 kg.

The main axis of the Kyamer Lungpa is east–west. The south-facing flank of the northern side of the nala, thus, gets the maximum exposure to the sun, causing the snowline here to recede earlier in spring than elsewhere and making available the first flush of grass. Later in summer, the snow on the north face of the southern flank of the nala melts, making those pastures available. Kyamer is a long and secluded nala and there was no great competition between the wild ungulates and livestock. The ewes and immature rams of the Tibetan argali occupied the lower flanks of the Kyamer Lungpa; the largest rams with their white throat fronts ruled the topmost reaches.

We crossed the Kyamer La and then Thratsang La (5,150 m), blinded by the fresh-fallen snow and sinking knee-deep in the snow drifts. It was particularly harsh upon our pack ponies. Below Thratsang, the valley opens out into the vast bowl of the inland-drained Tso Kar Lake. On my long trudge to the lake shore, I came upon a pair of 'chanku' – Tibetan grey wolf – chasing a female 'gowa' or Tibetan gazelle, her white patch of rump hair erect and fanned out in alarm as she disappeared over a crest, with the wolves in pursuit. The gazelle is now extinct in the Tso Kar region and is at present confined to a small population surviving in Kalak Tartar in the Hanle Valley, east Ladakh, Over my periodic visits to Hanle since 1970, I have found their numbers to be in slow decline.

Unlike the Tibetan gazelle of the Tso Lhamo plateau of Sikkim who are very confiding, the gazelle in Kalak Tartar take flight from a moving vehicle 500 m away and even further if the vehicle stops. This is a clear indicator of poaching from vehicles by the armed and paramilitary forces, who have all the control and the vehicles in that region. Kalak Tartar is part of the Changthang Wildlife Sanctuary, and as a member of the National Board for Wildlife, I had suggested that the road be closed and an alternative route for patrolling be used. As this never happened and is not likely to happen in the future, I fear that this dainty gazelle will become extinct in India's Western Himalaya.

To return to 1958, at Tso Kar we saw our first Tibetan sandgrouse – legs fully sheathed in feathers for protection against the cold – coming to drink at the inflowing freshwater streams at regular hours, as is the wont of all sandgrouse. Tso Kar then was a stark and desolate landscape, the lake almost three times larger than what it is now. Bar-headed geese and brahminy duck in bright nuptial plumage were then breeding on the lake on which we had camped. When we drew close, we were chased off by the threat displays of the nesting birds.

The Tso Kar bowl and the uplands north of it up to Kyamer Lungpa have one of the highest concentrations of the kiang or Tibetan wild ass and of the nyan. On subsequent visits, in vehicles, I have been able to obtain some of my best photographs of these animals in this region. In 2011, in the company of my family and one of the world's most outstanding wildlife painter, Robert Bateman, and his wife Brigit, we photographed in this region the black-necked crane, the Tibetan partridge and the kiang, and were even able to drive relatively close to the nyan.

In 1958, we trekked over the Taglang La (5,400 m), once more in knee-deep snow. By now we were fully acclimatized to the height and weather and were able to walk from Gya to Upshi on the Indus in a day. Today, one can drive on a tarmac road all the way from Tso Kar over the Taglang La to Upshi, in a few hours.

From the valley of the Indus we went up the Shang Nala, which is now in the Hemis National Park and holds one of the heaviest concentrations of bharal or blue sheep in Ladakh. One evening in Shang, my brother disturbed a snow leopard on her bharal kill. She climbed up a steep shale slope, where she was joined by two cubs that squatted on either side of her, providing a grand spectacle on the skyline.

In December 1995, I revisited Shang Nala. The wolf trap that we had seen in 1958 was still there at Sumdo, but was not in use. It was a wide well in which bait was placed; the predator would jump in to kill but would be unable to climb out. We reached Chakdo village at midnight, after a three-hour walk followed by a two-hour horse ride in brilliant moonlight, the horses slipping on hard ice in the frozen streams, almost throwing me off. Early morning on 4 December, with the temperature much below freezing, we went up to Chusurmo or the Sour Spring, spouting its mineral water and with a warm microclimate of its own. Around here the bharal congregate to eat the lichen and sparse vegetation. Looking down westwards into a vast bowl from the Pankur Ridge, we saw a group of four bharal. A mature, black-chested male in rut, neck outstretched, sniffed a ewe to determine if she was in oestrus. A younger ram inched towards them, whereupon the alpha male lowered his horns and lunged at the intruder, who then trotted away. Just then, my Ladakhi guide, lying prone beside me, whispered to me, 'Shan'! A long, lissom, grey form was snaking downhill towards the unsuspecting sheep, changing direction to take advantage of any cover on that open shale slope, halting when the sheep raised their heads and creeping when their heads were down. It reached a jumble of rocks from where it hoped to ambush the young ram that had been driven away. But the ram then turned to retrace its steps towards its amorous companions. Realizing that its object of pursuit was moving away, the snow leopard took its chance and charged, hurtling down some 60 m in a veil of dust and pebbles, the golden rays of the early morning sun behind us brilliantly lighting the unforgettable tableau.

The distance was too much. The bharal escaped. I, who had lain entranced watching the drama through my binoculars, woke up to the need of setting up a tripod and taking pictures. After a break to regain its breath, the shan strode along the hillside towards us, resplendent in its luxurious winter coat, swinging its oversized fluffy tail from side to side for balance. When it rested in the open in that brilliant sunshine, even the eagle-eyed Ladakhis could not spot it, though we knew where it was. When it faced us, only its creamish chest gave away the superb camouflage. After almost ninety minutes, it got up, climbed a perpendicular crevice that would have been challenging even for an ibex to traverse, and disappeared. My field note of that day records:

> This is a culmination of over thirty-seven years of trudging and riding at least a thousand miles in snow leopard country .... I have not seen a more wondrous sight in the animal world than a markhor standing statuesque atop a rocky pinnacle with a backdrop of precipices crowned with snowy peaks, his head topped by spiralling horns 50 in long, surveying the slopes below him, the only movement being the sharp mountain wind swaying the long tresses sweeping down to his knees. And second, this snow leopard, climbing up the precipice in morning sunlight, stopping periodically to survey his mountain domain, gusts of gale rippling his long, winter fur.

The mountain gods have been kind to me and I have had other sightings of the snow leopard, the last being in the company of my daughter Radhika, in February 2014 in Rumbak, Ladakh, the temperature reading minus 35°C at night. We saw a female with two large cubs twice, with shapu and incredibly tame bharal as a bonus.

But back to 1958: Our five-week trek culminated with the annual dance of the lamas at the Hemis Gompa (monastery), the largest in the Western Himalaya. A day before, near Martselang, we met a caravan with supplies for the border posts in the Chang Chen Mo Valley, manned by officers we had befriended when we stayed at the old Moravian Mission, which was then the army headquarters in Leh. Later, when we were in Srinagar, we learnt that this very caravan had had a skirmish with the Chinese at the Hot Springs in Chang Chen Mo, an incident which started the confrontation that culminated in the war of 1962.

I have been fortunate to have seen the dance of the lamas at the installation of the new rinpoche in 1989 at the Tabo Monastery, the oldest in the Western Himalaya, in Spiti, as well as the annual lama dance at the Thimphu monastery in Bhutan and elsewhere. However, for its colour, grandeur, backdrop and awesome impact, it is the dance at Hemis that remains the most vivid in my memory.

While the dance was on I looked up to the crags above, to see a bharal nanny with its kid, peering down at the spectacle in the Gompa quadrangle.

I have narrated at some length my trip of 1958, because Ladakh today is so different from the Ladakh of yesteryear. Motorable roads did not exist east of Hemis or westwards or northwards of Leh. The staple diet of the people was sattu (barley) and green tea, with blobs of dirty, delicious, black-hair-encrusted yak-milk butter, interspersed with copious doses of chang or barley 'beer' brewed in the gut of a goat, the peptides ostensibly residing in the long-dead intestine apparently giving it a special flavour and, certainly, a special odour. It remains my favourite drink in Ladakh.

Life and lifestyle in Ladakh had a certain timelessness and tranquillity that is hard to describe. Very little was available locally, other than yak butter and an occasional egg in the Changthang. Barter was more acceptable than cash. There were hardly any schools and the whole village would come and watch us in camp, hours on end, the adults turning their prayer wheels as if they were body appendages. There are few places or people I love more than Ladakh and the Ladakhis, even when so much has changed.

For me, the most significant change was in the behaviour of the fauna. In the aftermath of the 1962 conflict with China, the army and the paramilitary forces had moved in, in droves. Even the wild asses had become scarce and wary. Tales of slaughter of whole herds of bharal and ibex were common. On a trip in 1970, I came across remains of the rumen of shapu and ibex marking the spots where they had been butchered. It was difficult to approach within a kilometre of ibex in the Kanji Nala in Suru and of shapu in Hiniskot, below Fotu La. In the Changthang, I saw no bharal or nyan, not even their droppings.

In 1971 at a party in Delhi, I happened to meet the chief of the Indian Army, General S.H.F.J. (Sam) Manekshaw, later to become a field marshal. I complained about the massacres in Ladakh. Manekshaw asked me to meet him in office the next day. He listened patiently, then called in his stenographer and dictated a memo in my presence – any officer or jawan found hunting illegally would be court-martialled and it was the duty of the commanding officers to enforce compliance. This missive preceded the Wild Life Act of 1972.

When I revisited Ladakh in the mid-1980s during my second stint as director, wildlife preservation of India, the situation was noticeably improving. Animals were less shy and more widely seen.

A ready 'barometer' of hunting pressure over the years has been the number and the tameness of the shapu seen between Leh and Saspol, on the road to Kargil. For a long period, from the 1960s until the early 1990s, none could be seen. In June 1995, I photographed a golden eagle pinning down a struggling shapu kid with a broken back, on the plain between Pathar Sahib and the Magnetic Hill, above the spectacular junction of the muddy Indus and the blue waters of the Zanskar. These eagles swoop upon newborn kids, carry them in their talons high into the sky and then drop them, maiming them and rendering them immobile. In the years following this, I have seen a gradual increase in shapu numbers and their tolerance to human and vehicular presence in this region.

One haven for wildlife, even during the hunting epoch decades ago, had been the environs of the Rizong Gompa, opposite Khaltse on the Indus, in Ladakh. The narrow mouth of the nala opens out into a curving bowl of a valley, the bottom choked with willows and vegetation, the sides rising steeply into slopes of loose shale and crags. I camped in the Gompa (monastery) in December 1995 for four days and the forty lamas then residing there made me most comfortable. They were puritans – they neither smoked nor drank, nor did they eat meat, eggs or onions. Rizong is far from the main road and secluded, and it is buttressed by tall winding hillsides shielding it from the howling winds of Central Asia. This makes it an ideal Buddhist retreat. The presence of the Gompa in a predominantly Buddhist society, gives it sanctity. During the December stay, I used to see the wily chakor partridge roosting on the eaves of the Gompa, and even today, nowhere are the chakor so confiding as in this valley.

In 1995, Abdul Rauf, the forest ranger who accompanied me, estimated the number of shapu in the Rizong Valley to be around 300. They were in their period of rut, with the large rams sporting black chests, offset by white throat patches, a deep ochre-russet body pelage and white undersides. I also saw my first 'farrah', wild dogs in the Himalaya, in their winter pelage: three creamish-yellow-coloured animals with long bushy tails, chasing a singled-out shapu ewe, with the stamina and determination which is the hallmark of this species.

On every subsequent visit to Ladakh, I have always tried to go to Rizong and never have I failed to see shapu in this valley. In October 2006, I witnessed another chase, a large wolf going full tilt at a herd of some sixty shapu.

Some other cameos of Ladakh are etched in memory. In 1958, while walking along the Shisher Nala in the Indus Valley: the whistle of wind from the wings of a golden eagle dive-bombing to capture a shapu kid, its mother giving her shrill whistles in alarm. June 1995: a helicopter flight past Sasser Kangri, at 5,500 m the highest peak in Ladakh, and hovering over bharal in the Galwan Valley and over the largest ibex bucks I have ever seen, in the Nubra Valley. And on the same trip, experiencing a Himalayan Serengeti: 223 kiang scattered over the Spanggur plains, with black-necked cranes, brahminy duck and Tibetan woolly hare in the foreground, between Thag La and Chushul, south of the turquoise-blue Pangong Lake. In 2006, when my paramilitary hosts believed I had strayed into Chinese-occupied territory across the nala and were about to sound the alarm: a bunch of twenty-six argali rams, in the Kugrang Nala of Chang Chen Mo. In 2008: photographing the Himalayan fox, chiru, argali, kiang, bharal and wild yak and being threatened by a huge lone bull yak, also in Chang Chen Mo.

I cannot leave Kashmir without recounting my encounters with another marvellous animal on the western front – the Pir Panjal markhor, the largest wild goat in the world with corkscrew horns spiralling up to 64" in length. When my batch of IAS officers had our army training in Kashmir in 1961, I opted for a placement at a higher altitude, in the hope of being sent to markhor grounds. Sure enough, I was sent to Tangdhar on the Kishanganga river, right on the line of control (LOC), with the Pakistani pickets just across. The mighty Shamshabari massif towered above us. A very understanding commanding officer, Colonel Harish Bakshi of the Gurkha Rifles sent me to the remotest parts. But I saw no markhor. The next year, on the completion of my IAS training in Mussoorie, I went back to the Shamshabari Mountains on the invitation of Col Bakshi. The area was bristling with landmines, placed there after the Pakistani aggression in 1948, and I was ordered to remain on the paths. But markhor I did see, including an astounding sight of them silhouetted statuesquely along the skyline, undisturbed by the volleys of rifle fire from the firing range below. They are the wiliest amongst the wild goats and shun human presence, but they had come to learn that the area around the firing range was the safest for them.

In all my pursuits of wild animals, Kashmir is also where I perhaps came closest to being killed. I was following a male markhor along a ledge on the Champathar precipices of Shamshabari. The ledge became narrower and narrower, but intent upon pursuit, I kept edging forwards, only looking ahead. Then a piece of the rock face to which I was clinging came off in my hands. I let it go, and when I did not hear it thud for a while, I looked down, to see a sheer 400-metre drop. There I was, perched on a narrow ledge, clinging on to another rock with the other hand. It was an agonizing claw back to safety, with friable rock handholds and footholds.

In 1969, again at the invitation of (now) Brigadier Bakshi, I went after markhor in the Kajinag Mountains of Kashmir. On a ridge atop Ghoretal Nala on the LOC, markhor were reported to come to feed in a small marg or meadow that had sprung up in the wake of receding snow. My guides dug a hide overlooking the marg, just large enough to crouch in, and covered me with boughs of chir pine, with instructions not to even bat an eyelid if the markhor were looking in my direction. It was a fabulous tableau – forests of pine interspersed with meadows with craggy rocks and snow drifts above, topped by the stupendous pinnacles of the Kajinag peaks, the summer abode of the markhor males. Within half an hour of my internment in the hide, a resplendent male western tragopan pheasant strutted out to feed. Then a pair of Himalayan monal pheasants soared past giving their whistling call, the iridescent plumage of the male alight in the evening sun. They landed on the other side of the meadow away from the tragopan, and while the female scratched about the soil and pecked, the male kept whistling and displaying its erect crest feathers and horizontally held golden-russet tail. Then a male Kashmir musk deer strode out and started nibbling away at the fresh sprouts of grass. The light was fading and I had an hour's walk ahead of me to the camp. I have some superstitions: sighting an owl brings me bad luck and the involuntary batting of my right eyelid invariably brings me good luck. My right eyelid just would not stop fluttering that evening. So I waited longer in hope, till, when dusk was gathering, I had to stir out. In a last desperate try, I crawled up a slope and trained my binoculars on the skyline above me. I thought I saw the branches of a chir pine way above move, both horizontally and vertically. But there was no wind. It then dawned upon me that I was watching a feeding markhor with enormous horns. There were others as well. I crawled back into the hole, praying that the markhor would not move further to my right and above me, where they would certainly get my scent on the now upward-moving draft of wind. All the while, my right eyelid kept on fluttering feverishly! The markhor moved left and four of the younger males came down in a bunch to the marg at a trot. This is a classic ibex-markhor tactic, especially of the older males. They take great pains to ascertain the presence of danger when descending to eat and then come down fast in a group, usually with the younger males as the advance party.

Two more adult males, one with a freak, half-broken horn, came down. While the younger four had reached the meadow and were hungrily feeding, these two stood sentinel, watching both flanks, one looking intently at my hide, even as I lay agonizingly immobile. A while later, they relaxed and sedately moved down, by which time from the corner of my right fluttering eye, I could see two more. One a fine specimen, dirty creamish coat with dirtier swaying tresses drooping down to just above the fetlocks; creamish white mane, black beard and huge spiralling horns swaying with his movements – a truly grand sight. The other, the last of the eight, was more horn than body. His head drooped low with the weight of his enormous two-and-a-half curl horns, over a metre and a half long. His ribs were showing, the body had assumed a pale brown colour with skin devoid of hair in patches, and the black goatee was speckled with silver. Descending the steep slope, he rested on his haunches like a dog. As for alertness and the instinct of self-preservation, however, nothing had been lost. While feeding, if he found that he was at the edge of his group, he would quickly move to the centre. When two of the smaller males, including the sentinel, started sparring with each other, the biggest one took over the watch, standing statuesque with head raised in alertness. If only there had been brighter light for photography. Still, I could hardly sleep that night from the excitement of fulfilment.

Next day, I moved into the adjacent Malangan Nala, one of the most awe-inspiring and dangerous grounds I have seen. Here I was able to get some indifferent pictures of females and of a 'reend' (immature male markhor) licking the mineral-laden moisture oozing below rocky overhangs. But far more interesting was an afternoon spent watching a brown bear with her cub. After foraging for a couple of hours on a slope steep enough to suit a markhor, she scraped a depression in the ground and curled up in it to sleep. The cub lay most endearingly draped over its mother. After a while, the cub got up and started emitting plaintive, long-drawn calls. When the mother did not stir, it wandered off, then came back to lie upon her again, then took off once more, emitting those cries. This was repeated for a third time, the cub straying some 100 m away, whereupon the mother got up, strode up to the cub and slapped it, sending it squealing and rolling down the slope in a ball.

It then picked itself up and went back to its mother, who this time placed her huge paw over the cub to prevent it from any further meandering. Both then went back to sleep.

With the help of information from my local guides and my own observations, I guesstimated the total markhor population of the five major nalas of Kaj-i-Nag – Maidan, Ghoretal, Malangan, Gujar and Limbar – to be approximately 240 animals. In 2004, I revisited Kaj-i-Nag as the Wildlife Trust of India, of which I was then chairman, was undertaking an assessment of the status of the markhor and my colleagues Riyaz Ahmad and Yash Veer Bhatnagar enumerated a total of 280 to 330 markhor, with 180 to 200 in the Kajinag, twenty to thirty in the Boniyar Nala across the Jhelum, forty to fifty in the Hirpora Sanctuary on the Mughal Road and another forty to fifty on the southern flank of the Pir Panjal Range in Poonch (Ranjitsinh et al. 2005).

5

Bhutan

In many ways Bhutan is unique. In the nineteenth century, the rival temporal and spiritual power centres that had divided the country were united under one sovereign. In the twentieth century, the maharaja of Bhutan – unlike the others under British hegemony – became a King and the country joined the United Nations as a sovereign state. Sandwiched between two giants – China and India – it has not only retained its integrity and independence but has provided security, prosperity and quality of life to its people. Bhutan has no equal amongst the montane nations of the world, having maintained over the centuries its culture, traditions, values, and its natural endowments and beauty.

Buddhism and an enlightened monarchy, together with discipline and a relatively low rate of population growth have ensured that in no part of the habitable Himalaya has there been a lesser human impact upon montane ecology and biota than in Bhutan. Indeed, I would say that no habitable montane region in any of the seven continents or Oceana that I have visited, today remain as pristine as do major portions of Bhutan.

I have mentioned the unparalleled richness and variety of the large mammalian fauna of Kashmir. The Eastern Himalaya, on the other hand, rise too high and perpendicularly to provide the ecological transitional zone of high uplands extending into the Central Asian plateau. The great argali sheep, wild yak, kiang,

Tibetan antelope and gazelle are, thus, not real residents of the Bhutan Himalaya. The ibex did not colonize the Himalaya east of the Sutlej river. The brown bear stopped its eastward march in the Nepal Himalaya, and the Himalayan tahr remains confined to western Bhutan. But the more ample monsoon clouds from the Bay of Bengal provide greater rainfall to the higher altitudes of the central-eastern Himalaya, and hence, a much more profuse and diverse flora. The great range is also narrower in the east and its gradient steeper, providing a greater variation in ecology and biodiversity in a shorter distance of travel and altitudinal change. The bird life is far richer, and there appears now an unusual animal, the huge, ungainly but impressive rupicaprid, the mysterious Bhutan takin, the state animal of Bhutan.

When I first went to Bhutan in 1965, there were very few roads, sparse population and no hunters other than the royal family. I found black musk deer nibbling away unconcernedly just 20 m from me; and a male satyr tragopan, indescribably gorgeous in its shimmering crimson coat, tilted its blue-black head and gazed at me in wonderment five paces away. In all my wanderings in the mountains, I have never seen such a profusion of montane bird life and such numbers of confiding, large mammals, as in those early years in Bhutan – not in the Western Himalaya, Tian Shan, Altai, the Pamirs, nor in the Simien Mountains of Ethiopia. The only other comparable place would be the Tso Lhamo plateau of Sikkim, but only in respect of large ungulates. With the advent of the Chhukha Hydroelectric Project, came cheap labour and the start of surreptitious netting and snaring of birds and animals, and terracing of the hillsides for agriculture.

Bhutan has some of the most spectacular monasteries in the world, luxuriance of vegetation, awesome peaks and precipices, and its people of unparalleled courtesy, dignity, discipline and hospitality. It will remain my most loved nation after my own.

Maharaj Kumar Dasho Namgyal Wangchuck, the younger brother of the then reigning king of Bhutan, Druk Gyalpo Jigme

Dorji Wangchuck, was sent by the Government of Bhutan to be trained in the Lal Bahadur Shastri Academy of Administration at Mussoorie in 1961. We were there together for a year, and became friends. He invited me to Bhutan in the autumn of 1962. I had obtained my leave and my tickets, when the war with China began and the trip, of course, was cancelled. A year later, I was all set to go when an attempted coup nixed the trip once more. Bhutan appeared jinxed for me. In the summer of 1965, however, I went and spent over a month there, trekking extensively in the northern and central regions. My friend Namgyal had become Paro Penlop (governor of Paro), with the title of His Royal Highness.

I was housed in the royal palace of His Majesty the king at Dechencholing, some distance upstream of the Tashi Chho Dzong then being renovated, in the capital at Thimphu. The palace was a four-storey, quintessential Bhutanese structure, both outside and within, complete with traditional ornate furniture and drapery; but very comfortable. Above the entrance to my apartment, hung a fine, ten-point pair of antlers of a shou (misnamed the Sikkim stag), shot by His Majesty in the Chumbi Valley on the north-eastern boundary of Bhutan. There were a number of trophies of the chase – fine specimens of takin, bharal, chiru, serow, nyan, yak, bear and leopard. In the private chambers of the king, I was shown the skin of a tiger shot by the late father of His Majesty, the like of which I have never seen. It was not white, but very light coloured and had one stripe along the lower spine and just four short, narrow, faint stripes, close to each other on each side of the lower back and abdomen. There were a few stripes on the legs and face. Otherwise, the skin resembled more a lion or an oversized Tasmanian thylacine than a tiger. On a subsequent visit, I saw both the shou head and the tiger skin in the museum at Paro.

I was spoilt by the hospitality of the royal family. Paro Penlop was an avid fisherman, and though I myself never cared for the sport, I did join him and even landed some brown trout, most of which we released. Brown trout are a recent introduction to the

Bhutan streams and they were so numerous, that we got a strike almost every third cast.

Paro Penlop drove us to the top of the ridge which separates the Thimphu Valley from the Punakha Valley, past the impressive Simtokha Dzong (fort) where he lived. The road ended on the ridge and the rest of the journey to the Wangdue Phodrang Dzong and beyond was done on horseback and on foot. Luckily, I had Paro Penlop's sturdy hill horse with a proper saddle, covered with a padded Bhutanese rug. I, therefore, rode comfortably, unlike the agonizing hours spent on obstreperous, stunted ponies with wooden saddles that I had to ride elsewhere.

We crossed the Sankosh river over the most ornate wooden bridges I have ever seen – now, alas, washed away – and were made very comfortable in the Wangdue Phodrang Dzong by the dzongpen or fort master.

Next day, we rode to the very impressive Punakha Dzong and monastery, towering above the River Punakha, called Sankosh lower down. The walls were covered with paintings and silk thankas (religious paintings), the monks sitting in rows reciting their deep-throated, monotonous, haunting chant which is the hallmark of their prayer and worship. There was nothing then in Punakha but the Dzong. Now it has become a township.

From Wangdue Phodrang, we continued our march up the Pe Chu Valley into the Tang Chu Valley. Walking and riding allow one to savour the surroundings and to feel an affinity with the place, which is denied to the traveller in a vehicle. Apart from the stunning scenery, the bracing climate and vast vistas of virgin terrain, one had to stop, admire and photograph the multitudes of orchids, magnolias, rhododendrons and meadows carpeted with wild flowers. There were tracks of bear, leopard, sambar, barking deer and wild pig. We saw the black bear and dozens of the Himalayan brown goral which, contrary to what many field guides say, I found to be slightly larger and darker than the Western Himalayan grey goral and the bright ochre-red goral that I was later to see in Walong, on the Tibet border in Arunachal Pradesh.

But it was the takin that I had really come to see, for I had never seen one before. We camped for a week below a hill slope reputed to be their winter abode, spending whole days glassing the open grazing grounds and trekking from slope to slope. There were fresh hoof marks of takin herds and solitary bulls, huge and splayed, and whorls of their yellow and chocolate-brown hair, but never a sight of the animal itself. We were just a little too late. They had moved north on their summer migration, to the favoured spots at the top of the Punakha Valley, in what is now the Jigme Dorji Wangchuck National Park.

There was no dearth of interesting and exquisite birds – Bonelli's hawk eagle, black eagle and lammergeier in the sky; scarlet finches, Mrs Gould's and fire-tailed yellow-backed sunbirds in the foliage; blood pheasant, snow pigeon and snow partridge on the ground.

From an ornithological standpoint, however, there was a more interesting occurrence. Camped below the picturesque Shrill village in a lovely meadow, each morning I would see pairs of kalij pheasants pecking away at the droppings of our ponies. I could not quite identify the birds in Jean Delacour's excellent book *The Pheasants of the World*, which I was carrying. On the last morning as we were breaking camp, I borrowed the shotgun of Kado, Paro Penlop's man Friday who was accompanying us, and shot the male kalij. I later sent it to the Bombay Natural History Society, who had it identified by Dr Dillon Ripley, secretary of the Smithsonian Institute, Washington DC. It was declared to be a black or Moffitt's kalij. In Delacour's book, the distribution of this pheasant is recorded as: 'Still unknown ... From its intermediate characteristics between *Melanota* (black-backed kalij) and *Lathami* (black-breasted kalij), it might be inferred that this perfectly stable race inhabits the still unexplored part of Central Bhutan around the Mo-Chu (Punakha) Valley, between the known ranges of the other two' (Delacour

1964). Delacour's conjecture was correct. The *Handbook of the Birds of India and Pakistan* by Salim Ali and Ripley, subsequently published, was to record the status, distribution and habitat of the black kalij as: 'Unknown. Named from an aviary specimen of unknown provenance imported into California through a Calcutta bird dealer in 1934 ... only a single wild example ♂ so far obtained: Pechu Valley, Central Bhutan (c. 27° 30 N, 90° E), June 1965, by K.S. Ranjitsinhji of Wankaner' (Ali and Ripley 1969).

On the return journey on the Bumthang–Wangdue Phodrang road, we had an interesting interlude as we were marching up to the Makhushon pass. It was drizzling, when Kado suddenly whispered, 'Jh' (serow). I have always been intrigued and fascinated by this secretive, elusive, solitary and little-known rupicaprid. There it was, 150 m away, across a steep wooded valley, in full view of the frequented pathway, sheltering from the rain under a rocky outcrop. A foreleg was stretched out to support it against the gradient, the long pointed ears continuously batting away the flies. No camera. An overzealous porter had marched ahead with the bag, an hour earlier! A syce was dispatched, scurrying fast to intercept the advance party, while I watched in agony with my binoculars. The rain stopped. The serow stood up, shook off the droplets from its body and walked off to feed. The drizzle restarted; the serow hurried back and took shelter under the same overhang. The rain stopped and off went the serow again. An hour and a half later, the syce rushed up with the bag, panting with the exertion. He brought the rain back with him and so as I was taking out my cameras, the serow promptly returned to the shelter. I filmed and photographed it both while it stood there and as it strode off again.

Serow has a wide range, from the Himalaya through South-East Asia into Taiwan and Japan. They come in various hues. Specimens of the Western Himalayan race are larger in body size than those of Bhutan and the Eastern Himalaya.

I returned to Thimphu and after paying a courtesy call upon the two queen mothers and the sisters of Paro Penlop, amongst the most gracious and charming ladies I have met, it was decided that I should proceed to the Seijathang Valley for the takin. Situated on the north-eastern boundary of Bhutan adjacent to Tibet, Seijathang was regarded by Paro Penlop to be the ultimate haven for takin in summer.

There was hardly any human habitation upstream of the Dechencholing Palace in those days. We marched up from the palace grounds, and two-and-a-half hours later we were below the picturesque Cheri Gompa, situated atop a conspicuous hill on the junction of two streams. Thereafter, there were frequent crossings of the stream, and the sides of the valley became steeper and narrower. We camped at Parsho. The vista widened at Shodu village, where we reached the stunted rhododendron and high grass biome and saw our first musk deer and monal. In the five-and-a-half-hour trek between Parsho and Shodu, we had seen no vestige of human habitation; in fact, we had not seen a soul.

Below the Yale La Pass (5,218 m), we saw our first bharal and Himalayan marmots. It had also become bitterly cold, well below freezing point at night. The bharal here are slightly smaller than those of the Ladakh Changthang. The black throat patch on the adult ram is more prominent amongst the Bhutan animals and it appears at an earlier age as well.

My standby transport had changed from a mule to a yak and there was no 'royal' saddle for the yak. It was a huge, piebald, hornless animal. Perhaps, because it was hornless it was believed to be safer. There is no transport in the world to compare with the yak. It moves at its own pace and there is nothing that the rider can do about it, since the reins are in the hands of the handler, who literally pulls the animal by the nose and goads it by verbally abusing it constantly. If the rider tries to hurry up the animal by whacking it with a stick, as I have tried a number of times at my expense, the behemoth can suddenly spring to life with great alacrity and the surprised rider may get thrown. My hornless yak proved to be more obdurate than most. If prodded beyond a limit, it had the habit of simply sinking down to earth on all fours. I chose to walk most of the time. When utterly tired, I would lie down lengthwise on my chest on the broad back of the plodding yak to regain my breath and strength.

After a three-day trek we reached Lingzhi Dzong and the headwaters of the Sankosh river. More musk deer and bharal; the spectacular waterfall of Tanda and a valley of flowers below Gofu La. A shepherd told us of a bharal kill by a snow leopard three days previously, the feline remaining in full view for an hour. Another spoke of a white bear he had seen the previous year. Could this be the legendary Tibetan 'blue' bear?

Two days' march northwards brought us to the top of Yari La. We flopped down, dead tired. Behind us to the west stood Chomolhari, at 7,314 m the second-highest peak in Bhutan. In front, towered the peaks of Masang Gang (7,194 m) and Gangchhen Ta (6,794 m). On my left, a herd of forty bharal sat, chewing their cud. But of the utmost interest was the valley deep below us – the fabled Seijathang. Running north to south and hedged on all sides by steep slopes and towering peaks, some 800 m below us lay one of the most secluded, tranquil and pristine valleys I have ever seen. The valley floor was surprisingly broad and level, covered with greensward interspersed with rhododendron thickets, through the middle of which gurgled a fast-flowing stream. In the open patches, I could make out some sixty or seventy dark, ponderous animals with yellow saddles on their backs, milling around. 'Yaks,' I said in disgust. 'Dong khimse,' (literally, trident-horned, the Bhutanese name for takin) replied my guide Ton Thaka triumphantly. A peep through the binoculars revealed that the yellow patches on the backs were 'saddles' spreading on the massive withers of mature takin bulls. The females and immature males had smaller, or vestiges of, 'saddle' colouration on their backs, which grow with age in males, as in the case of the Nilgiri tahr.

The animals were grazing as well as licking exposed wet clay containing minerals, which makes Seijathang such an attraction for the takin. Some were sitting or even lying on the floor while others were sparring and chasing each other with their ungainly, lurching run. This was obviously their haven that provided all that the takin needed, including a very salubrious temperature and an absence of flies and insects.

I spent two absorbing days amongst the takin. We nearly got run over by two bulls when they charged down at us in a tunnel through the rhododendrons, confused and disturbed by our scent. It is difficult to describe the takin. The face in profile resembles that of the African wildebeest; the body of a large bull like that of the American bison.

In the autumn of 1974, Kalpana and I, accompanied by our Austrian friends Hellmuth and Francisca Reichel, visited Bhutan, again as the guests of HRH Namgyal Wangchuck, who had now become a minister in the government. His nephew Jigme Singye Wangchuck had succeeded his father and had been crowned as king.

This time we drove to Paro and Punakha and then trekked in the Black Mountain Range of Wangdue Phodrang province. There were fewer pheasants, barking deer and musk deer encountered on this trip than on the previous one. Above the treeline, the bharal were still plentiful, but not as confiding as of yore. Man had begun to impact wildlife and nature.

I went again to Bhutan in 1980, to Gaylephug, Bhutan Manas and elsewhere, but not to north Bhutan. Jigme Dorji National Park had been extended, becoming the largest contiguous protected area in the Himalaya. The estimated number of tigers in Bhutan has gone up from 151 in 1988 to 237 in 1993, the highest density predictably being in the foothills around the Royal Manas National Park.[1]

In February 2016, in the company of Karthikeya Ghorpade and others, I made an extensive tour of Bhutan. It was a revelation. There were multi-storey buildings in Paro and Thimpu; paved roads where we had walked and ridden horseback. Hardly any wildlife could be seen from the highways. From Paro we went into the Ha Valley to photograph the satyr tragopan pheasant without success, but did

---

[1] Dasho Paljor J. Dorji, '*Panthera tigris* in Bhutan', paper presented at the New Delhi meeting of the Global Tiger Forum, 1994.

get pictures of the monal pheasant on the premises of Gompas (monasteries) near Paro and Bumthang in eastern Bhutan.

On the river below the imposing Punakha Dzong, I saw and photographed for the first time in my life a resplendent wild mandarin drake, a vagrant in the company of ruddy Sheldrake ducks. Also in the Punakha Valley I was able to photograph the black kalij alive; in 1964 I had to shoot one to identify it, as mentioned earlier. In the Phobjikha Valley we saw the magnificent spectacle of black-necked crane congregations on their winter grounds, white with frost and snow in the early mornings.

My main interest, however, was the Jigme Dorji National Park, now 4316 sq. km in extent and straddling most of north-eastern Bhutan, and within it, the annual range of the Bhutan takin, the emblem of the nation. During the winter months the takin migrate south from their summer abode in the Seijathang Valley where I had seen them in 1964, down the Mo Chu river about halfway between Gasa and Punakha Dzongs. The park is a composite ecological entity, encompassing both the winter and summer abodes of the takin and the routes travelled to reach both. It also holds snow leopard, leopard, clouded leopard and the tiger, as well as the golden cat, leopard cat, marbled cat, Pallas's cat, bharal and musk deer.

We camped downstream of the park headquarters at Domji and I was able to photograph, albeit in bad light, and watch for hours groups of takin feeding, resting and jousting. On the precincts of the Cheri Gompa upstream of Thimpu where I had walked and camped in 1964, we drove up and photographed the brown goral, incredibly tame.

With modernization and the influx of outsiders, Bhutan has lost its wildlife once in evidence everywhere. However, a major part of the country remains a wilderness and barring the musk deer other mammals are not under threat of extinction. The gompas will remain safe havens for all animate wildlife, and Budhism and the Bhutanese culture will ensure that nature will not be routed in the country.

6

Madhya Pradesh

In December 1943, when I was five, my parents took me to Mandla, where my maternal uncle Maharaj Nagendra Singh of the Indian Civil Service (ICS), was the collector. His house stood right on the Narmada river and I would spend hours on the open verandah, watching the boats and the birds. I found the place and the aura of my uncle's position as collector very impressive. The collector and superintendent of police were then entitled to hunt even in the Banjar Reserve – later to become the Kanha National Park – of which I had heard so much about and had been promised a visit to. At that age, I announced that I would join the ICS and become the collector of Mandla.

On New Year's Day 1944, my family went to Kanha and left me sleeping in the house. I remember howling for the best part of the day, on that favourite verandah, vowing that when I was collector of Mandla I would have my revenge by not taking my parents to Kanha. Twenty-four years later I was to live in that same house, my parents would come to stay with us and we would go to Kanha.

In 1945, we visited Pachmarhi atop the Mahadeo Hills in Hoshangabad district, where Uncle Nagendra Singh again was the collector. We stayed in Narsinghgarh House, belonging to my mother's aunt, the Maharani of Narsinghgarh. The Mahadeo Hills are clothed in sal forests, the only 'island' of sal surrounded by teak forests in the world. The hills have sal forest fauna including the red junglefowl and painted spurfowl and, in the past, even the barasingha at the base of the hills. They also boast the highest peak in Madhya Pradesh, Dhupgarh.

Narsinghgarh House was way outside Pachmarhi town and surrounded by forests. Leopards came into the premises and a woman had been taken by a tiger, on the road between the house and Pachmarhi town, some weeks before our arrival. Each dark night I would gaze out of my bedroom window in wonderment at the sal trees festooned with twinkling fireflies. It was the forests and the fireflies that reconfirmed my resolve – to one day live in Madhya Pradesh.

I passed my Master of Arts examination from St Stephen's College, Delhi, in 1959 and decided to see and photograph all I could of the wilds of India, before being bound by the shackles of service. I photographed black bear in the Hamta Nala, and musk deer in the Solang Nala of the Kullu Valley; a tiger that used to pull down gaur bulls, the largest I have ever seen, in Sarhi, Madhya Pradesh; leopards in the Barda and Girnar Hills of Saurashtra; lions in the Gir; chinkara, great Indian bustard and wolf in Kutch; blackbuck and imperial sandgrouse in Gajner, Bikaner; hangul, black bear, serow and goral in Kashmir; wild buffalo in Manas; barasingha, rhinoceros and elephants in Kaziranga; gaur, sloth bear and more elephants in Bandipur, Karnataka and in Sathyamangalam, Tamil Nadu. Above the Bison Shola in the Nilgiris, overlooking the Silent Valley, I saw a male black leopard stalk a herd of Nilgiri tahr, shimmering black in the golden evening sun. I also saw there what I think was the critically endangered Malabar civet.

In 1961, I got selected for the Indian Administrative Service. I had opted for Madhya Pradesh, which then had a third of India's forests – and did not have my relatives in each district, which was the case with Gujarat and Rajasthan – and was allotted the state of my choice. In June, I went to the National Academy of Administration in Mussoorie for a year's training, interspersed with visits to Kashmir, my first visits to Periyar and Corbett National

Park, and surreptitious interludes evading lectures in the Academy to see goral on Benog Hill, west of Mussoorie, involving two hours of cycling and hiking each way.

In 1962, I was posted as assistant collector under training in Sagar, Madhya Pradesh, which I had earlier visited in 1956 when another maternal uncle, Maharaj Virbhadra Singhji, was a collector there. As a part of my training, I had to try criminal cases before I could be bestowed with first-class magisterial powers. Prohibition was then prevalent in Sagar. I had been given cases wherein the accused – mostly tribals – had been found drinking liquor, home-brewed from the local mahua flowers. The minimum punishment was one month in jail and the accused often confessed. However, the police never seemed to catch persons who illegally distilled liquor from molasses and sold it surreptitiously.

Sagar was a garrison town, being the headquarters of the Mahar Regiment, and we were often invited to parties where liquor flowed freely, the prohibition imposed by the state government not being applicable to army cantonment areas. I was then a teetotaller and would sip orange squash, but the district collector, my boss, enjoyed his whiskey. To make my guilt worse, the collector declared one room of our club as part of the cantonment, which promptly became a bar. Drinking in that room for all club members was 'legal'; stepping outside with your drink was not! We bureaucrats do know how to 'work the system' without actually breaking the law.

While there are no tigers in Sagar district today, it then held a very substantial population of tiger as well as other wildlife. The collector's secretariat maintained records of humans and livestock killed by wild creatures. The figures for the year 1962 were 318 livestock killed by tiger, 93 by leopard, 122 by snakes and 57 by 'other' animals, a grand total of 590.

Some 20 km south of the town Khurai in Sagar district, a leopardess had turned maneater. There were no forests here, but the scrub vegetation along the Bina river and the sugar cane fields provided cover. She had killed about nine people over a period of six months, mostly women and children. I was ordered by the collector to go and destroy the maneater. Accompanied by my old collegemate and batchmate Pratap Singh of Kunadi, later to become the director general of police in Madhya Pradesh, I went to Guwari village, where the latest human kill had occurred. A young schoolboy, eager to find out how he had fared in his examination, had gone after dark to find out his marks from his teacher, disobeying his parents who were worried for his safety. He never came back.

We were in luck. A young buffalo calf had been killed and partly eaten by the leopardess the night before. I put up a machan on a banyan tree 100 m from the village, there being no other tree with denser foliage in the vicinity of the kill. I was spied by the leopardess, either when going up to the machan or while sitting in it, for half an hour after it became dark I heard scratching on the bark of the banyan, as if an animal was climbing up towards me. I turned around in the machan to face it, whereupon the leopardess slithered back and jumped down. Two hours later, she returned to her kill and started feeding. When the spotlight was put on her, she got up to run. The bullet caught her a little behind the shoulder and she ran off in the dark. We followed with lanterns and torches and found her dead, which was the cause of great jubilation. It was foolhardy to follow the animal in darkness, but the frothy, pinkish blood indicated a fatal lung wound and the villagers were very impatient. If she had been alive, someone would surely have been mauled. We found that the leopardess had a gnarled forefoot with three nails that could not be sheathed, most likely an old injury caused by a foot trap. This was perhaps what caused her to become a maneater and why she could not climb silently and fast when she came after me in the machan.

Shikar was still in vogue. A collector or an assistant collector could shoot in any hunting 'block' that was not allotted to another hunter, and pay a royalty of ₹50 for a tiger and ₹25 for every leopard he killed.

There occurred in Sagar an incident which in some ways proved to be a turning point in my life. Word must have gone around that I had shot a maneater. I was asked to come and dispose of a large, querulous sloth bear which had developed a not uncommon penchant for slashing and mauling human faces, in the forests of Gaurjhamar. I stayed overnight in the forest rest house there and asked the villagers to drive out the animal towards me the next morning. As soon as the din of the drive began, one of the most magnificent male tigers I have seen trotted out into the nala I was covering. I saw him some 70 m away, heading towards me, his huge head swaying slightly with locomotion and getting larger. I slowly raised my .465 Holland & Holland double-barrel rifle, put the foresight bead on his head, and let him come. He never saw me sitting behind a rock. Some forty paces from me he turned slightly sideways, revealing the length and dimension of his superb body. I quickly shifted the foresight of my rifle to the junction of his huge neck and body and waited for him to come a few paces nearer. Early morning sunlight slanting from the side lit up his deep ochre-orange winter coat, his muscles rippling under the dazzling skin. He was almost level with me and now moving directly in front, less than thirty paces away. The bead of the rifle had now shifted to his shoulders and kept following him, leading a few inches in front to allow for the travel time of the bullet. He was dead meat, as the saying goes. But a curious thing was happening. My eye would not focus on that rifle foresight, but upon the magnificence of that tiger's coat. Repeatedly I tried to bring the eye back to focus on the foresight but involuntarily it would go back and focus on that tiger, and I just could not press that trigger.

Two conflicting thoughts were racing my mind. If I did not shoot the tiger, the word would unfailingly go around that I was too petrified to fire, sitting as I was on the ground. The other was the unwelcome thought of a crumpled mass of dying flesh in contrast with this vision of a gorgeous, living, feline grace. The rifle foresight followed the tiger all the way till it disappeared. I have never regretted the decision.

I would like to report that my hunting ended there, but this would be an untruth. However, this was the start of a period of extra restraint, of introspection, reticence and doubt, of 'softness'. To quote Winston Churchill after Dunkirk, it was the end of the beginning.

A few weeks later, I was driving to the Noradehi rest house, through some of the best wildlife habitats in the district. The eyes of my jeep shone on six pairs of eyes, of wild dogs, surrounding a beautiful white cow standing over a dead white calf. When the wild dogs would close in to feed on their kill, the cow would charge, whereupon some of the pack would rush in from the other side to grab mouthfuls. The wildlife enthusiast within me demanded that I leave the matter to nature and the predators to their prey, with no interference. But I was young and the pathos aroused by that brave cow was overpowering. The dogs were scared away and I went closer to investigate, but was chased right back into the jeep by that tormented cow. But there was not a scratch on her, when she could easily have been disembowelled and killed by the wild dogs that were being prevented from eating their kill (Ranjitsinh 1997). So much for the reputation of 'ruthless, fiendish killers' ascribed to wild dogs. Noradehi has since become a wildlife sanctuary, one of the largest in peninsular India, but the forests have been thinned out and there are no tigers and not much other wildlife surviving.

In Sagar, a male blackbuck fawn was brought to me. I named it Lindy, after the great fast bowler Lindwall, whom I had watched almost win for Australia that epic cricket test match at Lords, in 1953. Lindy was part of my household for over eight years, undertaking five transfers with some of my other pets – chital, chausingha and barking deer. From boyhood, I have always been inspired by the blackbuck, the black prince of the plains. Lindy provided me with so much affection and insight into blackbuck behaviour that I subsequently chose the species as the subject of my PhD thesis.

In the summer of 1964, I was transferred to Burhanpur, then a subdivision of Khandwa district, on the border with Maharashtra's Melghat. Burhanpur town had a population of almost 45 per cent Muslims and was a site of frequent communal tension, especially during Muharram and Holi, when Hindu revellers would wantonly sprinkle the unwilling Muslims with colour. It had been an important town during the medieval period, being on the route from Delhi to Daulatabad and south India. It had its own underground water supply from a spring almost 10 km away, through waterways installed during the Mughal era. Across the River Tapti was Ahukhana, literally meaning the abode of the blackbuck, a large complex enclosed by high walls. It was here that Mumtaz Begum, the favourite wife of Emperor Shah Jahan, was interned for her sixteenth childbirth, and where she whiled away her time hunting blackbuck, a pastime she was very fond of. When she died in childbirth, she was buried here, later to be removed and reburied in the Taj Mahal at Agra.

Burhanpur was a traditional training subdivision for IAS officers, before their promotion to the rank of district collector. The importance of maintaining law and order there caused the subdivisional officer and assistant collector to be given the rank of an additional district magistrate. Today it is a district on it own.

The impressive fortress of Asirgarh was in the Burhanpur subdivision, an important post to guard the north–south route in medieval times. Subsequently occupied by garrisons of the East India Company after the collapse of the Maratha Empire, the cemetery in the fort has a tomb of an English subaltern who was killed by a wild buffalo in about 1830. So, wild buffalo dwelt here in the early part of the nineteenth century. There was still plenty of wildlife in Burhanpur, and during my year's stay I would have seen no less than a score of leopards, half a dozen tigers, gaur, sambar and the rest. The open forest grassland terrain is particularly suited to that unique animal, the chawsingha or four-horned antelope. I also saw my first caracal, in the forest of Nawtha on the south bank of the River Tapti. This most elusive, elegant and lissom cat is now facing extinction in India.

My duties kept me constantly busy and I learned a great deal in

Burhanpur, especially with regard to maintenance of civic supplies, of law and order and human resource management. An incident where wildlife helped me in addressing an awkward law and order situation may be worth recounting.

Cattle slaughter was prohibited in Burhanpur, keeping in view the prospect of communal tension. Muslims, however, did surreptitiously smuggle calves into their houses and slaughter them, from time to time. One morning as I sat in court, I received a phone call from the local circle inspector of police. Right opposite the main Ram Mandir of the city, close to the main mosque, in a locality inhabited mainly by Muslims, the bones of a hind leg of a calf had been found that morning, in an open sewer. The Jana Sangh party, the progenitor of the present Bharatiya Janata Party (BJP), was very powerful in Burhanpur. A mob had gathered around the spot, the remains of the calf had been collected and a procession was marching with them to my office, led by the fiery lawyer Parmanand Govindjiwale, who practised in my court and later became a member of the Lok Sabha.

The procession arrived and the vanguard entered the crowded office. Govindjiwale, after his oratorical condemnation of cow slaughter, removed the cloth covering a large tray, to reveal the tibia–fibula bones, with the femur attached, of a hind leg, shorn of all meat and bearing the gnaw marks of a pi-dog. The lowest portion of the skin just above the hoof had not been removed and was still visible. It was piebald and not the usual plain white, brown or black. Human mind often works very fast under such circumstances and a sudden thought came to me. This is not the leg of a calf, I declared, but the leg of a nilgai. Then followed a small discourse about the colouration of a nilgai leg; that nilgai were not part of the cow family but of the antelope, but because of their resemblance with cows were called nilgai; that they are destroyers of agriculture and though not eaten by Hindus because of the name nilgai, they could be and were hunted on a licence and legitimately killed and eaten by Muslims and Harijans, etc. All this to buy time and defuse the tension. Govindjiwale and his companions knew I was a wildlife enthusiast and I think they also trusted me as an individual. Their oratory and effervescence subsided slightly. But Govindjiwale was a lawyer and asked the obvious question – how did the bones of a nilgai come into the middle of the town? Shaukat Ali had obtained a hunting licence and must have shot and eaten a nilgai and thrown away the bones, which must have been dragged around by the pi-dogs, I replied. Shaukat was the owner of the main petrol pump in town, and was fond of shikar. Also, he lived not too far from the spot where the bones had been found. But Govindjiwale was not giving up. Could he verify the facts from Shaukat Ali, he asked, looking straight into my eyes. Of course, I had to concede.

When the delegation had left the court, I hurried into my chamber at the back of it and called Shaukat Ali. I told him he had to lie to the demonstrators and say he had shot a nilgai and eaten it, disposing off the remains. Shaukat was most reluctant. They will kill me for killing a nilgai, he pleaded, and what happens if they find out later that he had not shot a nilgai? Before they finish you, I will seal your petrol pump and finish you, I threatened. To save lives one has to sometimes lie, I hissed, and asked whether he wanted human blood to add to the cow bones in the gutters of Burhanpur. Poor Shaukat complied: he apparently told the lie with a straight face, and the crowd dispersed.

There also occurred in Burhanpur a landmark event of another kind. I was camping in a tent in Jambupani near the Melghat Tiger Reserve, close to the present Amba Barwa Sanctuary of Maharashtra. As I sat with the villagers clustered around, disposing cases under the revenue law, news came that a tiger had killed a buffalo at a waterhole in the forest. Partly to please the villagers whose cattle the tiger had been killing and partly to test myself after having let go the tiger the previous year, I decided to sit up over the kill. I was not carrying my .465 Holland rifle. The tiger came after dusk and sat close by in cover. Some sambar hinds turned up to drink, smelt him, gave their shrill alarm calls and bolted, the tiger making a perfunctory rush at them. He came to eat the buffalo kill at midnight. He was almost directly below the machan and the bullet struck low, nicking a foreleg without breaking it. He rushed off, fell, got up and struggled out of that nala, giving the most appalling roars from pain. Then complete silence.

Next morning we followed first the blood spoor and then the pugmarks, which led into another nala across a ridge. I sent my trusted tracker Kana up a tree to peer into the nala. His shadow fell on a dense thicket below from which came a curious, ominous, rumbling sound, which rapidly increased in reverberating crescendo. I felt for a moment an overpowering desire to run, but that would be suicide. The tiger was lying 20 m from me, the distance of a cricket pitch. There was a deafening roar, followed by violent shaking of foliage. He broke complete cover about 14 m away, coming low along the ground, slightly uphill, with the early morning sun slanting straight into his eyes. I could only see the high-held tail, the forepaws, and the head becoming rapidly larger, ruff erect, mouth slightly open and emitting short, loud, rasping roars, eyes steel-grey in offensive aggression. I shall never forget those eyes (Ranjitsinh 1997).

Surprisingly, I felt no fear, just a curiosity about where he would maul me, knowing the untrustworthiness of my ammunition. I let him come a little nearer to be sure, since there was to be only one shot. The .375 Magnum bullet crashed into his skull above his left eye, destroying his skull and brain before lodging in his spine beyond. He collapsed in a heap 5 m from my feet and while the head remained inert and pinned under his body, I watched in amazement the hindquarters rise twice to come on. Relief, a little remorse, but most prominent of all a question in my mind: Was this really necessary?

There is an aspect of destiny and fatalism connected with this episode. I was on duty and not on a hunt, and was carrying my father's .375 Holland & Holland. The ammunition was old and on an average every third cartridge hang-fired. I had loaded the two best-looking cartridges while following the wounded tiger and had prayed that they would not hang-fire. They did not and I lived. The very next time I fired that rifle, the cartridge did hang-fire.

A week later, I went to Mumbai at the behest of my parents, saw my future bride Kalpana, and agreed to marry her. I still tease her that had that .375 Magnum cartridge hang-fired, she would have been married to someone else.

In the summer of 1965, on my return from leave spent in Bhutan, I was transferred to Bhopal and appointed undersecretary at the home department, in the state government of Madhya Pradesh. I now had the opportunity to work under three of my mentors: Eric Reinboth, R.N. Chopra and Suresh Mathur. I also came in contact with that unique personality, R.P. Noronha, the most 'non-sahib' ICS officer that, perhaps, ever was. He was the chief secretary of Madhya Pradesh, an ardent fisherman and a big-game hunter, who somehow took a liking for me that lasted till his untimely demise.

The 1965 war with Pakistan broke out and I was in charge of the X Section, dealing with 'coded' and confidential information. Having to work eight-hour shifts, two shifts a day, listening to reports of imaginary infiltration from gullible district collectors, sifting out the genuine ones, and reporting them each morning to Noronha and hearing his expletives, was an experience in itself.

Later that year, I got my first district, Dhar, near Indore. It was in Dhar that I got married the following year. This was also the first of three consecutive years of failure of the monsoon. As many as 130,000 people would come to work on specially started scarcity projects at ₹1.50 per day, or less if they could not complete the required quantum of daily work. Interstate and inter-district movement of foodgrain was banned and smuggling and corruption ensued. Rice had not been distributed in Dhar for some six months. So when my old friend and colleague, the late Mahesh Buch, the collector of Ujjain, asked me what I would like as a marriage present, I said two trucks of rice for my district. It was the best marriage present I received. Aid flowed in from various donors. There were stocks of milk powder, which I was only supposed to distribute to pregnant mothers. The milk powder started accumulating and even turning yellow. So I certified that there were 130,000 pregnant women and all the workers got free milk.

The fort of Mandu, with peripheral walls and battlements of over 70 km, the longest of any fort in the world, was in Dhar. Emperor Jahangir loved Mandu and it was here that Sir Thomas Roe, the emissary of the British Crown and of the East India Company, had met Jahangir and had also encountered lions. Lions, of course, and even tigers had vanished by the time I arrived at Dhar. But leopards were not uncommon.

The elegant lesser florican, the breeding male sporting a most striking black-and-white plumage with a lyre-shaped crest of neck feathers, would arrive on the grasslands of Dhar to breed in the monsoon. Later as the forest secretary of the state, I was able to declare one such breeding ground as a sanctuary near Sardarpur, in Dhar district.

There were large crocodiles in the River Narmada, which formed the southern boundary of the district. Boating along it one day, I asked the helmsman to peep into what was obviously a large den of a crocodile, of course, after ascertaining that it was not in occupation. The footprints of a crocodile were visible below the cave mouth. 'Tiger,' shouted the man, but there were no tigers anywhere in the area. What we found was most interesting – the striped legs of hyena puppies that had apparently occupied the cave when it was raided by a crocodile and the pups eaten, leaving a couple of pathetic bitten-off legs.

Dhar and its neighbouring districts are the lands of the Bhil tribe, amongst the most aggressive of all tribals and no friends of the forests and of wildlife. They had killed most of the wildlife and cut all the forests of the Nimar region. The highest number of murders and dacoities recorded in any single police station in India was in Alirajpur in Jhabua district, adjoining Dhar. Every year around Holi, the Bhils would congregate for the Bhagoria festival, where boys and girls could choose their partners and run away to get married. But it was also a time for them to consume extra amounts of mahua liquor and to release their pent-up aggression by shooting their arrows. A husband-wife team of doctors in Nisarpur town in Dhar district told me that in the 1965 Bhagoria they had to operate practically non-stop to remove arrows and stitch up eighteen people.

In 1966, just after our marriage, Kalpana and I pitched a tent in Dahi and participated in the biggest Bhagoria in the district. Targets were put up and prizes for archery announced. No one got hurt that year, though there were a couple of near misses when arrows from tipsy archers sailed way off target.

A couple of incidents occurred in Dhar that remain indelibly marked in my memory. Soon after my appointment as collector, word came in that a minor girl was being married off to a sixty-year-old widower. I quickly sent my most seasoned and trustworthy deputy collector to the spot to inquire about the girl's age, to stop the marriage if she was a minor and to talk to the girl and ascertain what she wanted, if she was not a minor. An hour later my man came back. The girl was not a minor; he had taken her aside and asked in private whether she wanted to marry the bridegroom or not. The answer was simple: 'My father has chosen a husband for me. It therefore must be the right choice.' The marriage had not proceeded and would be held back till I decided. I sent the deputy collector back to speak once more with the girl, in private. It was her life that was at stake and she must not be ambiguous. Her reply was exactly the same as before and we withdrew, for legally we had no right to intervene as the girl was not a minor.

The second incident happened in Dharampuri, on the banks of the Narmada. Just before the general elections of 1967, message came that two Muslim boys had raped a Hindu girl; a most potent prescription for a communal riot. Dharampuri was the birthplace of Rani Rupmati, the consort of Baz Bahadur, Sultan of Malwa. Both of them had perished when Akbar captured Mandu.

Along with M.K. Tiwari, the superintendent of police, I rushed to Dharampuri. The sub-inspector there, a very competent officer, said he could not proceed with the case as the girl was not prepared to file a complaint. The culprits had escaped across the border into Maharashtra, but his men were watching them.

We called the girl in and spoke to her alone. She was incensed but composed. She told us that she wanted to file a complaint, to have the offenders punished, but her father was not allowing her to do so. So we called the father in and spoke with him in private. He was worried as to who would marry his daughter if the news spread that she had been raped. His apprehension was genuine in the Indian scenario.

Just then the mayor of Dharampuri, a member of the Jana Sangh, came to meet us to say that if the father of the girl was worried about her future and if he could not find a suitor for her in their own community because of this occurrence, his son would marry the girl. The complaint must be filed, the rapists apprehended and punished, he stated. I said that I would like to ascertain the wishes of the boy himself, in person and in private. So the mayor brought his son. The boy was quite forthright. He would marry the girl not out of pity but because he felt that it was a right thing to do and that he was under no duress from his father or anyone else. What if you have second thoughts and back out after the complaint has been filed and the rape becomes public knowledge, I asked. He was prepared to take any sacred oath that I may want him to, he replied. This was the best option available, for whatever it was worth. So I asked him to go down to the Narmada with the police sub-inspector and take a vow with the water of the sacred river in hand that he would marry the girl, if she too was agreeable to this. That accomplished, the girl was sent for again. Would she be ready to marry the mayor's son, whom she knew, if no other marriage of her choice could be arranged? She coyly looked down, but would give no answer. When pressed again, she whispered a yes.

We asked the mayor and the girl's father to join us and made clear that whichever boy the parents of the girl selected to marry her, as is the tradition in India, he must be told of the rape. Only if he was prepared to marry the girl and the marriage was also acceptable to the girl, would it take place. If such a marriage could not be arranged, the mayor's son must fulfil his promise. All parties agreed. The father of the girl asked that I should perform the kanyadan, the giving-away of the bride ceremony, at her marriage and I agreed to attend it, wherever I might then be posted. The police sub-inspector left with his arrest party while the girl was dictating her first information report (FIR) at the police station. That night the culprits were arrested and brought in next morning. They were later sentenced, but by then I had left Dhar. However, the girl got married whilst I was still in Dhar, to a boy of her choice who knew what she had suffered. Her father and I jointly gave away the bride.

The state election of 1967 led to the defeat of the Congress. A conglomeration cobbled together under the leadership of Rajmata Vijayraje Scindia of Gwalior formed the government. I had been in Dhar for almost two years and, for the first time in my career, asked for a specific posting – Mandla.

Mandla district then included Dindori as well. It was a large district, mostly forested, encompassing both teak and sal forest biomes and an ecologically rich transitional zone in between. It was populated primarily by Gond, Baiga and Panka tribes. Its eastern boundary lay along the Maikal Range and one could then travel from Motinala to Amarkantak along this range for over 100 km without really leaving the forest. In between lay Baiga-Chak, a group of seven villages where the British administration had allowed the Baigas to practise regulated shifting cultivation, which should have been the model for Nagaland and other north-eastern states. Here, the Baigas cultivated the Baigani arhar dal, unequalled in taste and a great attraction for sloth bear, which lived here in numbers and were in constant conflict with the Baigas.

The Maikal Range ends with the Amarkantak massif, some 1,000 m above sea level and the single source of three large rivers of South

Asia – Narmada, Son and Mahanadi. Verrier Elwin, the colourful British missionary-turned-anthropologist who worked here during World War II, had found here, for the first time, people who had not heard of Mahatma Gandhi. In 1968, I descended into the deep forested gorge below Kapil Dhara, where the infant Narmada cascades to the plains, to investigate a rumour about the existence of a white tiger. This was once a part of the former princely state of Rewa and tribals in the valley still believed that they were the subjects of Maharaja Gulab Singh. They had not heard of Gandhi, Nehru and India's Independence. A little distance downstream in level forest, Maharaja Sadul Singhji of Bikaner, the brother-in-law of Gulab Singhji, had shot three cheetah in 1925.

Kalpana and I spent three of the happiest years of our life in Mandla, in that ramshackle old house perched atop the Narmada and where our first child Meenal, came to live with us after her birth in Mumbai.

Famine was still on, and thousands continued to work at the daily wage of ₹1.50 or less, including some tribals who were owners of over 50 hectares of land.

On the eastern boundary with Balaghat district, nestling below the Maikal Range, lies Kanha National Park, extending over 252 sq. km. Writing of Kanha a hundred years ago, Dunbar Brander, a doyen amongst the Indian hunter-naturalists of the last century, wrote: 'The tract contained as much game as any tract I ever saw in the best parts of Africa in 1908. I have seen 1,500 head consisting of 11 species in an evening's stroll' (Dunbar Brander 1923). In the middle of the reserve is the excavated lake Shravan Tal, where King Dasharath, the father of Lord Ram, is supposed to have killed Shravan by accident. Further to the east, on a hilltop above Kope Dabri, is Shravan Chita, where Dasharath is believed to have cremated Shravan and was cursed by his blind parents, from which originates the epic Ramayana. It was on the road leading from Shravan Tal to Nila Nala that I had seen my first tiger in Kanha in 1963, a large male named Behra, whom I filmed eating *Themeda triandra*, or red oat grass. Later that year on my next visit to Kanha from Sagar, I met George Schaller, perhaps the most eminent wildlife field biologist of the twentieth century.

Grasslands are the most productive ecotypes for wildlife the world over. If interspersed with patches of woodlands forming forest–grassland mosaics, the diversity of ungulate fauna increases appreciably. Sal forests on damp, level valley floors have patches of open high grasslands, a haven for the hog deer and the swamp deer or barasingha. But it is these rich, alluvial open 'maidans' that man occupies. By the time I had come to Madhya Pradesh, there were no maidans in any sal forests of the region that were not occupied or grazed upon, except those in the Kanha National Park. It was only here that the last remnants of the central Indian barasingha had survived. In 1965, Schaller had estimated their population at fifty-five. In 1968, I counted sixty-six, and seventy-two in the following year, all confined to the Kanha meadows, from Kanha village to Shravan Tal. The fawn numbers were also low. It was obvious that the species faced imminent extinction.

Baiting to attract tigers for visitors to see was still practised at Chuhri Hide and at Schaller Hide, where George used to bait tigers to observe them for his study. This baiting occurred in nala beds which held grass and water and were the most favoured spots for the barasingha, a preferred prey of the tiger. In 1967, sixteen barasingha were reported killed by tiger. Next year in a state wildlife board meeting in Kanha, the eminent wildlife photojournalist M. Krishnan suggested that we get specimens of the nominate race of the barasingha from the Terai and infuse new blood into the Kanha population. I opposed this move, on the grounds that the two populations were of separate subspecies and that we should do our utmost to save the central Indian subspecies, and went to the extent of saying that if it be really necessary, we may even have to remove tigers from the Kanha meadows, which was then the only habitat of the central Indian barasingha. Luckily, this was not necessary. The divisional forest officer in charge of Kanha, Deep Singh, agreed to stop baiting for tiger in the Kanha meadows and the number of barasingha killed by tiger dropped to just one in 1968.

However, by now it was clear that the barasingha, and indeed all the wild animals of Kanha, needed more space (Ranjitsinh 1997). Anthrax had reached Kanha, with three gaur and two chital succumbing to the disease. It was imperative to relocate the villages that occupied crucial niches in the middle of the park. The most important among these was Sonph. Its eighty-eight families cultivated 890 hectares of prime grassland, but its 900 head of cattle had an adverse impact on the same 120 sq. km of the park and were periodically killed by tiger. There being no funds available for the purpose with the forest department of the state, I approached my old friend Mahesh Buch, secretary of the Tribal Welfare Department of MP, and was granted ₹24,000 for the relocation of Sonph. The villagers were asked to choose from the plots of land available outside of the national park. Since Sonph was a forest village, each family had been allotted 10 acres of land, the headman having 20. Each family was then allotted twice the area of land it had in Kanha, in an area acceptable to the villagers. As I was the collector of the district, I could deploy a number of welfare schemes that were under my charge in the district, to the relocation site. The land was levelled with tractor free of charge; bullocks for ploughing and improved seed for sowing were also provided free of cost. Wells were dug for drinking water, and a school was built. Since tribals prefer to build their own houses, they were provided free bamboo and poles, and free transport in trucks to carry all their personal goods, including material from their existing huts, which also ensured that these huts were dismantled. Plots for residence at the new site were on a first-come, first-served basis. Within a month Sonph had been relocated. A week later, a tiger killed a buffalo, which had been too old to be shifted, on the precincts of the abandoned Sonph, and the barasingha moved into the abandoned fields and dropped their fawns there that monsoon, as the rain had transformed the fields into high grasslands. Since then, the Sonph maidans have been a stronghold of the barasingha. This was the first village to have been relocated out of any protected area after Independence and proved that relocation was possible, if enough incentive was given to the people and was beneficial for all.

Raunda village, a little to the north, was next to be relocated, and this vacated maidan too was quickly occupied by the barasingha. Thereafter, over twenty villages were relocated out of the extended Kanha National Park. The regeneration of suitable grasslands subsequent to the translocation of the villages had a dramatic effect upon the recovery of the barasingha. By 1985, their numbers crossed 500, though they have subsequently declined to less than 400. In 2016, there were almost 800 barasingha in Kanha, even after twenty of them were transported to the Satpura National Park in 2015.

But back in 1968, the survival of the barasingha was very much in doubt and I felt that its long-term survival could only be ensured by breeding them in semi-captive conditions, there being no captive specimens of this subspecies anywhere in the world. I selected a site close to Kanha village but quite hidden from it. It encompassed all the habitat requirements of the deer, both high and medium grasslands, marsh and sal forest canopy, extending over 77 acres. It would be easier to capture the deer here by simply driving them in from an open side, keeping them in the habitat itself without having to transport them to a zoo or safari park, where they would get domesticated and exposed to infection from other zoo inmates. Here in Kanha they would see their own kind, other herbivores and their predators, from within their enclosure. Their release would also be simple, entailing only the opening of a part of the fencing and letting them out.

In 1968, the administrative head of the Bhilai Steel Plant, G. Jagathpathi, later to become the chief secretary of Madhya Pradesh and my superior, came to Kanha. When I told him of my requirement of an enclosure, he promised to send from his factory the wire meshing and the iron poles required, at the price of scrap. But I still needed the money to buy the 'scrap', which the forest department of the state could not provide, there being then no scheme, either with the Government of India or with the state of MP, to assist conservation of a protected area.

In the winter of 1969, Fredrick Stoever, an American businessman, visited Kanha with his wife Renate. He readily agreed to donate $3,000, through the World Wildlife Fund, to build this enclosure. The work was assigned to the ranger, Jumman Khan, whose equal in integrity and loyalty I have not found. The work was completed in 1970, and five barasingha – two stags and three hinds – seven blackbuck and 155 chital were driven in. The chital were subsequently released. By 1981 when I returned to Madhya Pradesh as forest secretary, there were thirty-one barasingha in the enclosure, which I had named Stoever Stockade. From here, they were transported for the first reintroduction into the Supkhar meadows in Balaghat, in the then extended Kanha National Park. Others were let out in Kanha itself. The last survivors of the indigenous blackbuck of Kanha lived their last days in the enclosure. If only they had been released on the Bamni Dadar plateau, Kanha's blackbuck would in all probability have survived. Years later, the state government, at considerable cost and effort, captured blackbuck from the neighbouring district of Seoni and released them in Kanha. But the original stock, that had been isolated in Kanha and separated from other blackbuck for centuries, and had in all probability developed unique characteristics and adaptations suitable for Kanha, was now lost forever.

One morning in 1969, I saw ten tigers before breakfast, the largest number I have seen on a single outing. At about the same time, I saw a barasingha stag with twenty points on his massive antlers, the largest stag I have seen. I named him Maikal, after the Maikal Range, and tape-recorded his rutting call. When it was played back to him, he would immediately answer. His shed antlers are kept in the museum in Kanha.

Also in 1969 occurred a thrilling episode. I was camping at the Chaura Dadar rest house, on the western part of the Maikal Range, not far from Amarkantak, when news came of a cow having been killed by a tiger. I found the kill on a steep forested slope below a small cliff, at the edge of an escarpment. I made a hide and sat below the cliff. After dark, two tiger cubs appeared and started nibbling at the kill. My switching on a torch startled the cubs. They bolted, and one of them stumbled on the steep rocky slope and set up a series of long-drawn and plaintive yowls. I got up from my hide to have a better look and to locate if possible the distressed cub, when from above me came angry, purring growls of a tiger. The sound continued on a constant steady tenor, descending the slope behind me. I crouched back into the hide, turning around to face the sound. The source of the sound moved on to a large rock some 3 m away and a little above me. There was dappled light from a young moon and through the foliage I could make out the hazy form of the tigress, and could smell her distinctly. She remained perched on that rock for a minute or more, indecisive, but growling fiercely and continuously. She could have easily crashed through the flimsy foliage of the hide and collared me. But by now the cub was calling her more intently and loudly. The tigress stopped growling and gave two muted, short, bark-like grunts with a distinct clucking sound, which I have never heard, before or since. The cub stopped its pleading calls and the tigress moved down to it, making the same clucking growls periodically.

In 1969, I was able to persuade the MP state government to extend the Kanha Park from 252 sq. km to 318 sq. km within Mandla district, around Kisli in the west, Bhilwani in the east and beyond Raunda in the north. In June 1969, at about the start of the monsoon, I saw in the Kanheri maidan near Shravan Tal in Kanha a female lesser florican, and at the end of May 1971 I saw another female at the same spot. There was no other record of this bird so far east in India (Ranjitsinh 1984a).

In November 1969, the general assembly of the International Union for the Conservation of Nature (IUCN) was held in Delhi, inaugurated by Prime Minister Indira Gandhi, which I attended as a delegate of Madhya Pradesh. Indira Gandhi made a very pertinent remark in her inaugural speech, which revealed her approach to nature conservation. 'It is a sad commentary on our attitude towards Nature that we still talk of "exploiting" its resources,' she said. It was the most meaningful and effective wildlife conference I have ever attended. Project Tiger and the concern for the Kashmir hangul and other species owe their origin to this conference and it gave direction to Indira Gandhi's inherent interest in nature conservation. At her behest, the export of tiger skins was banned in the same month (Rangarajan 2009). The ban on the hunting of tigers followed a year later.

Delegates to the conference such as Sir Peter Scott, Kai Curry-Lindahl and F. Bourliere visited Kanha. We saw the Chuhri tigress and her two cubs sitting beside a large, disabled python which the tigress had recently mauled.

In 1970, with the help of my colleague the collector of Balaghat, I sent another proposal to the state government to extend the Kanha National Park south across the Maikal Range, into the adjacent Mukki forest of Balaghat district. This was prime tiger habitat and the forest villages like Sondhar, Ghorela and Bishanpura occupied grasslands, which, if vacated like Sonph and Raunda, would make available large habitats for the barasingha. It would extend the size of the park from 318 to 446.6 sq. km and, importantly, it would become the first protected area in the state that would straddle two districts.

Conversion to a national park meant the stoppage of forestry exploitation and of revenue, a proposition not very palatable to some forest officers. The Balaghat divisional forest officer (DFO) in charge of the proposed area reported that these forests held only five tigers – a deliberate underestimation – but also added that the forests themselves yielded an average annual revenue of ₹45 lakh. So, he claimed, to protect each tiger the state exchequer would have to forego ₹9 lakh per annum, 'in perpetuity.' Nobody had asked him to evaluate the annual outlay per tiger, but he gave it nonetheless.

With this nugget, the proposal was forwarded to the state chief conservator of forests at Bhopal, where it lay dormant.

Meanwhile, the government had fallen in Bhopal and Congress came back to power. I received from the State Department for Mines a notice of permission to prospect for copper, in an area between the Banjar river and the boundary of the Kanha Park, near Khatiya village. The licence had been given to a mining company owned by a younger brother of the new chief minister of Madhya Pradesh.

I replied that as the collector I was the officer in charge of mining operations in the district and the authority for granting both mining leases and prospecting licences. How was it that no application had been made to my office and that the state government *suo motu* had granted the permission to prospect, without even consulting me as collector and officer in charge of mining in the district? Besides, I pointed out, the area was adjacent to the Kanha Park and mining activity would be very detrimental to the wildlife.

A month later a rather brusque response came from Bhopal. Collector Mandla's points have been considered but he is directed to issue the prospecting licence. I then obtained from the excellent DFO in charge of Kanha, P.M. Rajwade, a letter to state how important the area, where the proposed prospecting was to be carried out, was and that the chital and other animals of the Kisli-Khatiya area had to pass through this tract to reach the Banjar river, which was the only source of water for the wild animals in the summer. From my side, I added that there was no copper located anywhere in the vicinity and that the nearest copper mine was 60 km away. Besides, I added, a brother of the owner of this mining company – also the youngest brother of the chief minister – owned a prominent shikar company and I stated that it would be very difficult to distinguish between a dynamite blast for prospecting, and a rifle shot.

That was the last I heard of the matter. The prospecting licence was never issued, but I was transferred from Mandla to Bhopal.

I was appointed deputy secretary, finance, reporting to Finance Secretary R.N. Malhotra, who was later to become the governor of the Reserve Bank of India and, undoubtedly, the most competent officer I have served under. The proposal of the Balaghat extension of Kanha was still stuck in the office of the chief conservator of forests of MP. With some effort on my part, it was brought to the State Forest Department and from there forwarded to the Finance Department for approval, but to another colleague in that department.

One day, I took the file from my colleague and carried it to the finance secretary. Malhotra never questioned how I had brought him that file since I was not dealing with forest matters in the Finance Department. But he did ask how he as finance secretary could be expected, for the sake of the estimated five tigers, to forego ₹45 lakh per annum, in perpetuity – which was a lot of money then – when he and I knew the dire straits of the state's finances. My own monthly salary, incidentally, was less than ₹2,000 at the time. I mumbled something about there being more than five tigers, and then blurted out: 'Sir, please approve this for my sake.' He looked up from the file, smiled and signed, and Kanha got its most important extension ever. For me it was a red-letter day and I shall always remain grateful to the memory of R.N. Malhotra.

7

Indira's India

In 1971, having opted for transfer from the state to the Central government, I was posted in Delhi at the Ministry of Food and Agriculture, Government of India. That vast ministry at the time included a tiny section that handled the subject of forests, then a state subject under the Indian Constitution. Within the subject area of forests, under an inspector general of forests (IGF), the minuscule component of wildlife was handled part-time by an Indian Forest Service (IFS) officer of the rank of an assistant inspector general (AIG). There were two deputy inspectors general (DIGs) handling forest matters and a post of a DIG (wildlife) had also been just created, but the incumbent was not found to be suited for the task. There was only one post in that forestry division for an IAS officer, that of deputy secretary, forests, whose job was to deal with administrative matters in the ministry and in the Forest Research Institute (FRI) at Dehradun, which, being run by the Union government, came within the purview of the Ministry of Agriculture. I was keen to occupy that post, but it was already held by another IAS officer and I was assigned as deputy secretary, machinery. IAS officers are meant to be the proverbial jacks of all trades and could be given a bewildering variety of jobs. There was even a fellow in charge of frozen semen (of pedigree bulls, of course!) in the Animal Husbandry Division of the Ministry of Agriculture. The practice provided a very wide spectrum of experience, also an escape route for some, but not for specialization.

India was then not manufacturing enough tractors in the country and, being short of foreign exchange, had imported RS09 tractors from a 'Rouble-zone' Balkan country. They proved to be defective; farmers from Punjab drove them in and left them to jam the streets of Delhi, but the country of origin would not take them back. As deputy secretary, machinery, new to Delhi and to the ministry, it was my job to handle the matter, for about four months.

In September 1971, Prime Minister Indira Gandhi, concerned about the declining wildlife of the country, called a meeting of wildlife personnel for a brainstorming session in her office. She had already banned the hunting of tigers and had a personal interest in conservation. From the government's side there was Karan Singh, Union minister for tourism and also the chairman of the Indian Board for Wildlife (IBWL), and the inspector general of forests, R.C. Soni. Kailash Sankhala of the Rajasthan cadre of the IFS, then working on his seminal book on the tiger under the aegis of a Nehru Foundation Fellowship, the redoubtable 'Billy' Arjan Singh of Dudhwa fame and Anne Wright of the World Wildlife Fund were also there. My batchmate in the IAS, Manmohan Malhoutra was a deputy secretary in the Prime Minister's Office (PMO). He had told the PM of my work in Kanha and at his behest I had shown her my wildlife movies. Though a deputy secretary, in conservation matters Manmohan reported directly to Indira Gandhi. He had earlier briefed her about some of my suggestions. I was also summoned to the PMO for the meeting.

Soni began by stating that since forests and wildlife were state subjects under the Constitution, they were the responsibility of the state government, and the Union government could only advise and encourage. This stand was supported by Karan Singh. Billy, as expected, attacked. 'What priority does wildlife have in your scheme of things, Madam prime minister?' he asked in his baritone voice. Indira Gandhi became defensive. She cared a great deal for wildlife she said, but wildlife could not take precedence over humans. Billy went on with his harangue over the plight of his beloved Dudhwa.

Indira Gandhi started getting restive, shifting in her chair and twiddling her pencil, which I was to learn later was her signal that her patience was getting exhausted. Wildlife ethologists call it displacement activity. That's it, I thought, she will never call another wildlife meeting.

My colleague Manmohan Malhoutra sitting next to me whispered that I should say something. So when Billy finished and she asked, 'So what can be done for wildlife?' I said that the situation was not so hopeless and the Central government could do a few substantial things. First, there was no uniform legislation for wildlife protection in the country. The provisions of the Indian Forest Act, 1927, under which the states operated, only dealt with hunting and the issuance of licences for this purpose. Maharashtra and a couple of other states had better laws of their own, but these too were inadequate. India needed a comprehensive wildlife legislation that would be uniformly applicable to the country and would actually address the protection of species and their habitats, the creation and management of protected areas, the control of wildlife trade and taxidermy and the rest. I went on to add that though the subject of forests and wildlife was in the State List under our Constitution, the Central government could legislate on a state subject under the provisions of Article 252, whereby if two states of the Indian Union passed a resolution in their respective state assemblies approving of a legislation on a state subject to be passed by the Central government, parliament could pass such a law. It would apply to those two states and subsequently to others who adopted it by a similar process, after its passage in parliament.

But which state would surrender its constitutional rights and powers, asked Karan Singh. 'I will ask the states to give us such a mandate,' replied Indira Gandhi in a low, clear voice.

By now she had turned to face me in her swivel chair. 'What else?' she asked. 'We only preach wildlife to the states,' I said. 'Their parks and sanctuaries are starved for funds. Why cannot the Central government start a central or centrally sponsored scheme, under which the creation of infrastructure and other "capital" expenditure in a protected area could be funded by the Government of India on an annual basis, while the maintenance of these assets and other recurring expenditure would be the responsibility of the states themselves? This would also enable the Central government to influence the quality of management in these protected areas.' Indira Gandhi nodded and asked Manmohan to take this matter up with the Planning Commission.

The meeting ended and I went back to the RS09 tractors. A week later, a memo arrived from Indira Gandhi, addressed to the minister for food and agriculture, Fakhrudin Ali Ahmed, later to become the president of India, saying that I should be placed in charge of wildlife. So I changed over from deputy secretary, machinery, to deputy secretary, forests and wildlife, in the Ministry of Food and Agriculture.

Soon after, Karan Singh in his capacity of chairman, IBWL, asked the only three people handling wildlife in the Government of India – AIG (Forests) N.S. Adkoli, who was reporting to me in wildlife matters in the agriculture ministry, A.G. Raddi, later to retire as principal chief conservator of forests, Maharashtra, whom Karan Singh had brought to his Ministry for Tourism to develop wildlife tourism, and me – to tour the north-eastern states and submit a report on the status and needs of wildlife there. We travelled by road from Imphal, through Manipur and Nagaland, to all the major sanctuaries of Assam, up to Jaldapara in West Bengal.

In Manipur, we went to the Keibul Lamjao Sanctuary, the sole habitat of the Manipur brow-antlered deer, locally called sangai. In 1950, it was believed that they were extinct. Then in 1959, the pioneering conservationist E.P. Gee had 'rediscovered' the species in Keibul Lamjao, south of the Loktak Lake, a morass of floating vegetation to which the deer had adapted, growing elongated hooves to support their weight. The sangai had survived in this last retreat as they could traverse the floating morass, called 'phumdi', which man and livestock could not. Based upon a sample survey, Gee estimated their number at approximately 100 in the Keibul Lamjao Sanctuary, extending over 10.75 sq. km.

Our party saw five sangai from the Pabot Hill in the sanctuary one early morning and again, based upon extrapolation, I guesstimated the total number at around fifty. Three years later, I realized what an overestimation that was.

In Kaziranga and Manas, with their profusion of rhino, elephant, hog deer and the rest, I met Sunjoy Deb Roy and P. Lahan, both of the rank of divisional forest officers (DFO) then. Among the early stalwart field conservationists of the country, they became my lifelong friends. In Kaziranga, I noticed that the barasingha there were morphologically quite different from those in Kanha as well as those in the Terai of the Dudhwa Reserve of Uttar Pradesh. In Manas, the grasslands of Pohu field would be crowded with hog deer and we took the exhilarating boat ride downstream from Mathanguri rest house to Kahitama, floating down with the current, disturbing wild buffalo, elephants and smooth-coated otters in the water; and hog deer, golden langur and sambar on the river banks. Manas Sanctuary also held a population of barasingha and of over fifty rhinos then. There were a substantive number of the rare Bengal florican all along its southern and eastern flanks. On the western flanks along the Kokrajhar district, there still were chital, the easternmost limit of the distribution of this deer in India. Manas also had clouded leopard, golden langur, pygmy hog and the hispid hare, which are absent in Kaziranga. Of the two, Manas is more important from ecological, faunal and floral standpoints.

This was my first visit to the Orang National Park in Assam and I was very impressed with its potential. Remote, small, neglected and overshadowed by Manas and Kaziranga, it still remains as unfulfilled now as it was then. Jaldapara in the northern duars of West Bengal held a high concentration of rhino, but lost thirty-two next year, when after the Bangladesh war and the disbandment of the Mukti Bahini freedom fighters, their arms were smuggled out to poach rhino in Jaldapara, with the help of a rogue mahout.

By this time, it had been decided to start a special project to preserve the tiger, an idea which had its origin in the IUCN Assembly of 1969, in Delhi, as mentioned earlier. Guy Mountford, a trustee of WWF and representative of the IUCN, had come to India. He addressed a gathering with Karan Singh in Delhi and announced financial support of a million dollars for the project, from the IUCN and WWF. It had been decided that the project would be handled by Kailash Sankhala, but he was still on a Nehru scholarship and could not join the government for some time. I was, therefore, appointed member secretary of the task force that was to initiate Project Tiger. The task force was chaired by Karan Singh. Inspector General of Forests, Kailash Sankhala, Zafar Futehally of the BNHS and others were members. Though not a part of the task force nor of the subsequent steering committee of Project Tiger chaired by Karan Singh, Indira Gandhi kept careful watch over the proceedings and gave directions to Karan Singh.

It was decided that initially only one tiger reserve was to be assigned in a state and that the selection was not merely to be on the basis of the tiger population that a protected area held, but its diversity, conservation value and potential as well. A deliberate effort was also made to cover the various habitat types that the tiger occupied in India. The existence of other endangered species was a vital consideration. The reserve was to be not less than about 300 sq. km in extent, within which neither forestry operations nor human habitation would be allowed.

Individual members of the task force were sent to nine selected areas to assess the situation and the potential of each, and also to ascertain if the state governments concerned were prepared to abide by the norms laid down, including stoppage of forestry operations in a minimum area. In Assam, Manas was preferred over Kaziranga, partly because the latter was already well protected due to its rhino, but mainly because Manas had greater faunal and floral diversity and greater potential if better preserved.

I was sent to Kanha, to Periyar in Kerala and Tadoba in

Maharashtra. Periyar and Kanha were easy and automatic choices, the respective states agreeing to our stipulations; forestry operations were in any case not being carried out in them. Tadoba was a problem: though it was a national park and the state government was ready to have it declared a tiger reserve, its size was inadequate. I wanted to include the adjacent forests of Andhari and Kolsa, but the state government would not agree. This was partly because of Maharashtra's reluctance to forego its substantial annual income from the teak forests of these two areas, in which the forest department also had carried out extensive teak and bamboo plantation. But there was also another reason, which was whispered to me. The then chief minister of Maharashtra, V.P. Naik, was a keen hunter and Kolsa was his favourite hunting area. So I did not recommend the inclusion of Tadoba as a tiger reserve. Zafar Futehally then selected Melghat instead. However, Tadoba later did become a tiger reserve, with Kolsa and Andhari included.

Karan Singh, chairman of the IBWL, brought up the question of renaming the national animal of India. He wanted the lion, which as represented on the Mauryan pillar capital was also the emblem of the Government of India, to be replaced by the tiger as the national animal. We had several discussions on the issue. I objected to the change on the ground that a national animal once declared, must not be changed, especially as India held the only population of the lion outside of Africa. Karan Singh argued that the lion was the emblem of England and since India had moved out from under the hegemony of that country and had the largest tiger population in the world, we should adopt the tiger. One day, he lost his patience with me and said I was objecting to the change since I myself came from the 'land of the lion,' Saurashtra! I replied that by that token one could say that he was favouring the tiger because his own pet name, given to him by his father Maharaja Hari Singhji of Kashmir, was Tiger! Karan Singh took my retort very sportingly, but insisted on the change. In hindsight, he was right. The national animal of India should have been the tiger all along. Apart from the fact that there are more tigers in India than elsewhere, the animal represents India much more than the lion. For, while the lion is confined to just one small part of the country, the tiger has almost a countrywide distribution, barring the arid west and the mountainous north. Also, no other country then had the tiger as its national animal.

Then there was the question of naming the national bird. I had proposed the great Indian bustard in the hope of saving that magnificent bird from extinction, which was impending even then. Karan Singh proposed blue jay or 'neelkanth', which is also the name of Lord Shiva. I objected as the bird was too small and not impressive. He dismissed the claims of the great Indian bustard with his own erudite finality: 'Ranjit, how can we have as our national bird whose name, if pronounced a little incorrectly, could spell disaster?' So we ultimately settled for the Indian peacock.

Indira Gandhi had tried to amend the Constitution to strike out the privileges and privy purses of the Indian princes, but had to suffer defeat in Parliament, whereupon she dissolved it and sought a fresh mandate from the country. She won a greater majority than her party ever had before and was very secure in office, with the Congress also ruling in a large majority of the states. Her letter of 12 April 1972, the first that she wrote to the chief ministers of all the states after being re-elected to power in 1971, was to request them to pass a resolution in their respective state assemblies to empower the Government of India to pass a comprehensive Central legislation dealing with wildlife conservation, a state subject then under the Constitution. She said: 'This is not a political issue. It concerns the survival of our natural heritage. It is hard to think of India devoid of its magnificent animals' (Ministry of Environment and Forests [MoEF] 2009). It may be difficult to believe in the current scenario, but eighteen states, including one with a non-Congress government, passed the requisite resolution in their assemblies without even having seen the legislation itself.

Meanwhile, I had been studying the wildlife laws of the Indian states who had separate Acts for this purpose, as well as those of other countries, especially developing countries in Asia and Africa. The state legislation which I thought most apt was that of Maharashtra, in which there had been considerable inputs from Humayun Abdulali and J.C. Daniel of the Bombay Natural History Society (BNHS), and others. Amongst the laws of other countries, those of Kenya, Indonesia and New Zealand had useful aspects that could be incorporated with modifications. The topics of trade and taxidermy were not dealt with sufficiently anywhere. I had no help in preparing a draft of the bill, except from my colleague and assistant, N.S. Adkoli. The draft was circulated to a few colleagues, but the papers were returned with no suggestions. After the Wild Life (Protection) Act, 1972, was passed, however, there were many critiques and debates over it, including by those to whom I had given the early draft for their suggestions.

When I had prepared a very rough format of the proposed Act, I went to the Department of Legislation in the Ministry of Law, in the spring of 1972. The deputy secretary and legislative counsel assigned with the task of drafting the Act in the Department of Legislation, V.N. Bhashyam, said he was too busy during the ongoing budget session of parliament and that I should come after the monsoon session was over, some five months later. I dictated a small note stating that the PM had desired that wildlife legislation be framed for the country, but the law ministry had conveyed that drafting of such legislation would not be possible till about September. 'The PM may kindly be informed,' I wrote at the end. All my superiors knew of the PM's interest in the subject and the file went up to the PMO with the signatures of the IGF, secretary agriculture and the minister for agriculture, without any comments. Within four days of my having dispatched the note, I got a call from Bhashyam. Could we meet the next day to start the process of drafting?

It was not an easy process. Neither Bhashyam nor I had a precedent, or an equivalent, or any real role model to help us. To his credit, Bhashyam agreed to almost everything I drafted and couched the provisions in better legal terminology. There were a few things he would not agree to. I wanted the title to be 'The Wildlife Conservation and Management Act'. But in the Constitution there are two words – wild life, and the Constitution mentions 'protection' of wild life and of forests, not 'conservation'. We would have to change the Constitution to bring these desired words into it and then I could have them in this Act, he said! A makna (tuskless elephant) is better than no elephant, I remember replying, and we settled for 'The Wild Life (Protection) Act, 1972'.

Indian jurisprudence, based on Anglo-Saxon traditions, is inquisitorial, not accusatorial. One is not guilty till proven guilty. But if one is caught with a fresh tiger skin or a rhino horn, how can one prove that the accused killed it or was a party to the crime? The Forest Act of 1927 and most other laws do not have any provisions to overcome such obstacles. But the Indian Evidence Act has a provision that if a person is apprehended with stolen property and the seizure of the same can be established, the burden of proof shifts and the accused will then have to establish that the seized articles were obtained legally. On my request, Bhashyam agreed to incorporate this provision in the wildlife Act. On his side, Bhashyam wanted to include the right of self-defence, which is a common provision in most criminal laws. But what if a person shot an elephant and then claimed that he shot it in self-defence, I argued? Who is there to see the act? So Bhashyam agreed to my suggestion that the right to self-defence could only be considered valid if at the time of exercising it the person concerned was not committing any illegality. In other words, for a person to use a weapon in self-defence and claim legal immunity, he must be where he was and carrying the weapon without having broken any rule or law. In protected areas, no one was allowed to carry any weapon without prior permission.

Controlled hunting was permitted in the original Act. I did not put the Nilgiri tahr in Schedule I of the Act and prohibit its hunting completely, as the largest population of the animal was then on private lands under the control of the Kanan Devan Hills

Plantations Company Private Limited (KDHP) of tea planters, whose game association allowed a few mature 'saddleback' males to be shot annually, for the sake of which they were saving over 600 tahr on their leased lands. The average annual kill was one to two Nilgiri tahr males (Ranjitsinh 1973). Conservation is a chessboard of compromise and some barters are worth it, provided, of course, they do not cross the proverbial Rubicon. The Tibetan antelope also was not put in Schedule I of the Act then, as the slaughter of the animal for 'shahtoosh' extraction in China was then not known and we wanted Jammu and Kashmir to adopt the Wild Life Act, which would have been very difficult if shahtoosh had been banned outright then. Further, every Changpa in Ladakh carried in his 'gumcha' sash the tips of the chiru horn, which were then used universally in Ladakh as sewing needles and there would be great harassment of these people if the possession became illegal. It was a fascinating, rewarding exercise, though taxing, as I had to do this after office hours, often working into the small hours of the morning.

The process was completed in about three months, and was circulated to all the ministries concerned of the Government of India for their comments and concurrence. The Ministry of Tribal Welfare came back to us with a poser – what about the traditional tribal rights of hunting and of carrying bows, arrows and spears? As for the right of carrying their weapons, I argued that they could not carry them in protected areas, which were then a minuscule part of the country's area, but could continue to do so outside. In the matter of the traditional rights of hunting, I conveyed that if such rights were recognized in any law, government order or decision of any administration, and had been put on paper, these would be incorporated in the Act itself and would be exempted from its provisions, much in the same way as the Coorgis were exempted from the Arms Act in British India. Only the administration of the Andaman and Nicobar Islands, a Union territory, came back with a notification which permitted the islanders of Car Nicobar to hunt without a licence. This was duly incorporated in the bill. Some of the other states made vague references to practices that were said to be prevalent, but had no recognition or approval.

The final draft came up for the approval of the cabinet. Neither IG (Forests) T.N. Srivastava nor Secretary (Agriculture) T.P. Singh, my superiors, had any insight on this legislation and so I, a low-ranking deputy secretary, was sent to the cabinet meeting. Minister Fakhrudin Ali Ahmed was away on tour, so the minister of state for agriculture, Professor Sher Singh was to pilot the bill in the cabinet. I had written out a note for him, mentioning the salient features of the bill and why it was essential.

In the meeting hall in the South Block secretariat in New Delhi, the cabinet secretary, the head of the ICS/IAS bureaucracy of the country, arrived and looked at the agenda. Who has come from the Ministry of Agriculture, he demanded rather imperiously. I presented myself, and when I said I was a deputy secretary, he queried aloud as to why my ministry could not have sent at least a joint secretary. Our forestry division has no joint secretary; the AIG of forests and I have been dealing with the subject entirely, I ventured. He gave no answer but asked me to sit at the far end of the room, as if I was unworthy to be anywhere near the hallowed table around which the cabinet sat.

The operation of the cabinet was most interesting. Indira Gandhi controlled her flock as a school 'ma'am' would her pupils. When Defence Minister Yashwantrao Chavan, a minister much senior to her, started whispering to Foreign Minister Swaran Singh, she pulled up the latter, saying that he should listen to the proceedings. When the item of the Wild Life Act came up, Professor Sher Singh started reading out the note that had been prepared for him. After about three minutes I could see Indira Gandhi fidgeting with her pencil, eyebrows knotted. 'Why are you giving us a speech, Professor Saheb?' she asked in Hindi in her low, flat, emotionless voice. 'This is a law which I myself have asked for.' The words are etched in my memory.

The discussion on the bill ended there, and the cabinet moved on to the next item. The cabinet secretary turned towards me and gave a wave of dismissal. A deputy secretary must not remain a minute longer than required in the sanctum sanctorum.

In September, the Wild Life (Protection) Bill, 1972, was introduced in the Rajya Sabha. In the morning of the day it was to come up for discussion there, I got a phone call from the PM's secretary, N. Seshan, not to be confused with T.N. Seshan who later became cabinet secretary. Why am I required, I asked Seshan. I was told that some scheduled tribe members of parliament had met the PM earlier that morning and had complained about the curtailment of tribal rights of hunting, as envisaged in the bill.

I walked over from my office in Krishi Bhavan to the parliament building next door, and there being hardly any security in those days, was soon ushered into her chamber. She looked up from her papers and with her now familiar slight scowl and drawl said, 'The tribal MPs are very annoyed with your Act.' 'What about, Madam?' I asked, and she replied that it was something over tribal hunting rights. I had been warned and was mentally prepared. 'We have inquired from all states and Union territories about the recognition in any form, of any such rights and only the Andaman administration has given us any validation, which has been incorporated in the bill,' I said, adding, 'if we give acceptance to any hunting practice merely on grounds of assumptions, practices of snaring and trapping, of paradh and akhand shikar (annual ritualistic mass hunts practised by tribal communities in Odisha and Madhya Pradesh, where the jungle is set on fire and wildlife driven into huge nets to be speared or killed with arrows) would be given legal sanction and the bill would have no effect whatsoever. Besides, if traditional tribal hunting practices are to be codified and permitted, why should not the same be done for other groups and communities who are also citizens of India? The princes of India have had traditional rights to hunt in their own states and, till the very recent amendment, even the Constitution permitted them to exercise these rights.'

The scowl on her face was getting deeper, but the argument, especially with regard to the sensitive subject of princes with its recent history, was reaching its mark. 'There is even a traditional right of hunting rhino, removing its heart and offering it to one's ancestors in the "tarpan" ceremony,' I continued. This was practised by the Ranas of Nepal, not the Indian princes, but if one just cites a grisly 'tradition' of some princes without stating the country to which they belong, it is not a complete lie, is it? If all these traditional rights are to be allowed, what is the purpose of having this Act, I asked.

By now she was twiddling the pen in her hand and I knew I must end. But the point had got through, one could see, especially regarding the princely privileges of hunting. She had not forgotten the defeat in parliament over the constitutional amendment for the termination of privy purses and privileges of the princes. 'Ask Seshan to fix up a meeting with the tribal MPs today and you explain the matter to them,' she said. I could not resist one more question. 'Madam,' I said, 'the bill is coming up for discussion in the Rajya Sabha this evening. I hope it will be passed in this session of parliament and not referred to a select committee.' She looked up straight into my eyes. The scowl had gone. In the same low, flat tone she simply said, 'Of course, it will be passed in this session.'

I asked Seshan to fix up a meeting with the tribal members of parliament in the early afternoon, as the PM wanted the discussion on the bill in the Rajya Sabha to go ahead as per schedule. Amongst the MPs who came for the meeting were Sahodra Bai, whom I had known from my Sagar days, and Mangru Uike, whom I had known from Mandla, as he had long been an MP from that district. They heard me out at length and raised some issues, but did not oppose the bill in parliament.

Around the same time, Indira Gandhi was also preparing to participate in the United Nations Conference on Human Environment in Stockholm, Sweden. Some people, including myself, were asked to suggest points for inclusion in her address. Ultimately, she wrote her own speech and my ideas certainly were not in her address to the conference, which she was the only head of government to attend, other than the prime minister of the host country, Sweden.

Within a week of the wildlife bill's passage in the Lok Sabha as well, I went to the Banff National Park in Canada as leader of the Indian delegation to the Eleventh IUCN General Assembly. Accompanying me was Kailash Sankhala, who had then joined the ministry as the first director of Project Tiger. Kailash presented to the IUCN assembly the first formulation of Project Tiger. Sir Peter Scott, chairman of the Survival Service Commission (SSC) of the IUCN, appointed me as a vice-chairman of the SSC, of which I was then the youngest member. It was good to meet up with friends I had made during the previous IUCN General Assembly at Delhi. From Banff, we moved to the Yellowstone National Park for the Second World Conference on National Parks to commemorate the completion of a century of the establishment of the world's first national park, Yellowstone. Patricia Nixon, then first lady of United States of America, had come to the Old Faithful Lodge in the park, to rededicate Yellowstone to the nation and to the world. Twelve hundred delegates from over eighty countries in the six continents attended the conference.

The commemoration ceremony was to be held at the junction of the Firehole and Gibson rivers at Madison Junction, where in 1870 the Washburn–Langford–Doane Expedition, sent by the United States' Congress to verify the reports of a natural wonderland, had made their last camp and decided that what they had seen did warrant a recommendation to the United States' Congress to establish a national park.

My friend Fred Stoever had come over from New York to join me and Kalpana. Fred had hired a car and while the rest of the delegates went in buses, he drove me and Kalpana from the Old Faithful to the Madison Junction, with a detour to see wildlife. It was late September and the rutting of the elk had begun. We saw a grand stag bugling. I got out of the car, in my suit and tie, and stalked up to the displaying stag. Yellowstone is, of course, a geyser land with fumaroles exuding steam, but also dotted all over are mudholes, well camouflaged in the grass. Intent on photographing the stag, I stepped into a mudhole and one leg sank up to the thigh. There was no time to go back to the Old Faithful Lodge to change. I arrived at the tumultuous gathering in a pied pair of pants, one unaffected and dark blue, the other caked in greyish yellow mud.

This appearance would hardly have mattered but for the fact that to dine with Patricia Nixon, the United States' secretary of the interior and governors of Idaho and Wyoming, on an elevated platform, was one representative from each of the six continents, who were also to be formally introduced to Mrs Nixon, in the full glare of lights on that platform. I had been selected to represent Asia. The weather had become bitterly cold. Open fires set up for the delegates helped in drying up that mud, but I was still piebald on the lower half.

Wolves had still not been reintroduced into Yellowstone and the elk were very numerous. A few weeks before our arrival we were told, a tourist unsatisfied with a bison bull grazing unconcernedly beside his car without raising its head and unmindful of his shouting, got out of the vehicle, walked up to the bull, placed his hand on the bull's hump and posed for his wife to take his picture. Whereupon the bull turned around, pummelled and gored him to death. Wild animals must not be feared; but they have to be respected for what they are and what they can do.

From Yellowstone the conference moved to the Grand Teton National Park, a strikingly beautiful landscape. I became friends with Eskandar Firouz, head of the Department of Environmental Conservation, Government of Iran, who invited me to Iran. He wanted to reintroduce the Asiatic lion, which had become extinct in his country during World War II. The Asiatic lion is the Persian lion – *Panthera leo persica* – and Iran must get it back, he announced. In exchange, Iran would give India the Asiatic cheetah, which had become extinct in our country. I agreed to the exchange, subject to concurrence from my government.

After photographing the American pronghorn antelope in Wyoming, mule deer in the Black Hills of South Dakota, USA, and moose in the Quebec Province in Canada, we went to Iran. In the Alborz Mountains, I saw my first wild goat (*Capra aegagrus*) amongst the snows of late autumn. In what was then the Tehran Imperial Reserve some 30 km east of the capital, we rode horseback and in an evening's ride in the reserve, must have seen not less than 800 Alborz urial (*Ovis orientalis*).

The Wild Life (Protection) Act had been notified and had come into operation by the time I returned to India in November 1972. One day I was suddenly sent for by Indira Gandhi. She said she had just returned from Anand Bhavan, her ancestral home in Allahabad, where she was informed that the family had a tiger skin, the possession of which was now illegal under the Act. 'The skin was presented to my grandfather Motilal Nehru by some UP zamindar. We haven't killed it', she added defensively. What can be done? I said that the thirty-day period for the declaration of trophies provided under Section 40 of the Act was now over. She should just lock away the skin and not tell anyone.

Under the Wild Life (Protection) Act, rules had to be framed by both the Central and state governments; and since the Act had mainly to be operated by the states, their rules had to be more comprehensive. Acts get passed but their rules normally do not get promulgated for years. So while framing rules for the Central government, I suggested that the Ministry of Law should frame a set of model rules for the states on the grounds of ensuring similarity of rules among states and expediting their passage. Though the ministry was reluctant to do this, my colleague Bhashyam was persuaded to draft a model set of rules for the states. The states adopted the model we sent them, almost in toto.

After word had been sent across to the Planning Commission by Manmohan Malhoutra of the PMO, I approached it to initiate centrally sponsored schemes to assist protected areas under the control of the states and Union territories. Two schemes were approved, one to assist national parks and the other for wildlife sanctuaries (much later, they were merged into one). Under these, the Government of India would fund capital works such as the construction of accommodation for the field staff, roads for purposes of patrolling, barriers on roads and delineation of boundaries, the purchase of vehicles, communication equipment, weapons, binoculars and the rest. The states would have to maintain and operate these, and bear recurring expenditure on staff maintenance, road repairs and fire control. Each year the chief wildlife wardens would come up with their plans, and based upon the importance of the area and of the items asked for, together with the past performance and utilization of funds, grants would be released.

India at the time was annually exporting 1.2 million snakeskins and 1.25 million skins of lizards, mostly of the genus *Varanus*. Also being exported annually were 5,000 common langurs and 40,000 rhesus macaques, for research and trial purposes. There were reports that some monkeys were being used as living dummies to test the impact of car accidents. In 1973, an exporter was caught trying to smuggle out the gravely endangered and endemic golden langur, coloured grey to resemble the common langur! Musk pods, crocodile skins, captured animals and birds were also exported. Ivory was imported. Animals which were protected under the Wild Life (Protection) Act were easy to stop export of, after the Act came into force. The monkeys, snakeskins and lizardskins took a little longer. Initially, their quantum was reduced. Subsequently, Vinod Pande, then the comptroller of exports and imports who later became cabinet secretary in the administration of Prime Minister V.P. Singh, agreed to totally ban the export of monkeys, snakeskins and lizardskins.

The export of monkeys was a lucrative business. They were caught in forests as the primates living in towns and in the proximity of humans carry human pathogens and are, therefore, not suitable for medical experimentation. The cost of capture, upkeep and transportation of one monkey up to New York was about $19. After quarantine, which cost another $4 per animal, it could fetch between

$180 and $220, males costing more. So there was a huge profit and only two companies were conducting this business in India. One of them offered me $50,000, to be deposited in a Swiss Bank – they would even open the account for me – if I would allow the previous full quota of 40,000 to be exported. This was the only time in my life I was offered a bribe.

Many more snakes were killed and skinned than the quota allowed for export, as a large number of them would be damaged or be unsuitable for export. Besides, it was obvious that many more were being exported than the permits allowed, with the connivance of the customs staff. The main snakeskin market was beside the then Calcutta office of the chief wildlife warden of Bengal and the smell and sight of the wares in it would have churned the stomach of the most hardened. The exporters made numerous representations against the ban on export on different grounds. First, it was claimed that they were shed skins of snakes. Then it was claimed that snakes were dangerous to humans and thousands of lives were being lost annually to these lethal pests.

Each time one had to argue with the exporters in the presence of superior officers and ministers. The last meeting took place in 1975, in the office of the redoubtable Babu Jagjivan Ram, the senior-most minister in the cabinet of Indira Gandhi, who had become the minister for agriculture upon appointment of Fakhrudin Ali Ahmed as the president of India. I argued that lizard export entailed the killing and skinning of the 'sanda – a desert lizard which is a primary predator of locusts. (This was not quite correct, because the lizard skins exported were mainly of monitor lizards.) Amongst the snakes, there were cobras and kraits whose venom, I argued, we required in the country to develop anti-venom vaccines. Even more importantly, a large portion of snakeskins exported were of dhaman or rat snakes, and I showed a published paper which said that one rat snake ate about eighteen rats and mice a month. Rats were then reported to consume almost 8 per cent of the cereal production of the country. I announced, a little theatrically, that though I personally loved the tiger, we were in the Ministry of Agriculture and for that ministry and for the country's agriculture the rat snakes and the lizards were more important than the tiger. Jagjivan Ram was convinced, and the ban on export remained.

On 1 April 1973, Karan Singh, chairman of the IBWL, launched Project Tiger in Corbett National Park. Kailash Sankhala was the director and to begin with there were nine tiger reserves – Manas, Periyar, Betla (Palamau), Corbett, Simlipal, Melghat, Kanha, Ranthambore and Bandipur. Sundarban and Sariska were added later.

Meanwhile, an important development was occurring in Kerala. I have mentioned that the KDHP tea planters were preserving the Nilgiri tahr on the uplands of the Rajamala–Eravikulam massif in the Kerala High Range, the highest point in the Western Ghats encompassing the tallest peak in India south of the Himalayas, Anaimudi, higher than even Dodabetta in the Nilgiris. The upper portions of Eravikulam and the adjacent Rajamala ridge in the Kerala High Range contain perhaps the most pristine ecosystem in India south of the Himalaya. Vast vistas of rolling 'downs' covered with greensward exist, interspersed with deep valleys choked with dense 'shola' forests that are amongst the richest in biodiversity, unaffected by human impact or the invasion of exotic species. The clear streams of the valley floors seethed with the only introduced species – rainbow trout. Though the KDHP had been paying an annual land tax on the whole estate, Eravikulam–Rajamala had never been planted nor cultivated, even by the original inhabitants, the Muduvan tribe. The only use had been fishing and selective hunting by the tea garden managers. The Muduvans were employed as game guards.

In 1971, the Kerala government revoked the lease given to the tea company by the Raja of Cochin. Non-utilization of Eravikulam–Rajamala for purposes of tea plantation, as stipulated in the original lease deed, was cited as one reason for the revocation of the lease. The Communist Party of India (CPI) that led the government in Kerala had promised the unoccupied land to the landless in the state. In 1972, the Supreme Court upheld the Kerala government's revocation of the lease and acquisition of land. The KDHP lost control over the area and poachers moved in. The High Range Game Association of KDHP stopped providing salt to the tahr in Rajamala, as the resulting congregation of tahr would fall easy prey to the poachers (Ranjitsinh 1973).

The Game Association representatives – Gouldsbury, Chengappa and Samar Singh – sent me an SOS and I went to Munnar with the Kerala chief wildlife warden K.K. Nair, a fine upright officer. We were taken up to the Poovar Hut at the top of Eravikulam, partly on a motorbike and the rest on foot. There was no motorable road then and I hope there never will be. It was paradise – tahr, sambar, elephant, rhododendrons in bloom and various hues of the shola forest.

From here we went to the state capital Thiruvananthapuram, and met Food and Forest Minister Baby John, who was over 6 feet tall. I pleaded that Eravikulam–Rajamala received over 600 cm of rainfall annually and, being 3,000 m high with temperatures dropping to below freezing point in winter, had never been inhabited, even by the Muduvans. If an attempt was made to cultivate it, the very thin nutrient-poor topsoil on the rocky surface would be washed away in the first monsoon and only barren rock would remain. It must become a national park, I urged. Baby John was most courteous and patient. But his party and the ruling Left Democratic Front (LDF) had announced a bonanza for the landless. Besides, he said in confidence, if the state government declared it a national park, the KDHP could revert to the courts and claim that while the lease had been revoked on the argument that the area was not used for agriculture as stipulated, now the government was itself declaring it a place for wildlife rather than cultivation.

So we went back to the KDHP to ask whether they would use the declaration of a national park as an argument to win back legal possession of the land. Gouldsbury and his colleagues confirmed what we already knew, that they were desperate and that what they had saved for over a century must continue to remain part of the national natural heritage. They said they would continue to pay for the Muduvan guards to protect the area, over which they had lost legal control, besides giving the state government an undertaking in writing that they would not agitate in court if the Government of Kerala declared Eravikulam–Rajamala as a wildlife sanctuary or a national park.

I returned to Delhi and reported this to the PMO. Indira Gandhi wrote a personal letter to the Kerala chief minister Achutha Menon requesting him to declare the area a national park. The matter, however, remained in limbo, the state government remaining indecisive for fear of a political fallout.

One day in the Ministry of Food and Agriculture, I had gone to Annasaheb Shinde, minister of state for food. Professor Sher Singh who held the portfolio for forests in the ministry being away on tour, Shinde was temporarily in charge of forests and wildlife. As I was about to leave, Shinde asked whether we had any work pending with the forest department of Kerala as its minister Baby John was coming to see him. So I recited the whole long story about Eravikulam, adding that the PM had also requested Kerala to declare the area as a national park but the state was hesitant. Shinde asked me to join him and John for the meeting.

It was a year of poor harvest and Kerala needed its staple – rice. The food and forest minister of Kerala had come to the food minister of the Union government to ask for the release of forty railway wagons of rice from the Food Corporation of India.

Shinde was an unassuming but a very determined man. It was a very fascinating, non-acrimonious discussion. Baby John mentioned the predicament of rice shortages. Shinde offered twenty-five wagons of rice straightaway but then asked about the declaration of the national park, with his disarming smile. Baby John looked at me, smiled and said the state was actively considering it, a standard phraseology in government. The negotiation went on in a very civil way – tahr in lieu of rice. The deal was ultimately settled at thirty-six wagons of rice for the declaration of Eravikulam National Park and Rajamala Sanctuary; part of the quantum to be released immediately, the rest after the declaration of the protected areas. Today, this barter sounds like a fairy tale. But it did happen.

Eravikulam–Rajamala has now become a showpiece for Kerala, with visitors eagerly asking to see the 'varai adu', now incredibly tame. There is a natural deficiency of salt in the soil and vegetation, which makes a salt lick a great attraction and a cause for their congregation in Rajamala. Once, watching and photographing a herd of Nilgiri tahr some 10 m away, I felt the urgent call of nature. No sooner had I turned around and started the process, there was a stampede behind me. I turned around to see ewes rushing towards me drawn by the smell of salt in the urine. Then came a large saddleback, brushing past me and nearly throwing me off balance in that state of dishevelment, taking possession of that fresh saltlick within touching distance! Never again.

Article 370 of the Indian Constitution provides that most laws passed by parliament will apply to the state of Jammu and Kashmir only after the state legislature adopts them. The Wild Life (Protection) Act, 1972, did not apply to that state, though it was most imperative that it should, not only for the magnificent wildlife the state itself possessed but also for the wildlife trade and taxidermy that was in practice there, which affected the whole country. Sheikh Abdullah had been released from custody and had become the chief minister. My batchmate in the IAS, R.K. Takkar, was then forest secretary of the state. I had persuaded him to move the state government to adopt the Wild Life (Protection) Act and a while later he informed me that the chief minister was agreeable and the needful would be done in the next session of the state assembly.

I then made a stupid mistake. Despite the passage of the Wild Life (Protection) Act, Kashmiri traders were still merrily plying their trade in India. Leopard, snow leopard and clouded leopard skins and products were freely available in furrier shops and we did not have any staff to enforce the Act, even in Delhi. It was most galling to see the open flouting of the law and I did not stop to consider the consequences of my action. Taking the help of my other batchmate in the IAS, V.K. Kapoor, then chief secretary of Delhi, officers of the Delhi administration, including two lady officers, were deployed as decoys to go and buy skins and stoles made from skins of animals listed under Schedule I of the Wild Life (Protection) Act from furrier shops in Delhi. One was in the Claridges hotel, the second in the state-owned hotel The Ashok, and others in Connaught Circle and in Chandni Chowk. All the operations took place at the same time, and after purchase, the shops concerned were raided by the police and the sold articles and receipts of sale seized.

This led to an uproar, and representations were made all around. I was sent for by Karan Singh and asked why furrier shops run by only one community – Kashmiri Muslims – had been raided. I replied that all the forty-three furrier shops in Delhi happened to be owned and operated by Kashmiri Muslims, so how could I raid the shops of any other community?

However, the Kashmiri fur-trading community represented before the J&K state government, and made it aware of the repercussions the provisions of the Wild Life (Protection) Act would have on their trade and livelihood. No effort on the part of the Government of India could persuade J&K to adopt the Act. Much later, in 1978, the state did pass its own Wild Life (Protection) Act modelled after the Central Act of 1972, the initiative being taken by the then chief wildlife warden of Kashmir, Mir Inayatullah.

The United States of America and other conservation-oriented countries had become conscious of the serious drain on wildlife resources caused by illegal trade, patronized mainly by the affluent countries. A conference was convened in Washington in 1973, which led to the promulgation of the Convention on International Trade in Endangered Species of Wild Fauna and Flora (CITES). The first list of species sponsored by India for inclusion in the various appendices of the convention was prepared and forwarded.

Meanwhile, the same year, I had been appointed as the first

director, wildlife preservation of India under the aegis of the Wild Life (Protection) Act of 1972. The first enumeration of tiger in India had taken place, under the guidance of Saroj Raj Choudhury, who had started the first training course for wildlife officers of the states in the Forest Research Institute at Dehradun. Based on the pugmark method of counting, a total figure of 1,827 tigers had been estimated in the country.

Wildlife was in the news and for the first time it was an emerging aspect in the national consciousness. Reports of tiger kills and tiger poisoning as a consequence were frequent. Eight lions were poisoned on a single kill in the Gir. The cattle compensation scheme started by my maternal uncle Maharawal Lakshman Singhji of Dungarpur seemed to be the best option. In consultation with some of the prominent chief wildlife wardens of the states, a scheme was mooted for compensation for livestock killed by lion and tiger, modelled on that of Dungarpur. If cattle were killed where they were legally permitted to stay or graze, the owner of the animal killed would get the full value of the animal. In national parks grazing was not allowed and, hence, livestock killed in a national park would not qualify for compensation. Unfortunately, the officers and staff took very long to determine the monetary value of the animal killed and to sanction the compensation, and there were kickbacks involved as well. So owners did not get compensated for months and the purpose of the scheme was partially defeated.

In 1998, when I was in charge of the tiger programme of WWF International, a cattle compensation scheme was started on similar lines in the forests around the Corbett National Park of Uttarakhand. The funding was given by WWF International, but the actual operation was carried out by the Corbett Foundation, an NGO. A reward was offered to anyone bringing news of a tiger or a leopard kill to the officers in the foundation, who were to proceed to the spot immediately in vehicles provided under the project. The value of the dead animal was assessed on the spot by the village elders. Half the compensation was paid immediately, the other half three days later, if no carnivore was found poisoned. A local person was to be employed on daily wages to watch over the kill to prevent it from being skinned by Dalits and from being poisoned to kill the carnivore. In the year and a half that I was in charge of the WWF programme, the number of livestock killed and compensated for crossed 1,600, and no case of poisoning was reported. From 1998 to 2014, compensation was paid for exactly 12,094 kills of tiger and leopard and not a single carnivore was killed or poisoned (Corbett Foundation 2015).

By the early 1970s it was evident that wildlife and the protected areas of the country required specialized management. The Indian Forest Service was geared for the exploitation and preservation of forests, not wildlife. Indeed, the job of the chief wildlife warden of a state had been regarded as a pariah post, outside the mainstream work of forestry. It was a job to be avoided and anyone posted there regarded himself sidelined.

But in that decade the situation changed. Officers assigned wildlife jobs had no fear of being bypassed and sidelined in career and promotions. Wildlife was becoming high-profile and officers manning protected areas were getting media exposure. At the core, as role models in the service, were stalwarts of the highest integrity and dedication – Saroj Raj Choudhury, Kailash Sankhala, Sunjoy Deb Roy, P. Lahan, S.P. Shahi, H.S. Panwar, Fateh Singh Rathore and Pushp Kumar, to name a few. I would wish to pay a special tribute to Saroj Choudhury, arguably the most outstanding of the low-profile, little-known officers of his time. I categorize conservationists into three levels. The first includes those who remain unflinchingly loyal to the cause of conservation even if they have to suffer for it in their life and career. Next, there are those who remain committed till the point where they are personally affected adversely, in their career or otherwise. The last group comprises those who take up the cause because they love wildlife, but are also motivated by their own ego and the desire for publicity and recognition. They would, of course, make no personal sacrifice for conservation. Understandably, there are very few who would fit in the first category. Saroj was certainly one of them.

Specialization in the field of wildlife conservation and particularly in the management of protected areas, as in other aspects of forestry and forest management, is a prerequisite – then and now. If a special wildlife wing could be created in each state manned by people who have opted for wildlife conservation as a career and are committed to it, and who are then retained in that post for a certain minimum duration so that they can be trained and allowed to dedicate themselves to their protected areas without frequent transfers, a great deal could be achieved. It would have to be ensured that these officers do not stagnate and suffer in their career. There were discussions whether there should be a separate cadre for a wildlife service or whether it should form a sub-cadre of the Indian Forest Service.

In late 1973, I had prepared a small note on the subject for the PMO, advocating that protected areas must not suffer a diarchy of control, where wildlife would be the responsibility of a park or sanctuary director and forestry operations would be with a territorial DFO in the same protected area. Manmohan Malhoutra sent the note to the PM, and in December 1973, a note came to the Ministry of Agriculture signed by Indira Gandhi, suggesting the creation of a special service or agency for wildlife management. I reproduce it here (see next page).

Prime Minister Gandhi also wrote separately to the chief ministers. Kailash Sankhala and I had initiated notes on this as well. Using these notes the then IGF K.L. Lahiri wrote a detailed proposal, largely supporting the idea of specialization in wildlife management and the strengthening of the wildlife wing in the states, at the same time emphasizing the primacy of the Indian Forest Service in this regard.

The cadre controlling authority of the Indian Forest Service (IFS) then was the Department of Personnel, which examined the proposal and opined that it was possible to have a viable wildlife sub-cadre of the Indian Forest Service. The states were consulted,

PRIME MINISTER'S SECRETARIAT

In the last few years wildlife conservation has made significant progress. A new legal frame-work has been enacted in the shape of the Wildlife(Protection) Act 1972. Project Tiger is under way and the States are more responsive. There is also larger financial allocation for wildlife programmes in the Fifth Plan.

I feel that the time has now come to introduce more specialised management for our parks and sanctuaries. At present, personnel are posted there in a haphazard manner without regard to expertise, aptitude or special dedication. Also postings are of such short duration that experience and expertise cannot be adequately built up. Many officers who have received wildlife training abroad or in Dehra Dun are being used for other jobs.

Throughout the world, wildlife management is becoming increasingly specialised. Our conservation cannot yield the desired results without a similar effort on our part. I should like some constructive thinking to be done on the possibility of creating a specialised Wildlife Service or agency. One possible approach with which I am in broad sympathy is enclosed, which might be studied and refined further by the Department of Personnel in consultation with the Inspector General of Forests.

Once a concrete scheme has been drawn up, the matter will have to be taken up with the States. I am writing to the Chief Ministers also.

(1) Creation of a Wildlife Department under the Forest Department at the Government level in those States which have large and important areas of wildlife. In the other States, there may be a separate Wildlife Wing under the Chief Conservator of Forests.

(2) Forest officers and field staff may be given an option to come to the Wildlife Service. Some special pay may be offered as an incentive. However, once having opted for it, these officers will not be allowed to go back to the regular forest line unless their promotion prospects within the Wildlife Service are blocked. The structure of the Wildlife service may itself be devised in such a manner that adequate promotion prospects are available. Alternatively, an officer may be given promotion in the Wildlife Service as and when his promotion in his parent Service becomes due. This will ensure long tenure, specialisation as well as attract people with the necessary commitment and enthusiasm.

(3) Personnel may be drawn from the Indian Forest Service, State Forest Services and to the extent that there is a shortfall from the open market or from other services. Special training will be imparted to these personnel in wildlife management. In addition, Government of India could offer to provide specialists on deputation as Consultants or Advisers.

(4) National Parks and Sanctuaries will be managed by the Wildlife Service exclusively, and all staff and activity will be under their control.

(5) If for commercial reasons, a State Government is unwilling to stop exploitation within a national park or sanctuary, it will be the duty of the Wildlife Service rather than the Forest Department to conduct and supervise timber felling etc. Such an arrangement will ensure that damage to wildlife is minimised.

Sd/- Indira Gandhi
27/12/1973

Minister of State (Shri Mirdha)
Copy to: 1) Minister of Agriculture
2) Cabinet Secretary.

but before a final decision to create a wildlife sub-cadre could be reached, Emergency was declared by Indira Gandhi in June 1975, and the matter was not pursued.

At this point I was selected to join the United Nations Environment Programme (UNEP) at their headquarters in Nairobi. When I returned to Delhi in 1985, I was appointed as a joint secretary in the newly created Ministry of Environment and Forests (MoEF). The MoEF had become the cadre controlling authority of the IFS. The IFS itself had stonewalled against the creation of a sub-cadre; indeed against the development of specialization in wildlife and in any specific field of forestry within the IFS. They felt it would weaken their service; I feel it would have made the service more effective and professional and, thus, more relevant and stronger.

In the 2006 report of the National Forest Commission chaired by the former Chief Justice of India B.N. Kirpal, and of which I was a member, there were five recommendations for creation of sub-cadres within the Indian Forest Service, to deal with wildlife and protected areas and other special fields in forestry. There was a note of dissent against these recommendations by the inspector general of forests and another IFS officer (MoEF 2006).

To return to the 1970s: After our discussion in the USA, Eskandar Firouz was already initiating steps for the reintroduction of the Asiatic lion in Iran, in exchange for the Asiatic cheetah. At that time there were approximately 260 wild lions in India and about 250 wild cheetah in Iran. Indira Gandhi had approved the exchange programme. Eskandar had appointed Paul Joslin, who had recently done his PhD on the Gir lion, to select sites for lion reintroduction in Iran and to prepare a plan. For India, it was a more difficult task to select a suitable site for cheetah reintroduction because of demographic pressures and the acute shortage of open-plains-living wild ungulates in the country. For, unlike in Africa, where the cheetah has over fifty species of mammals as prey, in India its main prey are the blackbuck and chinkara, and to a lesser degree the young of wild pig, nilgai, chital and chawsingha, where their habitats overlapped those of the cheetah. When the numbers of blackbuck and chinkara had plummeted in the plains, the cheetah had had an uphill task for survival. We were nonetheless making progress in the matter, but then I moved to the UNEP and, more importantly, Indira Gandhi got involved in the Emergency and was then defeated in the 1977 election. The regime of the Shah of Iran also fell and Eskandar Firouz was imprisoned by the new regime for some years.

However, while I was still director, wildlife preservation of India and negotiations for the lion–cheetah exchange were under way, we received in 1974 an intriguing request from Iran. His Imperial Highness Prince Abdorreza Pahlavi, the younger brother of the Shah of Iran, wanted to come to India to personally 'collect' for his museum a stag each of the swamp deer and hog deer. Prince Abdorreza was an avid hunter and had one of the largest collections of trophies in the world in his palace 'museum' in Tehran. India needed Iranian oil; we also wanted the Iranian cheetah. My batchmate in the Indian Foreign Service, Hamid Ansari, then the Indian ambassador to Iran and now the vice-president of India, stressed that allowing the collection of these trophies was important for bilateral relations. The Wild Life (Protection) Act had been passed, under which the rare and localized swamp deer or barasingha was in Schedule I and completely protected. Restricted hunting of some species was then still permissible under the Act, and I, therefore, recommended that if Prince Abdorreza wished to come to 'collect' a hog deer, it could be arranged in Assam. However, the swamp deer being a highly endangered species, hunting for even scientific purposes could not be allowed, we conveyed. We offered that we would take the first opportunity of acquiring a good stag killed by a tiger, if its skin on the neck and forequarters was not damaged. If His Imperial Highness should let us know how the specimen was to be mounted in his museum, the skinning of the barasingha tiger kill could be done accordingly. We never heard anything further from the prince.

In the summer of 1973, I went for the first time to the Andaman Islands. With the exception of the Ujung Kulon National Park in

Java, I have never seen such pristine, climax lowland dipterocarp forests anywhere as then in the Andamans. The Jarwa tribe had not been 'tamed' and we had to be careful traversing the forests of South and Middle Andamans. Of the six tribes that were the original inhabitants of these two groups of islands, the Onges of Little Andaman, the Shompens of the Great Nicobar and the Car Nicobarese of Car Nicobar who have converted to Christianity, were akin to the tribes of neighbouring Sumatra. The three other tribes of the main Andaman archipelago – the Jarwas, the Andamanese and the Sentinelese of North Sentinel Island – are of African origin. The most populous of the three were the Andamanese, who had the most contact with settlers from India, and as a result contracted their diseases to which they had no immunity. They had been reduced to a total population of twenty-three when I went to their only settlement on the North Passage Island. The Sentinelese were hostile to the settlers from the mainland and remain so till now, throwing spears at those who approach their shores. When I flew low over their settlement in North Sentinel Island in 1995, they came running out with their spears. The greatest conflict, however, was with the Jarwas in the Middle and South Andamans and more were killed in these encounters than were reported.

Interestingly, the Jarwas pursued and hunted the indigenous Andaman wild boar but would not kill the far more prolific chital, which had been introduced in the Andamans in the early twentieth century and had become the most numerous wild mammal in the archipelago, a pest which was destroying the local vegetation. On Interview Island where the forest had been clear-felled for forestry purposes, I saw herds in the open 'maidans'.

The chital of the Andamans had undergone an 'island attenuation', a shrinkage in size common to such introductions, in the space of some seven decades. A stag would not weigh much more than 50 kg and a hind about 10 kg less. They had developed dark circles around their eyes, for reasons unknown. Originally introduced on Ross Island, which was the headquarters of the governor of Andamans during the colonial period, they became so prolific that they were considered a pest prior to World War II. They colonized all the main islands of the Andaman Archipelago from Landfall Island in the north to Rutland Island in the south. Chital meat was being sold in Port Blair at a cheaper rate than goat meat in 1973. They had interbred with the introduced hog deer, exactly what had happened when Maharaja Ganga Singhji of Bikaner introduced the two species in the totally alien habitat of Gajner. I saw a flock of chital eating ficus fruits which had dropped on to the altar of a derelict, roofless church on Ross Island. The British had introduced a pair of leopards to curb the chital population. Fortunately, the pair turned out to be both males and, thus, the propagation of another preposterous introduction to rectify an earlier absurd one did not happen.

There were saltwater crocodiles near Diglipur in North Andaman. They were still being hunted then and, therefore, were shy. Their skins were being shipped to Madras. Instances of human and stray dogs being killed by crocodiles were then still common.

With the help of dogs, we were able to bring to bay an Andaman wild boar, larger than the pygmy hog but much smaller than the mainland wild boar. The boar had backed itself into a very dense thicket of stunted pandanus, grunting at the dogs and threatening them. They have short bristles on the back and rump, but these are totally absent on the nape and on top of the head. The wild pig of the Little Andaman I found to be larger in body and to have longer and narrower snouts than the specimens from the main Andaman Islands, with slightly shorter hooves and secondary hooves. They also had sparser body hair and, more noticeably, no bristles on the dorsal ridge and hardly any hair on the jaws, making them altogether different from the *Sus barbatus* of Malaysia. The colour of the Little Andaman pig is also much lighter than that of its counterpart on the main Andamans. It was reported that the pigs of Havelock Island, the largest island in Ritchie's Archipelago east of the main Andamans, were longer and bigger than elsewhere. The Suidae of the Andaman and Nicobar Islands need to be studied and classified before they get genetically mixed through interbreeding with domestic swine, which have been brought in by the settlers and by the Nicobarese themselves as they are avid keepers of domestic pigs.

In a swamp close to Hut Bay on Little Andaman, amongst a flock of about a 100 lesser whistling teal and a dozen cotton teal, I saw about twenty Andaman teal, my first in the wild. They were the most confiding of the duck there and allowed approach to within 30 m. The Andaman teal (also known as the grey or oceanic teal) is endemic to the Andamans, inhabiting freshwater lakes on the archipelago, which are not very common on the islands and were the first areas to be settled by humans. A well-known haunt of this bird was a freshwater lake on Neil Island in Ritchie's Archipelago. By 1973, the teal had disappeared from here after the lake was occupied by settlers from Bangladesh, who were refugees from the war of 1971. The Andaman teal is now amongst the most threatened birds of India.

Barking deer had also been introduced by the British administration, but not being as gregarious and prolific as the chital, nor as good swimmers, had not colonized the Andamans as effectively. Still, they were not uncommon in the Middle Andamans, where I saw their pellets in the forest.

Another introduction, accidental this time, was of Asiatic elephants on Interview Island, from where they had colonized other islands. They had been brought in to assist in the extraction of timber by P.C. Ray, a contractor who had been given a lease for forestry operations. The Andamans were then one of the largest suppliers of wood in India and the sawmill on Chatham Island, near the capital Port Blair, was reputed to be the largest sawmill in southern Asia. Relations with P.C. Ray soured and he filed cases against the government, which I had to handle as deputy secretary in the Ministry of Agriculture, the Andamans being a Union territory. Forestry operations leased to him were stopped and the elephant went feral, bred and spread.

In the summer of 1974, the IBWL chaired by Karan Singh with

Salim Ali and Dharmakumarsinhji as vice chairmen, appointed a committee headed by Dharmakumarsinhji with myself as member secretary to search for a second home for the Indian lion. I visited Todgarh and Jaisamand sanctuaries in Rajasthan to consider their potential. An experiment to create a second home for the Asiatic lion outside of Saurashtra, carried out in the Chandraprabha Sanctuary near Varanasi in Uttar Pradesh had failed fifteen years earlier. The IBWL had decided to try again, and Dharmakumarsinhji had suggested the two sanctuaries in Rajasthan, but I found them unsuitable. I felt that the most appropriate second home then was the Barda Hills near Porbandar in Saurashtra, which had had lions till the 1880s. But the Government of Gujarat was not prepared to declare Barda even as a wildlife sanctuary at that point of time. They had, however, accepted my suggestion to establish the Little Rann of Kutch as a sanctuary to protect the habitat of another species endemic to Gujarat, the wild ass. At 4,841 sq. km, it became in 1973 the largest wildlife sanctuary in the country.

By this time it was only too evident that it was imperative that India's protected areas should encompass all the diverse biomes and habitat types, and cover the last refuges of localized and endemic species. An attempt had already been made in this direction in the selection of the first tiger reserves, as mentioned earlier. The country's protected areas, however, did not adequately cover marine, coastal, montane and grassland-arid ecosystems, and the fauna and flora of these eco-types and those endemic to them. Though the Little Rann of Kutch had been established as a sanctuary, it was almost entirely a salt pan. It was essential to identify suitable areas in the arid west of the country where desert parks and sanctuaries could be established, to save both the eco-types and the endangered species dependent upon them, particularly the gravely threatened great Indian bustard. With this end in view, I undertook in 1973 a survey of the districts of Barmer, Jaisalmer, Jodhpur and Bikaner in Rajasthan, with the chief wildlife warden of Rajasthan and its director of tourism. The paradigms for consideration were that the areas should not be in the command area of the Rajasthan canal then under construction; that they should not be adjacent to the Pakistan border and not required for military purposes; that they should be relatively free from demographic usage and, if possible, they should be located so as to take advantage of the zeal and commitment of the Bishnoi communities living on these lands; that the area should be accessible for management; and of course, that it should contain wildlife populations, especially of the endangered species.

The greatest conservation asset of western Rajasthan is the Bishnoi community. However, their lands did not hold any permanent populations of the great Indian bustard. So our team selected a rectangular area of about 160 sq. km east of the Jaisalmer–Barmer road, near Devikot, for the establishment of a desert national park. It was mostly fallow land with very little cultivation. Only four villages and the peripheral lands of just five others were situated in it, which then could have been easily resettled. There were two enclosures in it of 5 sq. km each, made under a pasture development scheme. The topography was representative and we saw chinkara, houbara bustard, desert fox and eighteen great Indian bustard. Kailash Sankhala, who was soon to return to Rajasthan as its chief wildlife warden, selected a site further west, which made the area of the Desert National Park much larger but more difficult to manage because of the existence of a large number of villages and the consequent conflict with human interest. Today, only two enclosures near Sudasiri contain a vestige of the fauna of the desert and are the last refuge of the great Indian bustard in the state.

We also recommended the creation of a sanctuary at Jamboji in Bikaner district, the headquarters of the patron saint of the Bishnois, and another at Doli, some 50 km west of Jodhpur city. This Dhava–Doli area of about 40 km then held 1,000 to 1,500 blackbuck and the tract of about 150 km around it a total of about 3,000 antelope. We ourselves saw over 400 blackbuck in just 1 sq. km around the tube well at Doli. Here we met Sobha Ram, a combination of Bishnoi priest, patriarch and blackbuck guardian angel.

In the mid-1960s drought had struck Rajasthan and other parts of India for seven consecutive years. The Bishnois of Doli village pooled their meagre funds to hire water tankers to bring water for 'their' blackbuck, at the height of the successive droughts. Presided over by Sobha Ram, they also bored a tube well. At the height of summer when water was unobtainable, the blackbuck hovered around the village well, to lick the droplets that fell off the bodies of bathing women and accumulated on the masonry floor. In the worst period, Sobha Ram did not waste even the water with which he washed his cooking utensils. He left the vessels outside his hut with the dirty water in them and the blackbuck came and licked them dry. Then, in June, two blackbuck died. Sobha Ram vowed that he too would die, that he would not drink till his patron deity relented and sent rain. On the second night of his fast, it rained; an occurrence to which the villagers bore testimony (Ranjitsinh 1997).

In late 1973, Kalpana and I visited Bonn, West Germany, where I attended a conference convened by the World Wildlife Fund. We then took the opportunity to go with our friend Helmuth Reichel to see the chamois and the Sardinian mouflon in the Alps in Carinthia, Austria. With other friends Peter and Adrienne Jackson and Fred Stoever, who had joined us, we proceeded to the Gran Paradiso National Park, in the Aosta Valley in the Italian Alps, to see the Alpine ibex (*Capra ibex ibex*) and more chamois. Gran Paradiso is one of the grandest parks I have seen, with scenery and wildlife to match. But it also holds an iconic status in the history of conservation. The Alpine ibex had been exterminated in its entire range in the Alps. Less than fifty survived in the Gran Paradiso, which was then a hunting reserve of the king of Italy, at the beginning of the twentieth century. At about the same time, lions in India were also less than a hundred, as mentioned in an earlier chapter. With effective steps taken for their preservation, both species were saved. The surplus populations of ibex from Gran Paradiso have been reintroduced and spread out into former habitats in Italy, France, Germany, Austria and Switzerland, and now there are over 20,000 spread over the

Alps. There is a lesson in this for all of us – while there is life, there is hope; if there is a pair, we must not despair, as even two can make a multitude. But the habitat must exist, as also the determination to save the species.

The game guards of the park were not regularly paid in those days. Italians are a volatile people and if the wildlife staff had not received their dues when the autumnal hunting season arrived, the guards would allow hunters to poach the very ibex they had assiduously protected in the rest of the year, as a mark of protest! Two decades ago the guards of the Valmiki Tiger Reserve of Bihar did not receive their salaries for almost two years, but thankfully they did not resort to the same tactic.

Around this time the situation in Keoladeo Ghana National Park in Bharatpur was getting critical. Daily, thousands of cattle used to invade this small park to graze, the buffalo even wading into the wetlands to join the Siberian cranes in the winter. At the same time, the nilgai, blackbuck and wild pig from the park would raid the crops in adjacent fields. When I had been drafting the Wild Life (Protection) Act, I had occasion to meet Raj Bahadur, then a member of parliament from Bharatpur and a minister in Indira Gandhi's cabinet. He was so fed up with the problem that he told me that the Government of India should take over the Keoladeo Park. At his behest, the Rajasthan state government was considering the proposal. For this reason, I had made a provision in Section 38 of the Act, under which the Government of India could operate a sanctuary or park transferred to it by a state, or declare one in any area similarly transferred. The Rajasthan government then decided not to transfer Keoladeo Ghana but asked for funds from the Central government to build a wall around it, to prevent wild animals from walking out and damaging crops. Under the newly approved scheme of Central assistance to national parks, we offered to support the project financially over a period of time, provided that the state government did not allow livestock to enter the park through its gates. Rajasthan would not promise this and so Central aid was not forthcoming, whereupon they commenced building the wall with their own funds. Later, when I was no longer director of wildlife preservation, the wall was completed and livestock were not permitted to enter. There was public agitation and a confrontation, ending with police firing in 1982 in which lives were lost. But the ban on livestock entry remained.

In 1972, Gujarat had been placed under president's rule and K.T. Satarawala, a very upright IAS officer interested in conservation, had been posted as advisor to the governor. He launched the Gir Project and sought advice from the Bombay Natural History Society and individuals including myself. The area of the Gir Sanctuary was extended by 147 sq. km and 592 families of cattle owners or maldharis were resettled outside of the sanctuary with their livestock, to pave the way for the establishment of a human-settlement-free national park. A wall around the periphery of the sanctuary was started, supported financially in part by the Central government, to prevent entry of cattle, ultimately resulting in a peripheral wall extending to 380 km. I am reasonably certain that had it not been for the president's rule, all this would not have been achieved, especially the shifting of the maldharis en masse, despite the favourable conservation milieu of that time.

Meanwhile, Billy Arjan Singh had been writing to the prime minister about the problems of Dudhwa. We were directed to take up the matter with the Government of Uttar Pradesh. The chief conservator of forests, UP, there being no principal chief conservators then, was G.N. Singh, a classmate of Billy, but how they disliked each other! In that era, a forest officer took pride in the revenue he earned from the forests under his charge. The inspector general of forests in the agriculture ministry received a reply from G.N. Singh that UP obtained an average revenue of ₹85 lakh annually from the forests of Dudhwa. If the Government of India wanted UP to declare Dudhwa a national park whereby forestry operations would have to stop, it should compensate the state of UP with the same amount on an annual basis, presumably in perpetuity.

I put up a note stating that the PM had expressed a desire that Dudhwa should become a national park, and the reply received from the chief conservator of UP was being enclosed, ending with a mention that the PM may wish to see this. The note went to the PMO after the perusal of the IGF, secretary (agriculture) and the minister. A week after its dispatch, I received a phone call from Lucknow: the letter from the chief conservator may be ignored; UP was declaring Dudhwa as a national park. It was learnt that upon seeing the note Indira Gandhi phoned the chief minister of UP, H.N. Bahuguna, and the rest, as the cliché goes, is history. No individual has contributed so significantly to the creation and conservation of Dudhwa as Billy Arjan Singh.

Another matter of serious concern was the plight of the three crocodilian species in India – the gharial, the saltwater crocodile and the freshwater crocodile or mugger. All three had been extensively exploited for their skins and killed whenever they got entangled in fishing nests. The mugger and more so the 'saltie' can be dangerous to human life and there is an unfortunate universal antipathy towards crocodilians. After an all-India survey, a report from renowned herpetologist Romulus Whitaker had just appeared stating that there were perhaps not more than fifty breeding pairs of gharial left in the country. The gharial require flowing streams, which were fast being dammed up, including the Ramganga Dam that submerged the most productive portions of the Corbett National Park and affected what was then the only safe gharial population. By this time, the gharial had disappeared from the Manas river and was on the verge of extinction in the Brahmaputra.

In 1973, the Ministry of Agriculture received a project proposal from the Food and Agriculture Organization of the United Nations (FAO) to start a commercial project for the breeding of crocodiles in the Delhi Zoo, for harvesting and selling their skins. With some effort, I was able to persuade the FAO to approve a modified project to breed all the three crocodile species in captivity for release into the wild, with a footnote that if the species then became safe and surplus in the wild, we would harvest them in captivity. I suspect the FAO knew all along that that would not happen, but they cooperated. Robert Bustard, a renowned crocodile and turtle expert, was selected to oversee the project, and arrived in 1974.

Bustard surveyed tracts of rivers where the gharial was still known to survive – the upper reaches of the Chambal river in Rajasthan and of the Girwa in Uttar Pradesh, and the lower reaches of the Mahanadi in Odisha. Viable populations were located at Rawatbhata on the Chambal river, above Katerniaghat on the Girwa river and at the Satkosia gorge on the Mahanadi. However, we could not locate gharial nests anywhere. One day, I got a phone call from Bob Bustard that gharial eggs would be available in the upper Nepal portion of the Girwa, but we had no permission to obtain them. It would have taken far too long to get permission from Kathmandu through the 'proper channels', by which time the nesting season would have been over and a year lost. I, therefore, advised Bob to get the eggs from where he could, but to make sure not to get caught. The eggs arrived, were hatched at the newly established breeding centre at Kukrail near Lucknow, and four years later the young gharial offspring were released in Katerniaghat, which became a sanctuary. It is today, perhaps, the best place in the world to see large numbers of gharial, together with the Gangetic dolphin. It certainly eased my conscience to see sizeable numbers of gharial upstream in the Girwa, in Nepal, in 1998. Effective protection in the Katerniaghat Sanctuary has helped the saurian and other wildlife on both sides of the international border.

More captive rearing centres for the gharial and the freshwater crocodile were established near Morena in Madhya Pradesh and for the mugger at Sasan in the Gir National Park in Gujarat, near the Kamleshwar Reservoir, which now has one of the densest populations of the mugger in the country. Bob Bustard took up residence at the Satkosia gorge in Odisha and supervised the breeding of both the gharial and the mugger. He also trained herpetologists who became assets to conservation in India – B.C. Choudhury and L.A.K. Singh amongst them.

For the saltwater crocodile, all were convinced that the best place was Bhitarkanika in Odisha. The Sundarban of West Bengal, which, combined with the Bangladesh Sundarban is the largest mangrove area in the world, was already protected as a tiger reserve. Besides, Bhitarkanika was richer in biodiversity than the much larger Sundarban and held some of the largest 'salties' in the world, including perhaps the largest skull on record, in the possession of the Raja of Kanika. So a captive-rearing centre for the saltwater crocodile was started at Dangmal and Bhitarkanika became a sanctuary. Bustard then reported the mass breeding of the olive ridley turtle at Gahirmatha, close to Bhitarkanika. We were successful in persuading the Government of Odisha to declare the Gahirmatha Beach as a sanctuary and later to involve the Indian Coast Guard in patrolling offshore when the olive ridley 'arribada' arrived to breed there each spring, to prevent the traditional catching of turtles for the Kolkata market.

While the crocodile project was under way, the director for fisheries in the Ministry of Food and Agriculture, who sat in an office a few doors away from mine, issued a circular that if crocodiles got entangled in any nylon nets of fishermen – nylon netting having come into fashion lately – they should be killed to save the precious nets. When I protested, he said that crocodiles ate fish and so were an enemy of fishermen. I showed him a published paper saying that the Nile crocodile helped the Nile perch by eating the catfish which preyed on the perch, and said that in India too the crocodiles were the main predators of catfish and, hence, were a help to fishery. His reply was that the paper applied to the Nile crocodile and not to the Indian crocodilians!

The crocodile captive breeding and rearing project became the most successful wildlife conservation project of its kind in India, perhaps in Asia. Its ramifications were multiple. Not only were the three crocodilian species gravely endangered, they were feared, despised and not really regarded as creatures worth protecting. There were neither river sanctuaries nor specific sanctuaries for any of the crocodilians and they received incidental protection only because some of their habitats were in protected areas, like the Ramganga in Corbett National Park, Kamleshwar in the Gir and the channels of the Sundarban Tiger Reserve. Even the renowned conservationists of the country knew little of crocodilian ecology and the officers and staff of the forest departments of the states knew nothing about captive breeding and rearing for release into the wild, of any species.

It was fortunate that we started with crocodiles, as their captive breeding is relatively simpler than that of any other animal. Though there is a variation amongst the species, the eggs of a mugger, if hatched at a temperature of 31 to 31.5 degrees Celsius, would produce both male and female hatchlings; if hatched at 31.5 to 33 degrees, the hatchlings would mainly be males; and if hatched between 28 to 31 degrees most of the hatchlings would turn out to be females. Hatching at 33 to 34 degrees could result in freak offspring, and at temperatures above 34 degrees the embryos would die. This provided an opportunity for virtual mass production of whatever sex one wanted in a given clutch of eggs. And there is more. About 90 per cent of crocodilian hatchings do not reach maturity in the wild. If, however, they are kept in captivity for about three years and have grown to about a metre in length when released, the chances of these sub-adults reaching maturity and a breeding age are about 85 per cent. Besides, the technique of catching fish is instinctive in them, not taught by the parents as is the case with feline carnivores. Crocodiles reared in captivity and fed only dead fish will start catching fish for themselves when released in the wild. Crocodiles have not changed in about three million years as they have already evolved to perfection, the ultimate survivors.

The crocodilian metabolism is so low that an adult can survive on a daily diet of a kilo and a half of fish, which is what a cormorant needs per day! Young crocodiles need much less, which makes their rearing relatively cheap. The breeding and rearing centres became so prolific that restocking wild populations was more extensive and intensive than earlier expected. This was accompanied by an increase in populations in the wild due to the establishment of a number of riverine and estuarine sanctuaries – Chambal, Katerniaghat, Ranganathittu, Indravati, Coringa, Bhitarkanika and protected areas in the Andamans and elsewhere. By the time I returned to Delhi for my second stint as director, wildlife preservation, in 1985, the populations of all the three crocodilian species had become safe in the wild and we were in a position to advise the states to shut down most of the breeding centres and to stop Central funding, retaining only a few to maintain the knowhow and the techniques now learnt, especially for the gharial. The Madras Snake Park was also breeding these saurians and they were getting far too numerous there. During my second tenure as director, wildlife preservation of India, Pakistan approached us for captive gharial, as they had by then lost the species in the Indus, and we allowed export to Pakistan from the snake park.

Apart from ensuring the survival of the three crocodilian species, the major ramification of this project was a widening of the vision and the concept of conservation, hitherto confined to larger mammals and their habitats. For the first time, riverine and estuarine habitats were protected for non-mammalian conservation, giving protection thereby to a multitude of other species, including endangered ones like the Gangetic dolphin, otters and the mahseer, and the nesting sites of rare birds like the Indian skimmer and of the river terrapins.

In the autumn of 1974, I went to Australia, New Zealand and Papua New Guinea. The bird life, especially of the parrot family, was amazing. In the Fiordland National Park on the South Island of New Zealand, I saw the conservation project for kakapos, which are partially flightless, ground-living and one of the largest parrots in the world. Further north in the Mount Cook National Park, I saw my first Himalayan tahr, introduced in the early part of the twentieth century and now far more numerous on that island than in the whole of the Himalaya. Regarded as pests and 'noxious animals' like other introduced species such as the European chamois, some thousands of tahr had been culled from helicopters and otherwise from Mount Cook National Park alone. Near Lake Taupo in the Tongariro National Park on the North Island of New Zealand, I saw another introduced species, the Japanese sika deer (*Cervus nippon*).

In Australia, apart from seeing the bewildering variety of kangaroos, wallabies, wallaroos and the exquisite corals and marine life of the Great Barrier Reef off Green Island near Cairns, I went into the 'outback' of Queensland. We flushed a dingo (*Canis dingo*), the most hated animal in Australia. My host, a police officer, pulled out his rifle and cut loose at the galloping canid. At the shots, there rose to the sky in a radius of some 300 m around us, thirty-eight Australian bustards, almost identical to our great Indian bustard.

The Ministry of Agriculture, with the assistance of the FAO had initiated a project to survey the forest resources of India, with a view to establish forest-based industries. A helicopter had been provided for aerial survey. Heading the project was J.J. Dutta, IFS, later to be the chief wildlife warden in Madhya Pradesh during my tenure as forest secretary. We arranged that the survey for Manipur should take place in March 1975, the driest month of the year when the water level in the Keibul Lamjao Sanctuary would be at its lowest and the floating morass of vegetation, the 'phumdi', would have settled on the soil.

Circling low over Keibul Lamjao with Dutta for forty-five minutes, we could count each animal, the Manipur brow-antlered deer (sangai), hog deer and wild pig. We could find just fourteen sangai – five stags, six hinds and three fawns. This was the total world population of the animal, which made the sangai the rarest large mammalian taxa in the whole world. The population of Central African white rhino, now extinct in the wild, was then sixteen in the Garamba National Park of the Democratic Republic of the Congo (Ranjitsinh 1975).

Next morning I went around the sanctuary, appealing to the local people to save the sangai, their sangai, and to not graze their livestock in the sanctuary. Keibul Lamjao is the only place in the world for the sangai, I said. It is the only place in the world for our cattle to graze was the reply. I returned to Delhi, made my report on the situation to the PMO and requested the Government of Manipur to upgrade the Keibul Lamjao Sanctuary to a national park and declare the sangai the state animal of Manipur. By this time Manmohan Malhoutra had left the PMO and had been succeeded by another college-mate, Salman Haidar, later to become the foreign secretary of India.

Indira Gandhi asked me to visit Manipur every few months. She took up the matter with the Government of Manipur. In 1977, Keibul Lamjao became a park, the sangai became the state animal and the population of the deer increased to over 100. When I went back to Keibul Lamjao in 1993 and surveyed the sangai again from a helicopter, the count was ninety-eight, thirty-eight stags, forty-eight hinds and twelve fawns. The night before, a group of enthusiasts had come to see us and asked us not to disturb the sangai unduly in the census. They said that there were over 100 non-governmental organizations (NGOs) dedicated to the sangai and Keibul Lamjao. A dance called 'The Dancing Deer of Manipur', mimicking the prancing of the sangai over the floating phumdi grass had been evolved in the Manipur style of dance. The people had come to identify with their deer.

The year 1975 was also momentous for me personally. The Gujarat government nationalized the forests of my father Pratapsinhji, which had been kept as private property by my grandfather Rajsaheb Amarsinghji as part of the agreement when the princely state of Wankaner merged with the Union of India in 1948. Part of the forest was behind the palace at Wankaner and though the leopards had become extinct by then, wolves, nilgai, hyenas and chinkara were still present. The other forest was Rampara, 34 sq. km in extent and associated with my boyhood memories of wildlife. The legislation of the Gujarat government, for acquiring these private forests as well as those of other former princes of Gujarat, had come to the forest division of the Ministry of Agriculture and I was aware of it. One day, Father called me and my elder brother to ask as to what we should do with these private forests before they went from our control. We had seen other forests of Wankaner state vanish after the merger of the state and only our private forests had remained reasonably intact. Some of the other former princes were already extracting timber and other produce and selling these before surrendering the forests. All three of us agreed that we would not do the same, but hand over the forests with their tree cover intact. This was the right decision. Later in 1988, during my second stint as director, wildlife preservation of India, Government of Gujarat was persuaded to declare Rampara a sanctuary and today lion reintroduction is being contemplated there and the leopard and sambar have returned.

The Stockholm Conference of 1972 had led to the creation of a United Nations agency to deal with the environment – the United Nations Environment Programme (UNEP), which also dealt with forests, wildlife and ecology, thereby competing with the much older FAO. My five-year term with the Central government was nearing completion and instead of returning to my state of MP and being assigned the usual potpourri of jobs earmarked for IAS officers, I was keen to specialize in environmental and nature conservation. I, therefore, wished to join the UNEP and was facilitated in this by Kai Curry-Lindahl of the IUCN, who had joined UNEP and who had seen my work in Kanha. In the summer of 1975, when I was leaving to join the UNEP and went to say goodbye to Indira Gandhi, Emergency had been declared. I met her, accompanied by Salman Haidar, in her private office on Akbar Road close to the spot where she was assassinated in 1984. She inquired about the status of the Manipur deer and suggested that I should come back to India and serve here, after my stint with the UNEP. That was the last time I met her personally.

My post of director, wildlife preservation of India devolved upon another IAS officer, Nalni Jayal – dedicated, unassuming and unsung. It was he who helped Indira Gandhi with the forty-second amendment of the Constitution in January 1977, whereby forests and wildlife became concurrent subjects, instead of purely state subjects as of yore. Now, the Government of India has concurrent powers with the states to legislate on these subjects. Jayal was also in charge when, on the return of Indira Gandhi to power in 1979, the Forest Conservation ordinance followed by the Act were mooted, which have largely reduced the rapid decline of forest lands in the country.

There is an anecdote pertaining to Indira Gandhi and wildlife, which is perhaps little known. Her Congress party had been totally routed in the election of 1977 and she had lost her seat in parliament. Under the new Janata government, she was arrested for her role in the Emergency and was being taken in custody, to the Sultanpur Bird Sanctuary near Delhi. This was ironic, as Sultanpur had become a sanctuary mainly at the instance of Indira Gandhi. A railway line had to be crossed for the motorcade to reach Sultanpur and as a train was approaching, the gates of the railway crossing were closed. Indira Gandhi was allowed out of her car and she went and sat on the parapet of a culvert, very dejected and depressed. She was very soon recognized, a crowd collected and people began calling out her name and cheering. The officials who were with her say her demeanour changed as she realized that she was not a total national reject, that some segments still admired her. By the time she reached Sultanpur, she apparently was a different person and the old grit to fight back was returning. Did the road to a wildlife sanctuary pave the way for her return to power?

In hindsight, one can say that the decade following 1972, for the most part of which Indira Gandhi was the prime minister, was perhaps the most significant epoch of all in the post-Independence conservation history of the country.

8

The Wilds of Asia

In August 1975, I reported at the UNEP headquarters in the Kenyatta International Convention Centre, Nairobi, where I underwent training in the workings of the organization. Maurice Strong of Canada, who had been the first head of UNEP, had resigned and M.K. Tolba of Egypt had taken over. As part of my training, I was sent to the College of African Wildlife Management at Mweka, Tanzania, the only institute of its kind then in the Eastern hemisphere. It ran a diploma course in wildlife management for students and a certificate course for in-service personnel. Elephant control in national parks and fire as a tool in park land management were then hotly debated subjects, as they remain even now.

I travelled to Tsavo, Amboseli, Nakuru, Aberdare, Mt Kenya and Meru national parks and Shimba Hills, Maasai Mara and the Malindi Marine National Park and Reserve, revisiting many areas I had seen on a visit to the country eleven years earlier. In Tanzania, I went to Ngorongoro and Manyara, Tarangire and Serengeti national parks. These are some of the greatest wildlife refuges in the world. But there had been changes since my 1964 visit. I did see eighty-three lions, but not a single leopard or cheetah despite making efforts to find them. This time I saw only twenty-two rhinos and barring Amboseli, these were only in the Tanzanian parks and, significantly, confined to areas around park headquarters and guard posts. In 1964, I had seen more rhinos in just three days in a hunting area in the Machakos district of Kenya. In 1975, I did not see any elephant bull carrying a pair of tusks that could have been heavier than 50 kg; on the earlier visit I had seen pairs of tusks twice that weight.

My stay in East Africa convinced me further of the importance of grassland ecosystems, among the most ignored in the world, particularly in Asia. Of Africa's total area of about 29 million square kilometres, 1.3 million is classed as grasslands. Desert grasses are amongst the most advanced types of grasses and are able to support human and animal life where none otherwise would survive. Grasses provide a superb integrated representation of prevailing climatic and soil factors and are a prime insurance against soil erosion. They form the largest family of living plants in the world, and their uses – from pulp to protein production – are endless. On them have existed, from Pleistocene times, the greatest wild animal biomass the world has ever known.

Grasslands, therefore, are not only the greatest natural resource of Africa, but also one of the most important land systems the world over. Yet, it is ironic and somewhat surprising that these are some of the most misused areas in the world and grassland ecology some of the least understood. No other land system has been so modified by man – both in extent and in character. Today, the grasslands of the world are the greatest food production areas for mankind. I advised UNEP that grasslands should be one of their focal points of interest as desertification then was. Unfortunately, this did not happen, as it has not happened in India either. The bureaucracy in the UN is as influenced by politics as are departments of national governments.

At the end of 1975, UNEP opened a regional office for the Asia-Pacific region at Bangkok, Thailand, and I was posted there as a regional adviser.

We had been very concerned about environmental degradation in India. But the situation in other countries of South and South-East Asia was even more alarming, particularly the pace at which forest cover was being lost. In Thailand, the proportion of area under forests had reduced from 58 per cent in 1952 to 33 per cent by 1978. In the Philippines, about 9 million hectares amounting to one-third of the land area of the country was susceptible to erosion. Some 200 million shifting cultivators in the region were annually burning 8 million hectares of forests a year. This was affecting about 300 million hectares of forests in the Asia-Pacific region and Asia was losing 5 million hectares of forests each year (Ranjitsinh 1979).

Protected areas covered 2.79 per cent of the total area of Asia. Bhutan with 18.79 per cent had the maximum percentage and China, Burma and Bangladesh with less than 1 per cent had the lowest proportion of protected areas in the entire region (Ranjitsinh 1989b). India then had 3.93 per cent – less than Nepal, Pakistan and Sri Lanka.

A very rewarding concomitant of working with UNEP was the opportunity to visit a large number of protected areas in Asia and beyond, and to meet conservationists in both government and outside. One such individual whom it was a privilege to know was Boonsong Lekagul of Bangkok. Boonsong reminded me of Salim Ali. Both were pioneer conservationists in their respective countries; both had been hunters but soon converted to become father figures for wildlife conservation. Both were basically birdmen but their conviction and compassion encompassed all of nature. Both were childlike, guileless and self-effacing. Salim Ali gave all his earnings to the Bombay Natural History Society; Boonsong gave his for the acquisition of wildlife habitats for conservation. Most important of all, in all their conservation efforts they wanted nothing for themselves, only for the cause they passionately believed in.

Boonsong told me the tale of the Schomburgk's deer recounted in a previous chapter. It is worth recording here how this animal of Thailand became extinct. Named neua saman by the Thai, the stags carrying antlers with as many as twenty-eight points, this deer occurred (in historical times, at least) only in the flood plains of the Chao Phraya river on which Bangkok stands. Like the swamp dear, the brow-antlered deer and the much smaller hog deer, it preferred alluvial grasslands to which it was highly adapted. The neua saman paid the penalty, as did other deer, for its over-specialization to arable lands most wanted by man for cultivation. By the beginning of the twentieth century, Schomburgk's deer was already gravely endangered. Even after the Duke of Bedford's emissaries returned empty-handed twice from Thailand, as recounted earlier, there were still stray instances of dead Schomburgk's deer turning up in Bangkok, and Bedford sent his men again to Thailand.

This third time, Rangsit sent them to the forests in the west on the Burma border. More sambar, more disappointment and failure. None knew that the Neua Saman was not a forest but a grassland animal. All the while that the country was being scoured, remnant stragglers of Schomburgk's deer, according to Boonsong, still lurked in the high grasslands in what is now Soi Asoke off Sukhumvit, which is where I lived and where Boonsong told me this story, a bare 8 km from the Royal Palace.

Then came the Second World War. The last specimen of Schomburgk's deer in captivity, belonging to a temple near Bangkok, was killed by a drunken Mon tribal in 1938. Thus became extinct a magnificent animal which carried more true tines, or branches, on its antlers than any other species of deer. This is another instance to show that, in developing countries at least, interest in and commitment to conservation must come from those in power.

In December 1975 when I arrived in Thailand, the country was going through one of its periodic phases of democracy. The previous military regime had recently been overthrown following an incident curiously related to wildlife. The ruling military junta had made the Khao Yai National Park, a premier protected area in the country, their holiday retreat, with luxurious villas for the presiding generals. They had built a beautiful golf course in Khao Yai with noticeboards that said 'Beware of golf balls' on roads that went past the golf greens, perhaps the most incongruous signage I have ever seen in a protected area. These 'greens' were well kept and watered and I have seen numerous sambar and barking deer on them after dark. But the generals were not satisfied with making

Khao Yai their playground; they wanted to hunt in the park as well. They shot a gaur and left for Bangkok, leaving their minions to bring home the meat. The helicopter was overloaded with gaur flesh, and crashed and killed the occupants, en route to Bangkok. University students in Bangkok, galled by the injustices of military rule, gathered in an open ground in front of the university and the Royal Palace, adjacent to the temple of the Emerald Buddha. They refused to leave, so the army brought in tanks, hemming in the congregation from all sides. Tempers flared and in the resultant firing students were killed. King Bhumibol, revered by the people like a deity, came from his palace to his ancestral home, ordered food for the starving students, called in their representatives and, after hearing them, dismissed the military regime.

Being perhaps the best park close to Bangkok, Khao Yai was our frequent destination on weekends. The Thais love waterfalls and Khao Yai has its share of them. Besides, I have never seen so many great pied hornbills anywhere else. Near Chiengmai in the north, we visited the montane national parks of Doi Suthep and Doi Inthanon, the latter holding the highest peak in Thailand and some of the last of its goral population.

Another favourite was Khao Sam Roi Yot National Park, rising abruptly from the sea in the Kra Isthmus. For someone accustomed to seeing the serow at altitudes above 3,000 m in the Himalaya, it was a novel experience to find them here. I have a photo of a serow below a cliff with the sea shimmering behind and a blurred image of a white-bellied sea eagle which had barged into the photo frame.

In association with representatives of the FAO and IUCN, I helped prepare the first conservation strategy for Thailand. In this context, we travelled to a number of protected areas, notable amongst them being the lovely Phu Kradueng clothed in tropical pines, Nam Nao, Huai Kha Khaeng, which was then reported to hold the last population of wild buffalo in Thailand and where we saw fresh footprints of tiger, and to the Tarutao Marine National Park with its fish and corals.

In early 1976, I returned to India as the IUCN and WWF – which were financially assisting Project Tiger – desired a review of the project on its completing three years. The three-member committee for the review comprised Paul Leyhausen, chairman of the Cat Specialist Group of the Survival Service Commission of the IUCN, Colin Holloway of the IUCN, and me from UNEP. I travelled to five tiger reserves – Melghat, Kanha, Simlipal, Betla and Ranthambore, as well to as to Dudhwa to meet Billy Arjan Singh. The conservation status of these protected areas had definitely improved and what was most inspiring was the enthusiasm of the younger officers now in the field.

In Simlipal, I stayed with the redoubtable Saroj Raj Choudhury and his pet tigress Khairi, whom Saroj loved like a daughter. Apparently, Khairi took a liking to me and would follow me to my room, to hug and play. She would not unsheathe her claws, but I think tigers do not have adequate control over their dewclaw, the fifth one a little higher up the foreleg. Whenever she would hug or gently slap me with her paw, she would tear my clothes and scratch the skin with her dewclaw. Early morning she would enter my room and circle my bed. I would feign sleep, whereupon she would jump on to my bed and put her face a few inches above mine. If that was not enough to make me get up, she would sit on my legs, all 160 kg of her.

Khairi had grown up with a chowsingha fawn and they had been great friends, chasing and playing with each other. In three years, the antelope had grown to some 15 kg, Khairi to about 150 kg. One day, both were sitting side by side when the antelope took off to initiate a chase and play. Khairi grabbed him as she must have done scores of times earlier, but this time she broke his neck. Saroj buried the chowsingha in the garden; Khairi sat beside the grave for three days without food. Saroj tried to train Khairi to live freely in the wild, without success. She continued to live in his home until one day she killed and ate a pi-dog that had entered the premises, got rabies and died. I saw Saroj soon after. He had lost interest in life and did not live long thereafter.

Akhand shikar, the ritual tribal hunt was still going on in Simlipal and animals could only be seen at night. In Kanha, villages were being relocated under the able leadership of H.S. Panwar. In Melghat, driving from Dhakna–Kolkaz to Chikhaldara, I saw a caracal in daylight, not too far from the nearby forests of Burhanpur where I had seen one in 1964. In Ranthambore, it was good to meet up with Fateh Singh Rathore and to see the improvement in both habitat and fauna that one man's dedication had been able to achieve in such a short span of time. In Betla, it was the chief conservator of forests, Bihar, S.P. Sahi, who was the moving spirit for wildlife conservation in Bihar. There was a unique record in Betla, which should have been maintained for all parks – of the flow of water in the rivers emanating from the region at the time when it was made a tiger reserve and three years later. The monsoonal rivers, where in the past the water flow had stopped by September, were now flowing till December or later; those in which the flow previously stopped by the end of December were now alive till the end of March, and those that had previously stopped flowing by about the end of March had become perennial. If this is what watersheds can achieve by the establishment of protected areas in the country, national parks and sanctuaries have a great deal more to contribute to the national weal than the preservation of fauna and flora.

In Dudhwa, the wildlife situation had also improved, especially in the Sathiana area where the swamp deer were thriving under the care of Billy Arjan Singh. Billy also showed me a unique landmark in Sathiana, a commemorative stone marking a site where the ranis of Singhai had committed sati after their husband, the raja, had been killed by a tiger he had wounded. I know of no other instance of sati caused by a carnivore. I also went to the nearby Kishanpur forests and saw the swamp deer and the hog deer near Jhadi Tal, and recommended that this area must also be covered in a future tiger reserve.

The first draft of our report, most of which I wrote on a non-stop flight from Bangkok to London, was refined and augmented by my senior colleagues. The report was submitted to Karan Singh, the chairman of the steering committee of Project Tiger, and the recommendations that were then made hold good to this day. However, most of them were not adopted. We in India, especially those in government, believe that we know everything and that there is hardly anything that we need to learn from others, especially foreigners. A critique of our report was published by a very senior officer of the Indian Forest Service, which revealed the general mindset. Leyhausen had done his doctorate on small cats and Holloway his on forestry. 'What do they know of tigers?' the author asked. As for Ranjitsinh, he continued, 'He is only an IAS officer!' Period. No comments on the contents of the report!

In late 1976, I attended a conference of the IUCN Standing Committee at Kino on the Baja California, Mexico, surrounded by nesting frigate birds and other avians. I took this opportunity to visit the Mayan sites on the Yucatán Peninsula of Mexico, to see the alligators and the bird life of the Everglades National Park in Florida, the wintering whooping cranes (*Grus americana*) on the Gulf of Mexico in Texas, the awe-inspiring Grand Canyon National Park and its confiding mule deer, and the immense sequoias of Yosemite National Park.

An FAO conference in Kathmandu, Nepal, provided an opportunity to revisit the Chitwan National Park. Patrolling by the Royal Nepalese Army had certainly had an impact, the rhino population had increased and it was good to see gharial on the River Rapti.

Soon after, in Japan, I had the opportunity to visit the Nippo Kaigan Quasi-National Park and see the Japanese macaque (*Macaca fuscata*). On Hokkaido Island, the red-crowned cranes (*Grus japonensis*), revered by the Japanese, were flying in to be fed on the snow.

In 1977, the United Nations Conference on Desertification was convened in Nairobi, under the aegis of UNEP. M.S. Swaminathan was appointed chairman and I was assigned to assist him. Israel had the best techniques of water management and of overcoming desertification, and its representatives were keen to offer them to the Arab countries and others. However, politics prevailed, Israel's offer was ignored and its speaker heckled.

Around this time, on behalf of UNEP, I made visits to Manila to offer technical assistance in conservation to the Philippines government and to seek financial support from the Asian Development Bank for UNEP's projects. On one occasion I was able to go to Mt Iglit–Baco National Park on Mindoro Island. It entailed a very arduous walk uphill for over eleven hours and camping in an open shed on a cold night. Early next morning, on a small pond up in the mountains was a pair of the Philippine duck (*Anas luzonica*), which Delacour calls one of the most beautiful of the mallards (Delacour 1974, Vol. II). I also saw a couple of the Mindoro sambar (*Cervus unicolor barandanus*), very similar to the mainland sambar but much smaller. However, despite two days of hard trekking on those *Imperata* grass-covered uplands, I was not able to see the tamaraw (*Bubalus mindorensis*), the iconic small wild buffalo of the Philippines, endemic and highly endangered.

UNEP sent me in 1997 as part of an international team of experts to advise the Government of Sri Lanka on the conservation ramifications of the project on Mahaweli Ganga, the largest river on the island. With its legacy of Buddhist traditions and perhaps also as a result of British rule, Sri Lanka was one of the foremost nations in southern Asia in the field of nature conservation. With 11.39 per cent of the land under its protected areas system, Sri Lanka was second only to Bhutan in this regard in Asia. It then had eleven national parks and fifty-six other categories of protected areas, but ten of them were less than 20 sq. km in extent. Lack of trained personnel, tourist overuse of certain segments of the parks and infestation of exotic weeds was prevalent, as in India. The misidentification of domestic and feral buffaloes as wild buffalo was another problem. Yala National Park alone had 15,000 such buffalo. Nonetheless, the profusion of wildlife and the confiding nature of the animals and birds were remarkable. Though the elephant tusks in the museums in Colombo and Kandy bear testimony to the ivory once carried by the elephant bulls in Sri Lanka, the island attenuation syndrome together with the capture of tuskers in the past had resulted in only about one bull out of ten carrying smallish tusks. The rest of the males are makna or tuskless bulls.

However, the star attraction of the Sri Lankan parks is the leopard. Being the master predator on the island, the leopard has assumed the role played by the tiger or lion in India. Sri Lankan leopards are largely diurnal, non-arboreal, non-cryptic and bold. I saw them in Yala and Ruhuna, but in those pre-insurgency days the best place to see a leopard anywhere in the world, more than even those leopards up the trees around Seronera in the Serengeti, Tanzania, was the Wilpattu National Park in north-western Sri Lanka. I have seen five males in one morning before breakfast, and eleven in a whole day, while my friend Thilo Hoffmann, long-time resident in Sri Lanka, has seen thirteen in a 32-km drive through Wilpattu. Another wonderful area was the Horton Plains above Nuwara Eliya, commanding a wonderful view of Adam's Peak, the highest point on the island, and holding seventeen of the twenty-one endemic bird species.

I also had the opportunity to go to the Maldive Islands, and to admire its corals and marine life. Though at the time tourism was not rife, it had begun changing the landscape as individual islands and atolls were leased out to resorts. One resort had started a bizarre form of shark tourism, where a bare-breasted woman went underwater in a cage to feed the sharks, while a clutch of tourists were lowered in another cage to watch the spectacle. Whether the tourists were ogling at the sharks or at the 'mermaid' is another issue, but such ventures not only endanger the lives of others, but also grossly habituate wild animals to humans and should never be permitted.

In 1978, the Government of West Germany, as it then was, convened a group of experts to help prepare the Convention on

Migratory Species. There was a representative from each of the six continents, and I was invited from Asia. En route, I accepted a long-standing invitation to visit Israel from General Avraham Yoffe, who was in charge of the department of nature conservation of Israel. Yoffe was a legendary figure in conservation and a hero of the Six Day War. His ambition was to reintroduce into Israel all the animals mentioned in the Bible. In that direction, he had already brought the Somali wild ass into the Hai-Bar Nature Reserve at the edge of the Negev Desert, where I saw them with gazelles and other wildlife. Being an equid, the wild ass's metabolism is among the most efficient in the animal world and it can survive on the coarsest grasses and plants. These Somali asses had been raised in captivity and were fed lucerne and other green fodder. After release into Hai-Bar, green fodder continued to be provided to them, but in a few days the wild asses had started preferring the indigenous dry, thorny shrubs and grass. In the Ein Gedi Nature Reserve above the Dead Sea in the Jordan Valley, one of the lowest points anywhere on earth, Nubian ibex were numerous and very confiding. General Yoffe showed me photos of a male leopard that had moved into Ein Gedi and was preying on the ibex. Underwater in the Gulf of Aqaba, it was astounding to see the profusion and colours of the corals and marine life of the Red Sea.

In Bonn, as we drafted the appendices of the proposed Convention on Migratory Species and suggested amendments to the draft, I received news of the birth of our second daughter Radhika in Bangkok. Some eight years later, when I had returned to the Government of India for my second spell as India's director of wildlife preservation, the first conference of parties to this convention was summoned in Bonn and the host country honoured me by making me the chairman.

Soon after this, as part of a UNEP delegation, I went to China for the first time. Chairman Mao had recently died, but the stranglehold of communism was still very evident. In the entire trip of some twelve days covering rural areas and riverine tracts as well,

I saw only eighteen species of birds. The commonest bird was still the house sparrow, on which Chairman Mao had declared war for being an agricultural pest. We were taken to no protected wildlife areas, but I must have asked so many questions about the status and distribution of animals that our hosts in Shanghai asked me if I was very fond of cats. When I replied in the affirmative, he kindly offered to take us to a restaurant which specialized in cat meat. It was perhaps impolite, but I had to decline.

Later, I also went to Taiwan and apart from the National Palace Museum at Taipei, undoubtedly one of the greatest art centres of the world, I was able to visit the Yangmingshan National Park in the north of the island.

UNEP received its contribution from what was then the USSR in roubles, not in US dollars. Roubles could be spent only in countries which accepted this currency, and Mongolia was one of them. A combined mission, consisting of representatives of FAO, UNEP and the Government of Mongolia along with Russian scientists, including the eminent Prof. L.V. Zhirnov, met in Ulan Bator, the capital of Mongolia. The purpose was to assist the Gobi Gurvansaikhan National Park, at 5.3 million hectares one of the largest in the world.

We were taken to a forested reserve close to Ulan Bator, Bogdoula, established in 1778 – perhaps, the earliest area in the world to be declared as protected in modern times. We saw the Manchurian race of the Asiatic wapiti (*Cervus canadensis xanthopygus*), very similar to the American and the Tian Shan wapiti but slightly smaller.

At Ulan Bator airport I saw crates of vodka in our baggage. On my expressing surprise at the quantum, I was told that the supply constituted only the 'normal' quota for each member of the party – one bottle per person per day! When our vehicle broke down in the Gobi–Altai and we were asked to walk to camp some 10 km away carrying only our essential belongings, I lugged my heavy camera bag while my colleagues tucked their 'quota' of vodka bottles into their pockets and under their belts.

Przewalski's horse had just become extinct in the wild in the Gobi, the last sighting having been about seven years before our visit. But we did see the wild ass, or kulan (*Equus hemionus kulan*), though scattered, timid and only in small groups. At an oasis in the Gobi we saw a troop of seven wild Bactrian camels (*Camelus bactrianus*), lean, rangy and fast, quite different from their domesticated counterparts and even from the feral ones that range freely in Ladakh. The double humps on the wild camel are far smaller, perhaps there being less fat to store therein in the wild specimens.

We also came across scattered, small numbers of the Mongolian gazelle (*Procapra gutturosa*) and even fewer goitred gazelle (*Gazella subgutturosa*). We saw just one herd of the endemic and endangered Mongolian saiga antelope (*Saiga tatarica mongolica*), which demonstrated in a cloud of dust across the plain their reputation as one of the fastest land mammals in the world.

We were told that about 80,000 Asiatic ibex (*Capra sibirica*) lived in Mongolia, a sizeable number being in the Gobi–Altai. We did see some outstanding specimens. The Mongolian argali (*Ovis ammon ammon*) is amongst the heaviest-horned and largest-bodied sheep in the world and it was indeed surprising to see them on those rolling low hills and flat uplands. Their population in Mongolia was estimated at about 20,000. Close to Hailung Somon – supposedly the birthplace of the national hero Genghis Khan – in the Gobi, we flushed a flock of five houbara bustard, this being the summer habitat of the north-eastern houbara population, the other population being in the Arabian peninsula.

The young nation of Bangladesh expressed a desire, as Thailand had earlier, to formulate an environment strategy for the country. UNEP, jointly with the United Nations Economic and Social Commission for Asia and Pacific (ESCAP), was assigned the task and I was asked to head the team. Bangladesh had just undergone a military coup. I travelled by road from Cox's Bazar to Chittagong, through isolated patches of forests on hillocks, which are the eastern outposts of the Arakan Yoma Range. Elephants were still to be found here, travelling from one patch of forest to another. In the Chittagong Hill Tracts, denuded of its forests by slash-and-burn cultivators, I was shown a russet-coloured serow in captivity. Chittagong had a training college for foresters, a legacy of the former East Pakistan. I was taken to the Bhawal National Park north of Dhaka, a favourite retreat of the slain president Sheikh Mujibur Rahman, and virtually the easternmost limit of the sal forest in the subcontinent.

My work also took me to Pakistan more than once. Barring perhaps rural Russia, nowhere have I met such warmth, hospitality and camaraderie from the citizenry of any country as in Pakistan – from the waiters of the Holiday Inn in Islamabad to the man in the street in Rawalpindi to the elite of Karachi. S.M.H. Rizvi very graciously took me from Karachi to the Kirthar National Park, where he had a hut below the spectacular Kira cliff.

En route, I wanted to see the last remaining mugger crocodiles in Pakistan, at the shrine of Pir Mangho. Feeding these saurians on the premises of the shrine – Pir Mangho is considered the patron saint of crocodiles – is of special religious merit and meat is available for this purpose on sale. The caretakers of the shrine would shove the meat on your behalf down the open mouths of the satiated crocodiles, sometimes rupturing the membranes on the throat and causing their death – accounting for the very low numbers of these reptiles surviving. Even a crocodile can be loved or worshiped to death. When a crocodile died, it would be wrapped in a chaddar (cloth offered at the tomb of Mangho Pir) and ceremoniously buried (Ranjitsinh 1997).

From the sere, sandy, acacia-dotted plains of Sindh rises a rampart of hills, beyond which lies Balochistan. Ranikot, the fortress capital of the Amirs of Sindh, with fortifications extending to 70 km in circumference, is the second longest in the world after Mandu in India. Right across a plain rises another range peaking to 1,000 m above sea level – the Karchat massif, the mainstay of the Kirthar National Park.

The Amirs of Sindh were inveterate hunters of the 'sarha', the wild goat, also called the Sindh ibex or the Persian ibex, which I had first seen in the Alborz Mountains of Iran. When the last amir was defeated by the forces of the East India Company in the mid-nineteenth century and was a virtual prisoner of the British in Ranikot, he would seek permission to go across to shoot the sarha in Kirthar. The game guards of the park sat me in one of the shooting 'boxes' of the amirs, a semicircular wall of loose boulders, and staged a drive. In ones and twos wild goats appeared on the ridge above till there stood silhouetted against the sky forty-six males, some carrying horns well over a metre long. This wild goat carries one of the longest pairs of horns in ratio to its body height, towering above the animal in a huge, flaring circle. In 1979, I estimated the wild goat population in the Kirthar Park as between 500 to 600 (Ranjitsinh 1985b).

The other notable animal in Kirthar is the Balochistan urial (*Ovis orientalis blanfordi*), whose number I estimated at less than 100 on my two visits in 1979 and 1980. While stalking a small herd of the urial that had two fine rams with characteristic out-flaring, curling horns, I stumbled and fell with a heavy camera mounted on a tripod. Looking down, I found that I had kicked loose a large and perfectly formed mollusc fossil, a relict of the Cretaceous period over 100 million years ago when this land was under the Tethys Sea, before a chunk of the supercontinent Gondwana thrust itself against the Asian shelf to raise these uplands from the seabed.

Small groups of chinkara gazelle were frequently seen on the lower reaches of the Kirthar and we also flushed the see-see partridge (*Ammoperdix griseogularis*). I saw footprints of the plains wolf (*Canis lupus pallipes*) and a dead wild goat kid that had been strangulated in the expert manner of a feline. The fang marks on the throat were a little too large for those of a jungle cat and much too small for those of a small leopard. I am reasonably sure that kill was the handiwork of a caracal.

I was sent to Afghanistan in 1979 and though I had no time to see its wildlife and protected areas, I did visit the turquoise-blue lake of Band-e Amir, saw the Buddhas of Bamiyan, the largest rock-cut monuments in the world before the Taliban blew them into smithereens, and had a glimpse of Buzkashi, the wild game of horse chase with the carcass of a goat as the prize.

In the winter of 1979, I was sent for training to the East-West Center in Honolulu, Hawaii. Apart from seeing some of the island's unique and endemic bird life, including the rehabilitation of the Hawaiian goose that had been saved from extinction by the efforts of Sir Peter Scott and others, I was able to visit the spectacular Hawaii Volcanoes National Park.

In 1977, I had made my first visit to Burma (Myanmar), but only to Rangoon (Yangon) to meet government officials. I took the opportunity to call on U Tun Yin, the author of *The Wild Animals of Burma* and a pioneering Burmese counterpart of Salim Ali and Boonsong Lekagul. He had encyclopaedic knowledge of the wildlife of Burma, especially the endangered species. Like any conservationist who has devoted his life to this cause and sees in his twilight years that all that he had treasured and fought for in life in total dissipation, U Tun Yin was in a mood of utter despair. The Javan rhino (*Rhinoceros sondaicus*) was already extinct in Burma. U Tun Yin had kept track of the last one for several years in the forests of Moulmein district, even during the Japanese occupation of Burma during World War II. It was killed by Mon tribals in 1955. U Tun Yin went and measured its single 9-inch horn. A pair of Sumatran rhino (*Didermocerus sumatrensis*) he knew of in the same district had also been poached and he reckoned that there were then between thirty-four to thirty-eight Sumatran rhinos left in Burma.

While there were no true wild buffalo in the country, there were 6,000 to 7,000 wild elephants in the Burmese forests. Almost an equal number were held in captivity, used to operate the valuable teak forests of the country and for religious purposes. Elephants, of course, are a sacred animal for the Buddhist nation, so were less hunted than other animals. The tsine (the Burmese name for the banteng *Bos javanicus birmanicus*) was less pursued than the gaur or seladang, as its meat was less preferred. Yet, the numbers of the tsine were fast reducing. The military junta was in power in Burma and most of the hunting was done by the army. The animal most hunted was the sambar, whose meat was on open sale. Tigers were in sharp decline and tiger skins were on sale for some 3,000 kyats a piece in the trade corporation owned by the government. Poaching was quite rampant even in the so-called protected areas, but wildlife could still be seen in the Shwesettaw and Shwe-u-Daung sanctuaries.

The meat of the thamin, Burma's brow-antlered deer (*Cervus eldi thamin*), was not eaten as it was reputed to cause leprosy and leucoderma. But in 1980, I saw the makers of gold leaf in Mandalay, a thriving cottage industry, use the skin of the thamin for this purpose. Takin were still not uncommon in Kachin state, but local tribes pursued them with poisoned arrows.

Army control had led to the economic collapse and social decline of this most prosperous and self-sufficient country of southern Asia. The hotels were run down and even essential items were not available. I asked U Tun Yin what I could bring him when I next visited. His reply said it all – notebooks, ballpoint pens and aspirin.

When I revisited Burma two years later carrying these articles for U Tun Yin, the conservation situation had worsened. My attempts to visit protected areas met with problems, so I contented myself by going to Mandalay, the old capital of the kings of Burma, and by visiting the awe-inspiring cluster of innumerable, imposing pagodas in Pagan.

Malaysia, like Burma, was endowed with mineral and other natural resources. Having also been under British hegemony, it had inherited conservation conventions. Malaysia did not have the culture of non-violent Buddhism; still, not only was the country taking rapid economic strides, it had also evolved a conservation ethic and had established a number of outstanding protected areas.

A large part of the credit for this must go to the Malaysian Department of Wildlife and National Parks and its directors, notable amongst them being Mohd Khan bin Momin Khan. However, for any department of wildlife, nature conservation and national parks to be effective, especially in a developing country with a fast-growing economy, the government must not only select the right person to be in charge and keep him there for a long duration, but give him consistent support, not only financial but political. The Government of Malaysia had implemented these prerequisites and was a leader in nature conservation amongst the nations of South-East Asia.

Over my five-year period at the UNEP regional office in Bangkok, I had occasion to visit Malaysia four times. Mohd Khan became a friend and personally took me to a number of protected areas. In Krau Wildlife Reserve, I saw in daylight my first lesser mouse deer (*Tragulus javanicus*), larger than the Indian chevrotain. On the delightful three-hour boat ride to Kuala Tahan in Taman Negara, the premier national park of mainland Malaysia, I saw wild boar, pied hornbills and hairy-nosed otters (*Lutra sumatrana*). On boat rides on the lovely streams within the park – the Sungai Tehan and the Tembeling river – I saw sambar and more pig, malkohas and kingfishers. Walking about in the forest, darting mouse deer were not an infrequent sight. Twice we had good views of the agile gibbons (*Hylobates agilis*), swinging nimbly and swiftly along the branches, almost black in colour. Up the lovely rivulet Kuala Trenggan, I sat over a salt lick the whole night to see the Malayan tapir (*Tapirus indicus*), which I had never seen before. It came, but provided only a glimpse in the flashlight. I did, however, see five seladangs (*Bos gaurus*); large, dark and hulking like the south Indian gaur. They did appear to me morphologically slightly different from their Indian counterparts. The junction of the neck with the body appears higher in the seladang than in the gaur, the nape of the neck being more in line with the axis of the spine. Could a higher positioned neck be an adaptation of the Malaysian animal for having to browse much of its food, unlike the Indian gaur that grazes?

I happened to be in Malaysia when the egg-laying season of the leatherback turtle, the largest turtle in the world, had started on the coast of Trengganu, one of the biggest arribada congregations in the world for this species. Mohd Khan took me there and I spent the whole night going from one egg-laying female to the other. The first aspect of this turtle that strikes one, indeed staggers one, is its immense size. The average weight of those nesting females was over 400 kg, and a specimen weighing 725 kg had been recorded. There is an element of pathos and of incongruity about the whole egg-laying endeavour: the laborious task of hauling themselves on to the beaches and digging nests, often uncovering other nests in the process; the huge, gelatinous tears that they shed whilst they are laying and their helplessness on land. Once the laying starts, the turtles cannot stop the process and poachers can simply put a bag underneath them to collect the eggs for sale. The government has stepped in to guard the nests and a portion of the eggs are hatched in nurseries for release into the wild. I saw some of the eggs hatching on the beach and the hatchlings struggling to the sea in the night, in the glare of artificial light.

I was also able to visit Sarawak in Malaysian Borneo to attend a conference at Kuching, the state capital, made famous by an Englishman who had become an uncrowned king of the state, 'Raja' Bookes. I took the opportunity to traverse some of Borneo's forests and to visit the orang-utan rehabilitation centre at Sepilok.

Some facets of the information given to me by Mohd Khan are of interest even today. Malaysia spent over a million Malaysian dollars on digging 'elephant-proof' trenches, at about the same time these were being tried out in India. As in India, they proved to be only partially successful. Electric fencing was proving helpful, but the north-east Indian method of 'mela shikar', capturing elephants by noosing them, had proved a failure.

The director of wildlife of Sabah in Borneo, Datuk Lamri Ali, estimated the wild elephant population in Sabah to be about 500. Mohd Khan, who had himself taken a photograph of a wild Sumatran rhino, believed that there were between thirty and forty of these rhinos still surviving on mainland western Malaysia, about 400 seladang (gaur) and between 700 and 800 wild elephants.

Colonel Locke had estimated the tiger population in Malaysia to be about 3,500 in the middle of the twentieth century (Locke 1954). A quarter-century later, Mohd Khan believed there were only about 300 to 350 left.

A specimen of that extremely rare crocodile, the false gharial (*Tomistoma schlegelii*), had been caught a year before my first visit, at the junction of the Pahang river with Sungai Chenor, proving that the species still survived in the wild. It was tagged and released, caught again and released, only to be caught a third time at the mouth of the Pahang river some 320 km downstream. Amongst the crocodiles of South-East Asia, false gharials were particularly prized for their soft skins. Their over-exploitation and the destruction of habitat had rendered them almost extinct in the wild. There had been a population in the famous Samutprakan Crocodile Farm and Zoo near Bangkok, but they had been interbred with other crocodilians, where after the farm obtained fresh specimens from the wild and bred them separately.

A couple of aspects of animal adaptation were notable. In the Indian subcontinent, the leopard lives closer to human habitation and the tiger farther away, in heavier forests. In Malaysia, it was the other way around. There were fewer tigers in primary forests, which are too dense to support large ungulate populations, and more lived in logged forests and even in rubber and oil palm plantations, closer to human habitation, where they often preyed on livestock. The smaller body size of Malaysian tigers compared to their Indian counterparts, the occurrence of wild pig, a preferred prey of the tiger close to cultivation, and the high degree of melanism amongst Malaysian leopards, which make them more conspicuous than tigers in open areas, could also have been contributory factors. This behavioural adaptation was perhaps also caused by a morphological adaptation of the prey species. As is known, carnivores prefer animals that are at least their own body weight, going up to almost twice their own weight, and not those animals that are lighter or heavier than this (Ranjitsinh 1997). Dense tropical forests have very little ground vegetation for grazing; therefore, herbivores have adapted to browsing upon trees. Most trees are endowed with protective toxins and tannins. Hence, there are no wild ungulates in the weight range of 30–200 kg. Those below this weight range, the mouse deer and the barking deer, are selective browsers; those heavier, the sambar and the seladang, have a larger body size to counteract the effect of plant toxins and tannins. The one exception, of course, is the wild pig, which relies mainly on tubers and fruit. It is interesting that the Malay tapir whose closest relatives are in South America, providing yet another link with a common 'ancestral' home, the supercontinent Gondwana, is not preyed upon by the tiger despite its helplessness and a conspicuous black-and-white coat.

My work also took me to the islands in the Pacific – Fiji, Vanuatu, New Caledonia and the Solomon Islands, and twice to Papua New Guinea. In Nouméa, New Caledonia, still very French, I saw in captivity the unique flightless kagu, the only member of a bird family and genera. On Guadalcanal, which saw some of the bloodiest battles with the Japanese in World War II, halfway up Mount Popomanaseu, I saw the diminutive red-breasted pygmy parrot (*Micropsitta bruijnii*), exquisite and endemic, and at 9 cm, one of the smallest parrots in the world. Mount Popomanaseu at 2,440 m is the highest peak on the Solomon Islands and indeed in that part of the Pacific. In the capital Honiara, I happened to be in the same hotel as Jared Diamond, the outstanding ecologist and ornithologist who guided me in finding the pygmy parrot.

I happened to be in Mt Hagen, almost 4,000 m up in the Western Highlands of Papua New Guinea, when the sing-sing festival was on. This must surely be the most astounding human display of avian splendour in the world. One by one, groups from different settlements march in – rather, slowly swing in – accompanied by their individual drum beat and song. The participants, vividly painted and already on an alcoholic high, imbibe more as they dance in separate groups in that congregation, their sombre faces with red-shot eyes gyrating with their heirloom headdresses. It is these headdresses that are the cynosure of all eyes, and those wearing them know it. They are bedecked with a mind-boggling array of the most resplendent feathers of the birds-of-paradise. Amongst them I could identify the tail feathers of the blue bird-of-paradise (*Paradisaea rudolphi*), magnificent bird-of-paradise (*Diphyllodes magnificus*), Princess Stephanie's astrapia (*Astrapia stephaniae*), ribbon-tailed astrapia (*Astrapia mayeri*), the splendid astrapia (*Astrapia splendidissima*) and the black sicklebill (*Epimachus fastosus*). The iridescent chest feathers of the superb bird-of-paradise (*Lophorina superba*); the unbelievable and elongated head feathers of Lawes's parotia (*Parotia lawesii*) and of the king of Saxony bird-of-paradise (*Pteridophora alberti*) were also conspicuously present. Walking about in the valley forests, I was able to see the king bird-of-paradise (*Cicinnurus regius*) with its red head and white chest, fluttering on its short wings and with its long, wire-like tail feathers ending with emerald green rackets floating behind. I also saw a male Count Raggi's bird-of-paradise (*Paradisaea raggiana*) displaying, head down with its gold-tipped, saffron-red tail feathers fluffed up above, like a bouquet of flowers.

From a biodiversity standpoint, the most significant country in South-East Asia is undoubtedly Indonesia; extending from Sumatra in the west to Irian Jaya in the east, with its snow-covered, 4,884-metre-high Puncak Jaya, the highest mountain in South-East Asia. Indonesia straddles three biogeographic regions – Indomalayan, Oceania and Australasia – with the Wallace Line separating the Oriental faunal region from the Australasian. Indonesia also encompasses a major part of Borneo, as well as the unique island of Sulawesi with its endemic dwarf wild buffalo, the lowland anoa (*Bubalus depressicornis*) and the mountain anoa (*Bubalus quarlesi*).

I had a number of occasions to visit Indonesia. The Bali tiger, the smallest race of the tiger, had, of course, long become extinct, but the Javan tiger was still being vaguely reported in the Meru Betiri National Park. Leopards still persisted sporadically in Java, despite the island being one of the most densely populated areas in the world. It is one of the greatest riddles of zoogeography that though the leopard occurs on Java, it does not on the much larger and wilder Sumatra. So how did it colonize Java from mainland Asia without going through Sumatra?

At the eastern end of Java, and connected very tenuously to it by a narrow isthmus, is the peninsula of Ujung Kulon and on it is one of the greatest national parks I have been to. With the recent extinction of the last remnant population of the Javan rhinoceros (*Rhinoceros sondaicus*) in Vietnam and, thus, on mainland Asia, Ujung Kulon remains the last habitat of this second single-horned Asian rhino. The explosion of the volcano Krakatoa in 1883, the most cataclysmic natural phenomenon recorded in history, had sent a tidal wave 40 m high, the marks of which can be seen in Ujung Kulon even today. It destroyed all life including human settlements in Ujung Kulon but, fatefully, gave the Javan rhino a lease of life. After this holocaust, the rhino returned to Ujung Kulon over the narrow isthmus, while man returned only for sporadic settlement.

The Javan tiger (*Panthera tigris sondaica*) had already become extinct in Ujung Kulon when I visited, and there were then an estimated forty-five to fifty Javan rhino surviving. At Labuan port, since it was Ramadan we had to wait in the boat till the sighting of the moon was over. This gave me an opportunity to see a wonderful silhouette of a setting sun behind the iconic Krakatoa volcano. We passed the island of Pulau Panaitan, whose high point Gunung Raksa houses relics of statues of Shiva and Ganesha.

I was put up in the park guest house on Pulau Peucang, surrounded by a rainforest of beautiful, buttressed trees. Groups of the small rusa deer (*Cervus timorensis russa*), like miniature sambar, were around and I could watch them from my bedroom window. Stags standing 90 cm high, with antlers not exceeding 40 cm, would wallow and display. Their calls are a series of squeals, somewhat like a bugle. What was not so welcome was the presence of the tokay gecko lizard, named for its string of loud, staccato shrieks, which would keep me awake at night. I do not have an aversion to lizards,

Hunting cheetah of Maharaja Sayajirao, Baroda, CE 1890. This is the only known photograph of proven Indian cheetah, alive (top).
Copyright: Samarjitsinh Gaekwad of Baroda.

Raj Amarsinhji of Wankaner (R) with Jam Ranjitsinhji (Ranji) and Gir lion, CE 1907 (left).

Trophies of the Surguja royal family from a single winter shooting camp, 43 tigers (top) and 71 leopards (bottom).

Tigresses in Kanha National Park (NP), Madhya Pradesh: a charge in defensive aggression (note the orange colour of eyes) (top) and over a chital kill (bottom).

Leopards in Beda, Rajasthan (top and bottom).

Mothers and cubs: leopardess in Beda (top); and sloth bear in Daroji Sanctuary, Karnataka (bottom).

Sparring blackbuck, Velavadar NP, Gujarat (top).
Sprinting chinkara, Jamboji, Rajasthan (bottom).

Sambar stag, Satpura NP, Madhya Pradesh (top).
Elephant bull stripping and chewing bark, Corbett NP, Uttarakhand (bottom).

Great Indian hornbill in flight, berry in beak, to feed its family ensconced in a tree hollow, Valparai, Kerala (top and bottom).

A bird India lost: Siberian crane, Bharatpur NP, Rajasthan (top).
A bird the world may lose: great Indian bustard, Desert NP, Rajasthan (bottom).

Stags in rutting pelage: Sangai stag (note elongated hooves), Keibul Lamjao NP, Manipur (top); Ranjitsinh's barasingha, Kaziranga NP, Assam (bottom left); and Brander's barasingha, Kanha NP, Madhya Pradesh (bottom right).

Nilgiri tahr 'saddleback' male, Eravikulam NP, Kerala (top).
Pygmy hog, rare, localized, elusive. Manas NP, Assam (bottom).

Bharal ram: Gangotri NP, Uttarakhand (top).
Shapu rams in rutting pelage, Rezong Gompa, Ladakh (bottom).

Tibetan wild ass or kiang, mother and foal, Pangong Lake, Ladakh (top).
Tibetan gazelle or gowa males, Tso Lhamo, Sikkim (bottom).

Tibetan wolf in summer pelage, Chang-chen-mo, Ladakh (top).
Wild goat (Sindh ibex), Kirthar NP, Pakistan (bottom).

Black or Moffit's kalij pheasant male (top) and a young male Bhutan takin, Jigme Dorji NP, Bhutan (bottom).

European bison or wisent bull, Bialowieza NP, Poland (top).
Alpine ibex, Gran Paradiso NP, Italy (bottom).

but to have a multicoloured one the size of a small monitor lizard crawling on the ceiling above your bed, emitting those loud calls from time to time, is not very conducive to sound sleep!

Across a lovely sand-lined creek from Pulau Peucang, is a watchtower overlooking the meadow of Cijingkulon, cleared of its tree canopy to provide grass for the ungulates and a view for visitors. Herds of banteng (*Bos javanicus*) – cows buff-coloured, bulls dark chocolate to black, contrasting sharply with their prominently white buttocks – could be seen both morning and evening, grazing, nursing or resting and ruminating. I saw as many as twenty-three spread out on the Cijungkulon meadow.

Also present were wild pigs, the green Javan junglefowl and the elegant and gorgeous green peafowl with its pointed head-crest feathers. Hornbills were common. The crested serpent eagles here were similar to the dark phase of this species found in the Andaman Islands. White-bellied sea eagles were visible every day.

In a small speedboat named 'Kancil', the local name for a mouse deer, I travelled over a very rough sea to Cigunther, another artificially maintained meadow with a watchtower. Thirteen banteng and a wild boar were there. I went up the lovely, winding Cigunther stream for about 3 km, seeing two sets of fresh footprints of Javan rhino and those of a saltwater crocodile in the mud, and a green snake, resembling a viper, dangling from vines overhanging the stream.

At the airport in Medan on the island of Sumatra, I ran into Prince Bernhard of the Netherlands, who informed me that his country had conferred the Most Excellent Order of the Golden Ark upon me. I was on my way to the Bohorok orang-utan rehabilitation centre at the edge of the Gunung Leuser National Park, a premier park of Indonesia and a refuge of the Sumatran rhinoceros. Orang-utans seized from illegal traffic or possession were sought to be released into the wild. It was touching to see the parental care bestowed upon the baby primates by their keepers and the reciprocal affection they received. The released animals and some wild ones came to the feeding centres each day, where the captive ones were introduced to their wild cousins and to those who had been released earlier. A Sumatran tiger (*Panthera tigris sumatrae*) had killed a rehabilitated orang-utan some days before my arrival and I was shown his pugmarks. Serow (*Capricornis sumatraensis*) were reported nearby and I did see some siamang (*Symphalangus syndactylus*) in that dense tropical forest.

Like Malaysia, Indonesia was fortunate to have dedicated officers in charge of its Directorate of Forest Protection and Nature Conservation (PHKA), amongst them Effendy Sumardja and Widodo Ramono.

Many years later, I visited the Baluran National Park, at the north-eastern corner of Java. Its open forest and grasslands enable good sighting of rusa deer and of banteng. Nearby on the island of Bali, the wild banteng had disappeared even from Bali Barat, its premier protected area, but the domesticated cattle looked no different from the banteng.

From Bali, I joined the director of the PHKA on a field visit to Komodo National Park. We flew to Bima on the island of Sumbawa, followed by a three-hour drive to the port of Sape and a twelve-hour overnight boat ride to Komodo. As one circumvents Komodo with its desolate, high, jagged skyline in the pale early morning light, tall *Borassus* palms swaying in the sea breeze in the valley bottoms and *Imperata* grasses on the slopes, not a vestige of human habitation to be seen, it does appear to be the lost world. The tableau becomes more surreal whilst waiting for the 'ora'(Komodo dragon) to arrive. As the stench wafting from the goat carcass gets sharper, there is a rustle in the undergrowth followed by a hiss, and a huge shovel-shaped head is thrust out, pale yellow forked tongue flickering in and out of the mouth. One large unblinking eye stares at you; then with the turn of a dinosaur-like face, the other eye continues the scrutiny. A slow, measured amble to the carcass and the tearing of flesh begins. Soon others join in, some over 3 m in length, till there are fourteen around the goat, the larger ones keeping away the smaller with hissing and grunting, forked tongues flicking in and out all the while. My field note on the Komodo dragon (*Varanus komodoensis*) ends: 'A primordial monster in a primeval setting.'

The Komodo dragon is not just the largest lizard in the world. It is also the largest four-footed terrestrial reptile in the world and the only one which is the master predator of its terrain. In fact, it is the greatest living embodiment of the Age of Reptiles.

Confined to the islands of Komodo, Padar and Rinca, with some inhabiting the shores of the large neighbouring island of Flores, the 'dragon' has been able to take maximum advantage of its ecological niche and grown to lengths of up to 4 m. There are no other predators here, not even scavenger-hunters like jackals, hyenas or wild cats. The dragon has become a predator, stalking the rusa deer, pigs, even livestock and feral dogs. Their saliva contains venom which, once introduced into the bloodstream through a bite, causes death through slow poisoning. The 'ora' has just to follow the bitten animal and wait.

From Flores we had to return to Bali by boat, crossing the Wallace Line that lies between the islands of Lombok and Bali. The Wallace Line is the deep channel which probably prevented the Komodo dragon from marching westwards all the way into Asia and the tiger from marching eastwards possibly all the way to Australia.

At the end of 1980 on my completion of five years with UNEP, the Government of India asked me to choose – to either resign from the IAS and continue to work for UNEP or to return to India and continue with my service. I chose to come back to India.

9

The Forests of Central India

I returned to my parent state of Madhya Pradesh in January 1981. Chhattisgarh had not yet been formed, and MP was by far the largest state in India extending to more than 400,000 sq. km. As more than a third of it was under forest cover and the economy was rural, the Department of Forests had a special significance in the state.

Indira Gandhi was again the prime minister and the ethic of environmental conservation did partially pervade the states. I was informed in Bangkok that I should report in Bhopal at the earliest as the post of secretary (forests) was being kept for me despite political pressure. Madhya Pradesh was not unique in this regard. In the period that I was forest secretary in MP and had occasions to meet my counterparts in other states during meetings in Delhi, I found that there were thirteen others who were personally interested in the subject and were committed to conservation. Obviously, they had been specially chosen. Regrettably, this changed after the departure of Rajiv Gandhi, even during the regimes of subsequent governments under the Congress party. It suited governments to have more 'objective', non-committed forest secretaries.

I joined the state government of MP as secretary (forests and tourism). As tourism in the state was largely wildlife-oriented, barring the temples of Khajuraho, this combination of portfolios was regarded as appropriate. I was fortunate to be assisted by a team of very knowledgeable, honest and efficient officers – Chief

Conservator of Forests S.K. Seth and his assistants S.P. Dubey, M.B. Peter, R.C. Saxena, H.S. Panwar, J.B. Lall, W. Oak, V.K. Shrivastava, J.S. Solanki, J.J. Dutta, A.K. Dutta, P.M. Rajwade, L.K. Chaubey and others. In the Directorate of Tourism Probir Sen, IAS, was very imaginative and of great help.

The forest department was constantly under siege, with other departments such as industry, mining, agriculture, animal husbandry and even fisheries constantly demanding land and resources from forests. But what was far more pressing was the never-ending demand, as a matter of right, from the people themselves. There existed an ethic, an assumption, that the needs of all must be provided by the forests and these must be provided free of cost. There was a specific word for this free easement – 'nistar'. The prime role of politicians was to get maximum nistar for their constituents, by coaxing, cajoling or bullying. Whether the extraction of these resources was ecologically sustainable or not was not their concern.

Forest encroachment was another nightmare. Periodically, the state government would announce a settlement with existing encroachers with a deadline and a declaration that this was the final settlement and all future encroachments would be dealt with severely. In fact, these settlements merely encouraged a spurt in further encroachments, a process which was significantly slowed down by Indira Gandhi's Forest (Conservation) Act of 1981, but has again gained speedy momentum with the Scheduled Tribes and Other Traditional Forest Dwellers (Recognition of Forest Rights) Act of 2006, commonly known as the Forests Rights Act (FRA) and the recent devolution of the power to denotify small portions of forests to the regional offices of the Ministry of Environment and Forests, under the aegis of the Forest (Conservation) Act itself.

Collection of fuelwood was another threat to the very existence of forests in Madhya Pradesh. During the British regime, the rights of local villagers to remove fallen, dried fuelwood as headloads for personal domestic use but not for sale, had been recognized and recorded. After the initiation of electoral processes in independent

India, the application of rules was changed, first informally and later by formal orders of government. When I returned to Madhya Pradesh after an absence of almost ten years, orders existed that 'headloads' of 'fallen, dry' fuelwood could be removed and freely sold, there being no limit to such headloads upon an individual or upon any forest, even a reserve forest. Besides, what was called a headload could be carried on horse, mule or bullock cart, or even by vehicle or railway! Upon taking charge of forests, I had a quick survey done and found that over 17,000 such 'headloads' were being brought in daily into the city of Jabalpur alone. Gas was not so common in kitchens in those days and wood was the normal fuel for cooking.

The procedure was simple. The persons concerned would keep their axes hidden in the forest. They would go and cut their quota of wood and leave it to dry, then they would collect the wood they had cut and stacked some ten days earlier, which would by now be dry enough to be burnt, and bring it out. The whole process worked on a daily rotational basis. No wonder the extraction and sale of 'headloads' had become a thriving, mass cottage industry in MP. The forest guard, who also got his 'consideration' for turning the proverbial Nelson's eye, was getting remunerated for not going into the forest. He was also keeping the local politician happy by not taking cognizance of how the so-called fallen, dry wood was being produced. It was a cosy situation for all except the forests.

We prepared a detailed scheme under which we would make the Forest Development Corporation (FDC) of MP, which was under the aegis of the Forest Department, into mainly a fuelwood supply corporation. It would collect firewood from the state forests and sell it through depots in the various cities and townships. Individuals would be allowed to collect firewood for their own domestic use as before, but would not be allowed to sell it.

We took this proposal to the cabinet, which formed a special subcommittee under the chairmanship of Shiv Bhanu Singh Solanki, the senior-most minister in the cabinet. The subcommittee was asked to give employment to all those who were in this firewood trade.

Back we went to the drawing board. A statewide survey showed that there were over 43,000 people whose livelihood it had become to cut, procure and sell fuelwood; this did not, of course, include those who collected fuelwood only for their own personal domestic use. So we revised the scheme under which the FDC would gather the fuelwood from the forest, including from the timber then being harvested, and bring this to specified depots. From here those 43,000 persons whose livelihood this trade had become would be sold fuelwood at almost a no-loss-no-profit price and they could then go and sell this anywhere they wished. Only they, and no others, would be authorized to sell fuelwood. Those who collected fuelwood for their own personal use without selling it could continue the practice.

We went back to the cabinet and the scheme was accepted with one caveat: the present practice of collecting, transporting and selling 'headloads' of fuelwood would continue unabated! The forest department scheme should run parallel to the prevailing practice. Our scheme was to substitute the ongoing disastrous practice, not to supplement it or complement it, I argued. No go. I requested that, in view of this decision, the Forest Department may be permitted to withdraw the scheme, warning at the same time that the forests of MP, on which depended the livelihood of millions, would soon be mined out of productivity. This prognosis was stoically accepted and the withdrawal of the proposal allowed.

The supply of bamboo was another major problem. There are communities in MP, such as the 'Basods', that were once totally dependent upon making articles from bamboo – baskets, mats, screens, toys, etc. Barring some parts of Chhattisgarh, there is only one species of bamboo that occurs in MP and Chhattisgarh – *Dendrocalamus strictus*, which flowers gregariously and dies in 30–40-year cycles. When it flowers, the seeds are collected in large numbers by people who use and sell it for food. When it sprouts, hordes of cattle that graze everywhere in the forest eat the succulent shoots. When it grows a little more, it is an excellent source for making pickle. What may still be left is subjected to the scourge of man-caused fires which sweep through the forests thrice or more in a year. All the while, mature clumps of bamboo are harvested, legally and illegally, as 'nistar' to provide for hut construction, boundary fencing, basket weaving and as pulp for industry. No bamboo was being planted on private lands. So where were the bamboos going to come from to meet these huge needs? Yet, the state government had declared before my arrival that the needs of the 'Basods' would be adequately provided for. They would turn up at my office and house at all hours demanding truckloads of bamboo!

In 1983, I prepared a paper, after a month's study, showing that of the forty-five districts of the then Madhya Pradesh, only two, Bastar and Balaghat, had surplus of bamboo and that in both districts the cycle of flowering was due. What then? My estimation was that the state of MP would have to plan for an additional 4.6 million cubic metres (cu. m) of bamboo by 1991 and another 6.7 million cu. m by the year 2001, involving an additional plantation of 0.6 million hectares per annum. Since the state could never achieve these targets, I suggested social forestry on private and communal land and on refractory forests of the state, which would ease the pressure for fuelwood as well as for bamboo. Indeed, I had offered forest-based industries lease of refractory forests, for purposes of afforestation with the involvement of the local communities. However, the industry was only interested in good forests and the opportunity of harvesting their produce, not growing it themselves (Ranjitsinh 1983).

The leaves of another tree – the tendu – were rolled and stuffed with tobacco to produce bidis, handcrafted cigarettes, which was a major cottage industry and source of employment. It was also a major cause for corruption. A very upright tribal forest minister, Vasantrao Uike, had nationalized the exploitation of tendu. Corruption was reduced, but it still persisted. A year before my arrival in MP, the government had indulged in 'selective' allocation of annual rights of tendu collection in forest blocks and the uproar had not yet died down. In the following two years, I insisted on the auctioning of these collection rights, which was the appropriate method and also yielded more revenue.

There was another tree product that was also getting increasingly lucrative and troublesome at the start of my career as forest secretary – the seed of the sal tree, which is used in the production of cocoa butter, which is a base in chocolate production. But more on that later.

There were other damaging impacts upon forests from these over-exploitative practices. Fire is a natural phenomenon and the dry deciduous forests of MP and Chhattisgarh are ecologically adapted to withstand sporadic, occasional natural fires. Indeed, teak, the most commercially valuable tree in the region, can even benefit from occasional fires. But the forests of central India are subjected to three to five deliberate, man-caused burns in the drier six months of each year. The first fires are set around January to get a fresh flush of grass for livestock grazing. A month thereafter, fire again sweeps through to encourage a fresh growth of tendu leaves. The next month, fire is set to blacken the ground so as to enable easier picking of the white mahua flowers, from which local liquor is made. Later in the summer, if the forest happens to be of sal, fire is set twice, with an interval in between, to facilitate the picking of sal seed. No forest can thrive under such unnatural onslaught, especially the younger trees and bamboo, and regeneration of most tree species is adversely affected. When I returned to MP, the sal was already in regression in most places.

During the breeding season for ground-laying birds, including the peafowl and junglefowl, and for tortoises and other reptiles, there is no escape from fire. I tried to impose a condition that the tendu leaf leaseholders would make a deposit with the government, which would be refunded to them if there was no incidence of fire in their leaseholds and that it would be their duty to put out fires that may occur. The proposal was rejected.

In violation of the Wild Life (Protection) Act that prohibits commercial usage of biomass, which may have to be removed from a protected area for its better management, Orient Paper Mills was allowed to collect dead bamboo for paper manufacture from the premier Bandhavgarh National Park, after my tenure as forest secretary. When I returned to Delhi for my second stint as director, wildlife preservation of India, I was able to intervene and stop the practice.

It did not take me long to realize that in the prevailing circumstances not just wildlife but forests and, indeed, nature itself had a hope of long-term survival only in effectively managed national parks and sanctuaries. I, therefore, made it one of my prime objectives as forest secretary to bring as much area as possible under the protected areas system, and to include diverse, unique and representative ecotypes and habitats of endangered species. In hindsight, I think this was one of the best actions I have taken in my life.

From the Satna district in the west to Surguja in the east and straddling the districts of Rewa, Sidhi and Shahdol in between, lies one of the largest contiguous sal forests in the country. But between Dhubri in the west and Tamor Pingla Sanctuary in the east, there was no protected area in existence then. It was in these forests that the royal families of Rewa, Korea and Surguja had shot over 3,000 tigers in about thirty years, as related earlier. While the wildlife was now much reduced, the forests were still reasonably intact and there was great potential. In parts, it was amongst the best sal forests then surviving outside of the protected areas of India. On a survey of the area with Deputy Chief Wildlife Warden R.N. Mehrotra, I saw sloth bear, wolf, sambar, nilgai, barking deer, pigs and the tracks of a tigress. Unbroken forest continued up to the Ramgarh area of Korea, where the last cheetah in India had been shot in 1947.

I returned to Bhopal, demarcated the area to be covered under the proposed national park and since the area in question happened partly to be in the constituency of the then chief minister of MP, Arjun Singh, I sent the file to him to inform him of what I proposed to do. He complimented me on the proposal to establish a national park and then directed that it should be named after Sanjay Gandhi, the prime minister's younger son who had been killed in a plane crash in the previous year. I kept the file with me for a few days and at an opportune moment when Arjun Singh and I were alone, broached the subject of the naming of the park. I suggested that protected areas should be named on the basis of local place names, not after people. Besides, the proposed park included the Mohan forest range from where the white tiger named Mohan – the progenitor of all white tigers in captivity and the most famous tiger in the world then – had been captured. Mohan was still alive, in captivity for about eighteen years with Maharaja Martand Singhji of Rewa. I wanted the park to be called the Mohan National Park but Arjun Singh would not agree. I kept the declaration of the park pending for another few months before broaching the subject with the chief minister again. He told me that he had already told the prime minister that MP was establishing a national park named after her deceased son. Faced with this fait accompli, I recalled the old adage that a 'makna' was better than no elephant! So the Sanjay Gandhi National Park, with an area of 1,938 sq. km, was notified. My failure still rankles. Soon after, Mohan the white tiger died in captivity at Govindgarh and a holiday was declared in Rewa to mourn him. Some 467 sq. km of the park was in Surguja, which became part of Chhattisgarh when MP was split, and Chhattisgarh named its portion the Guru Ghasidas National Park after a locally revered figure.

There was a vague proposal long pending with the MP forest department to establish a zoo in Bhopal. It is an unfortunate tradition in India and elsewhere that every major city should have its own zoo, irrespective of the fact that it could have a perfectly good nature park nearby, where the citizens could have communion with nature and the young could develop empathy for wildlife. Besides, zoos in India normally have abysmal hygiene and veterinary care, and are run more like menageries than as modern zoological parks. The ChattBir Zoo near Chandigarh at that point of time had lion and tiger enclosures which held about eighty of these large cats, some hybridized, and which consumed almost 85 per cent of the annual wildlife budget of the state of Haryana.

Extending beyond the Shyamla Hill in Bhopal, where the anthropological Museum of Man was proposed to be set up, was a forested promontory jutting out towards the Bhoj Lake. Builders were already coveting the site for a hotel and some luxury houses. The Secretary (Urban Development), S.K. Sharma, agreed to allot the land for a zoo and Arjun Singh also concurred. I wanted it to be a theme park exhibiting animals of Madhya Pradesh alone, with large exclosures rather than enclosures to hold carnivores, while herbivores were to run free. So the Van Vihar National Park came about in Bhopal and J.J. Dutta and P.M. Lad contributed greatly to it. I tried to keep construction activity to the very minimum, a norm which has not been strictly followed subsequently.

A few months after the release of the ungulates on the premises of Van Vihar, I received an excited phone call at almost midnight from R.N. Nagu, the retired inspector general of police. He had seen a leopard on his way to his house on Shyamla Hill. I thought Nagu was hallucinating, but three days later a chital hind was found killed by a leopard. More kills followed, till we trapped the leopard and released it in the nearby forests of Kerwa.

One of the earliest sanctuaries I was keen to establish was Palpur–Kuno, which I visited soon after assuming charge as forest secretary. It had been a favoured hunting area of the Scindia rulers of Gwalior. In the 1920s Maharaja Sir Madho Rao Scindia had found the tract suitable for lion introduction and had brought African lions here, as he was not given Indian lions by the Nawab of Junagarh. The plan had not succeeded, as described earlier. The area had come under the sway of a series of notorious dacoits of the Chambal region.

By the time I went to Palpur–Kuno, there were hardly any tigers but the rare caracal was there, as were chital, four-horned antelope, chinkara, blackbuck and others. The area had great potential, and if the human settlements could be relocated, I felt it would become an outstanding protected area. The sanctuary was established in 1981 with an area of 345 sq. km.

I had been curious to see for myself why Maharaja Madho Rao had selected this forest for his lion introduction. The reason was clear: the prey was there and the habitat looked very much like the eastern Gir. I was convinced that there was no better place for lion reintroduction than Kuno, which was confirmed much later when the sanctuary was surveyed by the Wildlife Institute of India and chosen as the best available site for lion reintroduction.

The great Indian bustard had been in continuous decline throughout the country, but it did occur then in the Gwalior region, and there were no protected areas over its extant habitat in this region. In the monsoon of 1968, in the company of the renowned ornithologist Dharmakumarsinhji, I had seen both the lesser florican and the great Indian bustard in the Ghatigaon tract of rolling grassland-scrub forest, running along the side of the national highway between Gwalior and Shivpuri. Further south, between Jhansi and Shivpuri, the great Indian bustard had been recently reported in grasslands near Karera. Close by stood the imposing fortress of Narwar, near which Emperor Akbar had slain what was perhaps the first record of a white tiger and from where his favourite riding elephant had been captured (Divyabhanusinh 1986). Now there was only open grassland left.

In Karera, the land was mostly privately owned but left fallow, which allowed grass to grow in which bustards could nest. There were also a few government-owned grasslands open for public grazing. I went there with the commissioner of Gwalior, Ishwar Das, and the ornithologist, Lav Kumar Khachar. We not only saw the bustard but were impressed by the enthusiasm of the local people who were proud of their bird.

In May 1981, both Ghatigaon and Karera were notified in the same gazette, the former with an area of 512 sq. km and the latter covering 202 sq. km. Both protected areas made spectacular progress initially. The bustard numbers in Ghatigaon went up from eight in

1982 to twenty in 1986 and in Karera from fourteen to thirty-five in the same period, proving yet again that if effectively protected, even a slow-breeding species can make a dramatic comeback. In the Dihaliya Lake in Karera, even a vagrant Siberian crane appeared with other winter migrants, duck and bar-headed geese.

But we could not foresee what was to happen. First, an enthusiastic officer in charge of the sanctuary announced a cash prize for anyone showing bustard eggs. When I went there on a subsequent visit, a villager produced eggs and asked for his prize! If monetary incentives are to be given to local people, they should be for taking people to see year-old bustard chicks, not eggs, which if picked up, may be abandoned by the parents. This incentive was of course stopped, but by then the locals knew how and where to find the eggs, which they destroyed in retribution when they decided to take revenge on the sanctuary itself.

There was more in the offing. Taking advantage of the protection afforded in Karera, blackbuck from surrounding areas moved in and multiplied. From about 115 blackbuck in 1982, the numbers went above 3,000 in ten years. The resultant crop damage by blackbuck caused the local population to turn hostile against the sanctuary that was responsible for the increase in the antelope and also against the bustard that was responsible for the establishment of the sanctuary. The local people had no problem with the bustard, but they wanted the blackbuck to go. By then I was not dealing with wildlife even in Delhi, but I requested the Wildlife Institute of India to send a capture team to translocate the blackbuck. Barely three were caught. The people then took matters in their own hands, killed the blackbuck surreptitiously, destroyed bustard eggs and cultivated the grasslands.

Today, there are no bustards left in Ghatigaon nor in Karera and, in fact, nowhere in Madhya Pradesh. There is a lesson in this for all – that in areas inhabited by man, long-term conservation can only be achieved through not just the acquiescence of the local people but by their active participation, which is far more difficult to achieve than the establishment of protected areas. Though I was in charge of Karera only when its fortunes were on the upswing and watched helplessly when it was being destroyed, I will always blame myself, partially at least, for the failure of Karera, in not foreseeing its nemesis.

I was luckier with the other protected areas. Along the spectacular gorge of the Ken river in north Madhya Pradesh, lay the forests of Panna and Chhatarpur districts, fabled for tiger and large-antlered sambar. On the plateau above the Ken, lay the diamond mines of Panna, now being exhausted. I proposed to have a national park established on both sides of the river. Chief Wildlife Warden J.J. Dutta felt it would be more practical from the management viewpoint to have the park only in one district, Panna, with the river as a natural boundary. I argued that not only were there fine forests of Patori on the Chhatarpur side but that it would be wise to secure both banks of the river, otherwise human presence on the opposite bank would negate the safety and solitude of the bank on the park side and of the aquatic life in the river itself. We then both agreed to include the Chhatarpur forests on the upper reaches of the Ken, and Panna became a national park with an area of 543 sq. km in October 1981. In 1982, twenty-two tigers were reported in Panna. By 2000, the number had gone up to thirty-two; though later this was to suffer a drastic fall.

Adjacent to Panna and downriver, below the spectacular Raneh Falls, lay deep pools in the Ken that harboured the endangered gharial. Also in October 1981, the Ken Gharial Sanctuary was declared, encompassing 45 sq. km of the Ken river and adjacent land on both its banks. Later, this was included in the Panna Tiger Reserve.

A month earlier, another habitat of the gharial and one of the very few breeding sites of the endangered Indian skimmer was established in the Sidhi district. The Son Gharial Wildlife Sanctuary covered a 209-sq. km stretch of the river, with land on both sides extending up to 200 m from the shore. It has become a premier habitat of the gharial but faces constant threat from the sand-mining cartel.

The establishment of two more national parks in the year 1981, perhaps, gave me the most satisfaction of all. Running eastwards from where the River Tawa bisects it, the Satpura Range rises majestically to meet the rocky outcrop of the Mahadeo Hills. The Satpuras are home to some of the best teak forests in MP, meticulously managed from colonial times and a major source of revenue and of professional pride for the forest department. The Mahadeo Hills are clothed in sal forest, the only 'island' of sal surrounded by teak in India. On top is situated the hill station of Pachmarhi, with the peak of Dhupgarh, the highest point in MP, rising to 1,352 m above sea level and commanding a superb view of sal and teak forests extending to the horizon. Just below in a deep gorge is found the diminutive psilotum plant, endemic to Pachmarhi, which also has, perhaps, the largest number of the original, non-hybridized wild mango to be found anywhere on the subcontinent. The forests also have a second species of bamboo, the majestic 'katanga'. In the upper deep valleys were the rarest of the rare forests of India – pristine patches of teak forest that had never been harvested. In between the sal and teak biomes lay the transitional forest type richest in biodiversity, but dubbed 'mixed miscellaneous' as it lacks trees of commercial value comparable with teak and sal.

The forests also possess fauna of both sal and teak biomes. Forsyth, perhaps, the first white man to arrive atop Pachmarhi, records barasingha in the Denwa river valley below (Forsyth 1872). Wild buffalo were also present. Above Bori, at one waterhole in summer, I have seen together the red junglefowl and painted spurfowl of the sal forests and the grey junglefowl and red spurfowl of the teak. There was a very good population of sambar and gaur, including some white specimens, and also of tiger, leopard, wild dog, sloth bear and four-horned antelope.

The extensive array of rock shelters strewn along the range have some of the most exquisite and least-known rock paintings of the prehistoric era, bespeaking of the richness of the wildlife of the region. In the Chitrashala rock shelter near Churna, there

Roof of the World: Marco Polo sheep on December snows, Pamirs, Tajikistan (top and bottom).

Tadjik markhor pair above Amudarya (Oxus) river, Tajikistan (top).
Asia's largest *elaphus* deer: Tian Shan wapiti stag, Syrdarya river, Naryn Reserve, Kyrgyzstan (bottom).

Walia ibex, Simien Mountains NP, Ethiopia (top).
Mountain nyala with oxpeckers, Bale Mountains, Ethiopia (bottom).

Ethiopian wolf, Bale Mountains, Ethiopia (top).
Oryx beisa with carmine bee eater, Awash NP, Ethiopia (bottom).

Old 'tuskers' seek the safest spots. Elephant bull in Ngorongoro crater, Tanzania (top). Black rhino on Okaukuejo waterhole in floodlight, Etosha Pan NP, Namibia (bottom).

Young male lion and tortoise, Chobe NP, Botswana.

Leopard, Seronera, Serengeti NP, Tanzania (top and bottom).

Cheetah with cubs, Masai Mara, Kenya (top).
A pair of cheetah chasing warthog, Tarangire NP, Tanzania (bottom).

Sable antelope male, Shimba Hills, Kenya (top).
Red lechwe male, Okavango, Botswana (bottom).

A benign visage, Kruger NP, South Africa (top).
Leopardess, Moremi Reserve, Botswana (bottom).

Scimitar-horned oryx, Souss-Massa NP, Morocco (top).
Gerenuk, appropriately named giraffe gazelle, Tsavo NP, Kenya (bottom).

Inscrutable visage of a male 'silverback' mountain gorilla, the largest primate in the world, Parc National Des Volcans, Rwanda (top).
World's tallest sand dunes. Namib Naukluft NP, Namibia (bottom).

Denali NP, Alaska: Dall Sheep rams (top); and brown bear (right).

Killer whale (orca) pod in Kenai Fjords NP, Alaska (bottom).

Male jaguar, Mato Grosso, Brazil (top).
Vicuna, carrying the finest wool in the world. Pampas Galeras NP, Peru (bottom).

Polar bear scavenging reindeer carcass, Svalbard, Norway (top).

Adelie penguin pair, Antarctic Peninsula (left).

'Serengeti of the South'. King Penguin rookery, South Georgia, Antarctica (bottom).

The largest penguins of all: Emperor penguins tobogganing on Snow Island, Antarctica (top); and king penguin pair on Falkland Islands (bottom).

are two depictions in detail, one showing a porcupine, the other a hedgehog.

The tract was already well fortified with the construction of the Tawa reservoir. The backwaters of the Tawa and Denwa rivers provided a moat on the western and southern flanks. In the south lay the extensive forests of Betul district and in the east the massif of Pachmarhi rose sheer. I knew Satpura would become one of the greatest national parks of India, and had yearned to establish it as such from the time I had learnt in Bangkok that I was to take over as the forest secretary of MP. But there was a problem. Large tracts of its lowland forest had been handed over to the Forest Development Corporation, which had invested large sums in teak and bamboo plantations and had converted substantial tracts into man-made forests. From the remaining forests, the annual harvest of timber, including some of the best quality teak, was yielding large sums to the exchequer. It was one of the major sources of income for the Forest department.

I had been adopting a risky modus operandi, deciding with Chief Wildlife Warden J.J. Dutta the boundaries of national parks and sanctuaries and notifying them in the state gazette, and only thereafter informing the forest minister and the chief minister of the establishment of the protected area. After the imbroglio over the naming of the Sanjay Gandhi National Park, I took care to not even mention our intention of declaring a protected area to anyone until after it was notified. Also, the finance department was not kept informed in advance, as the stoppage of forestry operations pursuant on these declarations of protected areas meant a loss in annual revenue. We knew that if we sought the concurrence of the finance department, we would perhaps never get it. We were saved by the fact that there was no lessening of the total annual revenue of the forest department. The price of good timber was rising annually and as the stoppage of forest extraction happened in the protected area, the auction prices of harvested timber consequently went up in the neighbouring forests, following the age-old equation of demand and supply.

However, I did not know that this would happen in my first year as forest secretary. Many protected areas had already been established by our department in 1981. One day the Chief Conservator of Forests V.K. Seth, loyal and level-headed, came to my office. He said that he and the Forest Department appreciated my efforts in saving forests by declaring them protected areas, but if Satpura was declared a park, there was no way we could hide the loss of revenue, and the Finance Department would raise a ruckus, if we did not obtain its prior concurrence. He ended by saying that if I were to be shifted from the Forest Department as a consequence, this would be a loss for him and for the department. I hesitated.

After the monsoon my family and I went to Pachmarhi. Early in the morning we drove up to Dhupgarh. Looking westwards with the sun behind us, we saw the gorgeous, unbroken forest stretching to the tent-shaped Gutti Baba Hill 40 km away on the horizon, not a vestige of human habitation in between. The temptation was irresistible. On 13 October 1981, the Satpura National Park of 525 sq. km was notified, contiguous to the existing Pachmarhi and Bori sanctuaries.

Today, Satpura has become a premier park of the country and, fortunately, since tigers have not been 'tamed' there, it is not subjected to tiger tourism which is a bane of some other parks, where people only go to see tigers, which they can do easily in a safari park. They overrun the park and come away without having a communion with nature or developing an empathy for wildlife, which is what parks are for and what eco-tourism should be all about.

In his election campaign, Chief Minister Arjun Singh had declared that if elected he would hold a cabinet meeting in Bastar. A year after winning, he scheduled a cabinet meeting in Jagdalpur, the district headquarters of Bastar, in the autumn of 1981. I had never been to Bastar before.

Travelling almost a whole night from Raipur through Sitanadi Wildlife Sanctuary, seeing a tigress en route and a large bull wild buffalo early in the morning in Udanti, I reached Jagdalpur late the next night. At dawn, we drove to the Teerathgarh Falls in the Kanger Valley. Leaving the jeep, we went down to take pictures of the falls from below and on our return found my camera bag missing. We later found the bag abandoned with my cameras and telephoto lenses intact, only my watch and pen were stolen.

The Kanger Valley proved to be far above my expectations. Its flora is amongst the most diverse in peninsular India. Unlike the usual transitional forest type sandwiched between teak and sal biomes, huge sal and teak trees stand side by side in Kanger, with a profuse admixture of other 'miscellaneous' species – saja, bija, haldu, kusum, semal, pipal and banyan.

But there is another remarkable feature in Kanger – a series of underground caves, some as deep as 60 m and extending to 1,200 m in length. In them are amongst the most outstanding samples of stalagmite and stalactite formations in the Indian subcontinent, with life forms endemic to only these micro ecosystems. The remoteness of the area can be gauged from the fact that these were discovered only in the 1950s. It is tragic that these calcareous projections, formed over aeons, have been allowed to become icons of worship and smeared with vermillion. J.J. Dutta rightly wanted even the lower portion of the valley to be included in the park, which I was able to see only on a subsequent visit. The survey took some time and, thus, the Kanger Valley National Park covering 200 sq. km and 28 km in length of the valley, was declared in July 1982.

The ill-conceived Bastar Pine Project, whereby existing forests were to be felled and the land cleared for the planting of tropical pines to produce pulp for industry, in the middle of a volatile tribal area, was then raising controversy. I advocated closure of the project despite the investments already made, and fortunately it was later abandoned. Plantation for commercial purposes should be done on private lands or refractory and decimated forests, even if the yield will be much less, and not by cutting existing forests that may be less valuable commercially but are ecologically rich, especially if the local populace is dependent on these 'miscellaneous' or non-teak forests.

One could travel for hours in the extensive, rich forests and grassland-forest mosaics of Bastar without seeing a single wild animal. After the cabinet meeting I travelled through the Bhairamgarh forests to the Indravati river, below Abujmarh. On the way, we disturbed a chowsingha that just would not stop running for its life. In my entire life, I have not come across animals with as great a flight distance as in Bastar. When disturbed, they ran incredible distances at the maximum speed they could muster – testimony to the persecution they suffer from the local tribes. The central Indian barasingha had become extinct in Bastar by the time I went there, though I was given three sets of barasingha antlers. Usually rhesus macaques and langurs, in the few areas in India where they may be persecuted, escape by leaping from tree to tree. But in Bastar, a monkey disturbed in a tree would jump down to the ground and run like a hare, experience having taught it that it will be chased from tree to tree, and ultimately surrounded in an isolated tree, which will be cut down and the refugee killed.

I camped on the River Indravati in what was then the Kutru Wildlife Sanctuary. I asked the local village headman about wildlife in the area, including crocodiles in the river. He replied without prompting that there had been two types of crocodiles in the Indravati, the mugger that was still there and a long-snouted one that had disappeared a couple of decades earlier. From his description, I have no doubt he was referring to the gharial. This crocodilian occurs in the Mahanadi river system, but is not reported in the Godavari–Indravati system. Its awkward locomotion on land makes the gharial a very poor colonizer where travel overland is involved. But evidently gharials were once to be found in the Indravati (Ranjitsinh and Singh 2002).

I never saw the wild buffalo in the forest, but I saw their unmistakable, oversized hoof marks. I allocated some funds for improving the water-holding capacity of the tanks they drank from and wallowed in, and for other conservation measures. An area encompassing 1,258 sq. km covering the Kutru Sanctuary and other areas was notified as the Indravati National Park in 1981 itself. The next year it was declared a tiger reserve.

I took the opportunity to visit the Abujmarh plateau, still undemarcated in revenue records and still affected by man-eating tigers. The Maria tribe here practised shifting cultivation, but unlike in the northeast, it was more regulated. The forest regeneration was apparent and the streams still ran clear of silt. On my way up to the plateau from Orchha, I saw a single wild dog, the largest specimen of this species I have yet seen.

Many of the states of the country had still not declared their state animals and birds. I wrote to my colleague Kailash Sankhala, then chief wildlife warden of Rajasthan, that the most appropriate state bird for Rajasthan would be the great Indian bustard, as the major world population of this bird survived there. If he, however, did not wish to have it as the state bird, he should let us know so that MP could choose the bustard for itself. I think this prompted Rajasthan to declare the great Indian bustard as its state bird. For MP, Chief Minister Arjun Singh wanted the tiger as the state animal. At the time, MP did have the largest tiger population in India. However, I argued that the tiger was already the national animal and MP must have an animal unique to it. I suggested the central Indian barasingha, confined to the Kanha National Park, and he agreed. For the state bird, I suggested either the lesser florican or the paradise flycatcher. He unhesitatingly chose the latter.

Communion of mind, however, was not evident in another incident around that time. On the road between Tala and Umaria in Bandhavgarh National Park, a young cowherd was driving his herd of cattle one morning. A young male tiger, driven off by the alpha male nearby, attacked one of his bullocks. The brave man rushed up to save his animal. The tiger retaliated and killed him, but did not drag the body away, let alone eat the flesh, and just retreated into cover. The park director S. Hassan was categorical about the past conduct of that tiger and it was clear that he had only attacked when the cowherd got too close, with his stick raised to strike. A few hours later, Arjun Singh phoned me to ask whether I had declared the tiger a maneater to be destroyed. I explained the circumstances and said it was a retaliatory kill and that the tiger had not touched the body after the event, even when the others had run away and the tiger was alone with the body before the rescue party arrived. I added that we would watch the tiger closely and if he showed any future aggression towards humans, we will destroy him. Arjun Singh pointed out that recently when a crocodile had killed a girl in the Narmada at Marble Rocks near Jabalpur, I had it shot. I explained the totally different circumstances: the girl was in a boat dangling her feet in the water when the crocodile made a deliberate attack, caught her by the leg and pulled her down. It was also known to have made a previous unsuccessful attack. Arjun Singh then asked, sarcastically, 'Does a tiger have to kill and eat a man to convince the forest secretary of Madhya Pradesh that it is a maneater?' I just said, 'Yes, sir,' and he put the phone down, but he did not order the destruction of that tiger which of course he could have. I kept my fingers crossed for the next couple of months, but the tiger remained on good behaviour.

In May 1982, the Bandhavgarh National Park, then only 105 sq. km in size, was extended by a further 332 sq. km to take it to the Johilla river in the south, the Chandia forests in the west and towards Ghunghuti in the east. Villages were translocated from Bandhavgarh, as they continued to be from Kanha.

The Madhav National Park in Shivpuri, the second national park after Kanha to be declared in MP in 1955, was only 165 sq. km in area. It had been the favourite hunting grounds of the ruling Scindia family of Gwalior and from where record tigers had been shot by viceroys of India in the past. Tigers were long gone from Shivpuri, but it was a lovely park, on the national highway, with leopard, sambar, chital, chinkara and nilgai and lakes with crocodiles and migratory birds. Also in May 1982, a further 181 sq. km was added to this park, mainly towards the east.

Later that year, the north-western and south-eastern boundaries of the National Chambal Sanctuary, extending into the states of

Rajasthan, MP and UP, and now the best extant habitat of the gharial and of the endangered Gangetic dolphin, were rationalized and notified. In later years, the diversion of a huge quantum of water by barrages upstream, and by the industrial hub that Kota city had become poses a threat to the survival of the dolphin, gharial, turtle and other aquatic and avian life in the Chambal. In 2010, at my behest the standing committee of the National Board for Wildlife directed the Wildlife Institute of India to ascertain the minimum ecologic water flow required in the Chambal to sustain these endangered species. Political pressure currently has led to the flouting of these minimum levels.

The process of reorganization of the forest department was initiated in 1981, to make it more streamlined and professional and to identify and focus upon forest extension, production and other normal territorial functions. Certain new divisions and the splitting up of existing unwieldy ranges and jurisdictions were also contemplated. This was ably handled by A.K. Dutta, IFS.

N.D. Jayal, my successor after my first tenure as director, wildlife preservation of India, had followed my initiative and pushed for the setting up of wildlife wings in most states. Indira Gandhi had also lent personal support to this endeavour by writing to chief ministers. However, territorial control over the states' parks and sanctuaries, including financial powers of withdrawal and disbursal of funds, had not been transferred to the chief wildlife wardens and their staff, in most instances. So a diarchy of management persisted with all its pitfalls, wherein the logistic control over the protected areas continued with the territorial DFO, but the responsibility vested with the sanctuary warden. I set up the Wildlife Directorate of MP under a chief wildlife warden and transferred control of all national parks and most of the sanctuaries to the directorate. In some parks like Kanha, the process of transfer of control of buffer areas to park directors was also initiated.

It is an extremely difficult proposition to create new posts for staff. So instructions were issued that whenever a park or a sanctuary was established and the area transferred to the Wildlife Directorate, the posts of forest guards, foresters and rangers in existence over the area in question would also be transferred along with the area, to the Wildlife Directorate. The staff concerned would have the option to go the Wildlife Directorate or to move elsewhere to available equivalent non-wildlife posts. The wildlife posts left vacant, if any, would be filled by suitable personnel recruited by the Wildlife Directorate. The collection of minor forest produce from such a newly created protected area, if already auctioned, would stop from the financial year following its establishment. No vehicle would be allowed passage at night in parks and sanctuaries, except for the purpose of patrolling by the staff. The chief wildlife warden of MP would make entries in the annual confidential reports of territorial DFOs as to what they had done to conserve wildlife in their own areas of jurisdiction outside of the protected areas. After my relinquishing the post of forest secretary, many of these orders were either withdrawn or not allowed to be enforced.

A number of sawmills had come up close to forests. In daytime, they would function as flour mills; after dark, they would metamorphose into mills that sawed timber illegally cut and surreptitiously smuggled in. The forest authorities had no control over these mills adjacent to their forests, and even the Electricity Board officers could only disconnect electric supply to them if the operators failed to pay their dues, not if they changed a flour mill into a sawmill and back again. To deal with the situation, we drafted a new Sawmills (Regulation) Act, got the approval of the state cabinet in Bhopal and then got the concurrence of the Union ministry for power.

MP's director of tourism, Probir Sen, had started the annual dance festival at Khajuraho, with the iconic Kandariya Mahadev temple in the background. In the Department of Tourism, which was also my charge, we acquired the Jahangir Mahal in Orchha, originally built by Raja Bir Singh Deo Bundela to house his distinguished guest and patron, Emperor Jahangir. We converted the palace into a hotel. Bir Singh is notorious for having Abul Fazl (Emperor Akbar's friend, adviser and biographer) killed, at the behest of Prince Salim (the future Jahangir), near the Karera Sanctuary. But what distinguishes Bir Singh, in our context, is that he presented Jahangir with a white cheetah, the only one on record anywhere in either Africa or Asia (Divyabhanusinh 1999).

I took advantage of my position as secretary, tourism, to shut down the tourist lodges, which had been started in the forest rest houses within Kanha Park, and converted them into visitor centres and a museum. Tourist accommodation in India should be outside of protected areas, not in the centre of them.

Some years previously, I had brought to the notice of the eminent scientist and taxonomist Colin P. Groves the difference in antler formation and morphology between the barasingha found in Assam, those in the Terai region of India and Nepal, and those in Kanha. The latter two populations had already been recognized as separate subspecies – *Rucervus duvaucelii duvaucelii*, the nominate race in northern India and *Rucervus duvaucelii branderi*, the race in central India, named after the eminent naturalist A.A. Dunbar Brander, who had written about this population. On my visits to Kaziranga and Manas, I had observed marked differences in antler formation, in body, tail, head and ear shape, and in body size and colouration, between the Assam animals and the other two. I had published a paper describing the differences (Ranjitsinh 1980). Colin Groves subsequently came to India and examined specimens of all three populations. Later, he published a paper confirming the physical differences and named the new Assam subspecies after me, *Rucervus duvaucelii ranjitsinhi*. The reason he gave for assigning the name was: 'Ranjitsinh's name has been associated with many wildlife conservation projects in India and, recently, in Thailand; in the late 1960s his insistence and energy was primarily responsible for reviving *R. duvaucelli branderi* from near extinction and he has more recently been concerned in the still more difficult problem of saving the Manipur thamin (*C. eldi eldi*)' (Groves 1982).

The year 1983 was to prove a crucial one. I had already received hints that my tenure as forest secretary would not last too long, that I was treading on too many of the proverbial toes. The matter of transfer and posting was in fact a very lucrative 'industry' in MP. A person belonging to Gwalior could be posted 1,500 km away, in the south of Bastar. There were posts that offered better 'remuneration' than others. Quotas had been fixed for each MLA and MP, for each department of government, for recommending transfers and postings. Two periods of the year were fixed when transfers could take place on the recommendations of politicians, which I called 'open hunting seasons'. At these times, one would be pestered by phone calls from politicians at all hours, recommending transfers and specific postings. One could not take action against the persons themselves as there was no evidence, other than a phone call, that would stand scrutiny in court. For the posting of a particular person as a ranger in the Motinala Range in my old district of Mandla, I received recommendations from two chief ministers, another minister and four MLAs. The reorganization of the forest department was then going on, and I split Motinala Range into two to make the post less attractive.

Once I had to attend a meeting in Delhi. I chose to go after the last date of the summer open season had passed. But on my return to Bhopal, I was shown a written order from the forest minister, pre-dated to be within the prescribed open season, listing a large number of rangers to be transferred to specific ranges. Inadvertently, the secretary to the minister had given the wrong copy to the officer concerned in the forest department, for on it, scribbled in pencil, were the amounts to be levied on each beneficiary of the transfer. Tribals got a discount, OBC rangers got a greater discount, most likely because the minister himself belonged to this class, but the gold nugget was the entry: 'very poor – free'. Even in dishonesty there is room for compassion!

I took the paper to Arjun Singh who cancelled all the transfers and soon thereafter changed the forest minister. But there was an interesting aftermath to this drama. Those from whom money had been taken for the transfer orders started demanding refunds after the cancellation. Representatives of one of the 'aggrieved' accosted the minister on a railway platform, in public view, and would not let him board the train or leave the platform without a refund. As no cash was available on the spot, the refund was given by cheque, which was then produced on the floor of the Vidhan Sabha in Bhopal.

I had visited the forests on the Pench river in Seoni district in late 1982. The area had acquired a hallowed reputation in the accounts of R.A. Sterndale, J. Forsyth and A.A. Dunbar Brander. There was even a small Pench Wildlife Sanctuary of 118 sq. km on the Seoni side of the river. But the wild animal population was low and weeds such as *Cassia tora* and *Lantana camara* had invaded in the wake of extensive overgrazing by livestock. Still, the wildlife potential of the area was very evident, far above that of the adjacent Maharashtra forest around the Totladoh dam, which had already been declared a sanctuary. After some hesitation, I declared an area of 293 sq. km as the Pench National Park, with almost equal areas in both Seoni and Chhindwara districts. Animal numbers increased very rapidly and, today, Pench has become a premier park of India, despite its relatively small size, visited by a large number of tourists and holding substantial populations of tiger, wild dog, sambar, gaur, chital, pig and nilgai.

As the collector of Mandla district in the 1970s, I had frequently passed by deposits of fossils around Ghughua village in the Niwas tahsil of Mandla, not far from the southern boundary of the Bandhavgarh National Park. In early 1983, I heard that a medical doctor had collected a large quantity of fossils from the area, had broken them and used them to decorate the walls of his house in Jabalpur. I declared a cluster of eight sites as the Ghughua Fossil National Park. The fossils of the early Tertiary period, some sixty million years old, are mostly wood fossils but there are also fossil fruits and seeds that have been beautifully preserved. A unique feature is that some of the fossils stand upright.

In the northern corner of MP, adjacent to Rajasthan, lies the Gandhi Sagar Sanctuary, around a reservoir by the same name on the Chambal river. The forests had been greatly denuded but were the best in that locality and included the fort of Hinglajgarh, with its exquisite sculptures. I found otters in the waters. Its area of 225 sq. km was extended by another 369 sq. km in 1983.

The Kanha National Park had already been extended from its original size when I was the collector of Mandla, by additions in 1970, 1974 and 1976 totalling to 1,516 sq. km. The magnificent forests of Supkhar had already been added and barasingha had been reintroduced there from the Stoever Stockade of Kanha. Adjacent to this was another tract of forest that I was familiar with from my Mandla days, the forests on the River Phen, from Mangli to Mawai. The barasingha had gone from this tract a little before I took over as collector, but it still had gaur, tiger, sambar and the rest. In March 1983, the Phen Wildlife Sanctuary of 111 sq. km was established, and was later added to the Kanha Tiger Reserve.

Bandhavgarh had been extended on three sides as mentioned earlier, in 1982. To the north, and tenuously connected to it, lay a rich tract of riverine sal forest on the upper reaches of the River Son. The Panpatha Wildlife Sanctuary with an area of 246 sq. km was established here in 1983. In fact, three other sanctuaries were notified on that same date. One was the extension of the existing Ratapani sanctuary by 159 sq. km on the southern flank of the Vindhyas. Ratapani is now proposed to be declared a tiger reserve. The other two protected areas were created for the conservation of the monsoonal breeding grounds of the endangered and mysterious lesser florican. The first of these was the Sardarpur Sanctuary of 348 sq. km, an area which I knew well, being a part of my first district of Dhar. The second was the Sailana sanctuary of 13 sq. km in Ratlam district, a former property of my wife's uncle, Maharaja Digvijaya

Singhji of Sailana. This Sanctuary is now the best place to see the florican in central India. In May 1983, the Sarangarh–Gomarda Sanctuary, extending over 278 sq. km, was notified in the Raigarh district of what is now Chhattisgarh.

The most endangered large mammal in peninsular India now is the Asiatic wild buffalo. Apart from the usual threats of poaching and habitat destruction, the animal is afflicted by a danger whose import is still not fully recognized by the conservation community – genetic 'swamping'. Science is increasingly becoming aware of the importance of wild gene sources, especially of those species of fauna and flora whose counterparts have been domesticated by man – wild rice, wild citrus, wild mango, junglefowl, wild buffalo, wild horse, and others. Our domestic chicken is descended from the junglefowl, and there are more domestic buffalo in the world than any other species of domestic animals. Yet, these are the two species most affected by interbreeding with their domestic counterparts and are losing their wild genetic purity and identity.

The wild buffalo of South-East Asia disappeared around the time I was with UNEP, as did the Kouprey (*Bos sauveli*) from which our domesticated cattle have descended. Wild buffalo have also gone from Nepal and Bangladesh and the 'wild' population in Sri Lanka is obviously genetically inundated. When I visited Manas and Kaziranga between 1960 and '70, the wild buffalo were huge and largely saved from genetic 'swamping', except for the wild population along the periphery of these protected areas, where they came in greater contact with domestic buffalo. It was most interesting to see the change in the morphology of the wild buffalo from the southern borders of Manas in Bansbari, Bhuyanpara and Kokilabari, to those a few kilometres north in the Uchila grasslands in central Manas, and even more so further north in Bhutan Manas. In Kaziranga, the buffalo camps within the park, the 'khuntis', were relocated outside, for which the Government of India gave financial support. Some decrepit animals and, more importantly, the semi-wild stock that were the progeny of wild and domestic buffalo, stayed back. Though many of these were killed by tigers, those that survived continued breeding with the wild, as a result of which in my opinion there are no genetically pure wild buffalo now left in Kaziranga. In Manas, the Bodo takeover of the park in the 1980s resulted in a drastic decimation of the wild buffalo and the invasion of domestic herds, the result being the same as in Kaziranga and elsewhere.

I believe genetically pure wild buffalo now survive only in the Indravati National Park in Bastar and in Udanti Sanctuary, both in Chhattisgarh. There is a reason for this. Wild buffalo bulls are almost twice the size of the domestic bulls in that area. From time to time a wild bull would walk into a domestic buffalo herd, kill the herd bull if there was one and commandeer the domestic flock into the forest if he could. If anyone tried to prevent him, or to milk the domestic buffalo in his presence, the wild bull would threaten or even attack. The fetus of wild bull and female domestic buffalo union is so large that the majority of the offspring were stillborn or the mother frequently died giving birth. Of the progeny that survived, the males would become too large and obstreperous to be used as draught animals, which is their normal usage, and the females would grow up to reportedly produce less milk than the 'pure' domestic she buffalo. No wonder the local people disliked this intermingling and would take potshots at wild bulls that were aiming at a takeover of their domestic animals. Indeed, tribal communities that lived around wild buffalo habitats in central India kept cattle other than domestic buffalo.

By the time I came to Bhopal as forest secretary, there were a few isolated populations left of the wild buffalo in peninsular India. The largest population was in what became the Indravati National Park, established in 1981. Three small populations remained outside it. One was in Bhairamgarh on the Indravati, upstream of the Indravati

National Park. The other was southwards in Pamed, on the border with Andhra Pradesh, now Telangana.

In 1983, Bhairamgarh Sanctuary was established with an area of 139 sq. km and Pamed was also declared one, with an area of 442 sq. km. Both sanctuaries also had tiger, leopard and the other fauna of this region. Sadly, the wild buffalo is now extinct in both these sanctuaries.

The only central Indian wild buffalo population outside of Bastar and, thus, outside of Naxalite-affected areas was in the Udanti forests, east of the existing Sitanadi sanctuary. There was a problem and delay in its declaration as a Sanctuary, due to a previously sanctioned irrigation project in the area. Then a female wild buffalo fell into the pit dug for the masonry dam and, taking advantage of this, I was able to get the Udanti Sanctuary declared with an area of 231 sq. km. Today, it holds a population of only six animals – five bulls and one cow – but more of that later.

By now I had been forest, toursim and sports secretary in MP for two-and-a-half years. When I had taken charge, there were three national parks with a total area of 2,144 sq. km and twenty sanctuaries with a total area of 4,612 sq. km in the state, which then included Chhattisgarh. During my tenure, eight new national parks were added which have now become nine with the splitting of the Sanjay National Park. Of the existing parks, the area of Bandhavgarh had been more than quadrupled and Madhav National Park more than doubled, and there was a total addition of 5,292 sq. km to the coverage under national parks. Fourteen new wildlife sanctuaries had also been created during this period and three existing sanctuaries were extended, a total increase of 3,890 sq. km brought under sanctuaries. From 1983 till today, MP has added two new sanctuaries and Chhattisgarh one, an addition of a total area of 233 sq. km.

In my subsequent 'avatar' as joint secretary of forest and wildlife in the Ministry of Environment and Forests, a few years later, the forest minister of MP came to see me with a request that 'nistar' and minor forest produce collection including that of bamboos, should be permitted from within parks and sanctuaries, as what was left in the forests outside of these protected areas was now so reduced that the needs of the local people and of industry could not be met from them. This would have entailed the amendment of the Wild Life (Protection) Act, which of course I had no intention of doing.

In early 1982, I took some leave to spend time in Wankaner and in my main study area, Velavadar National Park, to complete my PhD thesis on the Indian blackbuck. Apart from an urge to study an exquisite and totally Indian animal deeply associated with my boyhood and youth, I felt a doctorate in animal ecology would give me a stamp of specialization and help with my future postings in my chosen field, rather than being assigned the assorted sundry jobs which await an IAS officer. There were several PhD dissertations being written on mega mammals, but few on the smaller ones.

By the beginning of 1983, the stoppage of commercial exploitation of protected forest areas and the stoppage or control of grazing within them was having its effect on the political dynamics of these areas. The chief minister had already told me to not establish any new protected areas, but when I told him that some were already in the 'pipeline' and for future ones I would take his prior concurrence, he did not object. Indeed, I was under considerable pressure to de-notify some of the sanctuaries as the Supreme Court order that no area of a park or a sanctuary could be de-notified without the prior concurrence of both the State Wildlife Advisory Board and the National Board for Wildlife, had not come about then. My own forest minister wanted a part of the Nauradehi Wildlife Sanctuary, which was in his constituency, to be de-notified; and my deputy minister of forests wanted Badalkhol Sanctuary in Raigadh district to be de-notified for the same reason. I realized the practical need for the rationalization of the boundaries of many protected areas, but was afraid of letting even a small area be de-notified as it would open the proverbial floodgates for de-notifications. I staved off the doom by saying that any de-notification of a protected area would require the prior approval of Prime Minister Indira Gandhi, and the ploy worked.

There were also other developments afoot. Sal seed was becoming increasingly lucrative. I wanted to auction the right to collect the seed, with penalty provisions for setting fire and for not checking consequential or incidental forest fires. Ultimately, I was ordered to bring the matter to the cabinet, which approved of collection of sal seed without auction. Soon after, I was transferred to the post of commissioner, Bhopal.

My hair had started showing the first streaks of grey. So my wife said the transfer was a blessing in disguise and that the new job would be far easier and less stressful. How wrong she was!

10

Bhopal, Gas and Union Carbide

The most glaring aspect noticeable in Bhopal was the rapid encroachment of municipal land by the illegal construction of veritable townships of shanties or 'jhuggis'. If the encroachers were evicted and resettled elsewhere on government land, they would dispose of or retain those properties and come back and build another jhuggi, often on the very land they had been removed from. As commissioner, Bhopal, it was my duty to supervise the revenue staff of the collector, whose job it was to remove and prevent encroachments. Soon after my assuming the new charge, we received orders that the existing jhuggis should be regularized and papers of their ownership rights be prepared for distribution by politicians. These regularized jhuggis were to be given free water and a minimum amount of free electricity; this when the Madhya Pradesh Electricity Board (MPEB) was in deep debt and short of electricity. To add to the irony, the government also directed that any further jhuggi construction should be 'strictly' prevented! Shades of past forest settlements and lessons for the future. I am a staunch believer in democracy, but have often naively wondered whether there could be an ideal democracy without vote banks and bank notes.

I went to see Arjun Singh and requested him to reconsider the order of regularization of encroachments, arguing that it would only give impetus to more such endeavours. What many politicians, even astute and experienced ones, do not realize is that there is no substitute for good governance, that the majority of people are not so gullible as to be taken in by 'sops'. An exception was Babulal Gaur, who as a lawyer used to plead in my commissioner's court and later became the chief minister of MP. He always supported the removal and prevention of encroachments. He won all his elections from the areas of Bhopal most affected by the jhuggis, succeeding there as a non-Congress candidate even in the face of the sympathy wave following the assassination of Indira Gandhi.

In November 1983, the Queen of England, Elizabeth II, and the Duke of Edinburgh, Prince Philip, came to India for the Commonwealth heads of government meeting. The Duke had expressed a wish to see the tiger and the lion in India. The Government of MP was playing host and I was deputed to arrange for his visit to Kanha, along with Chief Wildlife Warden R.C. Saxena.

As tourist accommodation within the park had been discontinued, the Duke was to stay in the Tourism Corporation Lodge in Mukki, in Balaghat district. November is a little too early for the start of the barasingha rut and in this month they are conspicuous by their absence from the meadows. However, the rut can be advanced a little if mud is available for wallowing. So I brought in water from a rivulet in the Sonph meadow in Kanha, to create an artificial wallow. Salt was provided in Bisanpura on the Mukki side of the park to attract the gaur.

The Duke was to arrive in his private plane at an airstrip near Balaghat on 19 November. The security personnel inquired about the route we would be taking in the park the next day so that they could go before us and 'sanitize' it from the security standpoint. I gave them the route and told them to do whatever they had to do by midnight; if they went in ahead of us early next morning and were going to hide behind sal trees, I would not bring the Duke on that route as it would be a worthless trip. They agreed.

Saxena and I received the Duke and escorted him to Mukki. I have never met a more suave conversationalist. He would speak with each person at the dinner table so that all would feel included. The twentieth of November happened to be his wedding anniversary and he could not have received a better gift than the sightings we had that morning. We left before dawn, seeing gaur, sambar, barasingha stags at the wallow in Sonph, and four tigers. Two more were located but the Duke was satisfied with the four he had seen. As we were having brunch at the Kanha bungalow, wild dogs brought a barasingha doe to bay in the Desi Nala in front of us, and pulled her down. On our return journey, I asked the Duke whether he would write a foreword for my forthcoming book *Beyond the Tiger*, and he readily agreed.

Dinner had been organized in his honour in Delhi and I was asked to attend. At the end of it, I said goodbye to the Duke, whereupon he asked me why I was not accompanying him next to the Gir forest to see the lions, which he knew was near my home in Wankaner. I replied that though my home was in Gujarat, I was serving in Madhya Pradesh. My batchmate Hamid Ansari, now the vice-president of India and who then happened to be the representative of the Ministry of External Affairs at the dinner, pulled me aside and said I must go with the Duke. Hamid said he would speak with the chief secretary of MP and get his permission, which he did.

Next morning, I joined the Duke and Maharaja Fatehsinhrao Gaekwad of Baroda, who was then the president of WWF India. The former flew us in his private plane to Keshod, from where we drove to Sasan in the Gir forest. We were driven around, saw crocodiles in the Kamleshwar reservoir, a handsome sambar stag and the customary chital, and then went to see the famed Kathiawadi horses in Sasan. No lions. I took the park director aside and asked why we were not seeing lions, for which the trip had specially been arranged. Lions are the easiest large cats to see in India. He replied that they had earmarked two prides and a pair of males, but since the approach and the environs of neither had been 'sanitized' by the security personnel, he could not take us to them. As there was no one to overrule the security officers and take personal responsibility, we never got to see the lions. At lunch, the Gujarat government representative presented the Duke with a photograph of the Indian lion. The Duke turned to Fatehsinhji and me and said: 'I believe it. I do believe that the lions are here!'

The end of 1984 proved to be, perhaps, the most traumatic phase in my career. In the morning of 31 October, I learnt that Indira Gandhi had been assassinated. Spurred by the news of the rampaging, retributory, anti-Sikh vigilantes in Delhi, mob violence broke out in Madhya Pradesh. A fire set to burn two shops owned by Sikhs in Indore also burnt the old Rajwada Palace of the Holkars of Indore and in the process destroyed the only repository of the Malwa school of painting, the Durbar Hall ceiling inlaid with ivory and the silver puja vessels of Ahilyabai Holkar, revered as a saint in central India and the creator of the iconic ghats on the Narmada at Maheshwar. In the Bhopal division under my charge, Sikhs were killed in Betul district and in Raisen.

In Bhopal city, a mob set out with similar intent in the old part of the city. The police force had been spread out all over to maintain law and order and only one platoon was with me and the DIG of police. We blocked the road but the mob came on. The DIG advised me to step aside as the crowd seemed determined to press forward. However, I could not help tarrying on the road. When they were close, the leaders asked us to move. I asked them what they wanted to do, and they replied that they wanted the Sikhs to be taught a lesson. I said that one of the Sikh assassins of Indira Gandhi had already been killed and the other would be duly punished. Besides, I added, when a tiger or a leopard turns a maneater it has to be destroyed. I myself have shot maneaters. But in the name of a maneater one does not destroy innocent tigers, nor does one try to eradicate the race of the tiger.

In a face-off with a wild animal in a defensive aggression mode, there is a moment when the aggression either subsides or escalates. The signs of this are easy to notice in the great cats, indicated by the colour of the eyes, the movement of the tail and ears, and more. With humans it is also body language that one must look for. I noticed that the crowd hesitated, the shrillness of the voices lessened. So I pressed on, saying that it is always the innocents who get hurt. Look what happened to the sacred vessels of Ahilyabai, and so on and on. Time had to be bought and the anger defused. The crowd gradually dispersed as more police reinforcements arrived. No Sikh casualty or property damage occurred in Bhopal city. I thanked my stars and tigers, and felt the worst was over. Little did I know the respite would be only for a month, till that fateful early morning on 3 December 1984.

'At 1.55 a.m., I was woken by a phone call from the City Kotwali Control Room. ASI K.P.S. Chauhan informed me in a gasping voice that there had been a gas leakage in the Union Carbide Factory and people were running away. The gas was causing serious irritation of the eyes, people were finding difficulty in breathing and effects were being felt even in the control room. SP Swaraj Puri also then spoke with me confirming the story. I told Puri I would be coming to the control room as soon as I could, whereupon he told me that my coming to the control room was futile since the telephones were jammed. He also informed me that ADM Prajapati had reached the control room. I, therefore, decided to make all the phone calls that I could and alert as many people as possible who could be of assistance in this emergency, before proceeding to the control room myself' (Ranjitsinh 1984c).

Quoted above is the opening paragraph of a report I prepared and submitted to the late Brahma Swaroop, chief secretary of Madhya Pradesh, soon after 3 December 1984. Reams have been written about the accident and are still being written over thirty years later. I do not wish to write what is already in the public domain, nor of which I have no personal knowledge. However, since I have never published anything on the subject before and avoided the media during the episode, I will describe here my experience as an active participant in the aftermath of the tragedy and the first non-Carbide employee to enter the premises of the factory that morning. There are aspects which may, perhaps, be not known.

Let me continue with the gist of my report cited above. I first phoned Dr M.N. Nagu, director of health services in MP, an old friend from my Burhanpur days, informed him about the accident and asked him to alert all the concerned medical officers and institutions. I next phoned J. Mukund, works manager of the Union Carbide factory at Bhopal. His wife said he had just left for the factory, so I asked her to tell him to call me back urgently. Then I phoned Brigadier Garg, managing director of Straw Products Ltd whose factory was close to the Union Carbide factory, to find out more. Garg was gasping for breath, barely able to speak, and said the children of his staff were the most affected. Next was Brigadier N.K. Mayne, area commander of the army, whom I requested to put in service as many army vehicles as he could to evacuate people from the Carbide factory area and to make available the facilities of the military hospital, which was not far from the site. I also asked the commander of the Special Armed Force to send their paramilitary vehicles, and requested the Bharat Heavy Electricals Ltd (BHEL) factory nearby to make their vehicles also available for evacuation and asked them to provide gas masks if any were available. At that moment Chief Secretary Brahma Swaroop, who was my neighbour in the Char Imli locality, walked into my house. Mukund of the Union Carbide phoned me back and told me that gas from his factory had leaked but would be stopped within an hour. On my specifically asking him whether the gas could kill a person, Mukund replied that 'such an occurrence of death has never happened and there is no question of a person remaining behind after inhaling the gas as the sensation is intolerable.'

General elections were due and a fleet of cars was parked in front of the house of Bharat Singh, minister of state, Department of Home. Asking him to send these vehicles for evacuation, I left for the control room, driving my official car.

Going past the Lal Parade Ground of the police, my eyes started burning. A little beyond, in Jahangirabad, crowds were surging towards me. I was stopped a number of times by people wanting me to give them a lift in the direction opposite to mine and asking me where I was going. When I replied I was going to the control room, one man asked whether I was mad.

'On the Pul Pukhta Bridge over the lower end of the Lower Bhopal Lake, leading into the old city,' I wrote in my diary, 'my car headlights revealed an eerie, unworldly, Kafkaesque scene. A haze of white vapour hung over the ground like a thin veil. From it were emerging figures of men, women and children, mostly in white to add to the other-worldly illusion, panting and running as if in slow motion. Footwear lay scattered all over and shards of glass glittered from the light reflected off the white vapour. The vision will haunt me for the rest of my life. My eyes started to smart and water even more and I smelt that unwelcome but not too unpleasant odour. It was a smell I was to recognize for weeks thereafter, in hospitals and closed rooms, on the burqas of Muslim women and on the breath of dying men.'

In the control room, Superintendent of Police Swaraj Puri and Additional District Magistrate Prajapati and their colleagues were coping manfully, but the conditions were hardly bearable. Phoning Dr Nagu from the control room, I learnt of the first casualties. Two children and an old man had died at J.P. Hospital. So much for Mukund's assurance that the gas was not lethal. I phoned the collectors of the districts under my charge – Vidisha, Raisen and Sehore – to urgently send as many doctors, officers, staff and vehicles as they could. These started arriving in some three hours. The physical ill effects of the gas were worsening. Having to talk and shout incessantly over the phone to overcome poor telecom connectivity and the din in the control room meant that one inhaled more gas, which still hung like a fog in the control room and outside. A cold winter's night ensured that the heavy vapour hung low.

In a couple of hours in the control room, I had done what I could and needed to do there. Swaraj Puri and Prajapati were already in charge. So at the hint of dawn, I left for the Union Carbide factory half a kilometre away, with Additional Collector Khan and police officer A.K. Singh. We were the first government servants and, in fact, the first persons who were not employees of Union Carbide to enter the premises of the factory after the gas leak. Conditions within were chaotic. There were some who were trying to get succour at the small factory dispensary, mostly Carbide employees. Mukund was still unaware of the tragedy outside. The factory workers had got under showers and had escaped serious injury. Only Shakeel Qureshi who had jumped over the wall trying to escape – as he knew most of all what the gas meant – had broken a leg in the process and, thus, inhaled a fair share of the gas. It was then that I heard for the first time what the gas was – Methyl isocyanate (MIC). I was the commissioner of Bhopal but I did not know that a cyanide by-product was being used in that factory. Mukund also informed me, for the first time, that a way of counteracting MIC was putting a wet cloth over one's face. If only Union Carbide had announced that a few hours earlier, many lives would have been saved and much suffering allayed. In the office hung an award given to the factory for its industrial safety measures.

Mukund told me that there had been a violent chemical reaction in the plant, the reason for which he did not know. As a result, about twenty tonnes of a total stock of sixty tonnes of stored MIC had escaped, and the gas scrubber had been unable to cope with it. Expressing his regret at the situation, Mukund took me to the storage tanks. One of the three tanks in which MIC had been stored had developed a crack on the thick cement outer cover and a part of the top of the tank had caved in, with steam still emanating in that predawn light from those cracks, apparently from the water that had been sprayed on it. The tank was still hot to the touch on that early winter morning, despite the dousing.

When I came out of the factory, people living in the jhuggis around it, those who had not yet left, were running about in panic. I could sense the trauma and anger building up. I returned to the control room, and informed Swaraj Puri and the chief secretary of the developments. I also phoned the collectors of my districts who informed me that their contingents had left. I remembered that my development assistant and deputy collector Shrimal had previously been the drug controller in Bhopal. So I asked him to go around and have all the medicine shops opened.

The next stop was Hamidia Hospital, the epicentre of medical care for the gas-affected, as it was one of the largest hospitals closest to the Carbide factory. The scene was total mayhem. Thousands were thronging the premises, bringing in the dead and the dying. An officer accompanying me counted one case in critical condition being brought in each minute. The doctors could barely cope. The less critical they would ask to wait, the dead they just waved away. I proceeded to J.P. Hospital, met Dr Nagu and requested him to send out ambulances if available to fetch patients from the most affected areas. Traffic needed to be controlled and patients diverted to other hospitals, as the wards of Hamidia Hospital were already overflowing.

Another round to the Carbide factory and to the Kotwali Control Room from where I asked collectors of the Bhopal division to dispatch street cleaners, as the staff of the Bhopal municipality had decamped and there was every danger of an epidemic. My former colleagues in the forest department and the collector of Sehore, I.M. Chahal, were asked to arrange for fuelwood, inevitably needed for the cremation of hundreds. Home secretary of MP, K.S. Sharma, Dr Saxena and I toured the most affected parts of the city. At the Bhopal railway station, we saw six people lying out in the sun. Going closer, we found that they were dead. The railway staff informed us that they were beggars. We met the station master, who, during the gas leakage, waved on the trains which arrived there, not allowing the passengers to disembark. He himself was suffering grievously. Dr Saxena gave first aid to the affected people we saw. We picked up eighteen bodies that day, from the open, from a hotel and from closed rooms.

I reached home at 11 p.m. Kalpana and Radhika were only partially affected as our house in Char Imli was at a distance from the factory and my wife had wisely kept the doors and windows shut. She said later that I looked like a zombie when I walked in and my clothes were reeking of MIC. I had been away some twenty hours, but I think I aged twenty months in that time.

Early next morning, I received a call from an officer from the collectorate. The kin of those terminally ill and in coma before the gas leaked but had died subsequently wanted the death to be certified as caused by MIC. He wanted guidance as to what we should tell the doctors. I said we should certify all such as having died from the gas, for the gas had certainly preponed the death of even the terminally ill.

I had asked Jaimini Photographers in Bhopal to record all the unclaimed bodies in the hospital morgues. I have never seen such gruesome visages on any dead. They had died gasping for breath, leaving their faces horribly contorted. On 4 December, the photographs were put up in a lost-and-found bureau, set up opposite the Carbide factory, in the city Kotwali and in the city hospitals, for identification and claiming of bodies.

There were over 300 unclaimed bodies lying close together like logs of wood in the open makeshift mortuary in Gandhi Medical College. I had already spoken with the mayor of the Bhopal Municipal Corporation and the secretary of the Waqf Board to assist in the disposal of the dead. As I came out of the Medical College on 4 December early morning, I recognized the students of the Maulana Azad College of Technology standing in a huddle. I had played cricket with some of them in happier days, but had threatened to lock some of them up a couple of months earlier when they had got unruly and burnt a bus. As I stopped my car, they came up and asked if they could be of any help. So I suggested they could assist people in the disposal of their dead. When they replied in the affirmative, I said the Muslims amongst them should contact the Waqf Board to get coffins to bury the dead and those who were Hindus should contact the municipality and avail of the wood that was being provided for cremation. One of the students looked me straight in eye and said, 'Sir, there are no Hindus and no Muslims at this moment; we will all jointly help in the disposal of the dead.' This time it was not MIC that caused tears to cloud my eyes.

They were true to their word. One of them even died inhaling gas trapped in the lungs of the dead. Doctors who did autopsies were also affected by gases escaping from the lungs of the dead.

Late in the morning on 4 December, Prime Minister Rajiv Gandhi came to Bhopal and I escorted him with Arjun Singh through Hamidia Hospital. Patients were lying gasping on the floor, eyes closed, and the children were screaming. The PM was visibly moved, though I do not think he noticed a young man dying as he stood close by, talking with the doctors.

Dead livestock posed another problem. At my request both the army and the BHEL factory had provided cranes for their removal, which even involved breaking cow sheds and lifting the carcasses into trucks, as no manpower was available. The Department of Irrigation and the commissioner of Hoshangabad, Mrs Binoo Sen, arranged for the excavation of large pits on the Berasia road. Over 1,400 cattle were buried, with tonnes of lime to disintegrate the bodies.

Warren Anderson, president and chief executive of the Union Carbide Corporation (UCC) of America, the parent company of Union Carbide India Ltd (UCIL), came to Bhopal, was arrested, given bail and put on the plane back to Delhi, all on the same day. I got to know only after the event, when Moti Singh, the collector of Bhopal, told me in the evening. I was not informed, perhaps, because it was thought that I should not be disturbed in my relief work or, perhaps, because I had no role to play in the process.

There are some facets of this ghastly episode which are worth a mention. I did not see anyone shed a tear till the third day after the disaster. People stood in queues with inert bodies of children cradled in their arms. When their turn came and the doctor would examine and pronounce what perhaps they already knew, they would turn around like robots and march off, without a tear or a sob. People, when they recognized their loved ones amongst the white-shrouded bodies lying in the open in the makeshift mortuaries of hospitals, would pick up the body without emotion and leave. Trauma, shock. It was on the third day, when people started returning to Bhopal and recognized their dead from the horrific photographs put up on noticeboards for identification, that I saw people weep for the first time.

Kalpana says I also had turned into an emotionless robot. The dead just became numbers – 30, 80, 220, 860, 1,540 – and after the first day another dead body evoked little emotion. Every morning and evening, I phoned the chief secretary, giving him the updated figure of the dead. One morning, I overstated the figure by about twenty and when I came to know of the mistake, I phoned him back with the correct figure. He said he had already conveyed my earlier figure to the chief minister and by the evening the shortfall of twenty would in any case be exceeded.

For three days after the event, I could see no bird in the sky and even the birds in my garden in Char Imli had disappeared. Yet, where the livestock was being interned on Berasia road a few kilometres outside Bhopal, there were hundreds of vultures and kites circling overhead. This was, of course, before the drug diclofenac decimated the vulture population.

Though it was the first week of December, it became warm enough for a couple of days so that a pullover was not necessary. In Professor Colony on the Lower Bhopal Lake, where Jaya Bachchan's father then lived, my cousin Hitendra Kumari Dolatpur had a house. In her garden were ornamental sisal shoots, amongst the toughest of plants with leaves laced with strong fibre. The shoots on the outside of the clumps, especially the side facing north from where the white cloud of MIC had come, had become dry, dark brown and shrivelled up. The others in the same clump were noticeably better.

Bodies remained unclaimed till the third day in the open mortuaries of hospitals, as mentioned earlier. Despite two days in the sun and the temperature getting warm, I could not detect a smell of putrification. When questioned about this, a doctor said the MIC had eradicated all the pathogens in the bodies of the dead, so there were none left to multiply and cause the flesh to rot.

Those who had consumed liquor that night fared better than those who had not. One up for booze! The reason was twofold. Doctors and scientists said that alcohol in the blood inhibits binding of the MIC ingredients with the red blood corpuscles (RBC), which destroys RBCs. Secondly, those who had imbibed too much liquor were in too soporific a state to panic and run, which is what had caused people to pant and swallow more gas.

While livestock penned in their sheds died, chickens in their coops did not, though the gas was the heaviest on the ground at chicken-level. I do not know the reason for this.

Bhopal then got its drinking water mainly from Bhoj Lake, which also received on another side of it the sewage of the city. We had all suffered from the Bhopal 'belly' at one time or another. I had seen on both the Lower and Bhoj lakes a white shroud of MIC gas covering the water, early that 3 December morning. I felt sure that the gas had mixed with the lake water, polymerized and become a part of the city's drinking water supply. I requested A.N. Varma, then environment secretary of MP and later principal secretary of Prime Minister Narasimha Rao, to examine the water quality for MIC and also the pollution levels in fruits and vegetables grown in the vicinity of Bhopal. I was not made aware of the outcome, despite inquiries.

There were many who gave much of their time and effort to assist, and many of them risked exposure and suffered, including the doctors, the army, particularly Major Khanuja, the railway, police and civilian staff. There has been much controversy as to how and why the gas leaked, about what should have been done and who did what and who did not. It is easy to sit back in safety, comfort and hindsight and pass judgement. There had never been a holocaust of this magnitude and we were not prepared. That factory should never have been where it was and the sporadic leakages at the plant reported by R.K. Keswani and others, which had even caused one death, should have been seriously considered and the factory shifted. Those jhuggis around the factory also should not have been allowed to come up. But the fact is that the factory was where it was, surrounded by jhuggis, and the gas leaked on the night of 2 December 1984. What also matters is the effort and intention of individual players in that awful drama, with no experience, no preparedness and no forewarning.

What had leaked, vaporized or polymerized from tank 610 in the factory was not 20 tonnes as Mukund told me, but over 40 tonnes. Over 15 tonnes was reported to still remain in storage on the premises, excluding the polymerized portions lying in the cracked tank 610. All this had to be neutralized and S. Varadarajan, head of the Council of Scientific and Industrial Research (CSIR), had already warned the government that this process could lead to a second tragedy.

The general elections were imminent, and nothing could be more important to politics and to politicians. Efforts were made to assure the people, who had been trickling back into Bhopal after the exodus of 3 December, that neutralization was a safe operation and that they should remain in Bhopal. Their votes were needed and they could only cast them in Bhopal. The dates for the neutralization were also not announced to my knowledge, but the people heard rumours and there was a second exodus the day before the process was to begin. People started leaving in crowded buses, sitting on the rooftops. That night Arjun Singh phoned asking me to somehow stop the exodus. I replied that any stoppage by the administration would cause more panic and more people would leave. In any case, it was just as well that they left as it would make the handling of the neutralization and the care of the already affected that much easier. The people would come back to their homes if the operation went well, and that is what happened. As already mentioned, there was much more stored MIC on the premises than the 15 tonnes claimed by Union Carbide, and the process of neutralization took almost a week.

By now, gas inhalation was also affecting me. After medication, my eyes had stopped hurting. I have always been fit and a nonsmoker, but climbing that single flight of stairs to my bedroom was causing me to pant. There was also a persistent cough. I had called Dr L.D. Loya, chief medical officer of Union Carbide, to my house to hear from him as to what effect MIC could have and what antidotes should be adopted by the sufferers. I thought he would be more forthright if I spoke with him alone in confidence. He said that the gas affected the lungs but could not be absorbed in the blood. He was categorical that there was no cyanide content in the gas that could be assimilated in the body. Union Carbide was desperately keen to underplay the cyanide factor of MIC and of Sevin, the pesticide which was the end product of MIC and the raison d'être of the factory. Obviously, they wanted to underplay the medical gravity of the accident, long-term and immediate, to minimize their financial and legal liability.

Just about then, I heard of the findings of Dr Heeresh Chandra, who had been conducting autopsies. He declared that death was being caused by hydrogen cyanide, by cyanide poisoning. He took me to his operating room and showed me the light-coloured blood and cherry-coloured lungs of the deceased. Dr Chandra volunteered to cut up the brain to show me the alteration in brain coloration, but that I had no courage to see.

My diary records that on 8 December, Dr Max Daunderer of Tox Center eV. in Munich came to see me. He claimed that the only known antidote to MIC is sodium thiosulphate, of which he had brought a supply and would send more. He said this drug would have no side effects, would only help and not harm. He ended in all seriousness, with a statement in his Teutonic accent which will always remain in my memory: 'Believe me, sir; we in Germany know something about poison gas.' Shades of Auschwitz and Treblinka! Even in that morbid atmosphere, I could not help but smile. He later confirmed to me in writing that 'other antidotes to MIC are not known in the scientific world.'(Max Daunderer, Munich, Germany, personal communication, 25 April 1985.)

I took a number of sodium thiosulphate injections and I think they helped me. There were certainly no side effects. But by then a controversy was raging amongst the medical community, between those for and against these injections. I strongly suspect Union Carbide was lobbying against the injections as their administration would have been an admission of the presence of cyanide poisoning and, hence, an escalation in their culpability.

To my mind the most heinous crime of Union Carbide was not the abysmal maintenance and safety of its outdated equipment, its understaffing and unpreparedness, the cover-ups of smaller leakages in the past, or the cavalier attitude of its inadequately trained safety staff, unpardonable though these are. The most unforgivable offence in my opinion is that when the accident did happen, they remained intransigent, uncooperative and secretive about the magnitude of the medical impact of the gas. If only they had publicly announced that early morning that people should cover their faces with a wet cloth, so many lives would have been saved and so much suffering lessened. It was the district administration that made that announcement after Mukund told me in the factory that water would help, but by then it was very late. Carbide knew of the antidote. There had been a leak in their Danbury factory in the US, but they would not tell us what to do medically – nothing that would sound like an admission of the presence of hydrogen cyanide. The cost of compensation was a greater consideration for them than the loss of human lives, permanent injury and humungous suffering.

There was another visitation from abroad. Hordes of American lawyers descended upon Bhopal. There were no vacancies left in the better hotels of Bhopal and in the Jehan Numa Palace Hotel close to the Union Carbide guest house atop Shyamla Hill, up to four were sharing a room. These were experts on the law of torts and wanted signatures of the afflicted, so that they could file suits for compensation against the Union Carbide Corporation in America. The parties had to pay nothing, only sign away to the lawyer 40 or 50 per cent of what they would get from UCC in a court suit or settlement. Some lawyers even came to see me but I refrained from signing anything. Later, the Government of India by an Act in parliament assumed the role of claimant on behalf of the affected.

While the onus of medical care devolved upon the health authorities and hospitals, my job and that of the district administration was to provide relief. M.R. Sivaraman, the finance secretary, with the best of intentions sent officers in the city to give cash compensation for the dead, on the spot. Predictably, this process was hijacked by cheats. People took unclaimed bodies from the mortuaries to claim cash. Compensation was often taken by people who were not the closest relatives. I suggested immediate stoppage of this modus operandi. What people needed most was medical care, succour for the needy and help in the disposal of the dead, the figure of which had crossed 2,000. Cash compensation could come later, after some inquiry as to the bona fides of the claims.

With such influx of cash, liquor sales in Bhopal shot up exponentially. I was going home one night, when I saw, in the headlights of my car, a body lying sprawled on the road. I sent a wireless message to the control room to send a van to collect yet another cadaver. As I waited, the body began to move, so I countermanded my previous order and asked the control room to send an ambulance instead. The body slowly sat up. On going up to the man to help him get up, I smelt not MIC but alcohol on his breath.

Government declared the distribution of free rations to those ration-card holders who were affected – wheat, rice, sugar and cooking oil. It was my job to supervise this with the assistance of a very competent young IAS officer, Vimal Jhulka. Almost every evening, we met either at the Vallabh Bhawan Secretariat or at the chief minister's residence to review developments – medical status, relief measures, the needs and the actions required. The meetings were presided over by Arjun Singh and attended by the chief secretary and other senior officers concerned. Donated milk powder arrived and free milk was distributed to those who wanted it. I found people accepting this enthusiastically, as they said it helped their stomach acidity, most likely caused by irritation of the stomach lining by the ingestion of gas. So we multiplied the outlets of free milk supply.

But with the general elections fast approaching, the government suddenly, without any warning, let alone prior consultation, announced extension of the free ration scheme to all, irrespective of whether they were card holders or not. This was a boon to the jhuggi dwellers, but it was also a godsend for the unscrupulous. If there was a ration card on which the amount of relief given could be inscribed, one could keep some kind of check even in that chaos. Otherwise, one person could stand in a queue at ten different shops and get ten times his due. I objected but was overruled. The scheme continued until after I left Bhopal and a sum of over ₹20 crore was spent on it. There was not a similar problem with milk, as it had to be consumed on the spot and only a limited amount could be taken home.

What was more worrisome was the emergence of the long-term physical impact of MIC. Doctors were reporting an abnormal rise in the incidence of stillbirth, infant mortality and miscarriage. There was a substantial rise in the incidence of mental depression and lethargy, of resignation and morbidity. It was feared that the occurrence of neurological disorders and of cancer would increase, a fear that was substantiated later by studies conducted at KEM Hospital in Mumbai.

The mood of the nation changed from sympathy to blame and finding fault. Doctors accused each other. People and the press blamed the state and Central governments, and everyone blamed Union Carbide. The accused became defensive. Compensation became the key word, rather than care of the afflicted. A legal battle started, but before that I had left Bhopal and others much more knowledgeable than me have written at length about it.

My own health was not improving too much. Perhaps the daily visits to the affected areas and inhaling of latent gas in nooks and crannies and from clothes of people, may also have prolonged the malaise. In June 1984, I had had a general physical check-up at Jaslok Hospital in Mumbai. Amongst the tests was one of lung capacity and the physician who tested me complimented me on the state of my lungs, which he said was better than normal for my age. After the gas leak there was no question of my getting any leave for a medical check-up or to go and see my anxious parents, for some months. Then, in late March 1985, I was permitted leave. I was feeling much better, but I went back to that same machine in Jaslok Hospital. This time the test showed a 23 per cent loss in lung capacity. This, in fact, is the only 'benchmark' medical test of any affected person in that tragedy – of measured lung capacity before the inhalation of gas and three-and-a-half months after it, on the same instrument. And this for a person who went to the gas-affected area a couple of hours after the burst.

People ask me whether the lesson of Bhopal has been learnt by the nation and if one day there could be another Bhopal. The Ministry of Home Affairs set up a task force on disaster management to tackle future man-made and natural disasters and made me a member. Natural disasters do occur and the early warning and response systems often fall short of the requirement. But the real lesson of Bhopal, I feel, has not been understood, let alone learnt. And that is, do we really need a pesticide as lethal as Sevin? That pesticides kill agricultural pests and, thus, increase productivity is undoubtedly true, but in a real cost–benefit analysis does that truly compensate for the toxic poisons that will permeate our food chain? And when these agricultural pests get immune to even these highly toxic chemicals, just as human pathogens are becoming resistant to antibiotics, do we resort to making those pesticides more and more deadly, for both the pest and for man? Is short-term productivity more important than the long-term health of the nation?

It is a little known fact that at the time of the Bhopal incident, the Central Insecticides Board and Registration Committee of the Government of India was considering the banning of Sevin and twenty-four other highly toxic pesticides. Why did they hesitate? Lobbying from the manufacturers? Fear of a reduction in cereal yield? The Ministry of Agriculture banned the production of DDT for agriculture purposes, as it did diclofenac much later. But the production and use of DDT for anti-malaria spraying is still permitted and India still produces, perhaps, the highest quantum of DDT in the world. Why? To keep the DDT factories running? Are we even planning for organic or other substitutes that would, perhaps, not be so effective but would also not be so harmful? What are the ground rules of a genuine cost–benefit analysis and who decides? When will the people of India be consulted and given a choice?

11

Environment and Forests, Ganga and Narmada

By January 1984, I had completed three years of service in my parent cadre state of MP and was entitled to another deputation to the Government of India. My elder brother Digvijaysinhji was then Union minister of state for environment and he did not want to cause embarrassment by getting me into his ministry; and I did not wish to go anywhere else. So I stayed in Bhopal. After the 1985 election, however, Rajiv Gandhi appointed another minister of state and himself assumed charge of the newly created Ministry of Environment and Forests (MoEF). I moved to Delhi as joint secretary (forest and wildlife) in mid-1985, the Government of MP having released me when the aftermath of the gas tragedy was somewhat under control.

The MoEF was a legacy of Indira Gandhi, and to continue the tradition Rajiv Gandhi chose to keep the ministry under his charge. He was keen on the subject and each year-end would go to a forest retreat with his family and friends. The Forest (Conservation) Act (FCA) of 1980 laid down that no land designated as forest or any government land that held forests could be diverted to non-forest purposes without the prior approval of the MoEF. The diversion of every hectare of forest land for non-forest purpose required the written approval of the minister for environment, i.e., the prime minister of India. Rajiv Gandhi was prompt in the clearance of such files and rarely overruled our recommendations. Apart from being designated as joint secretary in charge of forest conservation and the handling of the FCA, I was made director of wildlife preservation of India, for the second time and put in overall charge of Project Tiger.

There was a groundswell of opposition to the FCA from the states, as for the first time the powers of diverting forests and forest lands to other uses were being assumed by the Central rather than the state governments. However, despite there being no penalty for transgression of the FCA in the initial stage of the law, the states to their credit did by and large abide by the provisions. Of course, the fact that the Congress party was in power in a majority of the states helped. The Act, for all its opposition, did stem the rapid depletion of forest lands and the conversion of forested areas to other purposes, which had been in progress since Independence. Forest lands were the easiest to get hold of for hydroelectric, resettlement, agricultural or for that matter for any development projects. The FCA for the first time brought to the fore the value of forests and of forest lands, and made the authorities and project proponents look for alternatives when they needed land.

Rajiv Gandhi took personal interest in the drafting of the Environment (Protection) Act (EPA) of 1986, in which I was involved as well. There were a number of meetings where he would review the progress and draft formulations. During one such meeting, we were considering the scope of cognizance of offences under the Act. We had provided that no court could take cognizance of any offence under the EPA except on a complaint filed by the Central government or by an officer authorized by it in this regard. Rajiv insisted that an affected private individual must also have the right to complain. Secretary, MoEF, T.N. Seshan, the quintessential bureaucrat, pleaded that it would open the floodgates of litigation and even the harassment and blackmailing of industrial establishments. Rajiv smiled but remained adamant, and rightly so. It was at his instance that Subclause (b) of Section 19 of the EPA was provided, whereby a court could also take cognizance of a complaint made by a 'person who has given notice of not less than sixty days, in the manner prescribed, of an alleged offence and his intention to make a complaint to the Central Government or the authority or an officer authorized.'

Revision of the National Forest Policy of 1952 was also under way and nearing completion when I arrived in the MoEF. It, however, took three more years to finalize and place it before parliament in 1988, and I had the privilege to contribute and to participate in the process. While the 1952 policy had emphasized the maximization of the productivity of forests, the 1988 one recognized the serious depletion that forests had suffered and the need to conserve them for their ecological significance and as a source of sustenance for local communities. Its principal aim was 'to ensure environmental stability and maintenance of ecological balance ... which are vital for sustenance of all life forms, humans, animals and plants. The derivation of direct economic benefit must be subordinate to this principal aim.' This was a paradigm shift in the concept of forests and forestry and helped change the outlook of foresters, albeit very slowly. The policy specifically provided that 'there should be no regularization of existing encroachments' in forests, which was reneged upon with the enactment of the Forest Rights Act of 2006.

The vast majority that the Congress party had obtained that swept Rajiv Gandhi to power in 1985, afforded him the opportunity to forge ahead with his personal interest in environment and conservation. The idea of cleaning up the Ganga emanated during his period of ministership. He was a good minister to work with – courteous, patient, considerate of various viewpoints and not over-assertive. One could be confident of his support if one took a pro-environment stand. Twice a year, he would chair the meeting of the Indian Board for Wildlife and I think he enjoyed partaking in it.

I had been appointed India's commissioner on the International Whaling Commission and attended its annual Conference of Parties at Bournemouth, England, in 1985; Malmo, Sweden in 1987;

Auckland, New Zealand in 1988; and San Diego, USA, in 1989. In my entire career, I have not partaken in wildlife conferences so politicized and so intensely and acrimoniously debated. The whaling nations – Japan, Iceland, Norway and Denmark – were arraigned on one side, the rest on the other. To overcome the moratorium on whaling, the whaling nations would give themselves permits to hunt whales for research, year after year, and countries like Iceland would then sell the whale meat obtained by them for 'research' purposes, to the insatiable Japanese markets. The Indian Ocean had been declared a whale sanctuary for a specific period, which when it came up for extension, the Japanese lobbied against. They even fielded some island nations who would vote for the whaling lobby.

India's standpoint on whaling always clashed with that of Japan. The Japanese wanted to give themselves special permits to hunt whales under the provision of 'Aboriginal Subsistence Whaling', which was accorded to the Inuit Eskimos of the Arctic region. The Japanese called their fisherfolk – with their radar-equipped, harpoon-carrying whaling vessels – aborigines of Japan. I, therefore, asked that the terminology of 'Aboriginal Subsistence Whaling' should be clearly defined, pointing out that such hunting must be by weapons and vessels traditionally used by aborigines of a country and that the meat produced must be used by the aboriginal communities themselves and not sold. The Whaling Commission set up a small group to define this form of whaling and appointed me chairman.

Before each meeting of the Whaling Commission, the Japanese ambassador to India would come to the MoEF and meet the minister and myself, expressing hope that India would side with Japan, or at least not oppose its proposals. This would be backed by the Ministry of External Affairs (MEA), Japan then being one of India's main providers of economic aid and a major trading partner. Matters came to a head when Rajiv Gandhi went to Japan and the Japanese prime minister N. Kishi made a personal request that I should not be part of the Indian delegation for the next meeting of the Whaling Commission, which was then imminent, as my interventions were causing great embarrassment to the Japanese. To his credit, Rajiv Gandhi never spoke to me about this, but the matter was taken up by MEA, which also gave directions to the MoEF that we should abstain from voting on contentious issues and not hurt the sensibilities of the Japanese in the forthcoming Whaling Commission conference at Auckland, in 1988. Particularly at stake was the continuation of the Indian Ocean sanctuary for whales.

In response, I put up a note to say that India had earned the respect of the international conservation community, including governments the world over, and we had received letters from Sir Peter Scott and many others acknowledging the contribution of India to the cause of the whales. If India now went to the Auckland conference and supported Japan tacitly, or even remained non-committed, it would be a blow to the stature and reputation of the country. Rather than that, India should refrain from participating in the forthcoming Auckland conference, and if our policy in the foreseeable future was to be harmonized with the interests of the Japanese, we should opt out of being a member of the International Whaling Commission and save ourselves some foreign exchange.

My note was forwarded to Minister for Environment Rajiv Gandhi. I had been cleared to go to the conference, but had not booked my ticket. On the evening of the day the conference opened, the file came back from PMO, with a handwritten note from Rajiv: 'The Japanese, I believe, have a problem. But the whales have even a greater problem. We should support the cause of whale conservation.' That night I caught a flight to Auckland.

I noticed a perceptible change in Rajiv Gandhi after the Shah Bano incident, when the Muslim and vote bank lobby within the Congress party persuaded him to move parliament against the Supreme Court verdict granting a divorced Muslim lady the right of maintenance. He became withdrawn, hesitant, unsure. These traits became even more pronounced after the unleashing of the Bofors controversy, when direct accusations were made against him of taking kickbacks from the giant Swedish arms manufacturer.

Soon, Rajiv gave up his charge as minister for environment and forests, appointing the controversial former chief minister of Haryana, Bhajan Lal, in his place. But before that, he took a major decision: approval of the controversial Narmada project. The project had been on the anvil for decades. The environment ministry had not been in favour of it and Rajiv had been appreciative of its viewpoint. Just a few days earlier, I had written a long note against its clearance, pointing out that a proper cost–benefit analysis had not been done, that irrigation projects have a tendency for huge cost-escalation once their administrative approvals have been given and that their track record in the past thirty years had been a delivery of only about 55 per cent of what they had promised by way of irrigation coverage. Also, the value of only the standing forests that would be submerged had been considered, when the actual loss of forests would be permanent. The file had gone to the PM, as he then still was the minister for environment.

A felicitation in honour of Salim Ali happened to be held in Delhi at this time. Indeed, this was to be the last visit of this indefatigable champion of Indian wildlife to the capital. As he sat close to Rajiv Gandhi on the dais, someone in the hall whispered to me that a group of members of parliament had met the PM and that he had cleared the Narmada project. What incongruous news on such an occasion. I have often wondered that if there had been no Shah Bano and Bofors controversies, would the Narmada project have been cleared then, or ever. I shall return to the Narmada later in this chapter.

India had become a signatory to the Convention on International Trade in Endangered Species (CITES) and had been elected to chair its standing committee. My predecessor in office, Samar Singh, had played an important role in its early deliberations. The headquarters of CITES was in Lausanne, Switzerland, where I had the occasion to chair the meetings of the standing committee, as also at Ottawa, Canada, in 1985 and 1986. CITES had unstinted support from countries like Germany, the USA, Canada, Australia and the UK. The South American nations sought quotas in millions for the export of the skins of the spectacled caiman. The countries of southern Africa wanted to export leopard skins and ivory. The problem was of 'look-alikes' – the difficulty in distinguishing Asian from African ivory and African from Asian leopard skins, with DNA sampling facilities not being readily available in those days.

Pakistan wanted an export quota for kuth, a wild tuber growing in the Trans-Himalayan uplands used for medicinal purposes. It was a rare plant and involved much traversing of the uplands and digging, resulting in soil erosion. In only one place in the world – Lahaul in Himachal Pradesh, India – was the plant cultivated. Based upon the average annual crop production in Lahaul, a quota for the export of kuth was fixed for India.

Despite the considerable lobbying and politicking in those early years, CITES was able to fulfil its mandate of controlling illegal trade to a significant extent. It was a privilege to meet and have the support of conservationists of the stature of Felipe Benavides, whose 'farming' of the vicuña for wool saved the wild animal in the Andes, and Joseph Forshaw, the author of the monumental work *Parrots of the World*.

The number of protected areas in India was now more than 400 and the need for a special institute to train the personnel of the state forest departments in the skills and methods of managing protected areas and in conserving wildlife was strongly felt. While I was still in Bhopal, it had been decided to set up the Wildlife Institute of India (WII) at Dehradun and a 'feeler' had been sent to ascertain whether I would want to be its first director. I knew my friend and colleague H.S. Panwar was keen on the job and I was still involved in the aftermath of the Bhopal gas disaster. As it turned out, Panwar's selection as director proved to be an excellent choice.

When I took over as a joint secretary, forest and wildlife, in the MoEF and as director, wildlife preservation, the WII was part of my charge. The acquisition of land for the premises, the design and layout of the building, preparation of the work syllabus and fixing priorities of research and training were all rewarding tasks to partake in. For a number of years, I was chairperson of the Research Advisory Committee of the institute. Some outstanding field biologists and wildlife managers joined the ranks of the WII – A.J.T. Johnsingh, Ravi Chellam, B.C. Choudhary, Yadvendradev Jhala, V.B. Savarkar, Mita Shah and others.

The number of staff sent to the WII for training from the states was always low. Many seats remained vacant in training courses and were then allotted to other countries in South Asia. We repeatedly took up the matter with the states, but to little avail. One excuse put forth was the cost that the states had to pay for the training. So I moved the finance ministry in Delhi and got an exemption from payment for the states. Still the influx of trainees remained very meagre and, what was worse, the few rangers and officers who did come were posted on non-wildlife jobs when they returned to their respective states after their training. The primary purpose of the WII – indeed, the prime cause for its creation – was training, and applied research was an ancillary objective. It is a sad commentary that the WII is now almost entirely a research organization that hardly imparts any training.

I twice moved a proposal in the standing committee of the National Board for Wildlife that the Government of India, through the MoEF, should extend financial support only to those protected areas that were under the charge of officers who had been trained in wildlife management, either at the WII or elsewhere. The proposal was not implemented by the ministry.

In 1988, W.A. Rodgers, a UN expert deputed to the WII, and H.S. Panwar put forth a most important report in two volumes. Titled 'Planning A Wildlife Protected Area Network in India', it analysed the existing protected area network of the country, pointing out the shortfalls in the matter of coverage of diverse habitats in the various biogeographic zones, the habitats of endangered species that still remained outside of the protected areas, and the corridors and linkages that were required to be established to ensure connectivity of habitats and the prevention, thereby, of their ecological isolation.

I joined Panwar and Rodgers in various regional meetings, where the chief wildlife wardens and other state officials were called. We requested them to actively consider the implementation of the recommendations of the report and enlarge their protected area network accordingly. As events proved, this was the last good opportunity to rationalize and expand the protected areas on an ecological basis.

Project Tiger was also under my charge. Panwar had relinquished his charge as director of the project to assume his post at the WII. R.L. Singh, a forest officer from Uttar Pradesh who had done good work in Dudhwa National Park, was appointed in charge of Project Tiger. Man-eating had assumed alarming proportions in the agricultural tracts of Pilibhit district in which Dudhwa is situated. Vast tracts were under sugar cane cultivation, into which tigers had moved, taking up permanent residence and were breeding there. They were rarely disturbed and had access to pigs and livestock in these fields. However, they also took to man-eating. The local Rai Sikh migrants from Punjab took retribution into their own hands and thirty-three tigers were found dead in a span of a few months, just before I assumed charge as director, wildlife preservation, for the second time.

Shortly thereafter, a question was asked in parliament as to the cause of death of the tigers of Pilibhit. The Government of Uttar Pradesh's reply was 'drowning'! I phoned the chief wildlife warden of the state to protest against this incredible response, pointing out that tigers have been known to swim through tidal currents 20 km or more from land, so how could they have succumbed in the shallow pools of the River Sharda and its tributaries? The warden then sent me the autopsy reports of tigers. The lungs of all of them were filled with water. Diagnosis: drowning. I am certain that what had happened was that when the poisoned meat the tigers had consumed started taking effect, they must have immersed themselves in water to assuage the burning in the stomach. As they died in water some of it would have entered their lungs. When I asked for the results of the examination of their viscera, the reply was that that it was not deemed necessary as the cause of death had already been determined – drowning!

I had moved the proposal to establish Dudhwa National Park as a tiger reserve. The UP government – this being before the separation of Uttarakhand from UP – was agreeable, since forest exploitation had already stopped with it having become a national park. I was, however, insistent that Kishanpur, which was then a sanctuary but was separated from Dudhwa, should be a part of the Dudhwa Tiger Reserve. Kishanpur contained Jhadi Tal, an artificial lake which then and even now contains the largest herd of the nominate race of the barasingha in India. The main herd in the Dudhwa National Park, in the Sathiana block, had been decimated and the other population was already confined with the reintroduced rhinoceros in the large enclosure at Salukapur. Besides, Jhadi Tal held a large population of hog deer and migratory birds, and Kishanpur also had its quota of tigers. But Kishanpur had large plantations of exotic teak planted by the forest department, which it wanted to exploit. The negotiations delayed the declaration of Dudhwa as a tiger reserve. Ultimately, the Government of UP relented and agreed to include Kishanpur, and Dudhwa Tiger Reserve came into being in 1986, with an area of 811 sq. km.

The next year, Kalakad Mundanthurai in Tamil Nadu, encompassing 800 sq. km and extending from lowland forests to the craggy habitats of the Nilgiri tahr on the edges of the Agasthya Malai Range, also become a tiger reserve. In 1988, Bhadra in Karnataka, which contained one of the most diverse forests in the Western Ghats, became a tiger reserve, with an area of 492 sq. km.

The Convention on the Conservation of Migratory Species of Wild Animals, which had been spearheaded by the Government of Germany and which I had assisted in its formative stage, had its

Conference of Parties in Bonn, West Germany, in October 1986. They honoured India by making me the chairman of the conference. The European nations were most keen to make Italy comply. Lying on a main flyway between Europe and Africa, the trigger-happy Italians inflicted a huge annual toll of the transcontinental bird migrations over the Mediterranean, each way.

In 1986, an important amendment was made to the Wild Life (Protection) Act of 1972. The 1972 Act had provided that all traders in wildlife declare their stocks and get them marked. They were to obtain trading licences and dispose of their existing stocks. But even fourteen years after commencement of the Act not only had the licensees not disposed of their stocks, but they were not prepared to cooperate with attempts to acquire the existing stocks through the agency of government undertakings. The reason was simple. The traders wanted to retain the facade of the declared stocks duly stamped and marked, which they could display to clients and use as a front to clandestinely sell illicit skins and other products in India and abroad.

The Amendment Act 28 of 1986 prohibited the trade in wild animals specified in Schedule I and Part II of Schedule II of the 1972 Act, or in any derivatives therefrom, after a period of two months from the commencement of the Amendment Act, or two months from the date of any future inclusion of any animal in Schedule I or Part II of Schedule II of the Act. All existing wildlife trading licences for internal trade would become invalid two months after the commencement of the amendment and no future trading licences would be granted. Notified government agencies were given an exemption to acquire the existing declared stocks to make articles only for sale abroad, for a period of two months. The same amendment also prohibited any further trade or manufacturing of articles from Indian elephant ivory and imposed control over the making of articles from imported African ivory.

There was considerable opposition to this ban, especially from the artisans of Kerala and Karnataka. But the Government of India held firm and the tiger, leopard and snow leopard skins and crocodile skin bags vanished from shop showcases at last. The ivory craftsmen took to whale bone, buffalo bone and wood carving.

One of the most barbaric forms of exploitation of wildlife, indeed of any life, is the procurement of frog legs, a delicacy in French cuisine. They are said to taste like prime chicken, but no taste could be worth the method used to collect them. The frogs are pulled apart alive, the hind legs collected in a basket, the rest of the body thrown away as waste. Being amphibians, frogs are tenacious of life. The bodies of the unfortunate creatures, minus the hind legs, lie alive and wriggling for hours or even days.

Frogs play an important role in vector control, especially of mosquito larvae. In the two decades following Independence, India had strenuously endeavoured to eradicate malaria and had succeeded to a remarkable extent. In the 1980s, however, malaria outbreaks were again being recorded in certain parts of the country, particularly in the south and east. In Kerala and Andhra Pradesh, malaria resurgence was found in areas where there was large-scale harvesting of frog legs. Three species of frogs were harvested and they were only for export. I came across a published paper showing the role of frogs in mosquito control. Armed with this document, I approached the Directorate of Exports and Imports to obtain a ban on the export of frog legs.

The export and import policy was revised every year, coming into effect 1 April at the start of a financial year and ending on 31 March the following year. The policy explicitly stated that if any item which was previously allowed for export was banned at the commencement of the next financial year, the government was under no obligation to allow the export of stocks of the newly banned item that might be lying with exporters or traders.

The ban on the export of frog legs raised the expected flurry of petitioning and posturing. Members of parliament on behalf of exporters approached Bhajan Lal, who had become the minister for environment after Rajiv Gandhi had relinquished the post. Bhajan Lal belonged to the Bishnoi community, totally vegetarian, whose active conservation of both fauna and flora have even entailed sacrifice of human life in the past. However, the minister wanted to make a one-time exception and allow the export of pending stocks of frog legs. I pointed out that this would set a very wrong precedent for any future ban on wildlife export. I mentioned my previous experience following the passage of the Wild Life (Protection) Act in 1972 and the banning of the export of musk. I had been approached to allow the export of existing stocks, which it was claimed amounted to 5 kg. When I refused, they approached Karan Singh, at whose behest I tried to collect the figures from around the country. The figure then reported was an unbelievable 45 kg of musk, whereupon the proposal for one time export had been rejected once and for all.

I pointed out to Bhajan Lal that the traders and exporters just wanted a loophole. Like the wildlife traders who did not dispose of their stocks for fourteen years till we had to ban all trade, they would keep the trade and export going on, legally or otherwise, and defeat the purpose of the ban. The meeting with the minister and MPs ended in a stalemate, with no clear decision. All the while I had to do all the arguing as my secretary, the articulate T.N. Seshan, had assumed a neutral role, not wanting to ruffle the feathers of our political bosses. However, the minister next day gave an order in writing that I should ascertain the stocks already lying in the country, awaiting export. I checked with the cold storage facilities concerned – 28 tonnes of frog legs.

Two more meetings followed, chaired by Bhajan Lal and involving up to three MPs, but the stalemate continued. Then a fourth meeting was convened by the minister, this time attended by another Central cabinet minister from Andhra Pradesh and the three MPs from south India. Again the same arguments and the same dogged denial. Then Bhajan Lal, affable and unflappable as ever, politely asked me what the options for a solution to this imbroglio were. I said there were three options. The first one was to accept my advice and reject the request for the export of existing stocks. The minister said that they had discussed that option threadbare already; what was the second option? I said that the exporters should go to court and if the court gave them a favourable order allowing export, I would put up a note to the honourable minister, recommending that we appeal against that court order. If he then gave an order in writing that we should not go in appeal, rejecting my recommendation, I would carry out the orders of the court. Bhajan Lal protested that this option would take too long, so what, therefore, was the third option? I replied that transfers and postings were the minister's prerogative, and the third option was that he should transfer me from my job as director of wildlife preservation under the Wild Life (Protection) Act and appoint another of his choice, who would do his bidding. There was a stunned silence. The meeting adjourned. Seshan, who had continued to remain silent, complimented me as we left. To the minister's credit, there was no change in his cordial attitude and courteous behaviour towards me. No permit for export was issued to that pre-ban stock of frog legs.

When time permitted, I took the opportunity to visit various protected areas of the country, especially the habitats of endangered species and those I had never been to before. In December 1986, I went to Balphakram and Nokrek National Parks of Meghalaya for the first time. In an area subjected to shifting cultivation, these stood out as amongst the last repositories of the state's immense biodiversity. When private forests across the country had been acquired, tribal landholders in Meghalaya still individually owned hundreds of square kilometres of outstanding forests. I could see scores of trucks transporting huge quantities of timber to the sawmills; it was also being smuggled into neighbouring Bangladesh. The Government of Meghalaya owned only about 3 per cent of the forests of the state, which was raised to about 5 per cent when the MoEF provided funds for the state to acquire forests from private holders, to add to the Nokrek and Balphakram national parks.

The Khasi pine, which grows in the uplands in the north-east, was then used for making cases for defence needs and for logs used in the renovation of the Mazagaon Docks of Mumbai. I took up the matter of using substitutes rather than pine wood and there was a change ultimately.

The railways had traditionally used wood for the sleepers below the railway tracks. The teak forests of central India had been destroyed to provide sleepers for the railway lines laid in the mid-nineteenth century, and subsequently sal logs were universally used as teak became scarce and increasingly valuable commercially. I approached Minister for Railways Madhavrao Scindia, whom I knew personally, and requested him to search for an alternative to sal wood sleepers. It took some time, but the railways did change over to cement sleepers. Further, when a lion was run over by the metre-gauge train going to Sasan in the Gir forest, I suggested that this train which hardly had any clientele should ply only in daytime and at slower speeds, and Madhavrao agreed.

In the summer of 1986, in a joint meeting with the director of the Wildlife Institute of India and the chief wildlife warden of Arunachal Pradesh, it was agreed that the WII would carry out an extensive survey of Arunachal to determine the status and distribution of its wildlife, especially its endangered species such as the takin, snow leopard, Sclater's monal and Szechenyi's monal-partridge or pheasant-grouse, the last of which was known to occur in the Upper Subansiri district of Arunachal.

In 1986, over forty rhinoceros were poached in Kaziranga alone. I visited the park in February 1987 with P. Lahan, then the conservator in charge of Kaziranga. R. Sonowal had just been appointed as the divisional forest officer (DFO) in charge of Kaziranga and matters had already improved. Forest guards were instructed to shoot poachers, and the message was understood. On this visit, I noticed a degeneration in the body and horn size of the wild buffalo, an obvious outcome of interbreeding with feral buffaloes that had remained behind in Kaziranga when the cattle camps had been shifted from the national park during my first tenure as director of wildlife preservation, almost fifteen years earlier. Between 1972 and 1974, ₹4.71 lakh had been paid by the Government of India to the district council of Mikir Hills (renamed Karbi Anglong) as compensation for declaring a portion of the hill district adjacent to Kaziranga, where animals sought refuge during the monsoon, as part of the national park. The Karbi Anglong District Council, after keeping the money for twelve years, returned it, saying they did not want an extension of Kaziranga. Nameri, Barnadi, Pobitora and Laokhowa sanctuaries had still not been fully transferred to the wildlife division of the state and I pressed the state authorities to take action on this and also to implement the six proposals for the extension of Kaziranga, pending for years.

At the time, the Siberian cranes still visited Keoladeo Ghana National Park in Bharatpur each winter. I proposed that the park authorities make a contractual agreement with the irrigation department whereby a certain minimum quantum of water be released each monsoon, via the Ajan Bund into the park, to ensure the maintenance of a minimum level of water and the influx of aquatic fauna essential to provide for the life support of avian fauna dependent upon it. Such an agreement did come about, but years later.

In Sariska, I noticed the prevalence of bovine diseases amongst the wild ungulates, especially nilgai. They had obviously contracted these from the livestock which still surreptitiously grazed in the tiger reserve. This was confirmed through the examination of blood samples. The field director, however, had only made a provision of ₹2,000 for annual veterinarian needs. I met with the collector of Alwar and requested him to mount a campaign to inoculate livestock all around Sariska. The situation had improved by the following year.

The forest contained within the Bala Qila Fort towering above Alwar city, represents the best extant undisturbed climax forest to be found anywhere in the Aravallis. It needs to be preserved as natural heritage, representing as it does the best example of the original Aravalli biota. I recommended that it should be included, together with its surrounding forests of Siliserh, in the Sariska Tiger Reserve, but that did not happen.

In 1985, famine had struck Gujarat once more. In violation of the provisions of the Wild Life (Protection) Act, I had given approval in early 1985 for cutting and baling of 7 million kg of grass in the Gir Sanctuary, to be supplied as far away as the Banni grasslands of Kutch; a further 1 million kg of grass was allowed to be cut by cattle owners living around the Gir. Traditionally, whenever there is a famine in Kutch or Saurashtra, all livestock in the region head for the Gir. It was to stall such an invasion with its concomitant danger of disease contagion that this very unusual step was taken.

In 1986, the monsoon failed again. This time there was no grass which could be harvested and sent out, and in the summer of 1987 there was a large-scale invasion of cattle into the Gir. Word reached Prime Minister Rajiv Gandhi and I was directed to go to the Gir immediately.

The scene I encountered was startling. Carcasses of cattle littered the countryside from Rajkot airport to the Gir. Even the then plentiful vultures were too satiated to touch them. This was the third year of a serial famine, the worst since 1899. An estimated two to four lakh cattle had invaded the Gir, haggard, decrepit and ripe for disease. One lion and two leopards had already been poached and poached venison was on sale in Sasan. From 27 July to 7 September 1987, the personnel of the forest department of the state – rangers, foresters and forest guards – went on strike. Once this was known, the floodgates of intrusion and destruction had been opened. I estimated that at least 10,000 trees had been cut. The Kamleshwar reservoir near Sasan had shrunk to two small pools in which I could count over forty large crocodiles. Shots could be heard each night that I was in the Gir. My field notes record that the Gir had been set back by at least a decade.

I sent a detailed note to the prime minister, suggesting both short-term and long-term measures, and he took it up personally with the Government of Gujarat. The recommendations – removing the invading livestock to cattle camps outside and extensively and continuously inoculating them; shifting the remaining cattle encampments from within the Gir and ear-tagging of the livestock that belonged to the Maldharis who lived in the Gir to distinguish them from illegal intruders; providing drinking water to wild animals; stopping night traffic on roads within the Gir Sanctuary and the control of tourism – were all addressed by the state government. The Gir recovered faster than I had estimated.

A proposal came from the Department of Fertilizers to the MoEF for permission to set up a gas-based chemical fertilizer factory at Chauth Ka Barwara, 28 km from Ranthambore National Park. A special committee, consisting of representatives of the state and Central Pollution Control Boards, S.K. Verma, the chief wildlife warden of Rajasthan and myself, was set up, asked to visit the spot and submit a report. We found that the distance of the proposed site was not 28 but 22 km from the borders of the national park, and on the windward side of it, with the prevalent wind direction for the major part of the year blowing from the site towards the park. Its effluents were to be emptied in the River Banas which formed the northern boundary of the tiger reserve. Work had already started at the factory site in anticipation of approval.

The standing committee of Project Tiger had earlier decided that no factory should come up within a radius of 30 km of any tiger reserve. The proposers of the factory project would not even tell us of their plans for future expansion. Our committee emphatically stated that the fertilizer factory should not be allowed at Chauth Ka Barwara, and despite considerable political pressure and lobbying, the MoEF held firm and the factory site was shifted.

During my visits to Ranthambore for this report, I took the opportunity to visit Sorsan near Kota and was very pleased to see that the local panchayat was safeguarding the great Indian bustard and the blackbuck. The bustard has since become locally extinct. However, I found that the fine forested valley of the Darrah

Sanctuary was overrun by livestock and the Jawahar Sagar Sanctuary on the Chambal had huge mining operations touching its premises.

On my two visits to Ranthambore in 1987, though I never saw any cattle within the precincts of the park, the fresh droppings of livestock and the telltale marks of browsing, lopping and grazing were unmistakable. This proved two things – that grazing was rampant and that the staff could prevent it, as they did when I paid a visit there of which they received advance notice. The local shepherds and cattle herders of Ranthambore were aggressive, and their boldness had been further accentuated at this point of time by the acquittal in court of the graziers who had murderously attacked the previous field director of Ranthambore, Fateh Singh Rathore, when he challenged them on finding them trespassing in the park.

There were other problems too. Fifty tourist vehicles were already catering to visitors in 1987, when four years earlier there had only been four. I recommended the regulation of tourism and the induction of guides to accompany each vehicle, and these suggestions were implemented. I also emphasized the need to stop grazing and illicit woodcutting and suggested that tourist traffic should be diverted to areas affected by these scourges, which would help keep them under control.

In the Sundarban Tiger Reserve too the number of tourists visiting annually had risen from 9,000 in 1984 to over 30,000 in 1987. It was imperative that norms and guidelines be laid down to regulate tourism in sanctuaries, parks and tiger reserves so that visitors could have a rewarding experience and a communion with nature, while causing the least possible damage and disturbance to the park and its inmates. Each protected area needed to have a separate prescription suited to it. I formed a committee under the chairmanship of S.K. Roy, a former director general of tourism, with Divyabhanusinh, regional vice-president of the Taj Group of Hotels, Mahendra Vyas and Nirmal Ghosh as members. They produced the first report of its kind for wildlife tourism, including guidelines, but this was not implemented by the state governments concerned.

The protected area network in the country predictably afforded a far greater coverage to forest biomes – deciduous, evergreen, temperate, coastal and others – under the control of the state forest departments. In comparison, the montane, grassland, wetland, rivers, arid and marine biomes and ecosystems were very inadequately represented in the country's protected area network. I was very keen that all ecotypes of the country should have adequate representation and all habitats of critically endangered species should be included in our protected area system, as I had long been convinced that our natural heritage, let alone wildlife, had a hope of long-term survival only in effectively managed sanctuaries and national parks. An important ploy was to use charismatic species as flag-bearers to save ecosystems and habitats by including them in our protected areas, just as Project Tiger had proved. I hoped to use the snow leopard to save the unique and unparalleled fauna of the Himalaya; the Gangetic dolphin and the gharial for the river ecosystems; the great Indian bustard for our dry grasslands and corals for our prime maritime coasts.

In 1985, permission had been given to two research scholars, Raghunandan Singh Chundawat and Joseph Fox, to carry out a survey of the snow leopard and associated species in the north-western Himalaya, based in Ladakh. In October 1986, India hosted the Fifth International Snow Leopard Symposium in Srinagar, Kashmir, where I took the opportunity to announce India's intention to start a snow leopard project, modelled after Project Tiger.

The report by Rodgers and Panwar in 1988 had shown that about 5 per cent of the 250,000 sq. km of the Himalaya then enjoyed protected area status, included in forty-six sanctuaries and ten national parks. In the Trans-Himalaya region, there were an additional two national parks, seven sanctuaries and seven wildlife reserves, covering a total area of approximately 9,000 sq. km. The snow leopard, however, was known to occur in only ten national parks and sixteen sanctuaries, covering an area of 18,627 sq. km, which it is pertinent to note had been increased to this level from

10,840 sq. km in the two-year period following the announcement of the snow leopard project in October 1986 (MoEF 1988). However, the report of Chundawat and colleagues had shown that approximately 98,000 sq. km of habitat was available to the snow leopard, of which only 18,627 sq. km or 19 per cent was then under protected areas (Chundawat et al. 1986).

The snow leopard project was envisaged as an eco-system endeavour on even a larger scale than Project Tiger, due to the availability of contiguous montane habitats. It was to provide for the protection of the apex predator, the snow leopard, and its co-predators, their prey and their habitats in both the Himalayan and Trans-Himalayan terrains. Fourteen reserves – Karakoram and Changthang Wildlife Sanctuaries and Hemis and Kishtwar National Parks in Jammu and Kashmir; Kanwar and Rupi-Bhaba Sanctuaries and the Pin Valley and Great Himalayan National Parks in Himachal Pradesh; Kedarnath and Govind Pashu Vihar Sanctuaries and Nanda Devi National Park in Uttarakhand, Khangchendzonga National Park in Sikkim and the Mehao Sanctuary and Mouling National Park in Arunachal Pradesh – were chosen as the initial sites for the scheme. It was to be a Central sector scheme modelled after Project Tiger, wherein the Government of India would provide 100 per cent of the approved non-recurring expenditure and 5 per cent of all the annual recurring costs, the rest to be borne by the concerned states.

I was also very keen to start a bustard project for all the four species of the Otididae family – the great Indian and houbara bustards, and the Bengal and lesser floricans. The Bombay Natural History Society (BNHS) had already prepared a project prototype. In 1989, however, the Planning Commission told the MoEF that it could have only one more project like Project Tiger and that too not with 100 per cent Government of India funding for non-recurring expenditure. The controversial T.N. Seshan had moved out of the MoEF and the then secretary, R. Rajamani, decided to initiate Project Elephant, which to some extent overlapped with Project Tiger. As for the snow leopard and bustards, in the absence of any specific schemes for them, it was decided to fund the protected areas where they occurred, under the two ongoing centrally sponsored schemes of assistance to national parks and wildlife sanctuaries.

The forests and wildlife of the Union territory of the Andaman and Nicobar Islands were the responsibility of the Central government's MoEF. In both of my tenures as director of wildlife preservation of India, I had attempted to give special attention and importance to these magnificent repositories of nature. As mentioned earlier, there are hardly any spots left in the world where forests and nature remain so pristine and virgin, especially with regard to lowland dipterocarp forests. The greatest destroyer of the forests of the Andaman and Nicobar archipelagos was the Government of India itself. Large swathes of forests in the North and Middle Andaman Islands had been exploited and the wood sent to the giant sawmill at Chatham, near Port Blair. The Union government was sponsoring settlements of migrants from the mainland in the Great Nicobar and other islands; the settlers moving in with dogs, some of which would turn feral; domestic pigs, which would interbreed with the indigenous and endemic wild pig species, and poultry. The Indian Navy wanted their own establishments and the extant human population was growing and wanted more land. Fishing fleets from neighbouring countries were exploiting the territorial waters of India in the Andaman Sea. On the Tillangchong and other islands, Thai poachers were collecting nests of the edible-nest swiftlet, prized for making soup in Chinese cuisine.

On a visit to the Andamans, I discussed at length with the authorities at Port Blair the various new protected areas that were needed. I was keen that entire islands and their foreshores be declared sanctuaries, the important ones amongst them being the large Interview Island with its feral elephants; Narcondam Island with its unique and endemic hornbill; the long Tillangchong Island with its breeding colonies of birds; Ross Island that had been the headquarters of the Andaman administration in the British period; North Reef Island with its rare, surviving freshwater lake holding one of the last surviving populations of the rare and endemic grey or Andaman teal; South Sentinel Island with its totally aboriginal Sentinelese settlement; and Megapode Island, a habitat of another very rare, unique and endemic bird, the Nicobar megapode.

The Andaman administration was extremely cooperative, accepting almost all my suggestions regarding the establishment of protected areas and adding more of their own. An unfortunate omission was Tarmugli Island, the largest extant island of Andaman and Nicobar which had never been inhabited and was, therefore, the best example of the pristine flora and biodiversity of the archipelago. The archipelago now has nine national parks and ninety-six wildlife sanctuaries; ninety-three of the latter were declared in a single government notification on 16 February 1987.

In late February 1989, I had gone to Assam in connection with the extension of the protected area network in the region, in the context of the Rodgers and Panwar Report of 1988, and to partake in the Rhino Conservation Task Force meeting. I was not taken to the Manas National Park as the Assam government had just then lost control over it. The Bodo militants, agitating for a separate Bodoland, had occupied 120 sq. km of the core area of the park, including the southern Panbari area and the west side of the Manas river. They had also occupied about 350 sq. km of the adjacent Manas Reserve Forest, of which about 250 sq. km was proposed to be added to the Manas Tiger Reserve and National Park, with the remaining 100 sq. km as the buffer zone. The militants had killed a game watchman and a mahout and wounded others, burnt a jeep and twenty government buildings in the park, and taken away the weapons and equipment of the wildlife staff.

On returning to Delhi, I submitted a detailed note to the secretary, environment, and to the minister stating that considering the magnitude of the insurgency and the past record of the Government of Assam in its inability to check forest encroachment in the Kokrajhar district, it would not be able to evict the Bodos from Manas and its environs. I recommended that the Government of India should send the army or paramilitary forces for this purpose. If the eviction was not carried out immediately, the insurgents would have time to settle in and with the onset of the imminent monsoon it would then be impossible to drive them out. I went on to say that Manas was 'perhaps the most important national park in the country' and that the matter should be brought to the notice of the prime minister, who still continued to be the chairman of the Indian Board for Wildlife.

Unfortunately, the Government of India did not intervene, Manas and its environs remained under the control of the Bodos for a number of years, and when they were finally evicted, they left behind a park which is a mere ghost of its former magnificent self and it has still not recovered almost two decades later. In the Pohu field in the Panbari grassland, where there were once so many hog deer that the ground appeared more saffron and ochre than green, one would be now lucky to see half a dozen. The remnant rhino and the eastern barasingha populations – numbering about fifty animals each – were wiped out, as were the ivory-carrying elephant bulls in Manas and its environs, which in the past produced many of the largest tuskers found anywhere in Asia. Manas at one time held the largest population of wild buffalo in the world, and the majority of them were unaffected by interbreeding with domestic buffalo. Today, one sees a few scattered individuals and even these bolt at the sight of a vehicle or a domestic elephant. On the other hand, gaur have shown an increase. It does not require much ingenuity to assess what happened – the Hindu poachers who killed buffalo to sell the meat were reluctant to kill gaur because of its affinity to the cow.

Later in 1989, I was promoted to the post of additional secretary and was given charge of the Ganga Action Plan (GAP), under the aegis of the MoEF.

Rivers in India have long been used as convenient dumping sites of municipal sewage and industrial effluents. Among the worst-affected is the Ganga, long revered as sacred and a part of the Indian culture and ethic. The Yamuna, which is the Ganga's main tributary and joins it at the sacred confluence at Allahabad, is even more polluted. After having water pumped out upstream of the city of Delhi, all the sewers of eastern Delhi empty into it. Further downstream at Agra, the metal foundries and the thriving shoe-making industries add more lethal muck into the river. The water of the Yamuna that reaches Allahabad is mainly from the river Chambal – then and now the best extant habitat of the Gangetic dolphin and gharial. Further downstream, the Ganga receives the sewage and effluents of major cities like Kanpur, Mirzapur, Varanasi, Patna, Bhagalpur and finally Kolkata. The 'cocktail' entering the river is further augmented by the run-off of chemical fertilizers, pesticides and insecticides from cultivated areas. By the time of the GAP, the waters of the Ganga and her major tributaries were not only not potable or usable for man or animal, they were not even safe for bathing.

Rajiv Gandhi in his dual capacity as minister for environment and prime minister had actively supported a special project for the clean-up of the Ganga. It was a pioneering project and K.C. Sivaramakrishnan had done yeoman service to kick-start it. When he was promoted as secretary to the government, I was posted in his place as director of GAP.

The states of Uttar Pradesh, Bihar and West Bengal, through which the Ganga flows, were to carry out and maintain the works funded by GAP. The overhauling of the existing archaic drainage systems and sewage treatment plants and the construction of new ones was initiated, but it was a Herculean task, made worse by the apathy of some state officials and the lack of civic sense and responsibility on the part of the polluting industries. Factories were required to install and operate state-of-the-art effluent treatment plants, which would be enforced and monitored by the state pollution control boards. In Kanpur, I found the highly polluting leather industries operating their treatment plants at varying levels of efficiency in the daytime, but shutting them off at night to save on their electricity costs!

In my capacity as director of wildlife preservation, India, I had already been associated with the biotic aspects of GAP. I had suggested that five aquatic faunal families – dolphins, otters, turtles, gharial and mahseer – be chosen as indicator species to ascertain the health of the river. Being at the top of their respective food chains, their status and distribution would indicate the status of the biotic health of the river water, and the body tissues of these animals would reveal the quantum of pollution that the various stretches of river received. Just as the return of the salmon into the Thames estuary was the surest indication that control measures for water pollution in London were succeeding, the state of the mahseer would indicate the health of the Ganga. The monitoring of the mahseer would also show to what extent they were being affected by the construction of dams and the consequent reduction of river flow. Initiating recovery plans for these five life forms would simultaneously ensure their survival and of other life forms, and directly help in the cleaning and maintenance of the water quality of the Ganga and its tributaries. Besides, in Indian religion and art, the gharial is the symbol of Goddess Ganga and the dolphin that of Yamuna.

Varanasi had its own problems vis-à-vis the Ganga. One of the oldest towns in continuous existence in the history of mankind, the destiny of Varanasi is inextricably interwoven with the river. Dying in Varanasi ensures a berth in heaven, according to Hindu belief, but one must be cremated on the ancient ghats on the river in the traditional manner, not incinerated in the electric crematoria that GAP was building. The ritual cremation of human bodies has traditionally been the livelihood of a single community, the Doms. To save wood, bodies would often be half-burnt and then immersed in the river. Besides, it was also considered culturally appropriate in Varanasi to set afloat carcasses of dead cattle, so that their souls too may ascend to heaven. Gharial and otters do not feed on carrion flesh, human or livestock, and it would be too dangerous to introduce muggers in the Ganga at Varanasi. So we introduced carrion-eating river terrapins that would be harmless to living beings. The Indian flapshell and softshell turtles were bred in captivity and introduced in the river. This proved effective in reducing pollution from carrion in the stretch of the Ganga around Varanasi.

Another interesting ecological experiment was carried out in Chhapra, Bihar, a mid-sized town with no industry. The sewage that emanated from Chhapra was organic, not industrial or chemical, and the quantum was also manageable. Fortunately, there was a fair-sized piece of government land available nearby. Instead of installing a costly sewage treatment plant, the sewage water was diverted to this plot of land where tree-plantation was already under way and more was initiated. The species used as a means of bio-purification was eucalyptus, known for its high capacity of drawing water from the soil.

Experts of the Thames Water Authority of England, who were helping the Ganga Action Plan, brought an interesting fact to my notice. They said that mosquitoes do not breed on the waters of the Ganga, however dirty and still, but that did not apply to the waters of its tributaries including the Yamuna. Indians have always held the waters of the Ganga sacred, assigning it all kinds of qualities. But this mosquito-repellent attribute, asserted by a scientist, was certainly novel.

In 1989, I visited the Gangotri Glacier, the source of the River Bhagirathi and hence of the Ganga, for the first time. Just below the glacier, which then extended far lower than it does now, I saw a confiding herd of thirty-one bharal, of which nineteen were rams. When I went again in 2009, Gangotri had become a national park and I had been asked by the standing committee of the National Board for Wildlife to report on the possibility of allowing a road to be built for defence purposes along its edges. This time I saw 117 bharal in eight herds, the most incredibly tame bharal I have ever encountered. But more noteworthy was their habitat occupation:

this is the only instance I have ever seen of bharal in scrub forest and tree cover.

※

In October 1989, I was invited by Chief Minister Gegong Apang of Arunachal Pradesh to accompany him on his travels to the wilderness areas of his remarkable state. We flew to the Tibet border on the north bank of the Subansiri river and the next day over Mouling National Park on to and along the Brahmaputra river, locally called Siang or Dibang, to Tuting and Gelling on the Tibet border again. Unlike in Nagaland and Manipur, and despite the practice of shifting cultivation, the forests on the hilltops were still dense and extensive, especially in Mouling National Park. These are tribal lands and Apang proudly told me that his tribe had agreed to part with the forests of Mouling so that it could become a national park. Indeed, it is one of the more extensive undamaged forests that I have seen in India. I was informed by the divisional forest officer that it held substantial numbers of clouded leopard, takin, serow, black bear and brushless porcupine.

Flying northwards along the Brahmaputra gorge, we flew past a spectacular, high waterfall opposite the village of Gelling near the Tibet border, reminiscent of the celebrated Angel Falls of Venezuela. We got magnificent views of the iconic solitary massif of Namcha Barwa, 7,758 m high, far north in Tibet. At both Tuting and Gelling, the villagers presented us with the skulls and horns of the takin and serow, which they said were not uncommon in the surrounding hills. The takin came down in the winter, while in the summer they migrated north into Tibet. The local people killed them with aconite poison derived from a plant found just below the permanent snowline; I could not get them to identify the plant.

We flew further east to the village of Singa, on the north-eastern corner of East Siang district and again on the border of Tibet, where there was more evidence of the occurrence of takin, black bear, leopard and musk deer. I was also taken to the Tawang Monastery, situated close to the birthplace of the sixth Dalai Lama and where the present Dalai Lama arrived in 1958, when he escaped from Lhasa. We flew east to Lum La on the border of Bhutan and north to Malum La through which the River Manas enters India from Tibet. We were told of the presence of musk deer, wolf and bharal and of an interesting custom amongst the neighbouring tribal communities. If anyone kills a wild animal, he cannot have sex with his wife for some days and the two have to eat in separate vessels. A puja must also be performed in the nearest monastery. The larger the animal the longer the period of abstinence, the longest being for the tiger, which is, therefore, not killed unless it makes a nuisance of itself. The shortest period of abstinence is for the musk deer, perhaps because it is one of the smallest and most desirable. Poachers perform their puja before they set off on their hunting forays, atonement in advance of the crime!

In the autumn of 1989, I drove from Delhi to Leh via the Sangla Valley Sanctuary and the Pin Valley National Park in Himachal Pradesh. At the Tabo Monastery, perhaps the oldest Tibetan Buddhist monastery in India, we were fortunate to witness the installation of a new reincarnation (rinpoche) as the head lama.

By 1990, the Bofors gun had found its mark and the government changed in Delhi. Rajiv Gandhi and the Congress party were defeated and V.P. Singh became prime minister, heading a coalition government. Maneka Gandhi was appointed the minister in charge of environment and forests. Her commitment to conservation was total and she was a formidable champion for the cause. However, being new to ministerial responsibilities, she was prone to being swayed by unverified rumours and the opinions of the 'chatterati'. She felt I was being 'wasted' on the Ganga Action Plan of which she did not have a good opinion, and within a year I was transferred from GAP to be an additional secretary in the MoEF. In the interim, she would consult me on wildlife matters.

One day she sent for me and requested that I speak with the chief wildlife warden of Kerala and have a 'poor' bonnet macaque in Thiruvananthapuram released from captivity. When I spoke with the officer concerned, he gave me an earful. The bonnet macaque in question, a grizzled old male, had a penchant for grabbing lunch boxes from small school-going children and biting them for good measure. The first time it had been interned for his misdemeanours, Maneka Gandhi had intervened and therefore the simian was released, whereupon it promptly returned to its old haunts and old ways. It was caught a second time, and Maneka Gandhi had phoned the chief secretary of Kerala who arranged for the monkey's release even further away, but it came back and continued its aggressive bullying and biting till captured once again. I requested the chief wildlife warden (CWLW) to release the thief one last time, way out somewhere in the forest. A week or so later the CWLW phoned to tell me that he had done my bidding and released the macaque some 20 km outside Thiruvananthapuram. Within three days the animal was back, had grabbed the lunch box of a nine-year-old boy and had also bitten him. The monkey was caught again, a court order was obtained from a magistrate to declare the animal dangerous to human life and it was promptly put to sleep forever. The officer was apologetic, but he said he feared an intervention this time from the chief minister or governor of Kerala, courtesy Maneka Gandhi.

As additional secretary in the MoEF, my main duties were pollution control, biosphere reserves and environmental clearances, but I continued to assist my colleague and friend Sunjoy Deb Roy, who had taken over as director of wildlife preservation of India.

The Wild Life (Protection) Act, 1972, had provided for special hunting licences for the shooting of some species of birds and animals. In that era when the hunting ethos still prevailed, the maximum we could achieve was a complete ban on all endangered and threatened species, with some outlets for the then powerful hunting lobby, mainly the shooting of migratory birds. The scenario had since changed in the intervening two decades, with the conservation ethos having spread throughout the country. So when I discussed with Maneka Gandhi the amendments to the Wild Life (Protection) Act, which were due and which I was handling, she insisted on the deletion of all hunting licences, and rightly so.

On 2 October 1991, Mahatma Gandhi's birth anniversary, a major amendment of the Wild Life (Protection) Act came into operation, after seeking approval of the standing committee of the Indian Board for Wildlife. All hunting was prohibited, barring the destruction of specific vermin in specified areas, and for research and scientific purposes. No wildlife, or products derived therefrom, could be transported without prior permission. Penalties for various offences were enhanced to make them more deterrent and non-governmental individuals were now given powers to file a complaint in a court of law in case of a violation of the Act. Provisions were made for the appointment of honorary wildlife wardens and for the payment of rewards to persons helping in the apprehension of offenders. Immunization of livestock living around parks and sanctuaries, provided for in the 1972 Act, was now made compulsory. The provisions of national parks and sanctuaries were extended to the territorial waters of the country, to help the establishment of coastal and marine protected areas, while safeguarding the interests of local fishermen. To protect the rights of local people, especially tribals, it was provided that no area could be declared as a national park or sanctuary until the rights of the people concerned were settled. To improve the prevalent abysmal conditions in Indian zoos, which were at best menageries, provision was made to set up a central zoo authority responsible for overseeing their functioning and management; only zoos that were recognized and which maintained their animals in accordance with the standards prescribed by the zoo authority would be permitted to operate. Activities which caused harm or disturbance to zoo animals became punishable offences.

A long-pending need was to give legal sanction to the requirements of CITES, of which India was a signatory and an active member. During my tenure as chairman of the standing committee of CITES in 1985–86, draft guidelines of the legal requirements of CITES had been prepared and forwarded to the governments of member countries for adoption. The MoEF had debated how to implement the requirements. I was in favour of a separate legislation to give effect to the requirements of CITES, as their incorporation in the Wild Life (Protection) Act would make this Act very complicated, sometimes contrary to its existing provisions. Most of all, the inclusion of a huge number of species, including plants, which did not even occur in India, would add to an already very long and complicated list in the appendices of the Act. It was, however, decided to incorporate the CITES provisions within the Wild Life (Protection) Act. As a consequence, the import of African ivory for commercial purposes was also banned. Maneka Gandhi gave unstinted support to the whole endeavour and piloted the amendment through parliament.

On 31 December 1991, I was once again in Arunachal Pradesh, at the army outpost at Kibithu, north of Walong on the Lohit river. The plan was to see and photograph takin. With me were Conservator of Forests Jawaharlal Singh, Wildlife Warden Pratap Singh and a Mishmi tribal guide, Prakash Mangu. We trekked up the Tho Chu river, a tributary of the Lohit, within sight of the Chinese picket across the border, seeing hoof marks of takin and serow in the snow. The Mishmi tracker Mangu had seen takin in this spot a month earlier, but they had apparently moved on. What I did see on this three-day outing, for the first and only time, were seven specimens of the red goral, whose distribution in India is confined to this corner of Arunachal Pradesh. They are woolly, with brownish-russet bodies and fawnish-mustard lower legs, face and throat patch. And though it was deep winter with extensive snowfall, the bird life was astounding.

A fortnight later, I went to Lakshadweep and was expertly guided by M.S. Syed Ismail Koya of the Department of Science, Technology and Environment, Lakshadweep. It was very disappointing to see the dredging of sand in the Kavaratti lagoon, the turbidity of which had killed all the corals. I was most impressed with the Suheli lagoon with its rich corals and fish, and recommended that Suheli Par should become a marine park, with Valiyakara Island, which has the best surviving indigenous vegetation in the archipelago, and the neighbouring Chariyakara as parts of it.

The highlight of the visit was Pitti Island, a flat sandbank rising from a deep sea, created by swirling currents around it that allow landing on the island only when the sea is calm and impossible in the monsoon. Its inaccessibility, assisted by the absence of predatory birds or animals, has led to its being home to some 20,000 birds of four species. Eggs laid in the monsoon survive, but those laid in other seasons still get stolen by humans. I saw over 10,000 birds of two species, sooty and noddy terns, the latter outnumbering the former almost six to one and allowing approach as close as 3 m. Pitti is a sanctuary; the only protected area of Lakshadweep, 'the Galapagos of the Indian Ocean'. It must become a national park, as must the Suheli lagoon.

A considerable amount of my time was taken up in pollution control. The pollution control boards of the states were not able, and in some cases like Gujarat, not allowed, to tackle the problem of pollution. One day, I received a call from V.S. Vijayan, who was heading a research project of the Bombay Natural History Society at the iconic Keoladeo Ghana National Park at Bharatpur. An industrial unit was spewing effluents that were flowing into the park wetlands, he said. I left for Bharatpur as soon as I could, instructing Vijayan not to inform anyone of my visit. Next morning, he and I went to the spot and collected samples of the turbid effluent emanating from the factory. Then we went into the premises and questioned the management on its acts of omission and commission. The manager insisted that Vijayan and I go into his office for discussion, which we did, leaving our chauffeur with the car. When we returned some twenty minutes later, we found not the turbid, fetid sample in the bottle, but aqua pura. When questioned, our chauffeur admitted that the staff had insisted that he also have some tea and so he had left the car unattended and the sample unguarded. I do not recollect an instance where I have been duped so easily or felt so foolish.

In the autumn of 1992, I went to China to attend the International Snow Leopard Symposium at Xining, Tibet, nestled below the formidable Qilian Mountains. I took the opportunity to visit the vast inland Qinghai Lake and the bird sanctuary upon it, and the nearby birthplace of the present Dalai Lama. At Xi'an Qinling Wildlife Park, I fulfilled my ambition to see the legendary golden takin (*Budorcas taxicolor bedfordi*), which is reputed to have inspired the Greek legend of Jason and the Golden Fleece. The bulky, mustard-gold males are indeed awesome.

To see Lhasa was another lifetime ambition. From Chengdu we flew past the Namcha Barwa massif, this time getting a grandstand view from the north. Everywhere in Tibet, Kalpana and I received special treatment, being Indians, with no entry fees and special guides in gompas and shrines. We were repeatedly asked about the welfare of the Dalai Lama, and for pictures of him. At the massive Sera Monastery outside Lhasa, where there were then only seven monks in residence, the head monk asked me whether I had noticed the vast numbers of the local Bhutia dogs sitting around Sera and Ganden Monasteries and whether I had seen any in Lhasa city. I replied in the affirmative to the first part of the question and no to the second, and asked the reason. The monk looked me straight in the eye and replied: 'The dogs seek shelter in Sera and in Ganden because the Chinese eat them in Lhasa.'

At the summer palace of the Dalai Lama at Norbulingka outside Lhasa, we were ushered into the bedroom where the Dalai Lama had spent his last night in Lhasa before his flight to India and which had become a shrine. On the vast premises that surround the palace complex, I saw pika and Tibetan woolly hares, incredibly tame. Then the pièce de résistance: the only sighting I have ever had of a free Pallas's cat.

In early 1993, I returned to Madhya Pradesh for the last time, on completion of my tenure in Delhi. The destruction of the Babri Masjid in Ayodhya in December 1992 had led to communal riots in many places, including Bhopal. The state government had fallen and president's rule had been promulgated in Madhya Pradesh. My senior colleague in service and the chief secretary of MP, N.S. Sethi, had phoned to tell me that the government was planning to put me in charge of forests and some other departments. I conveyed that I had certain plans for the Department of Forests that the state government should know in advance, one being that I would convert the Forest Development Corporation into a fuelwood distribution corporation, which would collect fuelwood from the forest and distribute it at supply centres, thereby stopping the notorious practice of the huge extraction and sale of 'headloads' of fuelwood, which I had failed to do in my tenure as forest secretary. Sethi heard me patiently and said he would bring this to the notice of the governor, in whose name the state administration was being run in the absence of an elected government. Two days later, he reverted to say that the governor had decided to appoint me as the chairman of the Narmada Valley Development Authority (NVDA), with the rank of a minister. Obviously, my agenda for the forest department was not acceptable; it was just as well that I had made known my plans in advance, rather than being put in charge of forests and then thwarted.

It was ironic that I should be put in charge of the implementation of the Madhya Pradesh component of the Narmada dam project, as I had opposed the approval of the entire project while in the MoEF. When the two dams in MP, the Indira Sagar in Khandwa district and the other at Maheshwar, had been approved, I had inserted as conditions for approval the creation of a national park in the Pamakhedi forests in Khandwa and a sanctuary at Maheshwar. The Government of MP had accepted those conditions, so in my capacity as chairman of NVDA, I invited the Wildlife Institute of India to survey the areas in question and propose the demarcation of the national park and sanctuary, which it did. The proposed Pamakhedi National Park also included some large islands that would be created once the reservoir filled and which would have been wonderful habitats for wildlife, especially for the endangered and neglected four-horned antelope, to which this Nimar region is so suited. Once received from the WII and finalized, I forwarded the proposals to the MP government for the notification of the two protected areas, offering from the NVDA funds to support the creation of the two. Not only did the state government hedge and hesitate while I was in the NVDA, it has not fulfilled its commitment to this day. In fact, the MP government has set up no protected area in the last two decades.

In Bhopal, I called a meeting of the non-governmental organizations (NGOs) involved and requested them to oversee and monitor the resettlement and rehabilitation of the people dispossessed by the two dams in MP and by the backwaters of the huge Sardar Sarovar reservoir in Gujarat. I felt that they with their rapport with the local people would do a better job than the government agencies. Their unified response was that since they were opposed to the project itself, they would not cooperate.

Medha Patkar, a notable opponent of the Narmada project, came to Bhopal to go on a hunger strike in protest. The newly elected chief minister of MP, Digvijaya Singh, had given her permission to stage it in New Market, a prime location in new Bhopal. Patkar occupied an island roundabout on the main road, where a large shamiana (open tent) was erected. Surrounded by her supporters, she spent days and nights lying on a mattress, in full public view. After some days of the fast, I asked the director of public health of MP to have her medically examined every day, to check whether her condition was declining and if there was any danger to her life and health. Every evening after these examinations I would get a report. Well after a week of her starting the fast, the doctor reported that though Patkar had lost some weight and was a little weak, there was surprisingly no significant decline in her physical condition.

Not doubting her commitment to her cause, but curious to understand the situation, I asked the police, who had Patkar and her colleagues under surveillance, whether she was really on a total fast. They replied that she and her party were under public view 24/7, during which she ate or drank nothing except water. However, as there were no toilet facilities at the arena, she did have to leave the place from time to time. Also, each evening she went to a friend's house for an hour or less to bathe. I asked a senior engineer of the NVDA to provide her with a portable toilet and a shower with hot water facility on the fast premises, and to convey to the lady that we were providing these amenities in view of her weak condition and to avoid her having to leave the premises for her daily bath. A day later she announced that she was breaking her fast because her main demands had been met.

In 1994, I was invited by the International Union for the Conservation of Nature (IUCN) to participate in their conference at Caracas, Venezuela. I took the opportunity to fly over the great Tepui (high plateau) of Roraima that inspired Arthur Conan Doyle's immortal novel *The Lost World*, and past the incredible Angel Falls, the highest in the world. At the end of the conference, I flew to Manaus on the Amazon, the most inland large navigable port in the world, where the dark waters of the Rio Negro merge with the murky Amazon.

Going up the Rio Negro in a fast-moving narrow speedboat, past ocean liners and Amazon dolphins (*Inia geoffrensis*) we arrived at Anavilhanas, the largest inland delta in the world, consisting of over 300 islands. I was a guest of the Brazilian Institute of Environment and Renewable Natural Resources (IBAMA), which is based in Manaus. My host, a crocodile researcher, asked me to have a swim in the river, but wary of the caimans, I declined. At night, he took me on a motor-powered canoe ride. The spotlight revealed hundreds of spectacled caiman (*Caiman crocodilus crocodilus*), including thirty-six pairs in the pool I had been invited to bathe in earlier that day! Later, at the mouth of a rivulet, we came upon a large black caiman (*Melanosuchus niger*); of all the caiman and crocodiles of South America it is one of the largest and, perhaps, the only one dangerous to humans. A large black reptile, striped with yellow, floating atop iodine-coloured water 3 m away, ruby-red eyes shining in the spotlight in an inky black night, appeared to me like a prehistoric version of a banded krait. Black caiman are rare and have been known to attack humans. My companion wanted to jump on top of it, tape its mouth shut, haul it into our narrow canoe and take it to the research centre for examination and tagging. What if it thrashes its tail and the boat overturns, I asked in a low whisper. The canoe will not sink, it can be turned upright and we can clamber in, he hissed. What about my cameras, I hissed back. No answer. So the crocodile remained in the river, a black-and-yellow apparition in inky water, but I did get some flashlight photos.

In Bolivia, I was to fulfil a boyhood dream of seeing Lake Titicaca, the highest navigable lake in the world, and in Peru the incomparable Inca city of Machu Picchu. Fred Stoever, my American friend, joined me for a cruise around the Galapagos Islands. Charles Darwin was finally convinced of the theory of natural selection and the evolution of species on this unique archipelago. The Galapagos penguins, the northernmost penguins which arrived on this archipelago with the cold Humboldt Current from the Antarctic and to which the Galapagos owes its rich marine life, were the first wild penguins I had seen. These and other species of incredibly confiding birds, land and marine iguanas, the huge tortoises, swimming with the frolicking seals, and the very remoteness of the Galapagos make a visit there like none other in the world.

In early 1995, I returned to Delhi as director general of Council for Advancement of People's Action and Rural Technology (CAPART), an autonomous organization mandated to assist rural technology and development through the medium of non-governmental agencies. This was a brief but unusual interlude, where I came into contact with dynamic, innovative, visionary and pioneering individuals on the one side and blatant cheats on the other. I blacklisted some 420 organizations that had misused and misappropriated the public money assigned to them. On the other hand, I had the privilege to work with Anna Hazare, who agreed to help us with watershed and water conservation programmes, which we started on a large scale.

On 15 April 1995, I joined S.C. Dey, the director of wildlife preservation of India, and S. Singsit, the chief wildlife warden of Manipur, to survey the Keibul Lamjao National Park of Manipur from a Chetak helicopter. This was my first survey since 1975. We flew over the park for fifty minutes and were able to locate and enumerate each individual animal and group of animals twice over, flying about 50–60 m above the morass, going lower when we saw any animal. We saw about eighty hog deer and two sounders of wild pig. I counted forty-three sangai – fifteen stags including nine mature dark-coloured ones, twenty hinds and eight fawns and yearlings accompanying their mothers. There were six groups of three animals each, seven groups of two each and eleven solitary animals.

Though the sangai numbers were not as high as claimed by the park authorities, the population had increased threefold since my survey of 1975, especially the ratio of mature stags, and the animals were also much less shy. The strip of cultivated land Thang Brel Maril, which bisects the park, had since been acquired and had become a sangai habitat, making the park a composite ecological entity rather than a bifurcated one. Consequently, the main population of the sangai had shifted from around the Pabot Hill to north of the Toya Hill, within the park. The high *Phragmites karka* grass had reduced, but 'Ishing-kambong' (*Zizania latifolia*), a favourite food of the deer, had increased.

The most notable feature was the increase in the water level after the completion of the Loktak project in 1983, impounding the water of the Manipur river at Ithai, the backwaters of which were flooding

Keibul Lamjao. As a result, Tombi Singh, then dean of the School of Science, Manipur University, told me that the floating morass of phumdi was indeed thinning. In the note I submitted to the MoEF on my return to Delhi, I wrote: 'The water table has become stable and permanently high. Due to the lack of fluctuation in the water table, the phumdi has less opportunity to settle on the ground in the dry season and to, perhaps, derive nutrients therefrom. There must be a continuous study of the phumdi dynamics. If the phumdi is indeed thinning as I had suspected it would in my article in the *Journal of Bombay Natural History Society (JBNHS)* in 1975, it is a cause of grave concern, since the entire future of this subspecies would depend upon their ability to remain afloat on the floating morass, which is responsible for having saved the sangai from extinction once its habitat on dry land was destroyed in Manipur.' Sadly, the grave prognosis not only proved correct, but is even more serious today.

A very encouraging development was that instead of the animosity that the park faced in 1975, the neighbouring communities were now very keen to save the sangai. I was approached by a number of people who urged me to help them save the animal and its unique habitat. A Sangai Protection Forum comprising of 215 members from nineteen local voluntary agencies had combined to form one organization and had started a public education and awareness campaign of their own.

In February 1996, I joined the chief wildlife warden of Manipur, Priyobor Singh, for another aerial survey of Keibul Lamjao. The grass was much higher than at the time of my survey of 1975, but the water hyacinth had been greatly decimated by a weevil and there were more hog deer in evidence. Lantana had been cleared from the Chingjao Hill within the park and the original vegetation was making a comeback. We counted thirty sangai from the helicopter – ten stags, of which four were large, fourteen hinds and six fawns and yearlings.

In December 1995, I availed of my last leave and took my family to the Andaman Islands. The marine national park at Wandoor had become a great tourist attraction. I took advantage of the aerial patrolling sorties of the Indian Coast Guard to visit the Great Nicobar and Campbell Bay National Park with its Nicobar macaques and megapodes. We also flew to the awesome and sheer Narcondam Island, the only home of the endemic Narcondam hornbill, skirting the entire Andaman archipelago, returning to Port Blair after flying low over the North Sentinel Island, the home of the Sentinelese who shun outside contact. When they saw our plane above, the men ran out of their huts, brandishing their spears.

We also flew over Barren Island, which is called so because it is barren and an active volcano. In fact, it had erupted whilst we were in the Andamans and provided an awesome sight of huge plumes of smoke, with flocks of snowy white and black pied imperial pigeons silhouetted against the smoke. I recommended to the authorities in Port Blair that Barren Island should be declared a protected area. It did become a sanctuary in August 1997.

On attaining the then age of superannuation of fifty-eight years in February 1996, I retired from the Indian Administrative Service, having served for thirty-five years.

12

Conservation Outside of Government

Retirement gave me the freedom to travel for pleasure to places I had always desired to visit, to see as many as possible of the unique forms of life the Earth supports. I continued to visit Indian parks and sanctuaries as well. On the morning of the new millennium, 1 January 2000, I was with my family in my beloved Kanha, watching barasingha wallowing and bugling in the Sonph meadow. I took the decision that I would devote the rest of my life to further the cause of conservation and, while travelling as much as I could in different parts of the world, to see the parks and species that I had never seen. Since my retirement, I had already been roped in to help with several conservation efforts at different sites in the country, which was a privilege.

In 1996, the Government of Gujarat was keen to accommodate the extensive exploitation of the Little Rann of Kutch Sanctuary for salt extraction, wanting as the saying goes, to have its cake and eat it too. The Gujarat Ecological Education and Research Foundation (GEER) had worked out various options and a seminar was held. I advocated that since salt mining which has been going on for centuries cannot be totally stopped, it would be advisable to earmark certain areas on the periphery which could be excised from the sanctuary for salt extraction, while the rest of the sanctuary could remain free from commercial exploitation. The water below the surface of the sanctuary is nine times more saline than sea water and, hence, the demand of these areas for salt extraction. But after some years of extraction of salt, the salinity of the subsoil water drops and the Agariya community, who traditionally practise this occupation, would move periodically to fresh spots. The Government of Gujarat, therefore, wanted changeable boundaries for the sanctuary, or to have the freedom to give mining leases within it, both of which options were illegal and unacceptable. So the old practice of mining within the sanctuary, which is in violation of the Wild Life (Protection) Act, continues.

In the summer of 1997, Claude Martin, then director general of World Wide Fund for Nature (WWF) International, whom I had known when he was researching barasingha ecology in Kanha and I was collector of Mandla district, wanted me to head a special unit for tiger conservation in India, under the aegis of WWF International, but based in the WWF office in Delhi. The international tiger population had suffered a significant decline, India being no exception, and the world was deeply concerned. WWF International had collected sizeable funding, especially from the Netherlands, the UK and the USA, and had given the money to WWF India, which the donors felt the latter had not been able to utilize adequately to contribute to tiger conservation to their satisfaction. Hence, their desire to set up a special separate cell in India and their wish that I should head it.

The special WWF International project, named Tiger Conservation Programme (TCP), had been in operation for over half a year. When I joined, I was ably assisted by Brigadier (Retd) Ranjit Talwar and Tariq Aziz, later joined by a well-known journalist, Usha Rai. In the field, I had the good fortune to work with S.K. Patnaik in Odisha, Arin Ghosh in West Bengal, R.L. Singh in Uttar Pradesh, R.G. Soni in Rajasthan, Rajesh Gopal in Kanha, B.S. Bonal in Kaziranga, and a number of other stalwarts. At WWF International, Chris Hails was my contact.

My predecessor as project head, Thomas Mathew, had rightly begun with support to the renowned tiger reserves – Corbett, Dudhwa, Palamau, Manas, Kaziranga, Bandhavgarh and Periyar. By now, tigers were mainly to be found in tiger reserves and in some of the other better-managed protected areas. However, these and other premier tiger reserves had reached, and in some cases had exceeded, their individual carrying capacity for tigers. They had been in operation for long and had received adequate funding from both government and the public. Their demands from the TCP were mostly for vehicles, riding elephants, computers and office equipment.

Yet, there were other protected areas, including some tiger reserves, which were languishing for lack of funds, though they had the potential for a dramatic increase in tiger numbers if given the required support, as was shown by many tiger reserves after the initiation of Project Tiger in 1973. The prime considerations for TCP support were the area's potential for maximum impact on improvement of the habitat and enhancement of prey and predator populations, the presence of dedicated officers on the job, and responsive state governments. The protected area in question must also be fully under the control of the state wildlife wing and, thus, not suffer from administrative diarchy. In Odisha, we selected Satkosia Gorge and in Madhya Pradesh, Achanakmar. Both had been under their respective state wildlife wings but had later been reverted to the control of territorial divisional forest officers (DFOs). In the case of Achanakmar, the reversion had occurred after I relinquished my position as forest secretary of MP. While Odisha agreed to our precondition and Satkosia went back to the state wildlife wing, MP procrastinated in the case of Achanakmar and the TCP refrained from providing support. Now both these protected areas have become tiger reserves.

In addition, we selected the existing tiger reserves of Kalakad Mundanthurai in Tamil Nadu, Namdapha in Arunachal, Periyar in Kerala, Sariska in Rajasthan, Sundarban in West Bengal, Tadoba–

Andhari in Maharashtra and Valmiki in Bihar. The last mentioned had been suffering at that point of time from non-payment of staff salaries for almost two years. Other protected areas selected for support were Mahananda in West Bengal, Pakke or Pakhui in Arunachal Pradesh; Nameri and Orang National Parks in Assam; Katerniaghat in Uttar Pradesh and Biligiri Rangaswamy Temple (BRT) in Karnataka. Many of them were then almost unknown, and did not provide the WWF much by way of publicity. But the impact on the ground was what mattered. Support was mainly for protection and law enforcement, supply of vehicles and communication and patrolling equipment, construction of checkposts and control of forest fires. Group insurance of the field staff, including the daily-wage earners, a novelty then, was initiated as was training in law enforcement.

Simlipal Tiger Reserve in Odisha, the most extensive contiguous sal forest in the country, has always been plagued by akhand shikar – ritualistic hunts by assemblages of over 500 tribal men, which start in late spring and continue till the onset of the monsoon, and in which swathes of forests are set on fire to drive all animals, large and small, into huge arcs of nets, to be killed with spears or with bows and arrows. The TCP gave funds to seek alternatives to this slaughter by way of providing supplies of meat and to spread awareness amongst the concerned communities. The ritual did not die overnight, nor was it expected to, but it did abate and taper off. Akhand shikar, involving large groups that continued hunting for weeks, got attenuated into 'potem shikar' with small parties quietly foraying out for a day and returning home by night. The field staff of Simlipal was assisted to strengthen their patrolling to prevent this practice. Gaon mukhiyas or village headmen were deployed to dissuade their own communities from such burn-and-kill campaigns.

In the monsoon of 1998, Kaziranga was severely hit by floods and 652 animals drowned, or were hit by vehicles as they sought refuge on the highway that skirts Kaziranga. Of these, forty-two were rhinos – thirty-nine swept away and three killed by poachers.

Hog deer, being smaller animals, were the biggest casualty and 506 perished. Seven elephants, twenty-three wild buffalo and nine barasingha also succumbed. TCP made available to the park authorities the WWF Tiger Emergency Fund for boats, night-vision binoculars, tranquilizing equipment and rewards for the local people who had rescued fifty-five animals.

When I revisited Orang National Park in Assam, a protected area with which I have always been impressed with despite its small size, I was sad to note that the wild buffalo had become locally extinct, as the barasingha had become some years earlier. Only six elephant bulls now remained in Orang. Exotic weeds like *Mikania scandens* and *Eupatorium odoratum* had invaded the park. The Bengal florican for which Orang is noted, were still as plentiful as before and there were twenty-eight tigers reported in an area of 78 sq. km of the park, the highest concentration of tiger reported in eastern India and surviving mostly on livestock. The DFO in charge, however, had received only ₹1,000 to run his jeep in the annual budget. The TCP support for Orang fulfilled a sore need.

In the Pakhui Tiger Reserve, the intrepid researcher Aparajita Datta was working on the association between forest regeneration and hornbills. She gave me a very interesting piece of information, that the serow in Pakhui were an important source of food for the tiger.

Invited to a conference on tiger conservation in Chitwan National Park in Nepal, I travelled by road from Delhi to Dudhwa National Park and crossed over to Shuklaphanta Wildlife Reserve in Nepal. A lovely little patch of forest, it held the largest number of the northern barasingha in Nepal; I counted 123 in that one drive. Shuklaphanta suffered from poisoning of its tigers and had lost three in a year. We also went to the Royal Bardia National Park where the rhino had been recently reintroduced, then into Valmiki Tiger Reserve in Bihar, which TCP was supporting, and then back into Nepal and Chitwan.

I was struck by the extent of deforestation and encroachment in the Nepal terai. The protected areas I visited had become virtual islands, isolated from the adjacent protected areas in India – Dudhwa, Katerniaghat, Sohelwa, Sohagi Barwa and Valmiki. Tigers were moving across the international borders and were, thus, a shared resource, but the managers of the protected areas had no contact with each other and, in fact, did not even know each other.

So the TCP convened an Indo-Nepal trans-border conference in Delhi, where it was agreed that a dozen identified routes that tigers followed while crossing the borders need more protection, the protected area managers would meet every three months, a communication system and sharing of information would be established between managers of these trans-border protected areas, and that there would be synchronized enumeration of tigers and other species. Other decisions were the establishment of a linkage between Royal Bardia National Park in Nepal and Katerniaghat in India and the harmonization of the Indo-Nepal Trade Treaty of 1996 with the requirements of CITES. Not all the above agreements were adequately implemented, but it was a worthwhile beginning that did have the desired effect and it should have been a precursor to similar efforts between India and Bhutan and India and Bangladesh (WWF 1999).

On New Year's Eve of 1998, just outside Dudhwa National Park, a tigress with three cubs killed a cow, dragged it into a sugar cane field 40 m away and ate it. The park authorities, who were informed next afternoon, came in the evening, saw the kill and left at night. They returned the next morning to find the tigress and two cubs poisoned to death. The third cub was found dead the next day, also poisoned. Earlier, two tigers had been found poisoned over a single kill outside Corbett National Park. In a two-year period, Andhra Pradesh had lost twenty-eight tigers to poisoning, according to official reports.

I, therefore, decided to launch a special scheme using funds from the TCP, wherein the NGO partner operating around chosen tiger reserves, on receipt of information of a tiger or a leopard kill, would immediately proceed to the spot, in most cases in a vehicle provided by the TCP. After ascertaining the market value of the killed livestock from the local villagers, a part of the amount of compensation would be immediately paid to the owner of the killed animal and the rest a few days later, if the predator was not found poisoned in the meantime. A local person was also frequently hired to watch over the kill to ensure that no attempt was made to poison it. If a watchman could not be found and there was a perceived threat that the carcass would be poisoned, it would be burnt.

The scheme was started in Dudhwa National Park under the supervision of the redoubtable Billy Arjan Singh. Subsequently, it was extended to Corbett, under the aegis of the NGO Corbett Foundation, run by Dilip Khatau, which did an outstanding job, giving compensation for 1,085 cattle kills out of a total of 1,260 that received compensation during my tenure as head of the TCP, from January 1998 to the end of 1999. The cattle compensation scheme was extended to Katerniaghat in Uttar Pradesh; Nagarjunasagar–Srisailam, Gundla Brahmeswaram, Eturnagaram and Pakhal in Andhra Pradesh; Palamau in Bihar; Ranthambore in Rajasthan and to Tadoba–Andhari in Maharashtra. Except for Palamau, the scheme, which mainly depended upon prompt response of the NGO partner concerned, worked beyond my expectations and not a single tiger or leopard was poisoned among the total 1,260 compensated kills (WWF 1999) The NGO in Palamau made fictitious reports of kills and simply pocketed the compensation money.

The traditional method of assessing tiger numbers was through identification of individual animals by their pugmarks. It had been used for the first all-India estimation of tigers in 1972 and in all the counts thereafter, including each year in individual tiger reserves barring the Sundarban and some others. Most tourists and officials who visit tiger reserves are only interested in the tiger, and the number of tigers found in a reserve was, and unfortunately still is, though to a lesser extent, the main yardstick for the evaluation of a park manager. So each year the manager would manipulate the 'census' based on the pugmark method of counting, to boost the tiger number in his park or sanctuary, till in some cases it reached numbers that could not have possibly survived in the given area. Hence, the photo-trap method was introduced, and some protected areas were equipped with flashlight cameras that photographed tigers and other animals that happened to cross a ray. Undoubtedly, this is a far superior method, though not proof against those determined to somehow show an increase in tiger numbers. However, most of the tiger reserves, almost all the other protected areas of the country and all habitats outside of the protected areas, did not then have access to camera traps then. Till such time as photographic facilities were made available on an all-India basis, the dual system of assessment of tiger populations would have to continue.

Secondly, I felt that the staff of the state forest departments, especially the officer class, was increasingly getting further and further from any contact with the ground realities. A forest guard was often not able to distinguish the pugmark of a tiger from that of a leopard and almost never able to tell the difference between the pugmark of a male and a female tiger. Having grown up with some wizards in pugmark analysis, I felt it would be a great shame if this craft died out. The field staff must be able to identify the pugmarks of all carnivores and the hoof marks of all herbivores. Besides, till camera traps became universally available, the pugmark method of enumeration would continue and so it must be refined and improved upon. I, therefore, asked L.A.K. Singh of Odisha to come out with a guide on tracking (Singh 1999).

On 14 August 1999, I went to see my cherished old friend Sunjoy Deb Roy, who was in hospital, suffering from cancer. He opened his eyes and called me 'sir', which I always objected to as he was older than me, and said that he was not well. After talking with him for a while, I took his leave and met his doctor, who said Sunjoy would not live much longer. I asked the doctor whether I could be of any assistance, to which he replied that Sunjoy was constantly asking for the water of Beki, which the doctor had never heard of. During Deb Roy's tenure in Manas National Park, we had often floated down the rapids of the river Beki in canoes, coming upon elephants and wild buffalo immersed in the water, causing them to threaten us, or splash out of water and escape. We would see golden langur on the Bhutan side, otters occasionally and hundreds of hog deer invariably. Sunjoy would get off at some favoured spots to indulge in his other passion, fishing for the golden mahseer.

Next morning, I phoned the field director of Manas at Barpeta and asked him to send an elephant across the Manas river to its offshoot the Beki and collect water from that stream, not from the Manas itself, and to fly it over to Delhi. The TCP would pay the airfare of the courier. The officer said what I already knew, that it was midmonsoon and the Manas was in flood. But his men would do their best for Sunjoy Dada. The next day a ranger from Manas National Park flew to Delhi with the water of Beki, but Sunjoy had died the previous night. I poured the water over his body prior to cremation.

The purpose of narrating this sad episode is to reveal a mindset that is uncommon today. Those rare souls who identified themselves with the national park or sanctuary where they worked did the most for that protected area, even if their careers suffered because of that devotion. Saroj Choudhury's name is synonymous with Simlipal, Fateh Singh Rathore's with Ranthambore, Kailash Sankhala's with Sariska, Hemendra Singh Panwar's with Kanha, and Sunjoy Deb Roy's with Manas. They were not scientists, nor trained in wildlife management themselves. But they identified themselves with their beloved areas, which they referred to as simply 'my park'. They fought for them and were prepared to risk their career prospects for them. To a lesser extent, perhaps, I too felt such affinity with the district of Mandla and its Kanha National Park. This kind of bonding with one's charge is rare now and I feel conservation in India is poorer for it.

All this while, a natural disaster of serious magnitude was occurring in the forests of Madhya Pradesh. Sal is one of the most important commercial timber trees in India, and sal-dominated biomes are among the most important ecological entities. They cover over 100,000 sq. km of the country, 25 per cent of which is in the states of Madhya Pradesh and Chhattisgarh. Sal forests are periodically affected by infestations of the wood-borer beetle *Hoplocerambyx spinicornis* (MoEF 1998b). Sometimes these attacks would assume epidemic proportions. My old district of Mandla had a long history of these afflictions and, therefore, at the onset of the monsoon each year when the borer beetle would get active, tree-trap operations were carried out. Saplings were cut in the jungle to attract the beetles, which would feed on the freshly released sap with great avidity, get intoxicated and lie in torpor. The local villagers would bring these beetles to the forest authorities for which they would be paid per insect, and the forest department would get an inkling of how abundant the sal borer beetles were that year. This practice, which had been in operation since the British period, was thought to be infructuous and was stopped in 1976. However, in the working plan for the forests of Mandla district operative from 1982–83 to 1996–97, which had been approved during my tenure as forest secretary of MP, both preventive and curative measures as prescribed by Beeson were to be practised in the sal forests of Mandla (Beeson 1941). This was, however, not implemented till after the infestation had become manifest, in the monsoon of 1996, when over two million beetles were captured.

In January 1998, the MoEF constituted a task force comprising forest officials, academicians, scientists and experts for a 'wider appreciation of the problem and the solution adopted by the Government of Madhya Pradesh and to test the efficacy as also the severity of the large-scale tree felling in the affected areas.' I was appointed a member of the task force, which had no designated chairman.

We travelled through the affected forests of MP and Chhattisgarh. I was horrified to see the extent of damage. Over three million sal trees in an area of about 300,000 hectares in the districts of Mandla, Balaghat, and Shahdol in MP and in Bilaspur, Surguja, and Rajnandgaon, now in Chhattisgarh, had been affected and over 800,000 trees had already been cut.

Three members of the task force, including me, were of the view that priority had been given to harvesting sal trees that had a lesser degree of infestation and, thus, could still be sold as timber, rather than to ones that were in the last stages of survival or were already dead. These latter should have been removed first or burnt, to do away with the insects within them, but then they would not have fetched the government any significant revenue. Trucks to transport trees were in short supply, so the infected logs had been stacked in depots within the forest, and the beetles from these logs had attacked the living trees around. In the Karanjia depot in Mandla, just below Amarkantak, the source of the rivers Narmada, Son and Mahanadi, we found 150 sal trees infected around the stacked sal logs. Some infected logs had been transported to railheads in Shahdol and elsewhere and, thus, the contagion had spread further. But the majority view – that what the state government had done was appropriate – prevailed in the report of the task force. We bureaucrats are very adept in avoiding the fixation of responsibility in our acts of omission or commission, of stating anything that may rock the boat.

To me this heartbreaking journey through the devastated forests I had loved and adored, was a revelation. In the Kanha National Park, the sal borer had hardly any impact and there were very few dead or dying trees. But the forests in the buffer areas of the park, which suffer demographic impact, were severely affected. In the Chada–Jalda–Bona sector of the Maikal Range, it was worse. As we got nearer to villages in the forest, the infestation increased, while it was much less deeper in the forests away from human habitation and biotic pressure. It is a known fact that when attacked by the larvae of the sal borer, the sal tree releases extra quantities of sap, locally called 'raal', to drown them. If the number of invading insects is manageable and the raal released is adequate, the defence mechanism succeeds and the tree survives. The quantity of raal released depends upon the vigour of the tree itself. Here was a visual proof of the adverse impact of biotic pressure upon the health and vigour of trees and other biota. The sal trees affected by biotic pressure did not have the vigour to repel the insect invasion; those saved from these pressures, including those in the pristine forests of Kanha, had that vitality. This viewpoint was inserted as a 'minority view' in the interim report of the task force (MoEF 1998a). In the final report, it was explained away by saying that the younger trees in the Chada area were vigorous enough to withstand the insect attack – belying the fact that it was not age but the distance from habitation that was the deciding factor – and that the infestation in Kanha was 'low' (MoEF 1998b). But why was it low in Kanha when a holocaust prevailed all around? And why did the old trees in Kanha, some of the oldest extant sal in Madhya Pradesh, survive, when older trees are supposed to succumb easily according to the 'majority opinion'?

During this period the chief minister of Madhya Pradesh, Digvijaya Singh, had constituted the Madhya Pradesh State Biodiversity Board, with himself as chairman. M.S. Swaminathan, the renowned agronomist, the architect of India's green revolution and a former chairman of the National Biodiversity Authority, was appointed an adviser to the board, which formed three standing committees on Biodiversity Conservation, Sustainable Use of Biodiversity and Equitable Sharing of Biodiversity. I was appointed chairman of biodiversity conservation, and was ably supported by J.J. Dutta, H.S. Panwar, Rajesh Gopal, Suman Sahai and others. Our committee made a comprehensive report saying that the state, which then included Chhattisgarh, had in the past twenty-five years lost 41,265 sq. km of forests altogether, and a further 48,450 sq. km of forest area had been degraded (MP Biodiversity Board, undated). The report pointed out that the livestock population had increased from thirty-one million in 1951 to forty-five million in 1992 and in addition, about two million heads of cattle migrated each year from other states and raided the forests of MP. Issues such as the unsustainable exploitation of forests for fuelwood permitted under the guise of 'headloads', the related man-caused fires, the ban on recruitment of forest staff, the long-pending non-settlement of rights and non-rationalization of boundaries of protected areas, the ploughing back of revenues from wildlife tourism into the local economy, the lowering of groundwater table over almost 75 per cent of the land area and more, were discussed in detail and solutions offered. It was also mentioned that the attitude of the state government towards its forests hitherto had been to treat them as Kamadhenu, the celestial wish-fulfilling cow that can be milched ad infinitum, without being sustained and supported. This attitude had to change – forests were renewable resources that required periods of recovery and sustenance. The report met with the same response as do most such reports – stoic, somnolent silence and business as usual.

In May 1999, I undertook a hurried survey of nine protected areas – Sitanadi, Udanti, Tamor Pingla, Badalkhol, Semarsot and Gomarda in MP (now in Chhattisgarh), Karlapat and Sunabeda Sanctuaries in adjacent Odisha, and the Palamau Tiger Reserve in Bihar. Commercial exploitation in sanctuaries, including the extraction of tendu leaves for making bidis had been stopped in the protected areas of MP in 1982, during my tenure as forest secretary, but had been restarted from about 1997 onwards. The pretext was that these protected areas had not been notified 'finally', despite the categorical direction of the Supreme Court that all national parks and sanctuaries in the country should have the settlement of rights done and their final notification announced in a specified time frame, now long over, and despite the 1991 amendment of the Wild Life (Protection) Act to the effect that if parks and sanctuaries were on reserved forests where private rights had earlier been extinguished, a second notification was not essential. Moreover, for the first time a minimum target of tendu leaf collection per protected area had been set. The result was there for all to see. As many as five fires were set in some forests of MP between February and June to obtain a fresh flush of grass for livestock grazing, collection of mahua flowers for making the local brew, the growth of fresh tendu leaves; and two more fires to facilitate the collection of sal seed from which cocoa butter, an ingredient in chocolate manufacture, is derived. No forest can withstand such repeated onslaughts of fire each year.

I found almost 90 per cent of the Sitanadi Sanctuary and over 60 per cent of the Udanti Sanctuary – now the only abode of the wild buffalo in this region – burnt black. The extent of damage from fire was almost the same in Gomarda, Semarsot and Tamor Pingla Sanctuaries and worse in Palamau. In my time as forest secretary of MP, the chief wildlife warden of the state had made entries in the annual confidential reports of the territorial divisional forest officers (DFOs), stating what they had done by way of wildlife conservation in their respective forest divisions. Not only had this been stopped soon after I left, but now the officer in charge of a protected area had to have his annual confidential report endorsed by the officer in charge of minor forest produce (MFP) collection, which depended on whether the former had fulfilled the quota of MFP collection set for the protected area under his charge. This, despite the fact that MFP collection was illegal under the Wild Life (Protection) Act. In my report to the government of MP, I called this a state imposition of illegality and a travesty of conservation. The practice was changed later (Ranjitsinh 1999).

A year later, in May 2000, I led a team of foresters and scientists from WII and BNHS to ascertain the status and conservation of the wild buffalo population in peninsular India – in Udanti and its environs and in Bastar, both then in Madhya Pradesh. The DNA of the wild and domestic buffalo is very similar. Yet, there is a great difference in size and in other morphological aspects, especially amongst the bulls of the two.

There are more domestic buffalo than any other livestock species in the world and their most common use is not for milch purpose but as draught animals, where size and strength are most important. Besides, man has increasingly come to realize the genetic importance of the wild counterparts of cultivars and of domesticated animals. Therefore, from the viewpoint of human welfare, the wild buffalo should be the most important wild animal in the world today.

Interestingly, man has driven the wild counterparts of the most common animals he has tamed, to extinction or near-extinction. The wild dromedary, kouprey and tarpans of Eurasia have been rendered extinct in the world, while Przewalski's horse was made extinct in the wild. Others such as the wild Bactrian camel and the Asiatic wild buffalo have been driven to near-extinction.

Thailand lost its last wild buffalo whilst I was in Bangkok. Nepal has also lost its only wild population in Koshi Tappu. S. Deb Roy and P. Lahan relocated the domestic buffalo from the cattle camps of Kaziranga with Government of India's financial assistance during my first tenure as director of wildlife preservation of India in the mid-1970s, but some animals came back to their old campsites, survived tiger attacks and mated with the wild ones. The Kaziranga wild buffalo have, thus, undergone a distinct morphological change. Manas, especially in its middle portion around Uchila, had some of the largest wild buffalo I have ever seen, but no more. The few that survived the takeover by the Bodo insurgency are genetically affected and attenuated. The only few wild buffalo that match the ones I knew in the past are on the Bhutan side of the Manas river. They have been wiped out in Orang and totally genetically attenuated elsewhere in Assam.

The only hope of saving the pure form of the Asiatic wild buffalo was in Chhattisgarh, in Udanti in Raipur division, and in Bhairamgarh and Pamed Sanctuaries and the Indravati National Park, which I had notified, in the Bastar division. Here the local tribal communities in the past kept no buffalo, only cows, for fear of takeovers by the wild buffalo bulls. The few domestic buffalo that did exist were so much smaller than the wild bulls that the chances of interbred oversized calves surviving at birth were remote. Hence, this population of wild buffalo had maintained its purity, but had been reduced to minuscule, scattered populations due to hunting.

My colleagues carried out the survey in Udanti, estimating the wild buffalo population in the sanctuary to be between forty-two and forty-four, which perhaps was an overestimation. Now there are five specimens left in the wild in Udanti, all bulls, with the only female, Asha, now in captivity, repeatedly producing male calves. This perhaps is an indication of genetic regression and collapse, a precursor to extinction of this population.

I travelled with the team through Bhairamgarh and Pamed Sanctuaries and traversed the entire area of Indravati National Park, camping in the open on the premises of different village mukhiyas (headmen), as all the forest rest houses had been burnt down by Naxalite insurgents. We could ascertain that the wild buffalo had become extinct in Bhairamgarh in 1988 and in Pamed in 1993, though the official records showed their presence in both these protected areas until 1998 (Ranjitsinh et al. 2000).

Our survey team saw only one animal, a large bull that came to the Indravati river at 4.30 a.m. But we saw some of their enormous hoof marks, quite distinct from those of domestic buffalo, in the sands of the Indravati and elsewhere. On that basis as well as on detailed inquiries from the local staff and the local people who knew each animal individually, we estimated the wild buffalo population in the Indravati National Park to be between twenty-five and thirty, in three separate clusters, with perhaps no chance of their intermingling. So the total population of the animal in peninsular India was estimated to be below seventy-five. Constantly harried, the only group that had a chance for a decade or more of survival was the Tekmetta cluster, in the remotest part of the national park, in its south-western corner on the Indravati river opposite the Kollamarka forest of Maharashtra. Here, in the dense forest and bamboo thickets in undulating terrain not preferred by buffalo, a cluster of ten to fifteen animals had sought refuge. Fortunately, some of them have crossed over into Kollamarka, which the Maharashtra government has now notified as a conservation reserve.

The wild buffalo have changed their lifestyle to survive. They have forsaken their beloved midday immersion in water, indeed even a drink of water in the height of summer. They trudge long distances to reach different spots on the Indravati river in the small hours of the morning to drink and bathe, and depart to travel long distances to hide for the day.

In Bastar, after the rice harvest in spring, the ritualistic communal hunt called paradh provides a prime occupation in the months before the monsoon. As in the akhand shikar of Odisha, huge, strong nets are strung for hundreds of metres, fires are set and animals driven into the nets to be speared or shot with arrows. Our party came upon such a hunt within the Indravati National Park. We marched up to the 'paradhis' and with the help of the forest staff confiscated the nets and put them in jeeps, whereupon the hunters grouped, gathered courage and advanced upon us menacingly. We drove off hurriedly, with the nets. After we left Indravati, the Naxalite insurgents systematically burnt the houses of all village elders whose premises we had camped upon during our travels in the park. Now no forest staff can safely enter the Indravati National Park. The Kollamarka Reserve across the Indravati river in Maharashtra provides the only hope for the survival of the wild buffalo in peninsular India, as the Udanti population is, perhaps, beyond redemption in the wild, as of now.

The gaur are even scarcer in Indravati than the wild buffalo. For those inveterate hunters, the Dandami Bison Horn Maria tribe, the gaur are the prize target. Apart from the large quantum of meat, the gaur provide horns that adorn the tribal headdress essential for their dances and ceremonies. The official number of gaur in the park, when we visited in 2000, was only nineteen.

Over the years, well-meaning persons have repeatedly told me that forests and wildlife have not been destroyed by the tribals but by foresters, contractors and industrialists. This utopian view should be discarded. Almost no community or group is blameless in the destruction and decimation of the forests and wildlife of India, directly or otherwise over the past century. Only the form and quantum of destruction vary from place to place.

After my departure from the MoEF in 1992, needs had arisen which required further incorporation into and amendments of the

Wild Life (Protection) Act of 1972, the last amendment having been in 1991. In September 1995, the ministry had appointed an interstate committee to review the Wild Life (Protection) Act and other laws, and asked me to chair it. Amongst its eighteen members were the principle chief conservators of forests of states; S. C. Dey, the additional inspector general of forests in the MoEF; the director of WII, S.K. Mukherjee; member secretary of the Central Zoo Authority of India S.C. Sharma; and representatives of the WWF and BNHS – Ullas Karanth, Ashok Kumar, Mahendra Vyas and Walter Fernandes. The member secretary was Kishore Rao, DIG in the MoEF and one of the ablest colleagues I have had the good fortune to work with. It was a very competent and committed group that gave me unstinted support. Our mandate was to make the Act 'more effective in terms of penalties, procedure and legal protection to forest, wildlife and staff.' We were also to recommend changes if we felt any were required, in related laws such as the Indian Forest Act of 1927, the Indian Penal Code, the Code of Criminal Procedure and others to make 'wildlife law enforcement more effective.'

The pro-conservation era in government was by now long over and state governments were determinedly opposing the idea of establishment of any new sanctuaries and national parks. I, therefore, felt that a third category of protected area, conservation reserves, could be envisaged on government land, forest or otherwise, in which there would be no acquisition of private rights nor stoppage of grazing, but where there would be a management committee in which the local people had strong representation and which could conserve landscapes, seascapes and connecting corridors between protected areas. I thought the state governments who were resolutely refusing to establish sanctuaries may agree to the creation of conservation reserves instead. These would be far better than not having any protected areas at all. Besides, it was clear that conservation in a democracy like India could only progress, indeed survive, with the involvement of the people, and conservation reserves provided the basis for such endeavours, more so than national parks and sanctuaries. This third category was to be in lieu of the 'closed areas' category which was already in the Act, but was serving no purpose.

India has a marvellous tradition of empathy for nature, of communities protecting fauna and flora on their own, without the support of government and other communities, and sometimes in spite of opposition from the others. The Bishnois of Rajasthan and Haryana are best known for their devotion to this cause, but there are others – the Lyngdohs in Meghalaya, the communities that preserve sacred groves in Maharashtra, the Jains of Botad and the Vala Kathis of Sorath, both in Saurashtra, Gujarat, and the villagers of Purushottampur and Vetnoi in Odisha, to name a few. Recognition of such traditional conservation efforts and provision of financial and logistical support to them was long overdue. A fourth category of protected area was, therefore, envisaged. A community reserve on communal or private land, provided that the community or landowners desired it, was to be governed by a management committee consisting of five representatives of the local community and one from the state wildlife department. It would elect its own chairman, who would also be the honorary wildlife warden of the community reserve.

When I mooted the idea of conservation reserves and community reserves to the committee members, there was some initial hesitance. Still, I drafted the provisions for these two new proposed protected areas and the committee not only accepted them unequivocally, but improved upon the drafts.

The Indian Board for Wildlife so far was not a statutory body, though the state boards were. This was deliberate. In 1972, the administration of forests and wildlife was a state subject under the Constitution. I felt that if the national board was also incorporated into the Act, the states that had not passed resolutions adopting the 1972 Act, including Jammu and Kashmir, would be reluctant to do so. Those exigencies were no longer prevalent and the incorporation of a national board was long overdue. It was given the designation of the National Board for Wildlife. The state wildlife boards were also restructured and provision was made for the appointment of private citizens as honorary wildlife wardens.

In the powers vested with the chief wildlife warden to permit hunting in exceptional cases, an additional provision was inserted that such hunting would only be permitted if the chief wildlife warden was 'satisfied that such an animal cannot be captured, tranquilized or translocated.' The Act of 1972 permitted the hunting of even animals listed under Schedule I of the Act, if the animal posed a threat to human life, but not to human property. But cattle-killing carnivores and crop-raiding herbivores had been eliminated under this provision. While maneaters must never be translocated and released, other carnivores that are causing nuisance to humans can be; though there is a likelihood that they, especially leopards, will make their way back to their original homes.

There had also been misuse of the provision in the Act that provided for the cutting and removal of forest produce from national parks and sanctuaries, if that was deemed by the chief wildlife warden and his state government to be 'necessary for the improvement and better management of wild life' in that protected area. Subsequently, an amendment had been made that this permission should be with the concurrence of the respective state board for wildlife, but the unwarranted exploitation for commercial purposes continued regardless. The Buxa Tiger Reserve in West Bengal, which had extensive exotic teak plantations, and the Dudhwa Tiger Reserve in UP, which had exotic teak and eucalyptus plantations, were being exploited on the basis of working plans. The flowering of the *Dendrocalamus strictus* bamboo in Bandhavgarh Tiger Reserve in MP and in Shoolpaneshwar Sanctuary in Gujarat prompted the respective state governments to sell the dead and dying bamboo to paper mills for pulp, on the pretext of the dry bamboo being 'fire hazards.' Thus, a provision was made in the amendment bill whereby any forest produce removed from a national park or sanctuary for the improvement and better management of the same would be 'used for meeting the personal bona fide needs of the people living in and around the sanctuary or national park and shall not be used for any commercial purpose.' Overnight the exploitation of these protected areas for 'improvement and better management' came to a halt.

The amendment bill of 2002 also provided that alteration of a boundary of a sanctuary or national park would only be made by a state government on the recommendation of the national board. No construction of commercial tourist lodges, hotels, zoos and safari parks would be permitted in parks and sanctuaries except with the approval of the national board, and zoos could only acquire from or transfer animals to recognized zoos. Officers were empowered to expeditiously evict encroachments; penalties for offences were enhanced, as were rewards to persons assisting in the detection of offences and apprehension of offenders. Vehicles, weapons and tools used in the committing of an offence could not be returned to the offender, on the compounding of an offence. The Indian Forest Act of 1927 makes wide provisions for compounding of offences and, being familiar with them, forest officers were prone to not only compound cases under the Wild Life Act, but to also return the weapons, vehicles and other seized articles after the compounding. The Wild Life Act permits some lesser offences to be compounded, but the confiscation of weapons and vehicles used in the perpetration of the offence is a greater punishment than the fines paid whilst compounding.

The amendment bill of 2002 became the amendment Act of 2003. To me it was a landmark. I had drafted the Wild Life (Protection) Act 1972 and had been associated with every significant amendment of it thereafter, even after my retirement from government service in 1996. However, since the 2003 amendment, I have not been involved with any amendments of existing laws or the framing of new ones by the MoEF. The omission I believe is deliberate, and the efforts thereafter have been to 'dilute' existing laws where I would have been a misfit and an obstacle. The one exception was the Wild Life (Protection) Amendment Act of 2006, which set up the National

Tiger Conservation Authority (NTCA), for which I was unofficially consulted and a few of my suggestions were incorporated.

In the meanwhile, the MoEF came forth with the Biological Diversity Bill of 2000. The legislation defines equitable benefit sharing of biodiversity, which is indeed its covert raison d'être. The bill does make pious proclamations, strategies and plans for conservation, without in any way providing for their implementation and the prevention of the ongoing rampant misuse, overuse and abuse of the nation's biodiversity. The law uses the catchword of conservation – sustainable use of biodiversity. But sustainable at what level – the present overly degraded level or after the restoration of the ecosystem and its biota to an optimum level? This is a question no protagonist of the 'sustainable use' mantra is prepared to answer. Another poser that is conveniently ignored in debates, as it is in the biodiversity bill, is: In the case of a conflict of interest between conservation imperatives and utilization, as invariably arises, what will prevail in protected areas and elsewhere? When called upon by the Parliamentary Standing Committee on Environment to give my opinion on this legislation, I placed before it these views, summing up by saying that the legislation was more about 'the loaves and fishes' of biodiversity and not about its long-term management and wise utilization.

In 2004, the MoEF came out with the draft National Environment Policy, in which the increasing tilt towards economic factors, in the guise of the ecological, was even more evident. When asked to give my comments on it, I described it as a 'white paper' on development and a document to facilitate environmental clearances. The policy does emphasize public participation and rightly so, but ignores its pitfalls. Joint forest management had worked very well in some places; in many it had simply led to forest encroachment. Under the heading 'Environmental Offsetting' there was a nugget: that there was an 'obligation to protect threatened or endangered species and natural ecosystems that are of special importance to sustaining life, providing livelihoods or general wellbeing. By that token, as long as a tiger or an elephant provided revenue through tourism, we were under 'obligation' to protect them, if not, they could be dispensed with. And there was much more. In my analysis, I concluded that if this was the approach and attitude of the Ministry of Environment and of the Indian government, the environment of the country would perhaps be better served if the MoEF was abolished altogether. Little did I realize that this was just a preview; it would get worse and far worse as the years rolled by.

The MoEF did propose the second National Wildlife Action Plan (2002–2016), in the preparation of which I participated. The plan enunciated the principle that 'every species has the right to live and every threatened species must be protected to prevent its extinction' (MoEF 2002). It addressed all the problems that nature conservation in India was then facing and suggested remedies and alternatives. But like most policy statements and strategies, it was short on implementation.

Next came The Scheduled Tribes and Other Traditional Forest Dwellers (Recognition of Forest Rights) Act (FRA) of 2006. I consider this to be the most harmful act or action undertaken by any government with respect to forests, in the history of India. The intention patently was noble, to rectify a 'historical injustice', but latently totally political, to create a vote bank. The protagonists of this law had enough administrative experience to realize the misuse it could and would be put to. Not only did they not care but they facilitated its misuse and abuse at the cost of the forests of the nation.

The ostensible purport of the FRA was to settle on traditional forest dwellers, including tribals, their traditional rights within the forest, including rights over land, which had been denied to them by the British and by the Indian government since Independence. But the very same section went on to say that these communities should have 'occupied' the lands – not owned, not inherited, not been in possession of for a given number of years, but occupied – prior to 13 December 2005, for which they would be given ownership rights. The law came into effort on 29 December 2006. There had been past settlements of encroachments in almost all states; a number of times in states like MP and Chhattisgarh. So there was really no need for such a settlement at the national level. But while the settlements at the state levels had been of old encroachments, this one gave acceptance to those who had occupied forest land just prior to the passage of the bill. Verification of the fact that the occupiers of forest lands had in fact occupied these prior to 13 December 2005 vested with the gram sabha whose electorate the occupiers were. All past forest encroachment settlements had led to a spurt in further encroachment, but none as humungous as this one. In Kerala, people were growing and selling palm trees, one or more years old, which the encroachers who occupied forest land after the prescribed cut-off date could transplant, to show occupation prior to that date.

The Act laid down that in critical wildlife habitats in national parks and sanctuaries identified by the state governments, the forest rights could be modified or acquired: the community, if agreeable, could be resettled outside in an area acceptable to it, and it would also receive a resettlement package.

It was imperative that critical wildlife habitats be identified in accordance with guidelines proposed by the MoEF. Jairam Ramesh, who then headed the MoEF, called a meeting to finalize the guidelines, to which I was invited. The minister, in what I felt was a predetermined stance, chose not to finalize the guidelines but to get more feedback. The guidelines, indeed, were not finalized till February 2011.

I wrote two personal letters in May and September 2005, with regard to the Forest Rights Act, to Sonia Gandhi who was the de facto head of the UPA, which was then in power. I pointed out the deficiencies in the bill and the danger of its misuse and abuse. I mentioned that the Act would not undo a historical wrong but 'regularize recent, on-going and even future encroachments including those done under the current Joint Forest Management programmes – 30,000 hectares in Andhra Pradesh alone'. The forest degradation that would follow the spate of encroachments that were happening in anticipation of this settlement would affect the forest-dwelling communities most of all. I added: 'In some cases tribal communities have preserved and not damaged the forests; in many cases they have done the opposite. In Bastar and the northeast are some examples of tribals who own the forests or have total usage rights over them and, yet, have destroyed them. There is, thus, no one universal formula. Forests are far too important a national asset to be allowed to cater to utopian concepts.'

The letter went on to ask, 'Does the forest belong only to the tribals, which constitute 8.2 per cent of country's populace, or do they belong to the nation as a whole? Apart from the tangible forest products, the first charge of which must accrue to all its neighbouring people and not to the tribals alone, what about the even more important intangible benefits of forests, water most of all? What about food security and what about the country's ecological security?' I ended by saying: 'What is most ironic is that the bill is being spearheaded by a political party which claims inspiration from Shrimati Indira Gandhi and Shri Rajiv Gandhi, but will totally subvert the Forest (Conservation) Act, the Wild Life (Protection) Act and the National Forest Policy of 1988, which are amongst their greatest legacies.'

I received no reply from Sonia Gandhi and I expected none.

When the bill was under consideration of the parliamentary standing committee, I was asked by its chairman K.C. Deo to make a presentation before it. At the end of it, none of the members refuted my arguments, but Brinda Karat, an MP belonging to the Communist Party of India (Marxist), archly asked whether I was an IAS officer and had I worked in the MoEF. When I replied in the affirmative, she replied that it was because of officers like me and my ministry that the FRA had been framed! Disallowing my intended retort, the chairman brought the interview to a close. The penchant of passing judgement on a person and his motives rather than on the substance of what he is saying is a malaise quite common amongst politicians and bureaucrats in India, but what was most comical was the arrogance and the self-righteousness with which Brinda Karat delivered her little homily!

In a recent study on the implementation of the FRA, its impact on climate change and on the vulnerability of forests and forest-dwelling communities in Maharashtra, some startling but expected facts have been revealed (TERI 2014). Until 31 May 2014, over 3.7 million claims for individual and community rights on forest land had been filed at the national level, out of which over three million claims had been settled. A total of 1.4 million titles had already been distributed to the rights holders, distributing 2.38 million hectares of forest land.

In just one area, the Gondia forest division of Maharashtra, a total of 100,000 individual and communal rights had been recognized till then, covering 0.3 million hectares of forest land. Of these, 1,748.45 hectares had forest cover in 2005 and 433.38 hectares had forest cover till 2012, according to satellite imagery. Thus, the deforestation took place after the settlement of forests. The study further states: 'A total of 14,668.96 hectares of forest land lost the opportunity of carbon sequestration. The loss of opportunity for annual carbon sequestration is 9,017 tonnes of carbon dioxide due to wrong recognition of individual rights under FRA in Maharashtra.' A study should be commissioned to assess the impact of the FRA on carbon sequestration in the country as a whole and how far it has set India back in controlling carbon emissions, in the fight against climate change.

In early 2003, the Government of India set up a National Forest Commission, the first and only one of its kind so far. It was headed by B.N. Kirpal, a former Chief Justice of India. Professor J.S. Singh of the Banaras Hindu University, Chandi Prasad Bhatt known for his association with the Chipko movement in the Himalaya, A.P. Muthuswami, a retired IAS officer from Tamil Nadu, and I were members. The director general of forests and special secretary, MoEF, were also members, with the additional director general of forests in the MoEF as member secretary. The terms of reference of the commission were to review and assess the existing policy and legal framework, forest administration and institutions; to suggest specific policy options for achieving sustainable forest and wildlife management and ecological security; to make forest administration more effective and to establish a meaningful partnership and interface between forestry management and local communities. The commission travelled to a number of regional centres, heard the representatives of all the states and considered suggestions received from all quarters in response to a formulated questionnaire.

The report of the commission dealt with policy and legal framework, ecological security and the emerging needs of forestry; constraints and threats; forest, wildlife and nature conservation; forests of the north-east; people's participation in forestry; agroforestry, social forestry and research; forestry institutions, forest administration and personnel management; forest-based industries; Centre–state and international relations; financial requirements and, interestingly, the aspect of forests in national resource accounting. I believe it was a very comprehensive report which contained 360 recommendations. It was mainly drafted by Professor J.S. Singh and me, and in the absence of Chairman B.N. Kirpal, who was ill at the time, I presented the report to Prime Minister Manmohan Singh.

The six recommendations that pointed out the infructuous nature of the Forest Rights Act and its potential for abuse and damage to forests and to the ecological security of the nation were not acceptable to Chandi Prasad Bhatt. The six recommendations pertaining to the restructuring of forestry personnel to ensure specialization and creation of sub-cadres within the Indian Forest Service in four fields of forestry – forest conservation, extension forestry, wildlife management and research and training – were opposed by four members of the commission, including the two belonging to the Indian Forest Service. The dissent note said: 'The creation of sub-cadre in IFS is neither required nor desirable. Creation of sub-cadre within a service will lead to fragmentation of service and is bound to create conflict. The objective can be achieved by career planning with greater emphasis on taking up specialization along with appropriate transfer and posting policy.' The perceived interest of the service took precedence over the obvious benefit to the nation's forests and, of course, neither the career planning nor the transfer and posting policy alluded to ensure specialization within the service has yet come about.

The report of the National Forest Commission, though accepted by the government, was like the majority of such reports, not implemented except incidentally.

All this while I continued to take every opportunity to visit wildlife areas, especially those I had not been to before and to observe species I had never seen. Having crossed the age of sixty, my first preference was to go to the mountains while I could still climb, 'before age overtakes us', to quote George Schaller.

In June 1998, I went to the Pin Valley National Park in Spiti, to watch ibex. Yash Veer Bhatnagar, who had studied the ibex in Pin, suggested that I time my visit to synchronize with the seasonal visit of the animals to the Gechang natural salt lick in the park. But I was late and the trip was ruined by unseasonal rain and snow.

En route, I stopped at the Tabo Gompa (monastery) that had recently observed its 1,000th year, to admire its magnificent murals, the like of which I have not seen in any gompa in the Himalaya of India or in Tibet. At Sumdo, the junction of River Spiti with the mighty Sutlej, I wished to see the skeleton of a male ibex that had been found on the left bank of the Sutlej and which was being shown as proof that the ibex lived there. As naturalists know, the Central Asian ibex had colonized the Himalaya from the north-west, and progressed eastwards till the Sutlej provided them with an insurmountable natural barrier. There is no record of ibex east of the Sutlej. The skeleton on the left bank mentioned above was perhaps of an animal that had been swept away by the river and deposited on that bank. The ibex skulls with horns that hang in the iconic temple atop a hill in Kamru village, the old capital of the rajas of Bushahr in the Baspa river valley, must also have been brought from across the Sutlej, not too far away.

I spent a week in the Pin Valley National Park, seeing ibex each day when the weather was clear, camping at Mikkim, Gechang and Thango higher up the Parahio Valley in the park. I was ably assisted by deputy ranger Kesar Singh and forest guard Padma Namgyal. The rutting season of the ibex was long over and the males had mostly separated from the females and kids. Ibex were shedding their underwool or 'pashm', and were constantly rubbing their faces and horns against their bodies to remove the bolls of underwool that hung on.

Taking advantage of the cover provided by sleet to approach a herd of fourteen males, bedded down with eyes closed to avoid the downpour, I patiently waited for the weather to clear, with melting snow trickling down my spine and stomach. But instead of clearing, the sleet turned to snow and I only got some indistinct pictures of curved horns rising above shimmering snow. Once with the sun shining, I was pinned to my spot by a herd of thirty-three ibex above me, twenty-eight of which were males, including six carrying horns 40 inches or longer. After almost an hour during which I cowered behind a stone, cramped and freezing, they got up, stretched themselves and slowly trooped over a ridge. Collecting my gear, I climbed as fast I could at that altitude of over 4,500 m to make it to the ridge from where I hoped to peep over and photograph them on the other side. Then I heard a sharp whistle of alarm. Looking up I saw a female had come back to the ridge top, which the herd had crossed, to check whether they were being followed, and had spotted me. The game was over.

The ibex in Spiti are the Trans-Himalayan ibex, akin to those in Ladakh, Central Asia and Mongolia, the true *Capra sibirica*. Not only are their horns longer than that of the animals south of the main Himalayan divide but are more divergent and flare out further at the ends.

Dogged by bad weather, I was still hopeful that the skies would clear and ibex males would came to the Gechang salt lick, as a herd of females and young had. Then one night it poured and water entered my tent, wetting all my clothes and even the sleeping bags. Pneumonia became a possibility and so we marched out, having to walk all the way down to the bridge over the Pin river at Attargu as the road had been damaged, seeing ibex sporadically all the way down.

We then proceeded to Kaza, the headquarters of Spiti district, and met Charu Mishra, who was working on a research project there. We went up to Kibber village, then reputed to be the highest village in the world connected by a motorable road over 5,000 m high. The Dalai Lama visits the Kibber Valley, as it is the final resting place of one of his preceptors. Close to Tashigang village above Kibber, we came upon a very confiding herd of twenty bharal, mostly rams. Two of the males carried some of the largest horns I have seen on a bharal – over 26 inches long and drooping down. The characteristic black throat patch was fading and the coats were turning brownish grey with age. They were 'going back', in hunter's parlance. The herd allowed us to approach them within 100 m.

On the return journey, we stopped over at the spectacular Ki Gompa, perched atop a pinnacle in the valley and commanding a superb view. We met the westernized head lama whom I had met on my previous visit, ten years earlier. He still spoke English with an American accent. While sipping yak-butter tea in his chamber, one could see eight bharal rams across the valley.

There are some riddles about Spiti to which I do not have answers. Why are there so few bird species to be seen, and hardly any waterbirds along the lake shores and streams, as compared to Ladakh? Why are there no otters? Is it because of lack of fish in the Pin and Spiti rivers? Why are there no marmots and so few pika hares? Why has the lynx not been reported in Spiti? Is it because of the lack of smaller prey? Why have the kiang not colonized Spiti, either from Ladakh or along the Sutlej river from Tibet? Why is the wolf so rare in Spiti, while the snow leopard is not, when there is an ample supply of bharal and ibex available on grounds which the wolf can easily course?

In the autumn of 2000, I visited my alma mater the Lal Bahadur Shastri National Academy of Administration at Mussoorie. There I met the then chief of the army staff General V.K. Malik, whom I came to know well later. When I mentioned that I was keen to revisit the source of the river Teesta in north Sikkim, he kindly offered to make arrangements, as being on the Tibet border, movement there is restricted. Gangtok, the state capital, had grown beyond belief since my previous visit a decade earlier, and I have never seen such a profusion of liquor shops as are to be found there. I was taken to the Thangu transit camp just below the Trans-Himalayan plateau, at an attitude of 4,400 m, to get acclimatized. Later, I camped in different army outposts on the plateau.

This was my first opportunity to see and photograph the southern kiang, smaller than the western kiang that I was familiar with in Ladakh. The latter has slightly more white coloration on its pelage. I also had the best opportunity so far to photograph the dainty 'gowa' or Tibetan gazelle, which here allowed approach within 100 m in a vehicle, as opposed to the gowa in Kalak Tartar Valley in Hanle, Ladakh, where they would bolt when they saw a vehicle 600 m away. I estimated the number of gowa in this upland area of north Sikkim to be between sixty and ninety, in the year 2000. They have increased since then, especially in the Kongra La Valley north of Bunker.

In the valley leading to the Kongra La on the Tibet border, I saw 130 Tibetan argali, locally called nyan. There were 124 on a single hillside in a loose conglomeration, a group of thirty rams sitting slightly apart as the rutting season was still a few weeks away. In February 2013, I saw 143 argali on the same hillside, and fifty-five in May. They were at ease as long as we remained in the vehicles, indicating that they were not shot at from vehicles. The nyan are the tallest sheep in the world, the males standing some 120 cm at shoulder, and next to the Mongolian argali, they carry the most massive horns amongst sheep. But both the Mongolian and the

Tibetan argali are overshadowed by the unbelievable spiralling horns of the Marco Polo argali of the Pamirs.

I saw for the second time the Sikkim snowcock, the state bird of Sikkim. But what was most rewarding was my first sighting of, and the opportunity to photograph at close range, the Tibetan sand fox.

With the disturbance and occasional killing of wild animals in Ladakh, Sikkim today is the best repository of Trans-Himalayan fauna in India, though it does not have the wild yak and the Tibetan antelope, nor the ibex and the shapu of Ladakh. The army units on this spectacular plateau, with its lakes and towering peaks of Gurudongmar, Paunhri and Kangchengyao (6,889 m), need to be complimented on their conservation efforts. Peeping over the ridges into Tibet, one sees practically nothing. It is obvious that the herbivores are persecuted there and seek refuge in this secluded haven.

In 2004, Project Tiger assigned me the task of assessing some of the tiger reserves in the east. I revisited the Sundarban Tiger Reserve after a lapse of eighteen years. The habitat looked the same, but ecologically it had changed. In five days, I travelled some 400 km in the reserve, but saw only four saltwater crocodiles of which only two were adults. There were also very few signs of crocodiles on the mudbanks. I also noticed a lesser quantum of birds, both species- and number-wise. The reason for both, perhaps, is that the waters in the channels of the Sundarban are now more saline than before, with the diversion of water from the Ganga, Brahmaputra and their tributaries leading to a greater ingress of seawater. I was told of the increasing incidence of saltwater crocodiles coming to breed on the sandbanks of man-made freshwater tanks, at Haldi camp and elsewhere.

Efforts were on to breed chital in captivity, for release into the reserve. I pointed out the danger of contagion from the captive stock to the wild population, which have not been exposed to these pathogens and, hence, have not attained immunity. Besides, the wild chital have adapted to the peculiar features of this mangrove habitat, which the captive-bred animals would find very difficult to do. The chital in the Sundarban live in small herds, as the advantages of living in large numbers that exist in the forest-grassland mosaics, such as Corbett and Kanha, are absent here. Smaller herds would be better suited to the limited open space and food availability in the mangroves, and would also be a better anti-predator strategy.

We went to the southernmost island in the reserve, Mayadwip, a wonderful wild island. The guard outpost was surrounded by a fence to keep out tigers. We found fresh footprints of four tigers, a tigress with a cub and two others. On landing on the beach, they had not gone after the few chital and wild pigs that live on the island, but they had circled around the fencing, looking for a way to get in. The Sundarban tigers are, perhaps, the only population that have not changed since the arrival of the breech-loading gun. They still regard man as their prey. However, the field director of the Sundarban reserve, Pradeep Vyas, told us an interesting fact. Though in its own mangrove habitat the tiger attacks humans, when it goes into human habitations around the reserve it only hunts livestock. Another interesting aspect to emerge is the fact that the Sundarban tiger hardly vocalizes.

I next visited the Namdapha Tiger Reserve, after a passage of nineteen years. Namdapha is amongst our most beautiful and potentially one of the richest, and yet amongst the most neglected, protected areas. It is on a protuberance of Indian territory jutting out into Myanmar, with the snow-covered peak of Dapha Bum (4,495 m) on its eastern end. The reserve is flanked by settlements of those inveterate hunter-trappers, the Lisu tribe.

The rest house at Deban is at an idyllic spot, commanding a superb view of the junction of the Dihing and Namdapha rivers. It was January and the weather most bracing. We camped at Farmhouse, a lovely spot on the Namdapha river. There were footprints of gaur, sambar, barking deer and wild dog, and of a female leopard or clouded leopard. Wild dogs appear to be the major predator in Namdapha, though the prey population is low.

During our march we came upon the huge flower of the Himalayan sapria (*Sapria himalayana*), which is now endemic to Namdapha and very rare. It is a unique plant, a complete root parasite with the flower representing the whole plant. It belongs to the family *Rafflesiaceae* noted for their large, red, cup-shaped flowers that smell like carrion. We saw the eastern hoolock gibbon, and the rufous-necked and Assam wreathed hornbills. I noticed, however, that there were fewer great Indian hornbills than before.

On a visit to Mizoram to assess the Dampa Tiger Reserve, I went for the first time to two of the country's remotest national parks, Murlen and the Phawngpui Blue Mountain. It was most depressing to see huge tracts of magnificent forests cleared and burnt for shifting cultivation or 'jhum'. Murlen National Park is just 100 sq. km of hilltop forest that survived jhuming; perhaps the richest and most beautiful upland forest I have ever seen, mostly composed of oak, bauhinia, some rhododendrons and a few Khasi pine. Together with the nearby Lengteng Wildlife Sanctuary, which contains the Lengteng Peak (2,148 m), the second-highest in Mizoram, Murlen is the only surviving habitat in Mizoram of Hume's bar-tailed pheasant, the state bird. On a walk through Murlen, we flushed a female Hume's and a female barking deer in its deep bright orange-russet coat.

We next proceeded to Phawngpui Blue Mountain National Park, on the border with Myanmar at the south-eastern corner of Mizoram. The park encompasses the Blue Mountain Peak (2,157 m), the highest in the state, with a rest house at Farpak, on a hilltop just a little lower. Built during the British regime, it is situated on a site like none other I have visited, accessible by an exhilarating drive along a steep road. This also happened to be the first visit to this rest house by the state chief wildlife warden, the lady divisional forest officer and even of the forest ranger in charge of the park.

We spent two nights at Farpak. I was very keen to see the goral reported on the southern precipices. Accompanied by the knowledgeable forest guard Thangtheva, we skirted the edge of the escarpment, peering down the cascading cliffs. We saw altogether five goral, a female with a suckling kid and three males, two of which put up a sparring match. The animals licked the overhanging rocks under which they sought shelter, obviously deriving mineral nutrients that had seeped through.

The goral in the Western Himalaya are grey; in Sikkim, Bhutan and western Arunachal Pradesh they turn brown, and then red in the north-eastern corner of Arunachal. Though the distance was over 200 m, the goral appeared to be distinct from the brown goral I had seen. The belly was light brown, separated from the darker greyish brown of the upper part of the body by a dark line. The dark dorsal line was also visible, as was the deep brownish-grey marking on the forehead. To me, the goral of the Blue Mountain National Park is more akin to the Evan's long-tailed goral (*Naemorhedus caudatus evansi*) of Myanmar, rather than to the brown goral (*N. goral hodgsoni*) of the Eastern Himalaya. Alternatively, it could be a distinct subspecies or kline, as it does not quite match with even the Myanmar goral.

Another sighting of interest was the nesting of the rare and elusive dark-backed swift, which Salim Ali described as 'enigmatical' (Ali and Ripley 1970). The only other known breeding site of this bird in India is around Cherrapunji in Meghalaya, once known to be the wettest place on earth. While the much more common large white-rumped swift builds its nests with mud on rocky overhangs, the dark-backed swifts nest in rock hollows which they fill with vegetation. We ascertained the presence of sambar, barking deer, serow and leopard in the park.

Like all non-Buddhist tribal tracts of north-eastern India in which wild animals and birds have been relentlessly pursued, Mizoram too has lost a major part of its wildlife. It was, therefore, most interesting to visit a safe haven encompassing a microcosm of Mizoram's wildlife. Seven kilometres outside the state capital Aizawl is a rehabilitation centre for drug addicts, run by K. Liamthanga and capriciously named 'Sinner's Friend'. The 40-hectare premises hold giant squirrels, serow, barking deer and leopard. A tiger reportedly passes through it twice or thrice a year. It is perhaps the only place in India, or perhaps anywhere in the world, where one can view at close range William's kalij pheasant.

Just outside Liamthanga's kitchen, rice is placed each morning and evening for the kalij to feed on, and one can photograph these gorgeous birds, as I did, from a distance of 5 m. To add to the drama, a white house cat kept stalking the kalij, which allowed it close approach before hopping away and enjoying the game as much as the cat did. Liamthanga told me that once the cat got too close, whereupon a male kalij pecked her so hard on the neck as to draw blood.

It would be of interest to note that, unlike in Africa, the elephant in India is killed only for its tusks in areas where Hinduism or Buddhism is the majority religion. As only the bulls of the Asian elephant carry ivory, the cows and maknas (tuskless bulls) are spared. This does not apply to Meghalaya, Mizoram and Nagaland where Christianity is predominant and elephant meat is not taboo. The elephant is, thus, today almost extinct in Nagaland and Mizoram, even in the Dampa Tiger Reserve.

In March 2009, I joined the takin survey in Arunachal Pradesh, conducted by the Wildlife Trust of India, whose chairman I then was. Making the rest house at Mayodia on the Roing–Anini road in the Mishmi Hills our base camp, I slid and trudged up and down those steep, slippery slopes, bivouacking in deep valleys. It was an unforgettable but rewarding experience. One trip entailed four-and-a-half hours of descent with a seven-and-a-half-hour ascent the next day. I heard the calls of hoolock gibbons, which are the one primate the local Mishmi tribe do not kill to eat. There is also a taboo against the killing of tiger. Whilst we were on the march one morning, we heard a gunshot. It was bright and sunny then, but it soon turned cloudy. There was thunder and a drizzle began. My Mishmi guide, Robi Mekola, told me that a takin had been shot. The Mishmis believe that when a takin is killed, there is always rain and thunder, whatever the season and however clear the sky may have been. Presently, due to the persuasion of an enlightened Mishmi leader, Ikram Icola, the Mishmis were increasingly sparing the takin and other wildlife.

Early each morning, we would hear the call of Blyth's tragopan (*Tragopan blythii*) or 'pehba' in the Mishmi language, an incredibly eerie, haunting musical call. But we never saw a specimen and birds, in general, were neither plentiful nor easy to see.

Then above Mayodia, in the deep valley bottom called Amehathu, Robi Mekola spotted takin in a large rubble-covered opening caused by a landslide. Just above the shale of the landslide was a natural salt lick, where the takin had congregated. Takin live in these forests in the winter, from about October to April, and have their young here. In the summer, they move northwards and to high altitudes where the rut occurs. But before they migrate they visit the salt lick. I was just lucky it happened when I was there.

We rushed down the steep slope. Looking upwards from the valley floor with its fast-flowing river, we could see thirty-nine takin, mostly females and young with some bulls. One huge bull with pronounced withers was in possession of the salt lick on the overhanging rocks, shooing away others who approached it. The light was very poor and the distance nearly a kilometre.

Next morning, the light was not much better and there was no way we could cross the exposed river and clamber up the open hillside on the opposite bank. But I did get some photographs – and wonderful memories – of sparring bulls, nursing cows and the grunting conversation they carry on, reminiscent of the tableau in the Seijathang Valley in Bhutan so long ago. I estimated the congregation to number between fifty-five and sixty.

After retirement, I had been nominated to the Indian Board for Wildlife – reconstituted as the National Board for Wildlife – and its standing committee, till 2013. Some occurrences during their deliberations may be of interest.

In 1998, the standing committee of the Indian Board for Wildlife appointed me chairman of a subcommittee to examine the trapping and trade in birds, as the trade in all wildlife had been stopped with the amendment of the Wild Life (Protection) Act. A representative of the All India Trappers Association, Abrar Ahmed of the WWF, and Vivek Menon of the Wildlife Trust of India (WTI) were members. The committee recommended that exotic birds not covered under CITES and WPA should be dealt with under the provisions of the Prevention of Cruelty to Animals Act of 1960. It also suggested ways in which communities traditionally dependent upon trapping wildlife for their livelihood – like the Sahariyas, Baheliyas, Dafers and others – could be provided with alternative means of income, but this still has not been done.

The standing committee also appointed a committee for preparing revised guidelines for wildlife tourism, with Divyabhanusinh, Mahendra Vyas and others as members, and asked me to chair it. We enunciated a basic principle for wildlife tourism, which I think is axiomatic: that protected areas are not for tourism but tourism must be for the protected areas; that tourism must complement but be subservient to the conservation interests of the protected areas, which must remain paramount. It noted that tourism can greatly assist in winning public support for a protected area, that each protected area must have its individual tourism plan, that park entry must be restricted and defined and that local people must be given overriding preference in employment and benefit. It also recommended that all revenues which accrue from park entry must be ploughed back for park conservation, not deposited with the state exchequer.

The standing committee was fast assuming greater importance than the main body of the NBWL, as it was in the committee that clearances of projects affecting protected areas were now being given and their numbers were rapidly increasing. Indeed, the standing committee has become a clearing house for development projects. When some of us protested that no wildlife issues were being considered in its deliberations and even the items pertaining to conservation were kept for the end, to be hurriedly discussed only if there was time, the minister of environment and forests, who was the chairperson of the standing committee, agreed to consider our items at the beginning of the meetings.

But much prior to that, I had a difference of opinion with T.R. Baalu, the Union minister for environment and forests in the government of Prime Minister A.B. Vajpayee. The approval of a cascade of projects on the Subansiri river in Arunachal Pradesh came up before the standing committee. Almost all of us non-official members of the committee were opposed to the projects. At the end, Baalu summed up by saying that he had heard everyone and he would decide. I retorted that the Wild Life (Protection) Act, under which the standing committee had been formed, gave no powers to the chairman to decide on behalf of the other members. Indeed, he did not even have a casting vote. The standing committee was an advisory body that must decide by majority, any dissident view must also be recorded, and the committee must be freely permitted to render its advice, in both letter and spirit. However, the chairman of this committee was also the minister in charge of the MoEF, in which capacity he had every right to overrule the advice of the standing committee, which was an advisory body, but must give reasons recorded in writing. The reconstitution of the NBWL and of its standing committee was due and I was, of course, dropped from their membership.

In 2010, when I was reappointed to the NBWL and its standing committee, the issue of the MoEF preparing and funding recovery plans for endangered terrestrial and marine species was taken up. Our mandate was to identify the species and to suggest guidelines for their recovery. We selected the snow leopard, bustards, dolphin, hangul, Nilgiri tahr, marine turtles, edible-nest swiftlet, Asian wild buffalo, Nicobar megapode, Manipur brow-antlered deer, vultures, Malabar civet, one-horned rhinoceros, Asiatic lion, swamp deer or barasingha and Jerdon's courser. The recovery plans, though now under way in most cases, have not received the priority they should have, as the MoEF has not pursued the matter with the state governments concerned to ensure effective implementation, nor granted sufficient funds.

A proposal came up before the standing committee to allow the setting up of a tiger safari park on 260 hectares of the Ranthambore Tiger Reserve, a small park where tiger sighting is frequent and where the number of vehicles allowed already give the impression of it being a grandiose safari park. The proposal was unanimously rejected and a policy decision taken not to allow safari parks in any protected area, but which has subsequently been overturned.

Himachal Pradesh has thirty-five national parks and sanctuaries, but many of them include human settlements and are of little ecological value. A rationalization of their boundaries was essential. A very comprehensive proposal prepared by the state's chief wildlife warden Vinay Tandon, who had previously worked with me in the MoEF, involved de-notification of substantial tracts in twenty-seven protected areas. These were to be compensated by the notification of even larger areas as sanctuaries, mainly in the Trans-Himalayan zone. After spot inspections by the director of WII, P.R. Sinha, and me, the proposal was agreed to, with the caveat that the notification of the new areas as sanctuaries would take place first and only thereafter would permission be given to de-notify the others approved for this purpose, thereby setting a very salutary precedent, which again is not being followed in subsequent years.

The Indo-Tibetan Border Police (ITBP) had proposed a number of roads in the Changthang Sanctuary of Ladakh, on the border with Tibet. The inspection team, consisting of Asad R. Rahmani of the BNHS and myself, had not recommended the building of the road from the Tso Moriri Lake to the international border at Chumar, on the ground that an alternative route was already in existence and the proposed road would affect the large breeding colony of bar-headed geese on Tso Moriri. We were, however, overruled by the majority in the NBWL standing committee. On the question of clearance of another road in the same vicinity, I had made its approval conditional to the diversion of a nearby road which went through the Kalak Tartar depression near Hanle, which held the only surviving viable population of the Tibetan gazelle in Ladakh that had been harried to a point where they bolted when they saw a vehicle over 500 m away. Here again, I was overruled. So I took up the matter directly with Ranjit Sinha, then the director general of the ITBP and, subsequently, the head of the Central Bureau of Investigation. I wrote him a letter about the gazelle and Kalak Tartar and went to meet him. He confirmed in writing that the field formations in the area have been instructed to accord all possible cooperation to protect the rare gazelle and to avoid the use of Kalak Tartar, unless it is very essential to do so.

A proposal came up before the standing committee to allow the establishment of a major port at Poshitara, near the sacred shrine of Dwarka, but in a crucial portion of the Marine National Park in the Gulf of Kutch, the first of its kind in India. The project also envisaged dredging of the rich coral beds to deepen the approach to the berths in the proposed port. After a spot inspection by Asad Rahmani and myself, we submitted a report saying: 'We are of the considered opinion that the country cannot have both the Poshitara Port and the Gulf of Kutch Marine National Park for the purpose it was established. The government and the nation would have to choose one or the other, but if the port was to take precedence over the park, that decision should be made outside of the MoEF'. The proposal was rejected.

In March 2010, in the fifth meeting of the NBWL chaired by Prime Minister Manmohan Singh, I moved a proposal that funding from the MoEF to the protected areas of the country should be restricted to only those under the direct control of their respective state wildlife wings and manned by officers trained in wildlife management. In a meeting of the standing committee in 1998, chaired by the then minister of environment and forests Suresh Prabhu, I had been assured that protected areas 'whose jurisdictional control does not vest with the respective wildlife wing in its entirety are not eligible to receive financial assistance from centrally sponsored schemes of the MoEF. But this was not happening. A total diarchy was creeping into the management of our protected areas, wherein financial and even partial administrative control was being passed on to the territorial DFOs. The main responsibility of the wildlife wing, as I once jokingly said, was being confined to answering questions in the legislative assemblies and in parliament. Further, hardly any staff were being sent by the states for training at the WII, which had been primarily created for this purpose, and training at which was now available free of cost to the states. As a result, the WII had become mainly a research institute and only about 3 per cent of over 600 protected areas of the country were manned by officers trained in wildlife management. In 2010, for the nine-month training course meant for officers, there were only two trainees from India; the remaining eighteen were from other South Asian Association of Regional Cooperation (SAARC) countries. This very untenable and unprofessional situation still persists, despite the personal letters that Jayanthi Natarajan, then minister in charge of the MoEF, wrote to all chief ministers.

Also in 2010, the de-notification of a large portion of the huge and unwieldy Nannaj Sanctuary for the great Indian bustard in Maharashtra, came up before the standing committee. Six new sanctuary areas, still much lesser in area than that of Nannaj to be de-notified, were offered in lieu. I stressed that these six be notified prior to de-notification of Nannaj, as in Himachal Pradesh, and that amongst the new areas priority must be given to the Kollamarka Sanctuary in Gadchiroli district for the wild buffalo and to the Mansingh-Deo Sanctuary near Pench, close to Nagpur in Maharashtra. The then chairman Jairam Ramesh overruled me with regard to the notification of new areas prior to the proposed de-notification, but Kollamarka did become a conservation reserve and Mansingh-Deo a sanctuary.

I repeatedly drew attention to the plight of the hog deer in the premier Corbett National Park. When I first went to Corbett in January 1962, there were more hog deer in the open areas than chital. After the construction of the Ramganga dam and flooding of the riparian grasslands, the habitat of the hog deer shrank drastically, and they were now confined to a few higher grasslands, the Dhikala Chaur being the main one. But this is also the main tourist zone. To show the tiger, elephant and chital herds to tourists, these remaining grasslands are repeatedly burnt, denying the hog deer the only habitat they can live and breed in. The lack of knowledge of grassland management has been a major drawback in our conservation applications and continues to remain so. Today, there are probably less than twenty hog deer surviving in Corbett, almost all confined to the fringes of the overcrowded, over-burnt and open Dhikala Chaur.

In 2011, Rahmani, Divyabhanusinh and I were deputed by the standing committee to assess a proposed road through the Kutch Desert Wildlife Sanctuary, which would skirt the only breeding site of flamingoes in South Asia, and also go through Khadir Island and past the Dholavira archaeological site of the Indus Valley civilization. As the area remained underwater during the monsoon, to keep the road above the monsoon flooding meant construction of 31 km of road on a raised flyway, with guard walls on each side of the road, implying a wall length of 62 km and pilons of not less than 6 m deep to reach hard ground below 3 m of silt. It would only be useful during the monsoon, as in the dry season the salt pans of the Kutch desert form almost a hard race track for vehicles. It would also alter the complex hydrology of the area and very likely affect the flamingo breeding site drastically. Our team approved the construction of a part of the proposed road and rejected the rest, as an alternative all-weather national highway was already available, involving a slight detour only in the monsoon. When the National Board for Wildlife and its standing committee were reconstituted in 2014, none of us three were appointed to them. The project was approved.

In the sixth meeting of the national board in September 2012, under the chairmanship of Prime Minister Manmohan Singh, Divyabhanusinh and I raised the issue of the small and very lopsided allocation of funds to the MoEF for wildlife conservation. While the then forty tiger reserves of the country had an allocation of ₹778 crore in the Eleventh Five-Year Plan, the remaining 631 protected areas of the country and all other centrally sponsored schemes for wildlife under the MoEF, including the recovery of endangered species and support to wildlife outside of protected areas, were allocated only ₹364 crore in the same plan. While not advocating any diversion of funds from tiger reserves, we strongly advocated the enhancement of funds for the other efforts. However, the much-skewed budgetary allocation still persists.

In 2012, a subcommittee under the NBWL standing committee had been appointed under my chairmanship to recommend rules of procedures and guidelines for the functioning of the standing committee. I was ably supported by Prerna Singh Bindra, a member of the standing committee, and other officials. A very comprehensive format of the power, duties, responsibilities and procedures of working was prepared. We suggested that the decisions of the standing committee must be by majority opinion; that project proponents must prove compliance of stipulations of past proposals that had been approved; that it must be certified that no work had been undertaken on the project in anticipation of approval; and that the MoEF should establish a mechanism to monitor compliance with the stipulations and conditions under which projects were cleared. There was also a subcommittee appointed to formulate guidelines for linear intrusions to be permitted in protected areas, in which M.D. Madhusudan of Bangalore was of great assistance to us. The reports of both these subcommittees came up for approval in the thirtieth meeting of the standing committee in September 2013, a day prior to the expiry of the tenure of our membership to the national board. Both these reports were not discussed, deliberately, and hence not approved. In the current circumstances, I do not think that either of them will ever be implemented.

I had been deputed to carry out a spot inspection of the proposal of the Sardar Sarovar Narmada Nigam of Gujarat to divert land from the Kutch Desert Wildlife Sanctuary, for the passage of the Kutch branch canal of Sardar Sarovar. The canal had been completed over land outside of the portion traversing the sanctuary, to present the standing committee with a fait accompli. In any case, the canal water is crucial to Kutch and no one would have rejected the proposal. However, the canal alignment bifurcated a fringe area of the Desert Sanctuary, cutting off some 26 sq. km of revenue land covered with *Prosopis juliflora*, which would have no conservation value after the construction of the canal.

So I recommended the de-notification of this segregated area and of the canal portion with the road running along it from the sanctuary. It would revert to the revenue department of the state. In lieu, I recommended that some 14.24 sq. km of revenue land near the existing Kutch Bustard Sanctuary, which was of only 2.2 sq. km, be transferred to the state forest department and declared as a sanctuary, contiguous to the tiny existing one. The land had already been identified as suitable for the three species of bustards that occur in western India – the great Indian, the migratory lesser florican and the houbara. No land acquisition was required as they were state lands. Besides, the Gujarat energy department had received 37.7 sq. km of land from the Adani Group when the latter acquired forest land for their special economic zone project at Mundra Port in Kutch. This land also vested with the state revenue department, so it would only have involved transfer from one department of the Gujarat government to another.

In 2013, I had sought an appointment and had met the then chief minister of Gujarat, Narendra Modi, and had requested him to save the Kutch population of the great Indian bustard, which then was the second largest cluster surviving in the world after the one in Jaisalmer, Rajasthan, and numbering less than twenty. He not only agreed to help but discussed conservation and grassland management for an hour. He also declared the initiation of Project Bustard in Kutch in his Independence Day address in Kutch, on 15 August 2013. But he then became the prime ministerial candidate of his party, moved to Delhi as prime minister and the bustard project did not take off.

My proposal for the Narmada canal was briefly discussed in that last meeting of the standing committee prior to its reconstitution, and was broadly concurred with. In 2014, just prior to the reconstitution of the National Board for Wildlife by the government of Prime Minister Modi, I received a call from a senior officer of the Narmada Nigam of Gujarat. Would I be prepared to change my opinion and recommendation pertaining to the de-notification of the Kutch Desert Sanctuary, in lieu of notification of other lands as a sanctuary for the bustard? I said I would stand by what I had earlier suggested, knowing what the Gujarat bureaucrat was hinting at. Of course, I was not renominated on the newly constituted National Board for Wildlife. The canal proposal was approved in the subsequent meeting, segregating 134 sq. km of the desert sanctuary and bisecting it, without any transfer of land to the Kutch Bustard Sanctuary.

Speaking of bustards, in 2011, the MoEF had appointed a committee to recommend rationalization of the boundaries of the huge Desert National Park (DNP) in Rajasthan, which was a park only in name. Asad Rahmani, Divyabhanusinh, Malkhan Singh (MLA) and others were members, and I was asked to chair the committee.

The DNP covers an area of 3,162 sq. km, of which a greater part, 1,900 sq. km is in Jaisalmer and the rest in Barmer district. The park includes seventy-three villages within its boundaries. Only an area of 50 sq. km is designated as forest land and the rest as revenue, an ideal recipe for administrative diarchy and mismanagement. I have rarely experienced such animosity towards a protected area anywhere as we experienced from the people living in and around the DNP. The thirty enclosures that had been constructed decades ago by the Central Arid Zone Research Institute of Jodhpur, which were once so rich in wildlife, were in total disrepair. Only the three around Sudasari in Jaisalmer district offered some hope to the beleaguered great Indian bustard and other desert fauna.

We recommended that the basic requirements of the villagers, now denied to them as the area had been declared a national park, should be provided. In remote areas, away from demographic impact, more enclosures should be made and effectively protected, as they offered the best hope for the bustard and for the Thar Desert biota. Windmills should not be permitted on the DNP premises, and tourism, though it could be greatly helpful, must be regulated. The local people, who must be taken into partnership, should be given additional facilities such as solar lighting and water tanks. Despite reminders from the MoEF, the Rajasthan government took little action on the report and today the number of the great Indian bustard in Jaisalmer district would be, in my opinion, below fifty, making it the species most likely and most imminently to become extinct in India and, thus, in the world.

Another species on the fast track to extinction is the Kashmir stag or hangul. Ever since the IUCN conference of 1969 in Delhi, when the predicament of the deer was largely publicized, there have been innumerable seminars on the hangul and on Dachigam. Reams of recommendations have been written, but the hangul population has kept reducing, from about 400 in 1969 to less than 200 now, almost all confined to Dachigam and its surrounds. Unlike most other species, the problem is not habitat loss or conflict with man, but poaching. Within Dachigam, the lowest grassland that the hangul once occupied in deep winter has long been handed over to a government sheep farm, as if there were no other meadows for this purpose in Kashmir. Every report, from that of George Schaller onwards, has recommended its removal. Then finally, in 2010 the Government of Jammu and Kashmir took a decision in cabinet to shift the farm, but this did not happen. So in a meeting of the Kashmir board for wildlife in February 2012, chaired by the Chief Minister Omar Abdullah, I beseeched him to take concrete steps to save Dachigam and the hangul; to begin with, to stop the illicit occupation of Dachigam by the Gujar graziers and to implement the decision of his own cabinet to shift the sheep farm. I went on to add, perhaps a bit too caustically, that if the hangul went extinct as was likely, Kashmir would be the only political entity in the history of the world to have lost its state emblem and state animal, in which eventuality it should declare the Merino sheep the state animal. Stung by the remark, the chairman ordered that the sheep farm be shifted before May 2012. When nothing happened even thereafter, I made a similar statement in the meeting of the Kashmir board for wildlife chaired by Chief Minister Mehbooba Mufti in late 2016. In March 2017, evacuation of the sheep farm has finally begun.

In 2012, when we drew attention to the dire straits of the hangul in a meeting of the standing committee of the NBWL, a group was appointed to evaluate the implementation of the Species Recovery Programme of the Hangul, funded by the MoEF. I was asked to chair the group, assisted by S. Sathyakumar of the WII and Prerna Singh Bindra. Our report pointed out that Dachigam must be more effectively protected from poaching with the help of the army, the local unit of which had adopted the hangul as their emblem, and that the army was ready to help. We recommended that the illegal occupation of the Tarsar–Marsar area of the upper part of Dachigam Park in summer by the nomadic Gujar graziers, and which was where the hangul had their fawns and where the deer were killed by the Gujars and their dogs, must be stopped. Instead, the army was prepared to allow the Gujars to enter their traditional grazing grounds in the Gurez Valley, provided the Gujars agreed to stay out of Dachigam. We drew attention to the understaffing of Dachigam National Park and the low morale of the existing staff, who were being bullied by the Gujar graziers that took advantage of the fact that the then forest minister was a Gujar. We suggested that the remnant small and scattered populations of the hangul outside of Dachigam, which the Wildlife Trust of India had identified, must be saved and nurtured. Also, since there was no captive population of the hangul anywhere and its extinction in situ was a distinct possibility, there should be a programme to breed and save the species in captivity. In conclusion, our report said: 'The fate of the hangul and its long-term survival depends almost entirely upon the will and commitment of the state government. Unlike the predicament of many endangered species, the involvement of the people is not a deciding factor and, in any case, the state government has not made any significant effort to garner public support to the cause of the state animal and the state emblem.' Once more, the report saw very little implementation on the ground.

In the Kashmir state wildlife board meetings and outside, I also persisted with the need to save the markhor, Tibetan gazelle, Tibetan antelope, western tragopan and other endangered species. As the Supreme Court had approved the making of the new Mughal Road over a portion of the Hirpora Sanctuary in the Pir Panjal Range, a habitat of the markhor, stipulations to the approval required the setting up of another protected area for the markhor. I urged the creation of the Kajinag National Park, in an area which has the largest population of the Pir Panjal markhor. At my behest, the minister of environment and forests, Jairam Ramesh, also requested the Kashmir chief minister to establish the Kajinag National Park, which did come about in 2007.

With the difficult political situation in the state of Jammu and Kashmir, neighbouring Himachal Pradesh now provides the best alternative for the conservation of the Western Himalayan fauna and flora. In meetings of the wildlife board of that state, therefore, I have been repeatedly emphasizing on the need to save the fauna of the higher and Trans-Himalaya, particularly the brown bear, ibex and the snow leopard. Himachal Pradesh has bred in captivity three species of pheasant: cheer, Himalayan monal, and the most endangered of all, the western tragopan. It is the only state to do so. But not a single bird has been released into the wild, underlining again the failure in conservation breeding of our state-managed ex situ endeavours.

In the meetings of the National Tiger Conservation Authority (NTCA), I have continually emphasized the need of training officers and staff in grassland management, which is totally lacking today. I believe that tiger conservation begins from the grass roots, literally and metaphorically. Only by managing and manipulating the grass during different seasons can one augment the prey species of the tiger – swamp deer, hog deer, chital and even pig – and thereby not only increase the carrying capacity of tiger in a given habitat, but also prevent the tiger from straying out of protected areas to seek livestock prey and, hence, come in conflict with man. The only management practice that is now deployed vis-à-vis grasslands is fire, without understanding its full implications or ramifications.

In 2013, the Supreme Court directed that lions be reintroduced in the Kuno Sanctuary, Madhya Pradesh, overruling the objections of Gujarat and laying down a time frame for initiating the project. The MoEF constituted an expert committee to give technical advice to the two state governments in the modalities of reintroduction based upon IUCN guidelines, to select individual animals for reintroduction and to monitor the implementation of the action plan prepared for this purpose. The chief wildlife wardens of Gujarat and MP, representatives of MoEF, Y.V. Jhala of the WII, Ravi Chellam, A.J.T. Johnsingh and I are members of this body.

However, the MoEF seemed to be in no hurry to implement the court orders. After Narendra Modi became the prime minister in 2014, it seems the ministry is only going through the motions in the matter of this translocation. Amongst some Gujaratis the impulse to maintain the monopoly of having the lion in their state alone is of pathological proportions. In a media poll in 2007, whilst the court case pertaining to lion translocation to Kuno was in progress, 97 per cent of the people queried in Gujarat did not wish the lion to go outside the state. But there is a conservation dimension to this pride and possessiveness towards the lions of Gujarat. During the May 2015 enumeration of the lion in Saurashtra, I travelled extensively over the current lion landscape, which has been enhanced from about 3,000 sq. km two decades ago to some 22,000 sq. km now. What impressed me most was not only the tolerance and indulgence, but the sense of pride and of possession with which the local villagers view the presence of lions in their neighbourhood. People whose livestock are killed by lions often do not claim compensation. When I questioned them whether they did not mind the lions killing their livestock, the usual reply was that the lions also killed the nilgai which was a pest for them and, after all, the lions owned the land as much as they did. The same indulgence and pride does not exist towards the tiger and leopard; indeed, the opposite is often the case. So, my concern is, if the lion is translocated outside of Gujarat, and Gujarat thus loses its 'monopoly', will this affect the conservation priority it now receives from the state government and the pride of ownership felt by the people? Only time will tell. But all the same, the lion must move to Kuno to provide an alternative population.

The 2015 enumeration revealed a very significant fact. Though the total lion population had increased by 27 per cent during the years from 2010 to 2015, the increase in the five protected areas – Gir National Park and Sanctuary, Girnar, Pania and Mitiyala sanctuaries – was only 6 per cent, while the increase outside of the protected areas in the Asiatic Lion Landscape was a startling 126 per cent. Obviously, the lion populations in the protected areas had reached the limits of their carrying capacities and the numbers outside were mushrooming and marching out to reclaim their former territories (Ranjitsinh 2014).

Amongst my recommendations to the Gujarat Government, conveyed verbally and in my above cited article, were to focus attention on the future of these 167 lions operating outside the protected areas. The extended habitat of the lion must be safeguarded by declaration of sanctuaries where the land was government-owned forest, by establishing conservation reserves in other government land and by notifying eco-sensitive zones on privately owned land under occupation of lions. Indeed, as the number of lions will inevitably increase in these outlying areas, government should facilitate this movement and secure these habitats – Shetrunjaya and Sihor in particular. The Barda Sanctuary, which I had proposed as a second home for the lion in 1974, must also be actively managed and lions translocated. Regrettably, Gujarat has implemented none of the above, even government forest lands adjacent to the Gir have also not been declared as protected areas. Yet, Gujarat steadfastly refuses to give away any of its lions, despite the directives of the Supreme Court.

The lions have become incredibly bold. They have been found on the roads of villages in daylight and on the streets of Junagarh city in the night. The pride with which people now hold the lion in, will allow them to tolerate the killing of livestock, to a certain degree at least. But they will not tolerate the killing of fellow humans. If that happens, heaven forbid, Gujarat will have to answer for its 'lion in the manger' policy.

13

Cheetah

'Reintroduction of large carnivores has increasingly been recognized as a strategy to conserve threatened species and restore ecosystem function. The cheetah is the only large carnivore that has been extirpated, mainly by over-hunting, in India in historical times. India now has the economic ability to consider restoring its lost natural heritage for ethical as well as ecological reasons. The venture must be viewed not simply as an introduction of a species, however charismatic it may be, but as an endeavour to better manage and restore some of our most valuable, yet, most neglected ecosystems and the species dependent upon them' (Ranjitsinh and Jhala 2010).

The way India is progressing and its population is spreading, it has long been evident that it would be unrealistic to presume that we would be able to save the country's biotic wealth and natural heritage in their entirety, during the transition from a developing to a developed nation. When posted in Mandla half a century ago, I had come to believe that species, biodiversity and, indeed, nature itself had a future only in effectively conserved protected areas. During my tenure as the forest secretary of Madhya Pradesh and twice as the director, wildlife preservation of India, I had endeavoured to bring under the protected area coverage as many ecotypes and habitats of species, especially of endangered species, as possible. The first nine tiger reserves were selected not on the basis of the number of tigers they held but because of the diverse habitats they represented. Subsequently, Project Tiger did succeed in bringing under its coverage a substantial segment of the different forest habitats of this great feline. But these tiger habitats do not constitute the totality of even our forest biomes, notably excluding the montane and the western xerophytic forests. The Himalayan uplands, grassland-scrublands and marine areas were the most under-represented in our protected area system during the 1970s and it was my constant endeavour to rectify these shortcomings. Marine parks did get established, but the other two types were not making much progress. As described in an earlier chapter, my attempts to initiate a snow leopard project to cover the Himalayan landscape and a bustard project for their diverse grassland habitats, both failed.

Grasslands are the most productive terrestrial ecosystems in the world and in India the most abused and overused ecosystems of all. Yet, they are the most important for the life support they provide to a large segment of human society and rural economy. Grasslands are also the sole habitats of some of our most endangered species, as mentioned earlier, including those in the arid west – the great Indian bustard, lesser florican, Indian wolf, desert fox and desert cat. The grassland-dependent species, both bird and animal, have suffered a more drastic decline than species adapted to other biomes, simply because the grasslands have undergone the most qualitative and quantitative decimation of all ecotypes in the subcontinent. Our grasslands have a phenomenal power of recovery if given a chance, which they are not. All this points to evolving a more rational management through regulation and conservation of some selected grassland-forest habitats as prototypes, from whose example other similar habitats could be subsequently saved. Maybe, I thought, as happened in the case of the tiger, a charismatic carnivore like the cheetah could elicit the public and government enthusiasm that the poor bustard had failed to arouse, to save some areas of grassland-forest ecosystems.

Though the last cheetah had been shot in December 1947 in the Ramgarh area of Madhya Pradesh, which is now part of the Guru Ghasidas National Park of Chhattisgarh, cheetah had been seen in the same area as late as in 1967 (Ram Chandra Singh Deo, son of Ramanuj Pratap Singh Deo of Korea, personal communication,1987). It is of interest that the last cheetah in India were found in sal forests of Madhya Pradesh, Chhattisgarh and Odisha into which they had sought refuge after being harried in the open grassland–forest mosaics, which are their preferred habitats. Sal forests have grassy meadows and open spaces where they could chase and run down their prey.

No other animal, perhaps, has a greater claim for *ghar wapsi*, for return to its homeland of the Indian subcontinent, than the cheetah. The only large carnivore and, indeed, the only large mammal to have gone extinct in peninsular India in historical times, the very vision of its return would give an impetus and a new dimension to Indian conservation, just as the conservation of the much despised crocodilians did to the conservation of riverine ecosystems and species in the 1970s. It would be an addition in the Indian conservation endeavour, not at the cost of any ongoing effort. Among the large carnivores, cheetah are likely to present the lowest level of conflict with human interests as they are not a threat to human life and are most unlikely to prey on large livestock.

Anything that we lose we tend to treasure more and crave to regain, as in the Biblical tale of the prodigal son. The reintroduction of the cheetah would be the return of India's prodigal species. Of course, it would be difficult and there would be many pitfalls and a possibility of failure at the initial stages. I knew I would be blamed for any failures, while success would be claimed by the government, but this was never an issue. Nothing worthwhile is achieved if one is not prepared to take the risk entailed. It was also argued that India should save its tigers and lions and the other species it has, rather than introduce another large species and add to problems. That is a Lilliputian argument. How would the reintroduction of the cheetah adversely affect the conservation of the tiger or the others? On the contrary, it would ignite the conservation imagination of a people whose single focus on the tiger has become static.

During my first tenure as director, wildlife preservation of India, I had negotiated with Iran for the exchange of our lion for their cheetah, but this did not fructify, and the governments in both India and Iran changed. During my second tenure as director, Iran was in no position to give away any of its decimated cheetah population and India was not ready to receive the animal. However, I had been able to persuade the Gujarat government to declare the large 'island' of Khadir in the Great Rann of Kutch as a protected area, as it had the potential of a cheetah rehabilitation site – isolation, no competition, ideal habitat, little demographic pressure. The prey base of chinkara, pig and hare needed to be enhanced, and that could not be achieved before I relinquished my post.

In the first decade of the twenty-first century, however, there were some encouraging developments. The Kuno Wildlife Sanctuary, which I, as forest secretary of Madhya Pradesh, had established in 1981, had been selected to be a second home for the Indian lion outside of Saurashtra. All but one of its twenty-four villages had been relocated in preparation for the arrival of the lion, and the level, open areas, where agriculture used to occur, had now turned into prime grasslands in which chital has proliferated. There were also nilgai, pig and some sambar, chinkara, blackbuck and four-horned antelope. The tiger, for which Kuno had once been so famous, had been exterminated and the stray animal that arrived did not tarry long.

But the lion-reintroduction programme for Kuno ran into difficulty. The Gujarat government did not want to lose its world monopoly of being the only home of the Asiatic lion. The state had lost its tigers in the second half of the twentieth century and during my second tenure as India's director of wildlife preservation, I had tried to persuade them to exchange some of their lions for tigers from Madhya Pradesh. This would not only have brought back the tiger to its former habitat, but would have made Gujarat and MP the only regions in the world to possess both lions and tigers. But no, Gujarat did not want the tiger.

So, lion reintroduction in Kuno had reached a stalemate. The chief minister of Madhya Pradesh, Shivraj Singh Chauhan, personally told me that if the lion did not come to Kuno, he would allow the twenty-three villages, which had been translocated out of Kuno to facilitate the lion reintroduction, to return. It struck me that the grassland-cum-open-forest mosaic of Kuno was an ideal habitat for the cheetah; in fact, this region had been prime cheetah habitat and a principal site for their capture in the Mughal era (Habib 1982). The prey was there and there were no resident tigers. The lions had no prospects of immediate arrival and even if they did come, they would not pose a problem for the cheetah, if the latter had already been reintroduced, had their first litter and, hence, become locally established. In southern Africa, where cheetah and lion introductions in private and public reserves are routine, the cheetah are introduced first and after a couple of years when they have bred there, the lions are brought in. In the animal kingdom, especially amongst carnivores, first occupation is the key criterion.

The minister in charge of the MoEF at that point of time happened to be Jairam Ramesh, a man with vision and dynamism. When I raised the issue of cheetah reintroduction, he was enthused.

The Asiatic cheetah survives today only in the arid western parts of Iran, notably in Dasht-e-Kavir, and their numbers have been reduced to an estimated sixty to eighty animals. Transport always entails a risk of animal casualty. Iranian cheetah are far too valuable in their own country and it would be morally and ecologically wrong to ask Iran for even a pair of their animals for reintroduction in India. However, the African and Asian cheetah are morphologically and genetically very similar, much more than the African and Asiatic lion. Cheetahs are believed to have evolved in southern Africa and spread northward and then eastward across Asia. While the ecological separation between Asiatic and African lion is estimated to have occurred about 100,000 years ago, that between the African and Asiatic cheetah is believed to be only 4,500 to 6,500 years old (Y.V. Jhala, personal communication, 2010). Eminent felid geneticist and author of the seminal book *Tears of the Cheetah*, Stephen O'Brien, established that cheetah have only slightly more genetic diversity than laboratory mice, which are purposely bred for their genetic similarity (O'Brien et al. 1985). So the best option would be to try and obtain specimens of the African cheetah.

We found that Namibia had the highest cheetah population in the world and specimens that prove to be troublesome to a farmer for being livestock killers, are permitted to be killed or captured by that farmer, who may even invite a hunter to eliminate the animal for a fee. Also, South Africa had farms and facilities where cheetah could be bred and reared and groomed for release in the wild. Animal casualties would occur in translocation and rehabilitation of species. Besides, the progeny of the founding population of the reintroduced species would need a fresh influx of bloodlines at regular intervals in future to prevent inbreeding. Namibia had the cheetah numbers to provide these future requirements.

In 2008, supported by a generous grant from the Maharana of Mewar Charitable Foundation of Udaipur, extended by Shriji Arvind Singhji of Mewar, I travelled to Namibia and South Africa with Vivek Menon, the executive director of WTI, whose chairman I then was. Our task was to survey organizations and facilities that would be best to source the cheetah from, and to identify the best expertise that would be available to assist us in the programme. We were most impressed by the Cheetah Conservation Fund of Namibia and its dedicated executive director Laurie Marker. We were extensively helped by Annie Beckhelling of Cheetah Outreach and Deon Cilliers, a scientist with the Endangered Wildlife Trust, both in South Africa.

Encouraged by the support and the continued interest of the government, it was decided to hold a consultative meeting on the prospects of cheetah reintroduction into India. This was convened in September 2009 at the idyllic oasis resort at Gajner, Rajasthan, a former hunting lodge of the Maharaja of Bikaner and famous for its duck and sandgrouse shoots. Our host was the generous Arvind Singhji of Mewar.

The meeting was attended by the chief wildlife wardens of Rajasthan, Madhya Pradesh, Gujarat and Chhattisgarh, Rajesh Gopal of the National Tiger Conservation Authority (NTCA), director of the WII, P.R. Sinha, and his colleague Y.V. Jhala, Divyabhanusinh (author of the only book on the Indian cheetah), Asad Rahmani of the BNHS, Stephen O'Brien, Laurie Marker, Annie Bechelling and other cheetah experts.

The two-day meeting concluded that cheetah reintroduction was feasible and that keeping in view the close genetic similarity between the Asiatic and African cheetah, the latter would be genetically suitable for reintroduction into India. Further, it was agreed that there should be collaboration between India and Iran to save the remnant cheetah population in Iran. Participating experts and organizations pledged their support in the sourcing, translocation and rehabilitation of the cheetah and the training of Indian personnel. The participants opined that reintroduction of apex carnivores should be seen as ecosystem conservation rather than merely species conservation and that this endeavour would be reclaiming a part of India's wonderful and varied natural heritage.

Seven potential sites for reintroduction were chosen. These were Palpur–Kuno, Nauradehi and Sanjay–Dubri in Madhya Pradesh and the adjacent Guru Ghasidas National Park, where the last Indian cheetah had been shot, in Chhattisgarh. The Shahgarh 'Bulge' in Jaisalmer and Chandan grasslands, both in Rajasthan, and the Banni and Narayan Sarovar areas of Kutch in Gujarat, were the other potential sites selected. The final selection was to be based on detailed surveys that were to follow.

Jairam Ramesh then gave me directions to prepare a detailed road map for the reintroduction of the cheetah in India. Under the supervision of Y.V. Jhala of the WII, a research team comprising

H. Gehlot, Priya Singh, Ushma Shukla, N. Mahar and S. Shrotriya carried out a detailed survey of the seven potential sites selected, in which I also partially participated. The team opined that Palpur–Kuno, Shahgarh and Nauradehi, in that order, had the best potential, though all three required preparation. It was estimated that Kuno had the capacity to sustain twenty-seven cheetah, which could be enhanced to thirty-two by the addition of 120 sq. km of contiguous forest that was available. With proper management of the buffer area that surrounds this sanctuary, the Kuno landscape had the potential to hold over seventy cheetah. Based on the surveys and collation of other data, Jhala and I submitted our report to the MoEF, covering the assessment of the seven potential sites, the shortlisting of three, and the road map for the implementation of the project (Ranjitsinh and Jhala 2010). We recommended reintroduction in Kuno at the outset, mentioning that 'this would not preclude the reintroduction of the lion once the cheetah population is established and the two reintroductions would complement each other. Indeed, Kuno offers the prospect of all the four large forest felids of India to coexist, as they did in the past' (ibid). This would make Kuno unique in the world.

In 2011, the MoEF constituted a task force for the reintroduction of cheetah in India, comprising the chief wildlife wardens of MP and Rajasthan, Y.V. Jhala, Divyabhanusinh, Brijendra Singh and Asad Rahmani, with Rajesh Gopal as member secretary and myself as chairman. The task force was to prepare a detailed five-year road map for the reintroduction and to initiate negotiations with the countries concerned regarding the sourcing of the cheetah. In the first meeting of the task force, Rajesh Gopal informed us that while the cheetah project would be a new component of Project Tiger with an allocation of ₹50 crore for the plan period, the cheetah project component had a separate allocation from the Government of India and would not result in diversion of funds from Project Tiger or any other ongoing scheme of the MoEF or of the NTCA (NTCA/MoEF, 2011). We were all emphatic that the funds for cheetah introduction should not be diverted from any ongoing conservation project.

In August 2011, Laurie Marker of the Namibia Cheetah Conservation Fund joined us on a field visit to Palpur–Kuno. Madhya Pradesh was represented by its energetic chief wildlife warden H.S. Pabla. The habitat and prey density had dramatically improved since I had last visited Kuno and Laurie Marker went to the extent of saying in her report that the prey density of Kuno was higher than in parts of Namibia and that the natural prey would be adequate for the reintroduced cheetah (Marker 2011). Ten animals (three male and seven female) were to be initially brought from southern Africa as founder stock and acclimatized in a large, fenced holding area, which was chosen in the Kuno grassland. From it, a coalition group of three or four males would be released from the holding area, followed by up to six females, their home ranges being much larger than those of the males and overlapping with other females. Marker generously offered to provide the founder stock free of cost. A professional would accompany the cheetah, or come even earlier, to train the local staff and to oversee the operation in its early stages. Federal Express International Inc. (FEDEX) approached me with an offer to transport the cheetah from Namibia to India free of cost.

An action plan for the cheetah reintroduction into Kuno was jointly prepared by the forest department of MP, WII and the Cheetah Task Force and submitted to MoEF (MP Forest Dept. et al. 2011). Jairam Ramesh had assured the state governments concerned that the Government of India would bear all the costs of the reintroduction, but stipulated that the respective states must augment the field staff where required. The action plan budget envisaged that 89 per cent of the total outlay would be spent on relocation of the remaining human population from the sanctuary, eco-development and habitat restoration; 6 per cent on improvement of the infrastructure; 4 per cent on protection, enforcement, monitoring and research; 0.5 per cent on training and consultancy charges and 0.5 per cent directly on the cheetah introduction itself, as the animals and their transport were being subsidized. The habitat improvement and human resettlement, upon which the main outlay was earmarked, would have helped future lion relocation and, most of all, the conservation status of the Palpur–Kuno sanctuary itself.

Then a chain of events occurred. Jairam Ramesh, who had showed initiative and personal interest in the reintroduction programme, was moved from the MoEF and his successor did not evince the same commitment. The NTCA, which was handling the project on behalf of the MoEF, also lost its verve. Behind the scene, other forces were at work.

Wildlife conservationists are a remarkable lot. Most of them, however, come to get associated with certain species or areas. They become very possessive of these, especially those aligned with the charismatic larger felines and become almost as 'territorial' as the predators whose cause they champion. This commitment is good when they fight for their respective protégés, but it does not help conservation when they fight turf battles with each other over their respective cats or areas.

In the sixth meeting of the National Board for Wildlife in September 2012, chaired by Prime Minister Manmohan Singh, the subject of cheetah reintroduction came up. No member opposed it. Karan Singh, who in the past had headed the Indian Board for Wildlife and the steering committee of Project Tiger, went on to say that the proposed cheetah reintroduction was the most exciting prospect in the field of Indian conservation. The reintroduction of both lion and cheetah was approved (MP Forest Dept. et al., 2011).

Meanwhile, a cat fight was brewing not only amongst conservationists, but far worse, between states of the Indian Union. A public interest litigation long pending in the Supreme Court, seeking its directive to the Government of Gujarat to allow the translocation of Asiatic lions from Saurashtra to Palpur–Kuno, was at last coming up for hearing. In its defence, Gujarat cited a number of reasons not to send lions to Kuno. Poaching in Kuno, its alleged lack of prey density, an alleged unsuitable climate, the recent extinction of tigers in Panna, the security of lions and expansion of their habitat in Gujarat, the emotional attachment of the local people to the lion in Gujarat, all were listed as arguments against relocation. Gujarat then also argued that Palpur–Kuno was to be the site for cheetah reintroduction and since lions would pose a threat to the cheetah, it was another reason why the lion should not go to Kuno.

I helped the MoEF in framing its reply, which was filed in the form of an affidavit countering the apprehensions and the arguments of Gujarat and clearly stating that cheetah reintroduction was in accordance with the IUCN guidelines 1998, that the IUCN had appointed a group to assist the cheetah reintroduction, that if cheetah reintroduction could precede the lion reintroduction, both the predators could coexist as they do in Africa.

The affidavit was filed in the Supreme Court in July 2012. In March 2013, the court passed its final order, patently not taking into account what had been affirmed in the affidavit of the previous year but accepting the recommendation of the amicus curiae, who apparently had been misguided by those who did not want the cheetah to be brought to Kuno. The Supreme Court directed that the lion must go to Kuno within a prescribed time limit, and held that the MoEF decision to introduce the African cheetah there first, followed by the lion, was arbitrary and illegal. Thus, the petition was quashed. A review petition is still pending before the Supreme Court.

The MoEF appointed a committee to oversee and guide the translocation of lions from Gujarat to Kuno, as directed by the Supreme Court, and I was made a member of it. However, as we have seen in the previous chapter, from the outset the MoEF did not evince any enthusiasm in implementing the directive of the court, which became even more evident after the change in government following the election of 2014. The time prescribed by the Supreme Court is long over.

So Kuno still awaits both the lion and the cheetah, with no immediate hope of receiving either in the near future. The protagonists in favour of bringing the lion to Kuno also seem to have lost interest. No one has gained, least of all the Kuno Sanctuary.

Someday, perhaps long after I am gone, the cheetah will return to India. The most difficult thing to eliminate is a good idea.

14

Conservation in the Twenty-first Century

How will nature fare in India in the twenty-first century? This is the question we should be asking. Instead, we are almost only worried about whether the tiger will survive. Conservation cannot be a single-species cult, however magnificent that species may be.

India has one of the lowest per capita forest areas in the world. It was 0.14 hectares per person two decades ago, and is less than 0.06 now. Between 1999 and 2004, the state of Mizoram had its forest cover reduced by nearly 844 sq. km, according to the Forest Survey of India; approximately 400 sq. km of forest is annually brought under jhum or shifting cultivation, adding to India's carbon emissions, instead of using the forest to absorb carbon (Lalthangliana 2004). After almost a century of debate, we have not been able to find an alternative to this suicidal slash-and-burn system of agriculture. Between 1947 and 1980, when the Forest (Conservation) Act came into force, the state of Madhya Pradesh, holding then the largest forest area of any Indian state, was losing 0.13 million hectares of forest per annum and according to some estimates, India was losing almost a million hectares of forests per year (Ranjitsinh 1984b). The Act brought some check to the rampant decline of forests in the country. In the quarter-century after that legislation came into force, the total area of forest land diverted amounted to a little over a million hectares.

Forests as 'carbon sinks' are deemed to be a major means of controlling climate change. Yet, in October 2014, the Government of India delegated substantive powers to the divisional forest officers of granting permission for the diversion of forest lands for mining and other purposes. In 2010, the MoEF had declared almost 30 per cent of the coal-bearing forest lands as secure from mining activity under the 'no-go' concept formulated by the then environment minister Jairam Ramesh. By adapting new criteria, the inviolate forest area, where mining continues to be prohibited, has been reduced from 30 to about 15 to 17 per cent (Vishnoi 2014).

The conservation psyche in India is of the passive type. People believe in the sanctity of life and the value of nature, but will not intervene to save forests and wildlife – with the exception of the Bishnois and a few other communities, and the 'chipko' movement in the Himalaya. There has been no 'green movement' in our country and the conservation of environment, forests and wildlife has never become a political issue. Active conservation in the form of legislation and its enforcement, of political support to nature conservation, has always flowed from the uppermost echelons of power, as mentioned earlier in this narrative.

It has been said that the difference between a politician and a statesman is that the former thinks about himself and today, the latter about the nation and the day after tomorrow. In no other area is this dictum more apparent than in the field of nature conservation. Any venture or effort that may cause loss of votes is a 'no go' endeavour.

One is repeatedly told that conservation of any species or area can only be achieved if that conservation can be justified by a tangible monetary benefit to the stakeholders, especially the local communities. Of what value is a wetland or a wild dog? And if direct benefit of a species or area cannot be proved, do these entities forfeit their right to exist? Is that good governance? However, studies have shown that the presence of a protected area does bring economic benefit to the communities in the vicinity.

Besides clean air, potable water is the most valuable commodity on earth. In a path-breaking study conducted by the Gujarat Agricultural University on the environmental and economic benefits emanating from the Gir ecosystem in Saurashtra, it was found that the Gir National Park and Sanctuary and its adjacent buffer area 'has a multifaceted impact on agriculture, mango orchards, sugar industries, livestock enterprise, tourism, carbon sequestration, ground water-table [sic], water quality and biodiversity, besides a large number of environmental benefits' (Gujarat Agricultural University, Junagarh 2002). Also taken into consideration in the assessment of the total economic value (TEV) of the Gir and its environs were the total expenditure incurred by the state government in the maintenance of the Gir protected area, damage caused by its wildlife to crop, livestock and human life, and the estimated production of agriculture, horticulture and animal husbandry had Gir been cultivated and utilized like the areas outside of the protected area. It was found that the net profit per hectare of cropped area was more than ₹35,000 in case of villages adjoining the Gir protected area, despite the crop damage by the wild herbivores, but was between ₹11,000 and 15,000 in villages more than 15 km away from the boundaries of the protected area, despite a reduction in crop damage from wild ungulates. While the forest department collected grass annually to the value of ₹3.9 million, the estimated consumption of grass by livestock and wildlife in the Gir protected area was of the value of ₹819.11 million. The estimated value of annual timber and fuelwood collection was ₹96.94 million. There was an improvement in water quality and a reduction of salinity ingress that is adversely affecting subsoil water in the region, and the rainfall in the areas adjoining the Gir protected area was found to be significantly higher than in areas over 15 km from its borders. The opportunity cost of the land of the Gir protected area, had it been utilized for agricultural purposes instead of being a national park and sanctuary, was estimated to be ₹181.47 million annually. But the TEV of the Gir area, computed after taking into account all the benefits and the costs, was found to be ₹21,105.88 million.

If more such studies of our parks and sanctuaries are conducted, it could be established that they are not merely environmental but economic assets. The benefits accruing from the providing of water flows and the improvement of subsoil water regimes alone would justify their establishment and existence.

To turn to what the future holds for forests and wildlife, it is instructive to consider the five major failures in wildlife management, which hampered India's conservation effort in the twentieth century, and continue to plague it in the twenty-first. I share the blame for our failure to rectify the mismanagement, though not for want of effort to do so.

These five failures, in what I perceive to be in ascending order of importance, are as follows:

1. While our field personnel have developed the methodology of capture of itinerant problematic large mammals, notably carnivores and elephants that come into conflict with man, we have not yet been able to evolve techniques of mass group capture of herbivores that cause damage to agriculture – notably nilgai, wild pig and blackbuck – and their translocation and rehabilitation. The result is that these species have come to be designated as pests and declared as vermin under the Wild Life (Protection) Act, to be destroyed at will. It is not that India is surplus in these species. They are only present in large enough numbers to be problematic in some areas of human habitation. Nilgai and wild pig could be captured in groups and translocated to prey-deficient protected areas, where they would provide sustenance for carnivores. Blackbuck could be transported to protected areas where their populations have been decimated and to areas away from cultivation, where they could even form breeding nuclei as part of a future programme for the reintroduction of the cheetah. This would be a far better option than allowing the destruction of these animals and reopening a hunting ethos that the nation has left behind. Indeed, in the

closing years of the twentieth century I had corresponded with the governments of South Africa and Namibia about the transfer of techniques of group capture in connection with translocation of nilgai and blackbuck. These countries are the world's leaders in mass capture of large mammals and their rehabilitation. They both offered to send their experts – one specializing in the capture of roan antelope and the other in impala; these animals being the closest approximations to the nilgai and blackbuck, respectively. They would in collaboration with the WII evolve and adapt techniques suitable for the group capture and translocation of nilgai and blackbuck, which then could be passed on to the wildlife wings of the states. I communicated this offer to MoEF, but instead the ministry wanted to send a senior officer to South Africa to learn the technique – literally a junket – and the programme fell through. The WII on its own has not made any effort to develop these methodologies either, despite my periodic proddings.

2. A major cause of loss of habitat is the failure of our forest and wildlife managers to understand the implications of forest fires and fire ecology. Not only are most of our deciduous forests subjected to three to five man-caused fires annually, but our protected area managers themselves set fire to the grasslands in their charge to facilitate the growth of fresh grass and to enhance wildlife viewing. Not only does this seriously hamper the breeding success of grassland-specific species like the swamp deer and the hog deer and deprive them of their habitats as mentioned earlier, but it destroys reptiles including snakes and tortoises and the eggs and chicks of ground-laying gallinaceous birds. Fire also destroys the soil microfauna and the humus that give productivity to the soil; causes compaction of the soil and reduces its water-retention capacity; damages the regeneration capacity of many plants including grasses, giving an impetus to fire-resistant exotic plants; is detrimental to the nutritious, perennial nutritious *andropogon* grasses and favours their

conversion to the less palatable, low protein annual *heteropogon* grass varieties. If fire ever managed to spread to an evergreen forest, it would permanently change its ecology and render it a semi-evergreen forest. Yet, we keep on setting fire to our forests and grasslands, mostly in the spring when large numbers of the ground-laying birds are nesting, for fear of a worse conflagration later in the summer which we are unable to prevent. A senior colleague of mine who trekked through the Garhwal Himalaya found 97 per cent of the forest burnt, with the roasted remains of reptiles and small mammals littered about.

3. Our third failure is the continuing abysmal understanding of grassland ecology and, hence, of its management. The fact that the most endangered species of the country are grassland-specific bears testimony to this predicament. The three resident species of bustards – the great Indian bustard, the lesser florican and the Bengal florican – all the three subspecies of swamp deer, the hog deer, Manipur brow-antlered deer, hispid hare, pygmy hog – the list is much longer. No recovery plan for any of our grassland-specific, critically endangered species will succeed unless we can develop and implement an appropriate management regime for each habitat. But there does not seem to be any move afoot to develop expertise in the management of different grasslands – monsoonal, arid, cold desert, temperate, riverine or flood plain, or tall, medium or short grasslands. There is a forest policy for India. There is even a bamboo policy and bamboo is a grass. But there is no grassland policy, despite India having the largest number of cattle in the world, with their population rising approximately at the ratio of 2:1 in relation to economic growth (Ranjitsinh 1984b). There is another dimension to this shortcoming. Tiger conservation – and for that matter any terrestrial species conservation – starts from the grass roots, as I have stated before, literally and metaphorically. Fifty years ago, India was deficient in food production and cereals had to be imported. Today, due to the efforts of the scientists of India's

green revolution, the country is exporting cereals, despite the exponential rise in human population and lessening of area under food crops. All of us know that the future of Indian wildlife depends wholly on the country's effectively managed protected areas, and their area is finite and highly unlikely to increase significantly. The solution lies in the management and manipulation of grasslands and fodder in the protected areas to enhance the carrying capacity of the ungulates and, thus, of their predator species, including the tiger. Simultaneously, biological control of exotic plant species like *Eupatorium odoratum*, *Lantana camara*, *Mikania scandens* and *Strobilanthes* which are overrunning and killing our grasslands and choking our native trees, needs to be evolved and implemented. Nothing tangible is being done in this regard. Obviously, the applications and the options available to the agronomist for the enhancement of food crop production would not be permissible to the wildlife biologist for the improvement of grasslands and the consequent enhancement of herbivore and carnivore populations. But is any effort being made in this direction at all? India has some outstanding experts in tiger ecology and their findings are very useful in tiger conservation. But what is perhaps most needed is applied research to enhance the prey species carrying capacity of our finite tiger and other habitats. Thus, in my candid opinion, research applications to better the qualitative and quantitative production of grassland habitats would be of much more benefit to tigers than the information emanating from the radio collars around their necks.

4. Conservation in India continues to be seriously hampered by the non-establishment of a cadre of trained and committed wildlife and protected area managers, who have chosen wildlife conservation as their career and wish to remain in that field during their working life. The wildlife wings of the states need to be far more professional than they are and need to have direct control over the protected areas. This is not to denigrate the

individuals in the field today, some of whom are outstanding, but the current system in operation where specialization and continuity in the conservation field are not encouraged, has to change. On the positive side, forest and wildlife officials are less revenue-oriented and more pro-conservation than those of yore. And both the politicians and the forest dwellers have come to realize that there is greater socio-economic benefit in the latter moving out of forests to resettlement outside, and in accepting the handsome rehabilitation packages being offered today. This trend, perhaps the best prescription of all for the long-term survival of protected areas, offers the most hope in their future management and in their continuation as ecological conservation entities.

5. Finally, the greatest omission has been the failure to instil enthusiasm in and obtain cooperation from rural communities for nature conservation, especially of people living around the protected areas. Also, adequate recognition and support is not given to those communities who are conserving areas and species on their own (Ranjitsinh 2006). The inherent belief in the sanctity of life and vegetarianism of the majority of India's populace has been mentioned earlier, as also the active conservation efforts of the Bishnois and some other communities. This has not been taken advantage of; indeed, the efforts of communities in the protection of species and areas have not been adequately supported by the government. With increase in education, urbanization and greater focus upon economic factors, the religious beliefs and sentiments that motivated these communities to carry on their traditional conservation practices were bound to lessen. Close to Gandhinagar, the capital of Gujarat, are fifty-two villages including Kadi, where a community of Jhalawari Patels were protecting some 3,500 blackbuck. The leader of the community told me that the blackbuck were causing them an annual loss of over ₹10 million in crop damage. The government should compensate them, or at least give them adequate recognition, so that the community would have the pride and motivation to

continue; otherwise, he said, once his generation was no more, the next would not suffer the loss in revenue and the blackbuck would go. That is precisely what happened. The Dafer community was invited in and tacitly allowed to exterminate the blackbuck, and now less than 200 remain. On the other hand, the people of Manipur have 'adopted' the Manipur deer or sangai, and the people of Saurashtra the lion. They will not countenance the persecution and destruction of these species. But we have not been able to replicate these people-led conservation scenarios elsewhere; there are no instances of local people feeling a sense of 'ownership' of the tiger or of the snow leopard. In a large democracy still affected by poverty, the surest – indeed, in some respects the only – insurance for long-term conservation is the active participation of the rural stakeholder communities.

If I had to list what I consider to be the major threats to forest and wildlife conservation in India, I would list the following, again in ascending order of priority:

First, the interbreeding of wild animals with their domestic counterparts is causing the former to lose their genetic identity. True, this affects only a few animals and bird species – the wild buffalo, the wild pig, the Asiatic wild cat and its subspecies the desert cat, the red junglefowl and grey junglefowl. This genetic ingress is far more prevalent in the plant world, leading to many an indigenous plant going locally or even totally extinct and causing large-scale mutations. I make special mention of this trend as it is a most insidious threat extremely difficult to control and which has escaped notice to a great extent. In the decades to come, we may have only feral pigs, feral wild cats and feral wild buffalo, like the 'wild' buffalo of Sri Lanka. In the plant world, we will, perhaps, not be left with true wild mangoes and wild citrus, to name just two under threat, the genetic loss of which and its long-term economic impact, would be immense.

The second major threat is the economic exploitation of wild species – the tiger, snow leopard, clouded leopard, Tibetan antelope or chiru, all species of bear, musk deer, civet cat, mongoose, pangolin, elephant, rhinoceros, otter, butterfly, orchid, sandalwood, red sanders – the list is long and appears to get longer each year, despite the efforts of the CITES secretariat and of the Wildlife Crime Control Bureau of the MoEF. The recipe and the remedy are known to all – as long as China wants tiger-bone wine and India the shahtoosh shawl, tiger and chiru will continue to be killed. And lest we delude ourselves, no amount of tiger and musk deer farming and no ersatz substitutes will suffice to satiate the demand. The demand itself must end, just as the demand for ostrich feathers did.

The third nemesis is the size and isolation of and, hence, the threat to our protected areas, which I have been repeatedly mentioning as the only havens of hope for the survival of our natural ecotypes, species and indeed of natural evolution itself. In a number of instances, the protected areas are the only places where nature itself will survive in twenty-first-century India. In Rajasthan and Gujarat, for instance, the only forests worth the name that still survive are confined to the states' parks and sanctuaries. But these protected areas are small, isolated from each other and surrounded by seas of humanity that, after having over-exploited and destroyed natural biota and forest lands outside, are now increasingly coveting and advancing into these remnant repositories – and politicians are facilitating their task.

Even within secure and well-managed protected areas, species are not necessarily safe in the long-term future. They are threatened by the classic ecological imperatives of island biogeography, for islands they indeed are to all intent and purpose. As David Quammen says, 'An ecosystem is a tapestry of species and relationships' (Quammen 1997). Chop away a portion, isolate a section and what remains is not necessarily a representative microcosm of the whole (Ranjitsinh 2006). 'If most of the area of the habitat is destroyed and a fraction of the area is saved as a reserve, the reserve will initially contain more species than it can hold at equilibrium. The excess will gradually go extinct. The smaller the reserve, the higher will be the extinction rates ... For instance, 134 of the 325 lowland bird species of New Guinea are absent from all oceanic islands no more than a few kilometres from New Guinea ... The number of species on an island decreases with increasing distance' from New Guinea shores (Diamond 1975). Why did two races of the tiger – the Bali tiger, followed by the Javan tiger, inhabiting a larger island than Bali – go extinct in recent times? Why did the relict population of the gaur in Bandhavgarh National Park and that of the blackbuck in Kanha National Park both go extinct, while both species continue to exist in their respective contiguous habitats nearby?

However, if one were to be asked to name the single greatest threat to conservation and to the survival of nature and of threatened species in twenty-first-century India, I would cite lack of political will and support. Indeed, there is political collusion in acts detrimental to habitats and ecosystems, leading to likely extinction of species and damage to ecological security. Unlike Africa, Australia, Europe and the Americas, landholdings in India are too small to provide refuge to wildlife. In any case all wildlife in India is owned by the nation, irrespective of whether it stands on private land or public. Thus, the onus of nature conservation rests with the state, and if the impetus for this is found wanting or, worse, if the state is itself jeopardizing conservation for the sake of political gain, a soothsayer would not be required to spell out the future. It can take just one person and less than a year to undo what may have taken a generation of collective effort to create.

As mentioned earlier, India has not lost any large mammal except the cheetah – and the Javan and Sumatran rhinoceros in the country's periphery – in historical times. India's conservation record so far has been remarkably good, considering its humungous population and problems. But the sad truth is that this is set to change and the twenty-first century will in all probability witness the extinction of a number of life forms, faunal, avifaunal and floral. With less than a hundred scattered specimens left in the world, the great Indian bustard is most likely to go extinct the earliest;

the peninsular population of the wild buffalo, perhaps the only true genetically wild specimens left in the world, may precede the bustard. The Malabar civet may already have gone extinct and if the caracal follows suit, it would hardly be noticed. The Kashmir hangul with numbers constantly hovering below 200, almost all confined to a single habitat and with almost everyone's hand against it, is a strong candidate for early extirpation, while the Manipur sangai, also below 200 in number, is another candidate despite popular support and adulation, as it continues to be confined to a single, tiny, fragile wetland whose ecology is changing. The Andaman teal and the Nicobar megapode, already affected by the island syndrome, are unlikely to withstand the increasing demographic affliction. Jerdon's courser, already presumed extinct till rediscovered some years ago and restricted to a single area, is unlikely to survive the twenty-first century. As things stand, the tiger is unlikely to go extinct soon, but the same cannot be said for the clouded and snow leopards in India. The elephant too will survive, but I doubt if tuskers would be very visible a century from now, as is the case in Sri Lanka (Ranjitsinh 1997). With the poaching of the ivory-carrying bulls, soon only the tuskless maknas may be left to procreate.

The cheetah went extinct in India because we then lacked the wherewithal to prevent extinction. If any species goes extinct now, it would be deemed as allowed to go extinct, because we now know its predicament and have the power to prevent it. Only the political will is lacking.

I have been fortunate in life. Most of my aspirations and wishes have been fulfilled. I crave for one great wish to be granted – that no life form should become extinct in India, in the twenty-first century at least.

Bibliography

Acharya, I.N. 1974. 'Saurashtra ma Jhala Rajyavansh na Shasan no Itihas', PhD thesis submitted to Saurashtra University, Rajkot.
Adams, A.L., 1867. *Wanderings of a Naturalist in India*, Edinburgh: Edmonston and Douglas.
Ali, Salim, and S. Dillon Ripley, 1969. *Handbook of the Birds of India and Pakistan*, Vol. 2, Bombay: Oxford University Press.
Ali, Salim, and S. Dillon Ripley, 1970. *Handbook of the Birds of India and Pakistan*, Vol. 4, Bombay: Oxford University Press.
Babur Nama, 1921. Translated by J. Leyden and W. Erskine, London: Oxford University Press.
Bacha, M.S., 2013. *Wildlife Protected Areas Infuse Ecotourism in Jammu and Kashmir*, Srinagar: Book Vision.
Beeson, C.F.C., 1941. *The Ecology and Control of the Forest Insects of India and the Neighbouring Countries*, Dehradun: Forest Research Institute.
Champion, F.W. 1927. *With a Camera in Tiger-land*, London: Chatto & Windus.
Champion H.K. and S.K. Seth, 1968. *A Revised Survey of the Forest Types in India*, Nasik: Government of India Press.
Chundawat, R.S., W.A. Rodgers and H.S. Panwar, 1986. 'Status Report on Snow Leopard in India', in H. Freeman (ed.), *Proceedings of the International Snow Leopard Symposium*, Seattle, USA: International Snow Leopard Trust.
Cardus, N. 1948, *Good Days. A Book of Cricket*, London: Rupert Hart-Davis.

Corbett Foundation, 2015. 'Interim Relief Scheme in and around Corbett Tiger Reserve and Surrounding Forest Divisions', unpublished, April.

Craighead, J.J. and F.C. Craighead, 2001. 'Life with an Indian Prince', *Archives of American Falcony*, Idaho, USA: Boise.

Delacour, J., 1964. *The Pheasants of the World*, London: Country Life Ltd.

———, 1974. *The Wildfowl of the World*, 4 volumes, London: Country Life.

Dharmakumarsinh, R.S., 1978. 'The Changing Wildlife of Kathiawad', *Journal of the Bombay Natural History Society (JBNHS)*, Vol. 75, No. 3, pp. 632–50.

———, 1986. 'Following the Lion's Trail: Trackers of Mytiala', *The India Magazine*, Vol. 6, No, 4, pp. 28–35.

Diamond, J.M., 1975. 'The Island Dilemma: Lessons of Modern Biogeographic Studies for the Design of Natural Reserves', *Biological Conservation 7*, Applied Science Publishers Ltd, England, pp. 129–46.

Divyabhanusinh, 1986. 'Earliest Record of a White Tiger (*Panthera tigris*)', *JBNHS*, Vol. 83, (Supplement), pp. 163–65.

———, 1999. 'Hunting in Mughal Painting', in S.P. Verma, (ed.), *Flora and Fauna in Mughal Art*, Mumbai: Marg Publications.

———, 2006. 'Junagadh State and Its Lions: Conservation in Princely India, 1879–1947', in *Conservation & Society*, Vol. 4, No. 4, Bangalore, pp. 522–40.

Dunbar Brander, A.A., 1923. *Wild Animals in Central India*, London: Edward Arnold & Co.

Fenton, L.L., 1924. *The Rifle in India*, London: W. Thocker & Co.

Forshaw, J.M., 1973. *Parrots of the World*, New York: Doubleday & Co. Inc.

Forsyth, J.J., 1872. *Highlands of Central India*, London: Chapman and Hall.

Fry, C.B., 1939. *Life Worth Living*, London: Eyre and Spottiswoode.

Gee, E.P., 1964. *The Wildlife of India*, London: Collins.

Groves, C.P., 1982. 'Geographic Variation in the Barasingha or Swamp Deer (*Cervus duvauceli*)', *JBNHS*, Vol. 79, No. 3, pp. 620–29.

Gujarat Agricultural University, Junagarh, 2002. 'Quantification of Environmental and Economic Benefits of Conserving Gir Ecosystem, Final Report', mimeo.

Habib, Irfan, 1982. *An Atlas of Mughal Empire: Political and Economic Maps with Detailed Notes*, Delhi: Oxford University Press.

Holloway, Colin, 1970. 'The Hangul in Dachigam: A Census', *Oryx*, Vol. 10, No. 6, December, pp. 373–82.

Kurt, F., 1978. 'Kashmir Deer (*Cervus elaphus hanglu*) in Dachigam', in IUCN, *Threatened Deer*: Proceedings of a working meeting of the Deer Specialist Group of the Survival Service Commission on the IUCN Threatened Deer Programme held at Longview, Washington State, USA, 26 September– 1 October 1977, Morges, Switzerland: IUCN, pp. 87–108.

Lalthangliana, R., 2004. Speech Made at the Conference of Ministers of Environment and Forests, New Delhi, mimeo.

Lekagul, B. and J. McNeely 1977. *Mamals of Thailand*, Bangkok: Sahakarnbhat Co.

Locke, A., 1954. *The Tigers of Trengganu*, London: Museum Press.

Marker, L., 2011. 'Results of the Fact Finding Mission to the Kuno Wildlife Sanctuary, M.P., India', mimeo.

Mayne C., 1921. *History of the Dhrangadhra State*, Calcutta: Thacker, Spink and Co.

MoEF (Ministry of Environment and Forests), 1988. 'The Snow Leopard Conservation Scheme', New Delhi: MoEF, Government of India.

———, 1998a. 'Interim Report of the Task Force on Sal-Borer Attack in Madhya Pradesh' New Delhi: MoEF, Government of India, January.

———, 1998b. 'Report of the Task Force on Sal-Borer Attack in Madhya Pradesh', April, New Delhi: MoEF, Government of India.

———, 2002. 'National Wildlife Action Plan (2002-2016)', New Delhi: MoEF, Government of India.

———, 2006. 'Report of the National Forest Commission', MoEF, New Delhi: Government of India.

———, 2009. *Indira Gandhi on Environment and Forests, Selected Speeches, Messages and Letters*, New Delhi: MoEF, Government of India.

Misra, P.T.P., 1911. *A Short History of Dungarpur State*, Calcutta: K.L. Gupta.

MP Biodiversity Board, undated. 'Integrated Strategy Paper on Biodiversity Conservation (Forest, Wildlife Grasslands)', unpublished.

MP Forest Dept., NTCA, WTI and Cheetah Task Force, 2011. 'Action Plan for the Reintroduction of the Cheetah (*Acinonyx jubatus*) in Kuno-Palpur Wildlife Sanctuary, Madhya Pradesh', mimeo.

Nripendra Narayana Bhupa, Maharaja of Cooch Behar, 1908. *Thirty-seven*

Years of Big Game Shooting in Cooch Behar, The Duars and Assam, republished as *Big Game Shooting in Eastern and North-Eastern India*, Delhi: Mittal Publications, 1985.

NTCA/MoEF, 2011. 'Minutes of the Meeting of the Cheetah Task Force for the Reintroduction of Cheetah in India, held on 30.09.2011', No. 15-35/2010, New Delhi: NTCA, 28.10.2011.

O'Brien, S.J., M.E. Roelke, L. Marker, A. Newman and C.A. Winkler, 1985. 'Genetic Basis for Species Vulnerability in the Cheetah', *Science*, Vol. 227, No. 4693, pp. 1428–34.

Quammen, D., 1997. *The Song of the Dodo*, New York: Touchstone.

Rangaranjan, M., 2009. 'Striving for Balance: Nature, Powers, Science and India's Indira Gandhi, 1917-1984', *Conservation & Society*, Vol. 7, No. 4, pp. 299–312.

Ranjitsinh, M.K., 1973. 'A Note on the Eravikulam–Rajamalai Sanctuary, High Range, Kerala', *Cheetal*, Journal of the Wildlife Preservation Society of India, Vol. 15, No. 2, Dehradun, pp. 50–55.

———, 1975. 'Keibul Lamjao Sanctuary and the Brow Antlered Deer – 1972, with Field Notes on a Visit in 1975', *JBNHS*, Vol. 12, No. 2, pp. 243–55.

———, 1979. 'Forest Destruction in Asia and the South Pacific', *Ambio*, Vol. III, No. 5, pp. 192–201.

———, 1980. 'Geographic Variation in the Barasingha or Swamp Deer (*Cervus duvauceli*, Cuvier, 1823)', *Cheetal*, Journal of the Wildlife Preservation Society of India, Vol. 22, No. 1, Dehradun, pp. 9–10.

———, 1982. 'Nature's Havens of Hope, National Parks of the Indomalayan Realm', *Cheetal*, Journal of the Wild Life Preservation Society of India, Vol. 24, No. 2, Dehradun, pp. 45–61.

———, 1983. 'An Analysis of Some Trends in Supply and Demand of Forest Resources, Government of Madhya Pradesh', mimeo.

———, 1984a. 'Occurrence of Lesser Florican (*Sypheotides indica*) in Kanha National Park', *JBNHS*, Vol. 80, No. 3, p. 641.

———, 1984b. 'Conservation of Nature and Problems of the Collector and SDO', *The Administrator*, Vol. 29, No. 4, October–December, Mussoorie, pp. 419–25.

———, 1984c. 'Personal Observation During the Bhopal Tragedy on 3 December 1984: Report to Chief Secretary of MP', mimeo.

―――, 1985a. 'A Possible Sighting of Blanford's Fox (*Vulpes cana*) in Kutch', *JBNHS*, Vol. 82, No. 2, pp. 395–96.
―――, 1985b. 'Kirthar National Park', *Sanctuary Magazine*, Vol. 5, No. 3.
―――, 1988. 'A Critique of Tiger Conservation in Asia', paper read at The Year of the Tiger conference at Dallas, Texas, USA.
―――, 1989a. *The Indian Blackbuck*, Dehradun: Natraj.
―――, 1989b. 'Overview on Conservation and Management in Critical Ecosystems in Asia and the Pacific and Strengthening Training Capacities', paper presented at the Regional Workshop on Strengthening Conservation and Management of Critical Ecosystems in Asia and the Pacific, organized by ESCAP/World Bank/UNDP, November–December 1989, Bangkok, Thailand mimeo.
―――, 1997. *Beyond the Tiger: Portraits of Asian Wildlife*, Delhi: Brijbasi.
―――, 1999. 'Interim Brief Report on the Field Visit to Some Protected Areas in the Chhattisgarh Region in Madhya Pradesh and in Adjacent Areas of Odisha and Bihar', mimeo.
―――, 2006. 'Status of Wildlife Conservation in the Indian Subcontinent', *JBNHS*, Vol. 103, p. 283.
―――, 2014. 'Reoccupation of Former Territories by the Asiatic Lion *Panthera leo persica, Meyer, 1826*, in Southern Saurashtra, Gujarat, India: A Vision for Future Management', JBNHS, Vol. 111, No. 3, pp. 161–71.
Ranjitsinh, M.K., S.K. Chauhan, S.B. Bhanubakode, K. Sivakumar, Asad Akhtar, V. Patil and S.C. Verma, 2000. 'The Status and Conservation of the Wild Buffalo (*Bubalus bubalis*) in Peninsular India', MP Forest Department, Wildlife Institute of India, BNHS and Bastar Society for Conservation of Nature.
Ranjitsinh, M.K. and L.A.K. Singh, 2002. 'The Gharial (*Gavialis gangeticus*) in Indravati River?', *JBNHS*, Vol. 99, No. 2, p. 330.
Ranjitsinh, M.K., C.M. Seth, Riyaz Ahmad, Y.V. Bhatnagar and S.S. Kyarong, 2005. *Goats on the Border: A Rapid Assessment of the Pir Panjal Markhor* (Capra falconeri cashmiriensis) *in Jammu and Kashmir: Distribution, Status and Threats*, Department of Wildlife protection, Government of Jammu & Kashmir, and Nature Conservation Foundation, Delhi.
Ranjitsinh, M.K. and Y.V. Jhala, 2010. *Assessing the Potential for*

Reintroducing the Cheetah in India, Noida: Wildlife Trust of India and Dehradun: Wildlife Institute of India.

Rogers A. and Beveridge, H. (eds), 1980. *Tuzuk-i-Jahangiri, or Memoirs of Jahangir*, Delhi: Munshiram Manoharlal Pvt. Ltd.

Sanderson, G.P., 1912. *Thirteen Years among the Wild Beasts of India*, Edinburgh: John Grant.

Shukla, Nathuram Sundarji, undated. *Jhalavanshavaridhi*, Bhavnagar: Anand Printing Press.

Singh, L.A.K. 1999. *Tracking Tigers: Guidelines for estimating wild tiger populations using the Pugmark technique*, Delhi: WWF Tiger Conservation Programme.

Smythies, E.A., 1942, *Big Game Shooting in Nepal*, Calcutta: Thacker, Spink & Co.

Stockley, Lt. Col. C.H., 1928. *Big Game Shooting in the Indian Empire*, London: Constable and Company.

TERI (The Energy and Resources Institute), 2014. *Study on Implementation of FRA and Climate Change Vulnerability of Forests and Forest Dwelling Communities*, Delhi: TERI.

Vishnoi, Anubhuti, 2014. 'Black Gold, Green Signal', *India Today*, 8 September.

Waddington, C.W., 1933. *Indian India*, London: Jarrolds.

Ward, A.E., 1921, 'Big Game Shooting of Kashmir and Adjacent Hill Provinces', *JBNHS*, Vol. 28, No. 1, pp. 45–49.

Ward, Col. A.E., 1923a. 'Game Animals of Kashmir and Adjacent Hill Provinces', *JBNHS*, Vol. 29, No.2, pp.318–23.

Ward, Col. A.E., 1923b. 'Small Game Shooting in Kashmir and the Adjacent Hill Provinces', *JBNHS*, Vol. 29, No. 3, pp. 653–58.

Ward, R., 1928. *Rowland Ward's Records of Big Game*, 9th edition, London: Rowland Ward Ltd.

WWF, 1999. *Tiger Conservation Programme, Three Years and Beyond*, Delhi: WWF.

Wynter-Blyth, M.A., and R.S. Dharmakumarsinh, 1950. 'The Gir Forest and Its Lions', Part II, *JBNHS*, Vol. 49, No. 3, pp. 456–70.

List of Species Mentioned in Text

FAUNA
Mammals

Afghan urial	*Ovis orientalis blanfordi*
Agile gibbon	*Hylobates agilis*
Alpine ibex	*Capra ibex ibex*
Amazon dolphin	*Inia geoffrensis*
Asiatic cheetah	*Acinonyx jubatus venaticus*
Asiatic elephant	*Elephas maximus*
Asiatic ibex;	*Capra sibirica*
Asiatic lion	*Panthera leo persica*
Asiatic wild buffalo	*Bubalus bubalis*
Asiatic wild cat	*Felis sylvestris*
Bactrian camel	*Camelus bactrianus*
Balochistan urial	*Ovis orientalis blanfordi*
Bali tiger	*Panthera tigris balica*
Banteng	*Bos javanicus birmanicus*
Barasingha, or swamp deer	*Rucervus duvaucelii*
(central India)	*Rucervus duvaucelii branderi;*
nominate race (terai)	*Rucervus duvaucelii duvaucelii;*
Assam	*Rucervus duvaucelii ranjitsinhi*

Bearded pig	*Sus barbatus*
Bharal, or blue sheep	*Pseudois nayaur*
Bhutan takin	*Budorcas taxicolor whitei*
Blackbuck (south-eastern India)	*Antilope cervicapra cervicapra*
(western and northern India)	*A.c. rajputanae*
Blanford's fox	*Vulpes cana*
Brow-antlered deer	*Cervus eldi eldi;*
Manipur race – sangai	*Rucervus eldii McClelland*
Myanmar race –	*Cervus eldi thamin*
Brown bear	*Ursus arctos isabellinus*
Brown goral	*Naemorhedus goral hodgsoni*
Caracal	*Caracal caracal*
Central African white rhino	*Ceratotherum simum cottoni*
Chamois	*Rupicapra rupicapra*
Chinkara	*Gazella bennettii*
Chiru, Tibetan antelope	*Pantholops hodgsoni*
Chital, or spotted deer	*Axis axis*
Clouded leopard	*Neofelis nebulosa*
Common langur	*Presbytus entellus*
Desert cat	*Felis sylvestris ornata*
Desert fox	*Vulpes vulpes pusilla*
Desert hare	*Lepus nigricollis dayanus*
Dingo	*Canis dingo*
Eastern hoolock gibbon	*Hoolock leuconedys*
Elk	*Cervus elaphus*
European bison or wisent	*Bison bonasus*
Evan's long-tailed goral	*Naemorhedus caudatus evansi*
Four-horned antelope/chowsingha	*Tetracerus quadricornis*

Gangetic dolphin	*Platanista gangetica*
Gaur (Indian bison, seladang in Malaysia)	*Bos gaurus*
Goitered gazelle	*Gazella subgutturosa*
Golden cat	*Catopuma temminckii*
Golden langur	*Trachypithecus geei*
Golden takin	*Budorcas taxicolor bedfordi*
Goral (western Himalaya, grey)	*Naemorhaedus bedfordi*
(eastern Himalaya, brown)	*N. goral*
(Arunachal Pradesh, red)	*N. baileyi*
Great Indian one-horned rhinoceros	*Rhinoceros unicornis*
Hairy-nosed otter	*Lutra sumatrana*
Hangul, or Kashmir stag	*Cervus elaphus hanglu*
Himalayan black bear	*Ursus thibetanus thibetanus*
Himalayan ibex	*Capra sibirica sakeen*
Himalayan marmot	*Marmota himalayana*
Himalayan serow	*Capricornis thar*
Himalayan tahr	*Hermitragus jemlahicus*
Hispid hare	*Caprolagus hispidus*
Hog deer	*Axis porcinus*
Indian fox	*Vulpes bengalensis*
Indian porcupine	*Hystrix indica*
Indian wild ass	*Equus hemionus khur*
Indian wild boar, or wild pig	*Sus scrofa*
Andamans race	*Sus scrofa andamanensis*
Japanese macaque	*Macaca fuscata*
Javan rhino	*Rhinoceros sondaicus*
Javan tiger	*Panthera tigris sondaica*
Jungle cat	*Felis chaus*

Kiang, (Tibetan wild ass) – western	*Equus kiang kiang*
southern kiang	*Equus kiang polyodon*
Kouprey ox	*Bos sauveli*
Kulan	*Equus hemionus kulan*
Ladakh urial, or shapu	*Ovis vignei vignei*
Leopard/panther	*Panthera pardus*
Leopard cat	*Prionailurus bengalensis*
Lesser mouse deer	*Tragulus javanicus*
Lowland anoa	*Anoa depressicornis*
Malabar civet	*Viverra civettina*
Malayan tapir	*Tapirus indicus*
Manchurian wapiti	*Cervus canadensis xanthopygus*
Marbled cat	*Pardofelis marmorata*
Markhor	*Capra falconeri*
Pir Panjal makor	*Capra falconeri falconeri*
Mindoro sambar	*Cervus unicolor barandanus*
Mishmi takin	*Budorcas taxicolor taxicolor*
Mongolian argali	*Ovis ammon ammon*
Mongolian gazelle	*Procapra gutturosa*
Mongolian saiga antelope	*Saiga tatrica mogolica*
Mongoose (common)	*Herpestes edwardsi*
Mountain anoa	*Anoa quarlesi*
Musk deer	*Moschus moschiferus*
Kashmir musk deer	*Moschus cupreus*
West Himalayan musk deer	*Moschus leucogoster*
Central and eastern Himalayan	*Moschus chrysogaster*
Black musk deer	*Moschus fuscus*
Nilgai	*Bocelaphus tragocamelus*

List of Species Mentioned in Text

Nilgiri tahr	*Nilgiritragus hylocrius*
Nubian ibex	*Capra ibex nubiana*
Pallas' cat	*Felis manul*
Pere David's deer	*Elephurus davidianus*
Philippine duck	*Anas luzonica*
Pika	*Ochotona*
Plains wolf	*Canis lupus pallipes*
Prezewalski's horse	*Equus ferus prezewalskii*
Pronghorn antelope	*Antilocapra americana*
Pygmy hog	*Porcula salvania*
Red fox	*Vulpes vulpes*
Rhesus macaque	*Macaca mulatta*
Rusa deer	*Cervus timorensis russa*
Rusty-spotted cat	*Felis rubuginosa*
Sambar	*Cervis unicolor*
Sardinian mouflon	*Ovis orientalis musimon*
Sarha (Sindh ibex)	*Capra aegagrus blythi*
Schomburgk's deer	*Cervus schomburgki*
Seladang, or Malayan gaur	*Bos gaurus*
Shou, or Sikkim stag	*Cervus elaphus wallichi*
Siamang	*Symphalangus syndactylus*
Sloth bear	*Melursus ursinus*
Smooth Indian otter	*Lutra perspicallata*
Snow leopard	*Uncia uncia*
Somali wild ass	*Equus asinus somaliensis*
Striped hyena	*Hyaena hyaena*
Sumatran rhino	*Didermocerus sumatrensis*
Sumatran serow	*Capricornis sumatraensis*
Sumatran tiger	*Panthera tigris sumatrae*

Tamaraw:	*Bubalus mindorensis*
Tarpan horse	*Equus caballus gomelini*
Tasmanian thylacine (extinct)	*Thylacinus cynocephalus*
Thamin, or Eld's deer	*Cervus eldi thamin*
Tian Shan wapiti	*Cervus canadensis songaricus*
Tibetan antelope	*Pantholops hodgsoni*
Tibetan argali, or nyan	*Ovis ammon hodgsoni*
Tibetan gazelle, or gowa	*Procapra picticaudata*
Tibetan grey wolf	*Canis lupus chanco*
Tibetan sand fox	*Vulpes ferrilata*
Tiger	*Panthera tigris*
Wallaby	*Macropus notamacropus*
Wallaroo	*Macropus robustus*
Wild dog, or dhole	*Cuon alpinus alpinus*
Wild dromedary	*Camelus dromedarius*
Wolf	*Canis lupus*
Indian wolf	*C. lupus pallipes*
Grey or Tibetan wolf	*C. lupus chanco*
Yak	*Bos grunniens*

Reptiles

Banded krait	*Bungarus fasciatus*
Black caiman	*Melanosuchus niger*
Dhaman, or rat snake	*Ptyas mucosus*
False, or Malayan gharial	*Tomistoma schlegelii*
Freshwater crocodile (mugger)	*Crocodylus palustris*
Gharial	*Gavialis gangeticus*
Indian cobra	*Naja naja*
Indian flap-shelled turtle	*Lissemys punctata*

Indian krait	*Bungarus caeruleus*
Indian soft-shelled turtle	*Trionyx gangeticus*
King cobra, or hamadryad	*Ophiophogus Hannah*
Komodo dragon	*Varanus komodoensis*
Leatherback turtle	*Dermochelys coriacea*
Lizard	*Varanus sp*
Desert lizard	*Euromastix hardwicki*
Olive ridley turtle	*Lepidochelys olivacea*
Saltwater crocodile	*Crocodylus porosus*
Spectacled caiman	*Caiman crocodilus crocodile*
Tokay Gecko	*Gekko gecko*

Birds

Andaman or grey or oceanic teal	*Anas gibberifrons albogularis*
Assam wreathed hornbill	*Rhyticeros undulatus ticehusti*
Astrapia bird-of-paradise	*Astrapia spendidissima*
Bar-headed goose	*Anser indicus*
Bengal florican	*Houbaropsis bengalensis*
Black eagle	*Ictinaetus malaensis*
Black Francolin partridge	*Francolinus francolinus*
Black sickle-billed bird-of-paradise	*Epimachus fastosus*
Black-necked crane	*Grus nigricollis*
Blood pheasant	*Ithaginis cruentus*
Blue bird-of-paradise	*Paradisaea rudolphi*
Blue jay	*Garrulus glandarius*
Blyth's tragopan	*Tragopan blythii*
Bonelli's hawk eagle	*Aquila fasciata*
Brahminy duck, or ruddy shelduck	*Tadorna ferruginia*

Chakor or chukar partridge	*Alectoris chukar*
Cheer pheasant	*Catreus wallichi*
Chestnut bellied Indian sandgrouse	*Pteroles exustus erlangeri*
Common crane	*Grus grus*
Coot	*Fulica atra*
Cotton teal	*Nettapus coromandelianus*
Count Raggi's bird-of-paradise	*Paradisaea raggiana*
Crested serpent eagle	*Spilornis cheela*
Darkbacked swift	*Apus acuticaudus*
Demoiselle crane	*Anthropoides virgo*
Edible-nest swiflet	*Collacalia inexpectata*
Eurasian sparrow hawk	*Accipiter nisus*
Fire-tailed yellow-backed sunbird	*Aethopyga ignicauda*
Golden eagle	*Aquila chrysaetos*
Goshawk	*Accipiter gentilis*
Great Indian bustard	*Ardeotis nigriceps*
Great Indian, or great pied hornbill	*Buceros bicornis homrai*
Greater flamingo	*Phoenicopterus ruber roseus*
Green/Javan junglefowl	*Gallus varius*
Green peafowl	*Pavo muticus*
Grey Francolin partridge	*Francolinus pondicerianus*
Grey hornbill	*Ocyceros birostris*
Grey junglefowl	*Gallus sonneratii*
Grey quail	*Coturnix coturnix*
Greylag goose	*Anser anser*
Himalayan monal	*Lophophorus impejanus*
Himalayan snowcock	*Tetraogallus himalayensis*

List of Species Mentioned in Text

Houbara, or Macqueen's bustard	*Chlamydotis undulata*
Hume's bar-tailed pheasant	*Symarticus humiae humiae*
Imperial or black-bellied sandgrouse	*Pterocles orientalis*
Indian peafowl	*Pavo cristatus*
Indian skimmer	*Rynchops albicollis*
Javan junglefowl	*Gallus varius*
Jerdon's courser	*Cursorius bitorquatus*
Kagu	*Rhynochetos jubatus*
Kakapo	*Strigops habroptilus*
Kalij pheasant – white crested	*Lophura leucomelanos hamiltonii*
black-backed	*Lophura leucomelanos melanota*
black-breasted	*Lophura leucomelanos lathami*
Moffitt's kalij or black kalij	*Lophura leucomelanos moffitti*
Nepal kalij	*Lophura leucomelanos*
William's kalij pheasant	*Lophura leucomelanos williamsi*
King bird-of-paradise	*Cicinnurus regius*
Kingfisher	*Alcedo bengalensis*
King of Saxony bird-of-paradise	*Pteridophora alberti*
Lammergeier, or bearded vulture	*Gypaetus barbatus*
Lawe's six-wired bird-of-paradise	*Parotia lawesii*
Lesser flamingo	*Phoenconaias minor*
Lesser florican	*Sypheotides indica*
Magnificent bird-of-paradise	*Diphyllodes magnificus*
Malkoha	*Phaenicophaeus tristis*
Mallard	*Anas playtrhynchos*
Mandarin duck	*Aix galericulata*
Mrs Gould's sunbird	*Aethopyga gouldiae*
Narcondam hornbill	*Rhyticeros narcondami*

Nicobar megapode	*Megapodius freycinet*
Noddy tern	*Anous stolidus pileatus*
Painted francolin, or painted partridge	*Francolinus pictus*
Painted spurfowl	*Galloperdix lunulata*
Paradise flycatcher	*Terpsiphone paradise*
Philippine duck	*Anas luzonica*
Pied imperial pigeon	*Ducula bicolor*
Pintail sandgrouse	*Pterocles alchata caudacutus*
Princess Stephanie bird-of-paradise	*Astrapia stephaniae*
Pygmy parrot	*Micropsitta*
Red junglefowl	*Gallus gallus*
Red spurfowl	*Galloperdix spadicea*
Red-breasted pygmy-parrot	*Micropsitta bruiji*
Red-crowned crane	*Grus japonensis*
Ribbon-tailed bird-of-paradise	*Astrapia mayeri*
Rufous-necked hornbill	*Aceros nipalensis*
Saker falcon	*Falco cherrug*
Satyr tragopan	*Tragopan satyra*
Scarlet finch	*Haematospiza sipahi*
Sclater's monal	*Lophophorus sclateri*
See-see partridge	*Ammoperdix griseogularis*
Shahin, peregrine	*Falco peregrinus*
Siberian crane	*Grus leucogeranus*
Sikkim snowcock	*Tetrogallus tibetanus acquilonifr*
Snipe	*Gallinago species*
Snow partridge	*Lerwa lerwa*
Snow pigeon	*Columba leuconata*
Sooty tern	*Sterna fuscata*

Splendid astrapia	*Astrapia splendidissima*
Spotted sandgrouse or waku-waku	*Pterocles senegallus*
Superb bird-of-paradise	*Lophorina superba*
Szechenyi's monal-partridge or pheasant partridge	*Tetraophasis szechenyi*
Tibetan partridge	*Peradix hodgsoniae*
Tibetan sandgrouse	*Syrrhaptes tibetanus*
Western tragopan	*Tragopan melanocephalus*
White-bellied sea eagle	*Haliaeetus leucogaster*
White-rumped swift	*Apus pacifus pacifus*
Whooping crane	*Grus americana*

FLORA

Acacia (gorad)	*Acacia Senegal*
(babool)	*Acacia nilotica*
Bamboo (Calcutta bamboo)	*Dendrocalamus strictus*
katanga bamboo:	*Bambusa arundinacea*
Banyan	*Ficus benghalensis*
Ber	*Zizyphus mauritiana*
Bija, or beeja	*Pterocarpus marsupium:*
Chir pine	*Pinus roxaburghii*
Dhava, or dhavda	*Anogeissus latifolia*
English oak	*Quercus robur*
Haldu, or kadam	*Haldina cordifolia*
Himalayan sapria	*Sapria himalayana*
Ishing-kombong or Manchurian wild rice	*Zizania latifolia*
Jamun	*Syzygium cumini*
Karamda, or karaunda	*Carissa carandas*

List of Species Mentioned in Text

Kardhai	*Anogeissus pendula*
Khasi pine	*Pinus khasia*
Kusum, or kosam	*Schleichera oleosa*
Kuth	*Saussurea lappa*
Mahua	*Madhuca latifolia*
Mango	*Mangifera indica*
Palmyra palms	*Borassus flabellifer*
Pipal	*Ficus religiosa*
Psilotum	*Psilotum nudum*
Rayan, or raiyan	*Manilkara hexandra*
Red oat grass	*Themeda triandra*
Reed grass	*Phragmites karka*
Saja, or saaj	*Terminalia elliptica*
Sal	*Shorea robusta*
Semal, or simul	*Bombax ceiba*
Teak	*Tectona grandis*
Tendu, or timru	*Diospyros melanoxylon*
Tropical pine	*Pinus merkusii*
Vilayati babul /kikar	*Prosopis juliflora*
Wild mango	*Irvingia gabonensis*

Index

akhand shikar, 123, 164, 278, 291
Ali, Salim, 23, 82, 143, 160, 173, 239, 309
Amarsinhji, 1-2, 4–5, 35
Andaman Islands, 121, 123, 140–43, 153, 181, 255–56, 274, 350
Arunachal Pradesh, 81, 248, 254, 261, 265, 277, 278, 309, 310, 313
Australia, 154, 179, 183, 240
author's experience
    Burhanpur posting, 92–97
    awkward law and order situation, 94–95
        shooting a tiger, 95–97
    Delhi posting, 111–14
        meeting of wildlife personnel, 112–14
        author's suggestions, 113
    Dhar, 97–101
    Kanha National Park, 102–10
    Sagar, 89–92
        shooting a maneater, 90
    encounter with a magnificent male tiger, 91
    controlling mob violence in M.P., 217–18
    pets, 92

Bangladesh, 115, 143, 151, 160, 170, 209, 247, 280
barasingha, 49–50, 58, 60, 88, 103–06, 108, 115, 140, 196, 200–01, 205, 208, 215, 216, 243, 257, 275, 276, 279, 313
bear, 17, 44, 47, 56, 57, 59, 62–63, 75, 78, 79, 80, 84, 88, 91, 101, 196, 261, 323, 348
Bharatpur, 4, 43, 57, 147, 249, 266
Bhavnagar, 1, 29, 33–36
Bhavsinhji, Maharaja, 33–35
Bhopal, 49, 109, 190–92, 204, 214–33
    gas leakage in the Union Carbide Factory, 218–33
Bhutan, 77–86, 160, 209, 283, 289, 309
Bijay Singhji, Rai Rayan Maharawal, 13–14, 15

Bishnoi community, 43, 47, 145–46, 246, 293, 340, 346
blackbuck, 3, 11, 17, 21, 31, 33–37, 39–41, 43, 46–47, 49, 50, 88, 92–93, 106, 139, 145–47, 192, 194, 251, 330, 342–43, 346–47, 349
buffalo, wild, 49–50, 88, 93, 115, 162, 166, 173, 179, 196, 209–11, 248, 257, 279, 288–89, 290–91, 313, 316, 347, 350
Bundela, Raja Bir Singh Deo, 204–05
bustard project, 254, 320, 328
bustard, great Indian, 12, 37, 42, 88, 118, 144–45, 154, 193, 201, 251, 253, 316, 319–21, 328, 344, 349

caracal, 17, 35, 37, 43–44, 93, 164, 172, 192, 350
cattle compensation scheme, 18–19, 135, 281
cheetah
  hunting of, 5, 33, 35–36, 39, 49–51, 102, 190, 327, 329, 333
  measures to save, 329, 331–38, 342, 349, 350
chinkara, 11, 16, 17–18, 31, 33, 35, 37, 38–39, 43, 44, 46–47, 88, 139, 145, 155, 171, 192, 202, 330
chital, 17, 21, 31, 32, 43, 49, 92, 104, 106, 109, 115, 139, 141–42, 143, 192, 202, 207, 216, 306–07, 317, 324, 330
Choudhury, Saroj Raj, 135, 136, 163, 263

chowsingha, 17, 22, 163, 200
communities protecting fauna and flora, 293, 346
Convention on International Trade in Endangered Species of Wild Fauna and Flora (CITES), 134, 239, 240, 264, 265, 280, 312, 348
crane
  black-necked, 67, 72, 86
  common, 35
  Demoiselle, 42
  Siberian, 147, 194, 249
  whooping, 165
crocodile, 43, 98, 142, 200, 202, 216, 250
  concerns regarding, 128, 149–50
Crocodile Project, 149–53, 306

deer
  musk, 57, 59, 74, 78, 83, 84, 85, 86, 88, 261, 262, 348
  hog, 43, 103, 115, 140, 142, 154, 160, 164, 243, 257, 272, 273, 279, 283, 316–17, 324, 343, 344
de-notify some sanctuaries, 212, 314
Deo, K.C., 299
Deo, Maharaja M.S. Singh, 47, 48
Deo, Maharaja Ramanuj Pratap Singh, 49, 329
Deo, Maharaja Ramanuj Saran Singh, 47, 49
Deo, Ram Chandra Singh, 49, 329
Dharmakumarsinhji, R.S., 3, 29, 31, 33, 34, 36, 143–44, 193
Digvijaysinhji, 33, 63, 208, 234, 269, 286

Director, wildlife preservation of India, 10, 19, 43, 51, 61, 71, 135, 140, 153, 156, 190, 203, 235, 255, 263, 272, 289, 327, 330
dragon, Komodo, 182–83
drugs and hunting, 36
Dudhwa, 112, 115, 148–49, 164, 242–43, 277, 280–81, 294
Duleepsinhji (Duleep), 6, 13

elephants, 50–51, 88, 115, 120, 131, 143, 158, 159, 167, 170, 173, 176, 191, 193, 244, 255, 257, 277, 279, 282–83, 297, 310, 317, 342, 348, 350
Elephant Project, 254
endangered species in India, 88, 116, 128, 140, 144, 151, 153, 161, 195, 203, 205, 208, 209, 248, 253, 263, 269, 323, 328, 344
Environment (Protection) Act (EPA), 235
extinction, threat of, 12, 29, 31, 37, 39, 43, 47, 50, 55, 66, 93, 103, 114, 126, 149, 200, 211, 251, 273, 279, 290, 310, 321–22, 329, 337, 347, 349–50

falconry, 35–36
Forest (Conservation) Act (FCA), 185, 234–35
Forest encroachment, 185–90, 256–57, 296, 298
forests, preservation of, 14–16, 136
frog legs, procurement of, 245–47

Gandhi, Indira, 60–61, 118, 122, 124–25, 127, 139–40, 156, 157, 184, 215, 217, 234, 299
and wildlife conservation, 2, 3, 107–08, 112–14, 116, 132, 137, 149, 155, 156–57, 185, 203
Gandhi, Maneka, 262–65
Gandhi, Rajiv, 2, 184, 224, 234–35, 236, 237–39, 246, 250, 258, 262, 299
Gandhi, Sonia, 298, 299
Ganga Action Plan (GAP), 236, 258–60
Ganga Singh, Maharaja of Bikaner, 28, 30, 39–40, 43, 142
gazelle, 35, 37, 38, 43, 46, 56, 66, 78, 168, 170, 172, 305, 315, 323
gharial, 44, 149–50, 153, 165, 177, 195, 200, 203, 253, 258, 259
goat, wild, 72, 73, 127, 172
grassland ecosystems, 159, 344

Himmatsinhji, M.K. (ornithologist), 37
hangul, 47, 54–55, 56, 57, 58–62, 88, 108, 313, 321–22, 350
hornbills, 29, 162, 175, 181, 308
hunting tricks, 41–42, 48, 50
hyena, 8, 9, 12, 17, 44, 98, 155

ibex, 47, 56, 57, 65, 69, 70, 72, 74, 78, 146–47, 168, 170, 172, 302–06, 323
Indian Board for Wildlife, 2, 51, 112, 236, 257, 264, 293, 311
see National Board for Wildlife also
Indian Forest Service, 111, 112,

136, 137, 139, 154, 165, 301
  wildlife sub-cadre, 137–39
Indonesia, 179–83
International Union for the Conservation of Nature (IUCN), 107–08, 116, 125–26, 165, 321, 324, 337

Khanji of Junagadh, Mahabat, 28–29
Kumar, Pushp, 136

Lahan, P., 115, 136, 248, 289
Lekagul, Boonsong, 25–26, 160, 173
leopard, snow, 47, 56, 61, 64, 67, 68, 69, 84, 86, 133, 245, 248, 253–55, 267, 304, 313, 323, 328, 347, 350
licences for
  hunting, 56–57, 94–95, 113, 121, 244, 263–64
  trade, 244
lion
  Asiatic, 27, 39, 126, 139, 144, 313, 325, 330, 331, 336
  Indian, 27, 28, 144, 192, 217, 330
lion–cheetah exchange with Iran, 139–40
Lynx, 17, 304

Malaysia, 174–77
maneater, 89–91, 202, 217, 294
Manekshaw, General S.H.F.J. (Sam), 70–71
markhor, 56–57, 69, 72–76, 323
Ministry of Environment and Forests (MoEF), 139, 234, 247, 251, 254–55, 265, 284, 286, 296–98, 313–16, 318, 320–22, 324, 334–35, 336, 337, 340
Mohd Khan bin Momin Khan, 174
Myanmar (Burma), 173–74
Narmada project, 239, 268–69
national
  animal, 117–18, 201
  bird, 118
National Board for Wildlife, 203, 212, 241, 260, 293, 317, 320, 336 *see* Indian Board for Wildlife *also*
National Forest Commission, 139, 236, 299, 300–02
National Parks
  Baluran National Park, Indonesia, 182
  Bandhavgarh National Park, Madhya Pradesh, 25, 190, 201, 202, 207, 208, 211, 277, 294, 349
  Banff National Park, Canada, 125
  Bhawal National Park, Bangladesh, 171
  Campbell Bay National Park, Andaman and Nicobar Islands, 274
  Chitwan National Park, Nepal, 165, 279
  Dachigam National Park, Kashmir, 322
  Desert National Park, Rajasthan, 145, 320–21
  Dudhwa National Park, Uttar Pradesh, 242, 243, 279, 280, 281

Eravikulam National Park, Kerala, 52, 133
Everglades National Park, US, 165
Fiordland National Park, New Zealand, 153
Garamba National Park, Congo, 154
Ghughua Fossil National Park, Madhya Pradesh, 207
Gir National Park, Gujarat, 150, 325, 341
Gobi National Park, Mongolia, 169
Gran Paradiso National Park, Italy, 146
Grand Canyon National Park, US, 165
Grand Teton National Park, US, 126
Great Himalayan National Park, Himachal Pradesh, 254
Great Nicobar National Park, Andaman and Nicobar Islands, 274
Guindy National Park, Tamil Nadu, 34
Gulf of Kutch Marine National Park, Gujarat, 315
Gunung Leuser National Park, Indonesia, 181
Guru Ghasidas National Park, Chhattisgarh, 191, 329, 333
Hawaii Volcanoes National Park, US, 173
Hemis National Park, Leh, Jammu & Kashmir, 67

Indravati National Park, Chhattisgarh, 50, 201, 210, 289, 290, 291
Jigme Dorji National Park, Bhutan, 81, 85, 86
Jim Corbett National Park, Uttarakhand, 61, 88–89, 130, 135, 149, 152, 280, 316
Kajinag National Park, Kashmir, 323
Kanger National Park, Chhattisgarh, 199
Kanha National Park, Madhya Pradesh, 49, 58, 87, 102, 103, 105, 106, 108, 201, 208, 283, 285, 349
Keibul Lamjao National Park, Manipur, 272
Keoladeo Ghana National Park, Bharatpur, Rajasthan, 57, 147, 249, 266
Khangchendzonga National Park, Sikkim, 254
Khao Sam Roi Yot National Park, Thailand, 162
Khao Yai National Park, Thailand, 161–62
Kirthar National Park, Pakistan, 171
Kishtwar National Park, Jammu & Kashmir, 254
Komodo National Park, Indonesia, 182
Madhav National Park, Madhya Pradesh, 44, 202, 211
Malindi Marine National Park, Kenya, 158

Meru Betiri National Park,
  Indonesia, 179
Mouling National Park,
  Arunachal Pradesh, 254, 261
Mount Cook National Park,
  New Zealand, 153–54
Mount Iglit-Baco National
  Park, Philippines, 166
Mukundra Hills National Park,
  Rajasthan, 46
Murlen National Park,
  Mizoram, 308
Nameri National Park, Assam,
  278
Nanda Devi National Park,
  Uttarakhand, 254
Nippo Kaigan Quasi-National
  Park, Japan, 165
Orang National Park, Assam,
  278
Panna National Park, Madhya
  Pradesh, 195
Pench National Park, Madhya
  Pradesh, 207
Phawngpui Blue Mountain
  National Park, Mizoram,
  308, 309
Pin Valley National Park,
  Himachal Pradesh, 254,
  302, 303
Ranthambore National Park,
  Rajasthan, 251
Royal Manas National Park,
  Bhutan, 85, 256, 282, 283
Sanjay Gandhi National Park,
  Madhya Pradesh, 191, 197
Satpura National Park, Madhya
  Pradesh, 105, 197, 198
Tarutao National Park,
  Thailand, 162
Tongariro National Park, New
  Zealand, 154
Ujung Kulon National Park,
  Indonesia, 140, 180
Van Vihar National Park,
  Madhya Pradesh, 192
Velavadar Blackbuck National
  Park, Gujarat, 33, 212
Wandoor Marine National
  Park, Andaman Islands, 274
Wilpattu National Park, Sri
  Lanka, 167
Yala National Park, Sri Lanka,
  166
Yangmingshan National Park,
  Taiwan, 169
Yellowstone National Park, US,
  125–26
Yosemite National Park, US, 165
National Tiger Conservation
  Authority (NTCA), 295–96,
  323, 333
National Wildlife Action Plan, 297
Nehru, Jawaharlal, 2–3, 64
nilgai, 7, 11, 16, 17–18, 19, 43,
  94–95, 139, 147, 155, 190, 202,
  207, 249, 325, 330, 342, 343

orang-utan, 176, 181–82

panther, 16-17, 31
Panwar, Hemendra Singh, 136, 164,
  185, 240, 241–42, 253, 256, 283,
  286
partridge, 3, 32, 36, 37, 65, 67, 81,
  172, 248

Patkar, Medha, 269–70
peafowl, 7, 181, 189
pheasants, 47, 74, 81–82, 85–86, 248, 308, 310, 323
Philip's, Prince, visit to see wildlife, 215–17
pig, wild, 3, 7, 11, 29, 34, 55, 80, 139, 142, 147, 154, 177, 178, 181, 255, 272, 307, 342, 347
poaching of animals, 61, 66, 115, 131, 147, 173, 174, 176, 209, 248, 250, 255, 257, 262, 278–79, 321, 322, 336, 350
poisoning of animals, 7, 22, 135–36, 174, 183, 242–43, 261, 279, 280–81
Pratapsinhji, 5, 6, 20, 24, 155
Project Tiger, 61, 108, 116–17, 125, 130, 163, 165, 235, 242, 251, 253, 254–55, 277, 306, 328, 334, 336 report of, 164–65
pugees (trackers) of Wankaner, 8, 9–10, 29
pugmarks, tracking through, 10, 20, 96, 135, 182, 281–82

rams, 65–66, 72, 172, 260, 304, 305
Ranjitsinh, M.K., 4, 5–6, 13, 27, 30, 31, 32, 33
Rathore, Fateh Singh, 136, 164, 252, 283
rhinoceros, 88, 173, 180, 181, 243, 248, 313, 348, 349
Roy, Sunjoy Deb, 115, 136, 263, 282–83

sal forests, 48, 50, 87–88, 101, 103, 105, 171, 189, 190, 196, 199, 208, 213, 215, 248, 278, 283–86, 287, 329
salt lick, 60, 175, 302, 304, 311
sambar, 10–11, 17, 19, 21–22, 26, 31, 32, 43, 49, 50, 80, 93, 95, 115, 131, 156, 161, 166, 174, 175, 178, 180, 190, 195, 196, 202, 207, 208, 216, 307, 309, 330
sandgrouse, 4, 37, 41–42, 43, 67, 88, 333
Sankhala, Kailash, 112, 116, 125, 130, 136, 137, 145, 201, 283
Scindia, Madho Rao, 44, 192, 248
serow, 56, 61–62, 79, 82, 88, 162, 171, 182, 261, 265, 279, 309
Shahi, S.P., 136
shapu, 56, 57, 65, 69, 70, 71–72, 306
Singh, Arjun, 190–91, 192, 198, 201–02, 207, 214, 224, 227, 230
Singh, Digvijaya, 269, 286
Singh, Karan, 112, 113, 114, 116–18, 130, 134, 143, 165, 246, 336
Singh, Manmohan, 301, 315, 317, 336
Singhji, Lakshman, 14–18, 19, 20, 46, 135
Singhji (conservationist), Maharaj Rana Udai Bhan, 43
Singhji, Raj, 21
shoots, cruelty in, 42
shoots, organized, 43, 45
Singh, Billy Arjan, 112–13, 148, 149, 163, 164, 281
Singh, Maharana Fateh, 45–46
stalagmite and stalactite formations, 199
state animals and birds, 59, 78, 155, 201, 306, 308, 322, 323

Swaminathan, M.S., 165, 286

takin, 78, 79, 81, 83, 84–85, 86, 174, 248, 261, 265, 267, 310–11
teak forest, 4, 13, 15, 87, 101, 117, 173, 189, 196, 197, 199, 243, 248, 294
The Scheduled Tribes and Other Traditional Forest Dwellers (Recognition of Forest Rights) Act (FRA), 185, 297, 299–300
tiger
    conservation, 276, 279, 323, 344, 345
    kills of, 48, 104, 135, 136, 140, 279, 280
    pet, 163
    white, 49, 102, 191, 193
Tiger Conservation Programme (TCP), 276–81, 283 *see* National Tiger Conservation Authority (NTCA) *also*
tourists, issues with, 205, 215, 252, 274, 281–82, 295, 317
trade in wild animals prohibited, 128–30, 244, 245–47, 263, 286–87
turtle (olive ridley), breeding of, 151
turtle (leatherback), egg-laying of, 175, 176

U Tun Yin, 173, 174
United Nations Conference on Human Environment in Stockholm, Sweden, 124
United Nations Environment Programme (UNEP), 156, 158, 159, 169, 170

Wangchuck, Maharaj Kumar Dasho Namgyal/Paro Penlop, 78–80, 83, 85
waterfowl, 21, 57, 58
whales, 236–38, 245
wildlife conservationists, 25, 43–44, 114, 115, 136, 152, 160. 173, 240, 336
wildlife conservation accounts of India in
    pre-Independence, 3, 11, 20, 25, 26, 57
    post-Independence, 10, 21–22, 23, 24, 29, 34, 45, 58, 105, 157, 186, 235
Wildlife Institute of India (WII), 240–42, 248, 269, 288, 292, 316, 335, 343
wildlife preservation
    factors harming, 1, 3, 17, 194, 347–50
    motivating factors for, 118, 137, 151, 318, 345, 347
Wild Life (Protection) Act, 118–24, 127, 128, 133, 140, 147, 189, 246, 247, 250, 263, 276, 288
    Amendment Act, 212, 244, 264–65, 291–92, 295, 312, 313
    in the state of Jammu and Kashmir, 133–34
Wildlife Reserves
    Ambanal Reserve, Rajasthan, 20

Bandhavgarh Tiger Reserve, Madhya Pradesh, 294
Banjar Reserve, Madhya Pradesh, 87
Buxa Tiger Reserve, West Bengal, 50, 294
Dampa Tiger Reserve, Mizoram, 308, 310
Dudhwa Reserve, Uttar Pradesh, 115
Gajner Reserve, Rajasthan, 43
Kanha Tiger Reserve, Madhya Pradesh, 208
Kollamarka Reserve, Maharashtra, 291, 316
Melghat Tiger Reserve, Maharashtra, 95
Namdapha Tiger Reserve, Arunachal Pradesh, 277, 307
Pakhui Tiger Reserve, Arunachal Pradesh, 278, 279
Palamau Tiger Reserve, Bihar, 277, 287, 288
Panna Tiger Reserve, Madhya Pradesh, 195, 337
Periyar Tiger Reserve, Kerala, 52, 130, 277
Ranthambore Tiger Reserve, Rajasthan, 130, 252, 281, 281, 314
Sariska Reserve, Rajasthan, 130, 249–50, 277
Shuklaphanta Wildlife Reserve, Nepal, 279
Simlipal Tiger Reserve, Odisha, 4, 130, 164, 278, 283
Sundarban Tiger Reserve, West Bengal, 130, 151, 152, 252, 277, 281, 306, 307
Tadoba–Andhari Tiger Reserve, Maharashtra, 25, 117, 277, 281
Valmiki Tiger Reserve, Bihar, 147, 278, 279, 280
Wildlife Sanctuaries
Amba Barwa Sanctuary, Maharashtra, 95
Badalkhol Sanctuary, Chhattisgarh, 212
Barda Sanctuary, Gujarat, 25, 30–31, 325
Bhairamgarh Sanctuary, Chhattisgarh, 211, 289, 290
Chandraprabha Sanctuary, Uttar Pradesh, 144
Changthang Wildlife Sanctuary, Ladakh, 66, 70, 254, 314
Darrah Wildlife Sanctuary, Rajasthan, 46, 251–52
Gandhi Sagar Sanctuary, Madhya Pradesh, 208
Gir Sanctuary, Gujarat, 148, 250, 251
Girnar Sanctuary, Gujarat, 325
Hirpora Sanctuary, Kashmir, 76, 323
Jawahar Sagar Sanctuary, Rajasthan, 252
Karera Sanctuary, Madhya Pradesh, 194–95, 205
Katerniaghat Sanctuary, Uttar Pradesh, 150, 153, 278, 280, 281

Keibul Lamjao Sanctuary, Manipur, 114–15, 154–55
Ken Gharial Sanctuary, Madhya Pradesh, 195
Kollamarka Sanctuary, Maharashtra, 200, 290, 291, 316
Kuno Wildlife Sanctuary, Madhya Pradesh, 45, 324, 325, 330–31, 334, 335–37
Kutch Bustard Sanctuary, Gujarat, 319, 320
Kutch Desert Wildlife Sanctuary, Gujarat, 319
Kutru Wildlife Sanctuary, Chhattisgarh, 200–01
Lengteng Wildlife Sanctuary, Mizoram, 308
Little Rann of Kutch Sanctuary, Gujarat, 275
Manas Sanctuary, Assam, 115
Mansingh-Deo Sanctuary, Maharashtra, 316
Mehao Sanctuary, Arunachal Pradesh, 254
Mitiyala Wildlife Sanctuary, Gujarat, 25, 34, 325
Nannaj Sanctuary, Maharashtra, 316
National Chambal Sanctuary, Madhya Pradesh, 153, 202–03
Nauradehi Wildlife Sanctuary, Madhya Pradesh, 212, 333, 334
Pania Sanctuary, Gujarat, 325
Panpatha Wildlife Sanctuary, Madhya Pradesh, 208
Pench Wildlife Sanctuary, Madhya Pradesh, 207
Phen Wildlife Sanctuary, Madhya Pradesh, 208
Rajamala Sanctuary, Kerala, 132, 133
Rampara Wildlife Sanctuary, Gujarat, 7, 10–11, 12, 156
Sangla Valley Sanctuary, Himachal Pradesh, 262
Sarangarh–Gomarda Sanctuary, Chhattisgarh, 209
Sardarpur Sanctuary, Madhya Pradesh, 208
Shoolpaneshwar Sanctuary, Gujarat, 294
Sitanadi Wildlife Sanctuary, Chhattisgarh, 198, 211, 287, 288
Son Gharial Wildlife Sanctuary, Madhya Pradesh, 195
Sultanpur Bird Sanctuary, Haryana, 157 S
Tamor Pingla Sanctuary, Chhattisgarh, 25, 190, 287, 288
Udanti Sanctuary, Chhattisgarh, 210, 211, 287, 288, 289–90, 291
Wankaner, xi, 1–12, 20, 24, 82, 155, 156, 212, 216
Wodeyar, Jayachamaraja, 51
Wodeyar, Krishna Raja, 51
wolves, 7, 12, 38, 55, 56, 66, 67, 72, 88, 126, 155, 172, 190, 262, 304–05, 328
Zoo, 105, 149, 177, 191–92, 264, 295

Acknowledgements

I would wish to record my gratitude to all who have helped me in life in acquiring the subject matter of this book, as well as in the writing of it. I can name only a few.

Foremost, my parents, Pratapsinhji and Rama Kunwer of Wankaner, for encouraging me in my pursuit of wildlife and for permitting me, from a very early age, to wander on my own in the wilderness. My maternal uncles, Lakshman Singhji, Virbhadra Singhji and Nagendra Singhji of Dungarpur were a great source of inspiration and from whom I learnt so much. Uncle Chandrabhanusinh of Wankaner, arguably the greatest rifleman of my era who taught me, treated me as a son and gave up shikar when, after framing the Wild Life Protection Act, I told him that I would be deeply ashamed if he was found transgressing it!

I owe a very deep debt of gratitude to my 'gurus', the 'pugees', trackers and shikaris of yore, from whom I learnt so much and who reposed such confidence and loyalty in me – Nathu, Bechar, Kunvro, Kano, Jivraj and Savshi of Wankaner; Haider Jemadar, Kanthad and Viram of Gir; Nania and Bheru Singh of Dungarpur; Sonu and Manglu Baigas of Kanha, the Gond and Baiga trackers of Sagar and Mandla districts.

I am also deeply indebted to my wife Kalpana Kumari and daughters Meenal and Radhika for not only tolerating my idiosyncrasies, but for encouraging me, accompanying me in the wild and for acquiescing in my long absences. Gratitude is due to Divyabhanusinh of Mansa, Mahesh Rangarajan, Rivka Israel, Manmohan Malhoutra, Samar Singh of Dungarpur, and at HarperCollins, V.K. Karthika, Antony Thomas and Blessy Augustine who edited the manuscript, made changes and gave suggestions of immense value, as also to Sunder Kanwal, Renjini Biju and granddaughter Yashasvini, who helped so greatly in the typing of this book.

About the Author

Dr M.K. Ranjitsinh belongs to the royal family of Wankaner. He joined the IAS in 1961. As collector of Mandla, MP, he helped save the central Indian barasingha from extinction. As secretary, forests and tourism, in MP, he established 14 new sanctuaries, 8 new national parks and more than doubled the area of 3 existing national parks, a total addition of over 9,000 sq. km. to the protected areas of the nation. He was the prime architect of the Wildlife (Protection) Act; was director of wildlife preservation twice and additional secretary in the Ministry of Environment and Forests. He was member secretary of the task force which initiated Project Tiger and he also initiated Project Snow Leopard; he helped save the Manipur sangai and other endangered species. The eastern subspecies of the barasingha is named after him. He worked with UNEP as senior regional advisor in Nature Conservation for the Asia-Pacific region. He has published numerous articles and two books, *Beyond the Tiger* and *The Indian Blackbuck*, which is the subject of his PhD thesis.

30 Years *of* HarperCollins *Publishers* India

At HarperCollins, we believe in telling the best stories and finding the widest possible readership for our books in every format possible. We started publishing 30 years ago; a great deal has changed since then, but what has remained constant is the passion with which our authors write their books, the love with which readers receive them, and the sheer joy and excitement that we as publishers feel in being a part of the publishing process.

Over the years, we've had the pleasure of publishing some of the finest writing from the subcontinent and around the world, and some of the biggest bestsellers in India's publishing history. Our books and authors have won a phenomenal range of awards, and we ourselves have been named Publisher of the Year the greatest number of times. But nothing has meant more to us than the fact that millions of people have read the books we published, and somewhere, a book of ours might have made a difference.

As we step into our fourth decade, we go back to that one word – a word which has been a driving force for us all these years.

Read.